The phenomenon of international entrepreneurship is undoubtedly important, and yet most academic research has continued to take either an entrepreneurship or an international business lens to study it. This new volume, edited by Fernhaber and Prashantham, is therefore particularly welcome as it brings together a wide variety of perspectives on this increasingly important topic. The range of issues it addresses, and the interdisciplinary approach taken, will make it a must-read volume on international entrepreneurship for many years to come.

Julian Birkinshaw, *Professor, London Business School, UK*

The balanced perspective between entrepreneurship and international business makes this book unique. Most international entrepreneurship (IE) writings are dominated by either an entrepreneurship or an IB perspective. The cross-disciplinary team of Fernhaber and Prashantham has created a comprehensive IE book that should be on the book shelf of every IE scholar.

Patricia P. McDougall-Covin, *Professor, Kelley School of Business, Indiana University, USA*

This book is timely as it deals with a major topic of emerging importance in the field, international entrepreneurship. The editors have developed a book that serves as a thorough compendium of the field and is written by experts in international entrepreneurship. As such, this volume is a major source of knowledge on which to develop a course in international entrepreneurship or as a source for launching a major research program. Thus, I commend this volume to scholars in entrepreneurship, international business and complementary fields who desire to learn about this exciting field of international entrepreneurship.

Michael A. Hitt, Professor, *Texas A&M University, USA*

The Routledge Companion to International Entrepreneurship

The domain of international entrepreneurship has continued to gain momentum in an era that sees entrepreneurship and globalization as critical issues in the world of business. Given the flourish of new research in this area, there is a need to provide an up-to-date perspective on the field and its future.

This volume draws together a team of experts purposely selected from both the entrepreneurship and international business fields to present a comprehensive resource on the cutting-edge conversations within international entrepreneurship.

This prestigious reference book will offer students and researchers an introduction to leading scholarship in international entrepreneurship and also serve as a catapult for future research.

Stephanie A. Fernhaber is Assistant Professor of Management at Butler University, USA. Her research focusing on international entrepreneurship has been published in the *Journal of International Business Studies*, *Strategic Management Journal*, *Journal of Business Venturing* and elsewhere.

Shameen Prashantham is Associate Professor of International Business and Strategy at Nottingham University Business School, China. His research on international entrepreneurship has been published in *Entrepreneurship Theory and Practice*, *Journal of International Business Studies*, *Journal of Management Studies* and elsewhere.

ROUTLEDGE COMPANIONS IN BUSINESS, MANAGEMENT AND ACCOUNTING

Routledge Companions in Business, Management and Accounting are prestige reference works providing an overview of a whole subject area or sub-discipline. These books survey the state of the discipline including emerging and cutting-edge areas. Providing a comprehensive, up-to-date, definitive work of reference, Routledge Companions can be cited as an authoritative source on the subject.

A key aspect of these Routledge Companions is their international scope and relevance. Edited by an array of highly regarded scholars, these volumes also benefit from teams of contributors which reflect an international range of perspectives.

Individually, Routledge Companions in Business, Management and Accounting provide an impactful one-stop-shop resource for each theme covered. Collectively, they represent a comprehensive learning and research resource for researchers, postgraduate students and practitioners.

Published titles in this series include:

The Routledge Companion to Fair Value and Financial Reporting
Edited by Peter Walton

The Routledge Companion to Nonprofit Marketing
Edited by Adrian Sargeant and Walter Wymer Jr

The Routledge Companion to Accounting History
Edited by John Richard Edwards and Stephen P. Walker

The Routledge Companion to Creativity
Edited by Tudor Rickards, Mark A. Runco and Susan Moger

The Routledge Companion to Strategic Human Resource Management
Edited by John Storey, Patrick M. Wright and David Ulrich

The Routledge Companion to International Business Coaching
Edited by Michel Moral and Geoffrey Abbott

The Routledge Companion to Organizational Change
Edited by David M. Boje, Bernard Burnes and John Hassard

The Routledge Companion to Cost Management
Edited by Falconer Mitchell, Hanne Nørreklit and Morten Jakobsen

The Routledge Companion to Digital Consumption
Edited by Russell W. Belk and Rosa Llamas

The Routledge Companion to Identity and Consumption
Edited by Ayalla A. Ruvio and Russell W. Belk

The Routledge Companion to Public-Private Partnerships
Edited by Piet de Vries and Etienne B. Yehoue

The Routledge Companion to Accounting, Reporting and Regulation
Edited by Carien van Mourik and Peter Walton

The Routledge Companion to International Management Education
Edited by Denise Tsang, Hamid H. Kazeroony and Guy Ellis

The Routledge Companion to Accounting Communication
Edited by Lisa Jack, Jane Davison and Russell Craig

The Routledge Companion to Visual Organization
Edited by Emma Bell, Jonathan Schroeder and Samantha Warren

The Routledge Companion to Arts Marketing
Edited by Daragh O'Reilly, Ruth Rentschler and Theresa Kirchner

The Routledge Companion to Alternative Organization
Edited by Martin Parker, George Cheney, Valerie Fournier and Chris Land

The Routledge Companion to the Future of Marketing
Edited by Luiz Moutinho, Enrique Bigne and Ajay K. Manrai

The Routledge Companion to Accounting Education
Edited by Richard M. S. Wilson

The Routledge Companion to Business in Africa
Edited by Sonny Nwankwo and Kevin Ibeh

The Routledge Companion to Human Resource Development
Edited by Rob F. Poell, Tonette S. Rocco and Gene L. Roth

The Routledge Companion to Auditing
Edited by David Hay, W. Robert Knechel and Marleen Willekens

The Routledge Companion to Entrepreneurship
Edited by Ted Baker and Friederike Welter

The Routledge Companion to International Human Resource Management
Edited by David G. Collings, Geoffrey T. Wood and Paula Caligiuri

The Routledge Companion to Financial Services Marketing
Edited by Tina Harrison and Hooman Estelami

The Routledge Companion to International Entrepreneurship
Edited by Stephanie A. Fernhaber and Shameen Prashantham

The Routledge Companion to International Entrepreneurship

Edited by Stephanie A. Fernhaber and Shameen Prashantham

LONDON AND NEW YORK

First published 2015
by Routledge
4 Park Square, Milton Park, Abingdon, Oxon OX14 4RN

and by Routledge
605 Third Avenue, New York, NY 10017

First issued in paperback 2022

Routledge is an imprint of the Taylor & Francis Group, an informa business

Publisher's Note
The publisher has gone to great lengths to ensure the quality of this reprint but points out that some imperfections in the original copies may be apparent.

British Library Cataloguing in Publication Data
A catalogue record for this book is available from the British Library

Library of Congress Cataloging-in-Publication Data
The Routledge companion to international entrepreneurship / edited by Stephanie Fernhaber, Shameen Prashantham. – 1 Edition.
pages cm. – (Routledge companions in business, management and accounting)
Includes bibliographical references and index.
ISBN 978-0-415-82919-9 (hardback) – ISBN 978-0-203-51716-1 (ebook)
1. Entrepreneurship. 2. International business enterprises. I. Fernhaber, Stephanie A. (Stephanie Ann), 1975- editor. II. Prashantham, Shameen, editor.
HB615.R6835 2014
658.4'21–dc23
2014036449

ISBN: 978-1-03-247734-3 (pbk)
ISBN: 978-0-415-82919-9 (hbk)
ISBN: 978-0-203-51716-1 (ebk)

DOI: 10.4324/9780203517161

Typeset in Bembo
by Cenveo Publisher Services

Contents

Figures

Tables

Contributors

Editors

Stephanie A. Fernhaber is Assistant Professor of Management at Butler University. Her research focusing on international entrepreneurship has been published in the *Journal of International Business Studies, Strategic Management Journal, Journal of Business Venturing* and elsewhere. Stephanie earned her PhD in entrepreneurship from Indiana University.

Shameen Prashantham is Associate Professor in International Business and Strategy at Nottingham University Business School China. His research on international entrepreneurship has been published in *Entrepreneurship Theory & Practice, Journal of International Business Studies, Journal of Management Studies* and elsewhere. Shameen earned his PhD in international business from Strathclyde University.

Contributors

Svante Andersson is Professor in Business Administration at Halmstad University. His areas of research include marketing, entrepreneurship and international business. He has published in journals such as *Journal of Business Venturing* and *Journal of International Marketing*. He has extensive international experience as an export manager and as a guest teacher and researcher.

Shiv Chaudhry is Professor of Marketing and International Business at Birmingham City University, UK. Research interests involve the Marketing/International Entrepreneurship interface, particularly ethnic minority-owned SMEs. Publications include: *Entrepreneurship and Regional Development; Journal of Small Business & Enterprise Development; Marketing Intelligence & Planning* and *Small Business Economics*.

Sylvie Chetty holds the Dunedin City Chair of Entrepreneurship, University of Otago and is a Research Associate in the Department of Business Administration, Uppsala University. She has published in *Journal of International Business Studies, Journal of World Business, Entrepreneurship Theory and Practice,* and *Management International Review* among others.

Dave Crick is Professor of International Entrepreneurship at Victoria University of Wellington, NZ. Research interests involve the Marketing/International Entrepreneurship interface, particularly addressing the public/private sector interaction. Publications include: *Entrepreneurship and Regional Development, International Business Review, International Marketing Review, Journal of Business Venturing,* and *Small Business Economics*.

Dirk De Clercq is Professor of Management in the Goodman School of Business at Brock University, Canada. He is also Research Professor in the Small Business Research Centre at Kingston University, UK. His research interests include new venture internationalization, innovation, and social exchange relationships.

Pavlos Dimitratos is Professor at the Adam Smith Business School of the University of Glasgow, UK. His research interests include MNE subsidiary activities, SME internationalization, and international entrepreneurship. His publications appear in *Entrepreneurship Theory and Practice, Journal of Management Studies, Strategic Entrepreneurship Journal* and others.

Eileen Fischer is a Professor and Tanenbaum Chair of Entrepreneurship at York University in Toronto. Her research spans both entrepreneurship and marketing and has been published in outlets such as the *Journal of International Business Studies, Journal of Business Venturing,* and *Journal of Consumer Research.*

Gary A. Knight is the Helen Simpson Jackson Chair in International Management at Willamette University in Salem and Portland, Oregon, USA. He has authored six books and more than 40 refereed articles in academic journals. He obtained his PhD in international business from Michigan State University.

In Hyeock Lee is an Assistant Professor of IB/Strategy in Quinlan School of Business, Loyola University Chicago. His research focuses on the location strategies of MNEs and new ventures with performance implication. Prior to joining academia, he was a Deputy Director at the Korean government.

Nicolas Li is a PhD candidate at the Adam Smith Business School, University of Glasgow, UK. He received his MSc from the University of Aberdeen, UK, and his BA from the University of British Columbia, Vancouver, Canada. His research interests include entrepreneurship and SME internationalization.

Jude Lieberman obtained her Masters in Business Administration at Portland State University, during which time she studied social enterprise in Andhra Pradesh, India. She provides consultation to entrepreneurs and nonprofits in the Portland area.

Joseph A. LiPuma is Associate Professor and Director of the International MBA program at EMLYON Business School in France. Joe's publications include articles in *Entrepreneurship Theory and Practice, Small Business Economics,* and *International Small Business Journal,* among others. He founded companies in four countries prior to his academic career.

Benedikt Maissenhälter is a researcher at Technische Universität München. His current research focuses on decision making at the individual and firm level in the context of internationalizing and financing decisions. Benedikt received degrees from the London School of Economics and the University of St. Gallen.

R. Scott Marshall is Professor of Management and Associate Dean for Graduate Programs at the School of Business, Portland State University. His research interests are social entrepreneurship and corporate voluntary disclosures.

Rod B. McNaughton is Professor of Entrepreneurship at the University of Auckland School of Business. His research focuses on the early and rapid internationalization of knowledge intensive firms. Rod previously held positions as Eyton Chair in Entrepreneurship at the University of Waterloo and as Professor of Marketing at the University of Otago.

Hana Milanov holds a Professorship in International Entrepreneurship at Technische Universität München. She conducts research at the nexus of literatures in entrepreneurship, international business and social networks. Hana's work has been published in *Strategic Management Journal, Journal of Business Venturing,* and *Academy of Management Perspectives* among others.

Anna Morgan-Thomas is Senior Lecturer in Marketing for the Adam Smith Business School at the University of Glasgow. Positioned at the interface between international marketing and information systems research, her research focuses on the digital transformation of the marketing function. Her work has been published in *International Marketing Review, International Small Business Journal* and *Journal of Business Research.*

Niina Nummela is a Professor of International Business at the Turku School of Economics at the University of Turku. Her areas of expertise include international entrepreneurship, cross-border acquisitions, interfirm cooperation, and research methods. She has published widely in academic journals, including the *International Business Review, Journal of World Business,* and *Management International Review*, among others.

Michelle Pagès developed a passion for social enterprise while studying and pursuing field work in Andhra Pradesh, India. She earned her Masters in Business Administration from Portland State University. Michelle currently works in adventure travel and is dedicated to creating livelihoods in international communities.

Cecilia Pahlberg is Associate Professor at the Department of Business Studies, Uppsala University, Sweden. She conducts research within international business and marketing and her most recent research project focuses on the impact from socio-political actors on multinationals in emerging markets.

Juan Pellegrino is a Lecturer in Management at the Christchurch Polytechnic Institute of Technology, New Zealand. He holds a PhD from the University of Otago. His research focuses on the co-evolution of internationalization strategy and learning of early internationalizing firms.

Christiane Prange is a Professor of International Strategy at EMLYON Business School in France. She obtained her PhD in Management from Geneva University, Switzerland, and has lectured as a visiting professor in more than 10 countries. She has published five books and several journal papers.

Erik S. Rasmussen is Associate Professor at the Department of Marketing and Management, University of Southern Denmark. His international entrepreneurship research has focused on current issues, contextualising case studies, domestic versus international new ventures and location choice.

A. Rebecca Reuber is Professor of Strategic Management at the University of Toronto's Rotman School of Management. Her international entrepreneurship research has been published in various outlets such as the *Journal of International Business Studies, Journal of Business Venturing,* and *Strategic Entrepreneurship Journal*. She is a member of the editorial review board of *Journal of Business Venturing* and *Entrepreneurship Theory and Practice*.

Josep Rialp is Associate Professor of Marketing and Market Research in the School of Economics and Business at the Universitat Autònoma de Barcelona. He has had different book chapters published and refereed articles in academic journals. He obtained his PhD from Universitat Autònoma de Barcelona.

Alex Rialp is Associate Professor of Business Organization at Universitat Autònoma de Barcelona (UAB). His research interests are focused upon the intersection of international business with marketing and entrepreneurship. He has authored different books, book chapters, and refereed articles in several academic journals. He obtained his PhD from Universitat Autònoma de Barcelona.

Alan M. Rugman was Professor of International Business and Head of International Business and Strategy at Henley Business School, University of Reading, UK. He had over 250 papers published in major referred journals on the theory of the MNE and its regional strategy.

Harry J. Sapienza is a Professor at the University of Minnesota. His work on international entrepreneurship has appeared in the *Academy of Management Journal, Academy of Management Review, Entrepreneurship Theory and Practice,* and *Journal of Business Venturing*.

Per Servais is Associate Professor of Marketing at the Department of Leadership and Strategy, University of Southern Denmark. He has published a large number of book chapters and articles, for example, in *Industrial Marketing Management, International Marketing Review, Journal of International Marketing, Advances in International Marketing,* and *International Business Review*. He received the H.B. Thorelli Prize from the American Marketing Association.

Siri Terjesen is Assistant Professor in the Kelley School of Business at Indiana University and a Visiting Research Fellow at Lund University, Sweden. She is an Associate Editor of the *Academy of Management Learning and Education* and *Small Business Economics*. Siri has published over 45 articles in entrepreneurship, strategy, and international business in leading international journals. Her research has been profiled in *Business Week, US News and World Report, Christian Science Monitor, CNBC Europe*, and other leading outlets.

Liman Zhao is a Research Fellow at the CEIBS Case Development Center. Her research interests cover social entrepreneurship and international entrepreneurship. She has presented her works on the "internationalization of social entrepreneurship" at the AOM Annual Conference and NYU Stern Conference on Social Entrepreneurship.

Advisory panel

Julian Birkinshaw is Professor and Chair of Strategy and Entrepreneurship at the London Business School. He is a Fellow of the British Academy, and a Fellow of the Academy of International Business. Professor Birkinshaw's main area of expertise is in the strategy and organization of large multinational corporations, and on such specific issues as subsidiary-headquarters relationships, corporate entrepreneurship, innovation, the changing role of the corporate HQ, organization design, and knowledge management.

Michael A. Hitt is a Distinguished Professor and holds the Joe B. Foster Chair in Business Leadership at Texas A&M University. He has published in leading journals such as the *Academy of Management Journal, Academy of Management Review, Organization Science, and Strategic Management Journal.* Professor Hitt is a founding editor of *Strategic Entrepreneurship Journal*, a former editor of the *Academy of Management Journal*, and former president of the Academy of Management.

Patricia McDougall-Covin is the Director of the Institute for International Business and the William L. Haeberle Professor of Entrepreneurship at Indiana University's Kelley School of Business. She and her co-author, Benjamin Oviatt, were presented the 2004 JIBS Decade Award for their article on the early internationalization of new ventures.

Acknowledgements

Any project of this nature is a collective effort and we are grateful to several individuals around the world for enabling this project to be undertaken.

A book is to a large extent as good as the chapters it brings together. We have been fortunate in being able to attract a set of contributors from both the entrepreneurship and international business domains, representing a wide range of geographical locations. We are grateful to all of our contributing authors who not only made the time for producing their respective chapters but also engaged wholeheartedly with the review process, taking on board comments and suggestions graciously and efficiently.

We thank our very eminent advisors, listed here in alphabetic order: Julian Birkinshaw, Mike Hitt and Tricia McDougall-Covin. They represent the fields of international business, strategy and entrepreneurship respectively and their comments during the conceptualization phase helped us greatly with arriving at an optimal level of depth and breadth. Their comments at the conclusion of the project were a great source of encouragement. We are truly grateful to them for associating themselves with this project, and for sharing of their time and wisdom.

Routledge has been a delightful publisher to work with throughout the process. We are grateful to Sinead Waldron and Terry Clague in particular for their prompt and efficient responses to our queries at various points in the project, and for monitoring the process in a thorough and courteous manner. We are pleased that such a well-regarded publisher has taken on the cause of serving the international entrepreneurship field with a *Companion*.

Last but not least, each of us thanks our families and home institutions for the support we receive at home and work, respectively, which has enabled us to carry out this project to its completion. We hope they are as proud of the end result as we are.

Postscript

After we went to press with this manuscript, and shortly after a stimulating 2014 AIB conference in Vancouver where Alan Rugman (a contributor to Chapter 12) was at his provocative best, we were deeply shocked and saddened to learn of his untimely passing. In the light of this development, we feel especially grateful to have had a contribution from Alan and his co-authors. We have both been influenced by Alan in the early stages of our careers – Stephanie took his doctoral course on international business during her PhD work at Indiana University where she got to know him well, and Shameen benefited from his active encouragement and advice as a junior academic following his return to the UK. The fact that Alan contributed a chapter to this volume on international entrepreneurship, a research domain that has attracted his criticism from time to time, is indicative of the kind of scholar he was: someone with strongly held views and at the same time a deep commitment to scholarly debate. That surely is exactly the sort of openness to dialog that is required to stimulate the further development of IE and the cross-fertilization between IB and entrepreneurship that we seek to foster through this volume.

Dedication to Alan M. Rugman by Siri Tirjesen and In Hyeock (Ian) Lee

We dedicate our chapter to our co-author and friend Alan Rugman (1945–2014) whose presence is greatly missed in our lives. Alan was a pioneering scholar in the field of international business and strategic management. His ideas helped to define research as well as practice and policy. Alan played a key role in building the universities where he was a professor, most recently at the University of Reading's Henley Business School, and earlier at Indiana University, University of Oxford, University of Toronto, Dalhousie University, and University of Winnipeg. Moreover, he was a President of the Academy of International Business (2004–2006) and was elected as Fellow of the Academy of International Business (1992) and Royal Society of Arts (1998). In the course of our research, we benefited from Alan's fondness for a good debate and desire to challenge existing ideas. He was masterful at finding the weaknesses, but also the gems, in others' arguments.

Moreover, we enjoyed Alan as a friend. We have known Alan since our doctoral studies in 2000 and 2002 respectively. During our years together in Bloomington, Indiana, we especially enjoyed our time with Alan and his wife Helen. In addition to being a truly dedicated scholar, Alan was extremely devoted to his family and other non-academic pursuits. We remember Alan telling us about how he and Helen have been together since university, and have enjoyed living and traveling around the world together. Privately, Alan would talk not just about the upcoming AIB or AOM conference – but also that he and Helen were looking forward to visiting the particular conference city and what they had planned to do. Helen accompanied him to nearly every conference, and devoted her life to supporting Alan and their son Andrew. Alan also shared a very special relationship with their son, and Alan's home office proudly featured a picture of he and Andrew, taken when Alan ran the London Marathon and Andrew came out to support him. When Alan and Helen moved back to the UK in April 2009, they looked forward to more time with their son.

We have many happy memories of Alan and Helen in their Bloomington, Indiana, home, which Siri and her husband Per purchased when the Rugmans returned to the UK. The Rugmans left a 'good luck' token over the fireplace which remains in the home. Alan also provided his desk and bookshelves so that we might have a home office, and some other furniture which he and Helen had since the start of their life together in North America (in Winnipeg in the early 1970s), and which he thought might bring us joy. This generosity was so typical of Alan and Helen – they were eager to share their time but also lives with others. Helen and Alan also invited Ian's family (including his two children, Bryan and Nayoon) often to their lovely home when Alan was Ian's doctoral supervisor at Indiana University. Alan's keen storytelling skills in the academic world also transcended to the private world and he entertained Ian's young children with wonderful stories. Helen always kindly made delicious meals and taught English to the kids. The Rugmans returned frequently to visit Bloomington. The Rugmans' last Bloomington visit came shortly after the birth of Siri's first son, Tor, of whom Alan was extremely fond. Alan proved to be quite a baby whisperer and entertained little Tor such that they were both giggling with joy. Alan treated Tor just as he did anyone else he was 'conversing' with – he was always so interested in who you were and what you were thinking and why, and took the time to get to know you. A testament to this is that Alan and Helen have many lifelong friendships all over the world.

We can fondly recall many conversations with Alan that were two-part: academic and non-academic. The discussion often began with a debate about a particular idiosyncratic component of international business. Alan might conclude this conversation with, "Alright now that we've settled that, let's talk about something else shall we?" and then the conversation might turn to anything else, outside of the academy. Alan was deeply intellectually curious in all areas.

Ian met Alan in a dream on the following day of his passing away, which happened to be Ian's forty-fifth birthday. Alan gave Ian, his former doctoral student, a small portable desk as a birthday gift in the dream. A desk stands for an academic world of research and teaching, and the dream illustrates that Alan still continues to give valuable things to his colleagues, even from heaven.

We are knocked sideways by the loss of a great scholar and a wonderful friend. We are truly blessed for our years of friendship and collaboration with Alan Rugman.

An introduction to the *Routledge Companion to International Entrepreneurship*

Stephanie A. Fernhaber and Shameen Prashantham

It is an exciting time for the field of international entrepreneurship (IE). No longer a field in its infancy stage, but rather characterized by exponential growth, IE scholars are crossing new frontiers in terms of knowledge being created. Scholars today are grappling with increasingly varied and complex questions relating to the role of effectuation within IE (Sarasvathy et al., 2014; Schweizer et al., 2010), locational issues pertaining to both home and host markets (Acs and Terjesen, 2013; Fernhaber et al., 2008), the post-entry speed and behavior of internationalizing ventures (Prashantham and Young, 2011; Sleuwaegen and Onkelinx, 2014) and international social entrepreneurship (Zahra et al., 2014), to name just a few. Special issues on IE in journals such as *Entrepreneurship, Theory and Practice,* the *Journal of Business Venturing* and *European Business Review* continue to be rolled out, seeking to push IE research to new heights. In addition to serving as a mechanism for greater knowledge accumulation and insight, the evolutionary stage of the IE field offers the opportunity to consciously reflect on *how* it is currently evolving and where we would like to see it go.

International entrepreneurship: the intersection of entrepreneurship and international business

One of the intriguing – and enjoyable – aspects of editing this book as a duo of an entrepreneurship scholar (Stephanie Fernhaber) and an international business researcher (Shameen Prashantham) was the discovery that we had somewhat different takes on the very exciting domain of IE research. For instance, we seemed to view the starting point of research in this area as being McDougall's (1989) article in the *Journal of Business Venturing* (JBV) and Oviatt and McDougall's (1994) award-winning article in the *Journal of International Business Studies* (JIBS), respectively. Mirroring this divergent perspective, the 2011 JBV special issue takes the 1989 JBV article as the genesis of IE whereas the chapter by Dimitratos and Li, who are international business scholars, takes the 1994 JIBS article as the starting point of its analysis. While this is perhaps understandable given the salience of these outlets to our respective fields, it may be symptomatic of greater underlying differences in perspectives and emphases. That, coupled with the arguable dominance of entrepreneurship scholars in shaping this area,[1] led us to believe that it was important to ensure that, to the extent possible, insights from *both* disciplines were brought to bear in this handbook.

Such an integrative perspective seems desirable for at least three reasons. First, although Oviatt and McDougall envisioned the IE domain as "the intersection of two research paths" (McDougall and Oviatt, 2000), they later acknowledged that "most of the citations to it [Oviatt and McDougall, 1994] come from entrepreneurship journals and entrepreneurship scholars" (Oviatt and McDougall, 2005: 7). Our domain needs cross-fertilization as they have argued (McDougall and Oviatt, 2000; Oviatt and McDougall, 2005). Second, we would suggest that this domain has the potential to catalyze greater insight for entrepreneurship scholars into phenomena that are affected by cross-border facets and for international business scholars into the entrepreneurship of international activity (Al-Aali and Teece, 2014; Teece, 2014). To do so requires moving beyond parallel research streams in each discipline to offering new explanatory power and insight due to cross-disciplinary conversations (Cheng et al., 2014). Third, contemporary developments in firms' strategy and technological prowess have meant that the phenomenon of new venture internationalization can no longer fail to explicitly take into account the influence of large multinational enterprises (MNEs) and the interfirm ecosystems that they orchestrate (Acs and Terjesen, 2013; Prashantham and Dhanaraj, in press). Research on the international new venture–MNE interface represents a fertile lacuna in IE research, and one that will be best addressed by synthesizing insights from entrepreneurship and international business.

As such, for both entrepreneurship and international business scholars, there is a need to break out of their respective bubbles and collaborate together. This is how we believe the field will truly move ahead. We gain hope at glimpses of this happening. What an exciting time as Patricia McDougall, an entrepreneurship-trained scholar who has played a central role in the IE movement, chaired the Academy of International Business meeting in 2013. Likewise, the fact that a renowned international business scholar such as Alan Rugman is not only contributing a chapter to this book, but has already written several articles that make reference or relate to international entrepreneurship (e.g. Almodóvar and Rugman, 2014). Key leaders such as these offer a great example for their respective fields.

The Routledge Companion to International Entrepreneurship: an overview

The motivation behind writing this book stemmed from the momentum in closing this divide further. Not only do we as editors represent the entrepreneurship and international business fields, but we have also carefully chosen an array of scholars from both perspectives. Moreover, we have asked our authors to play special attention to both fields in the writing of their book chapters. We are grateful for their cooperation and have enjoyed helping facilitate this process.

The sections of the book have been broken into four areas, which illustrate the changing knowledge streams and continuous evolution of the IE field. The first part explores the emergence of IE as a field. The opening chapter by Rialp, Rialp and Knight offers a detailed review of the field while categorizing the research topics by international business and more traditional entrepreneurship origins. Dimitratos and Li then utilize citation analysis in Chapter 2 to demonstrate the seminal articles in the international business, entrepreneurship and IE arenas. Both chapters are a great starting point in identifying potential gaps for future research as well as for attaining an understanding of cross-disciplinary perspectives.

In the second part of the book, insight is offered into a growing stream of research that focuses on the make-up of the international entrepreneur. While cognition has experienced significant growth within the entrepreneurship field, it also has noteworthy relevance within the international context. Milanov and Maissenhälter offer an insightful background and overview of cognition in Chapter 3 and then lay out its applicability to the IE arena, outlining low hanging opportunities for research throughout. In Chapter 4, Andersson discusses how the background, experience, knowledge and behavior of the entrepreneur influences new venture internationalization. Marshall, Lieberman and Pagès introduce the relevancy of international social entrepreneurship in Chapter 5, while Crick and Chaudhry wrap up the section in Chapter 6 with an insightful overview of the transitional entrepreneur integrated with an empirical analysis.

The third part of the book covers a range of strategic issues for entrepreneurial internationalization. In essence, these topics discuss *how* entrepreneurial firms are able to internationalize and in doing so, offer a combined entrepreneurship and international business perspective. Chapter 7 begins with an examination by Chetty and Pahlberg of the role of networks. This is followed by a very relevant discussion in Chapter 8 by Sapienza, De Clercq and Zhao on knowledge and learning, and in Chapter 9 by Prange on capabilities. Using the lens of entrepreneurship, IB and IE, Reuber, Fischer and Morgan-Thomas then offer up capabilities in Chapter 10 that underlie the success of international new ventures leveraging a digital platform. In Chapter 11, LiPuma addresses the role of venture capital in IE. This section is wrapped up by a thought-provoking Chapter 12 by Rugman, Lee and Terjesen in which the extent to which international new ventures are indeed global is examined.

Lastly, in the fourth part of the book, we conclude with a section devoted to understanding the implications of entrepreneurial internationalization as well as for future research design. In Chapter 13, Servais and Rasmussen explore both the performance and survival implications, while McNaughton and Pellegrino shift their focus to policy implications in Chapter 14. The final chapter by Nummela in the book takes an in-depth look into the design of IE research, and offers a series of recommendations which again can help spur future research.

It is our hope that emerging and existing scholars will utilize this book for reference purposes, but also for inspiration to continue the evolution of the IE field with a more holistic and interdisciplinary collaborative spirit.

Note

1 Anecdotal data support this observation. For instance, in the 2000 special issue on international entrepreneurship in the *Academy of Management Journal*, the majority of the contributing authors were from entrepreneurship (or strategy more broadly) rather than international business. Also, the scholars invited to comment on Oviatt and McDougall's JIBS Decade Award in 2004 were leading entrepreneurship scholars (Autio and Zahra). Furthermore, the most recent influential special issues on international entrepreneurship have been in leading entrepreneurship journals (*Entrepreneurship Theory and Practice*, 2011; *Journal of Business Venturing*, 2014).

References

Acs, Z. J. and Terjesen, S. (2013). Born local: toward a theory of new venture's choice of internationalization. *Small Business Economics*, 41(3), 521–535.

Al-Aali, A. and Teece, D. J. (2014). International entrepreneurship and the theory of the (long-lived) international firm: a capabilities perspective. *Entrepreneurship, Theory & Practice*, 38(1), 95–116.

Almodóvar, P. and Rugman, A. M. (2014). The M Curve and the performance of Spanish international new ventures. *British Journal of Management*, 25(S1), 6–23.

Cheng, J.L.C., Birkinshaw, J., Lessard, D. and Thomas, D. C. (2014). Advancing interdisciplinary research: insights from the JIBS special issue. *Journal of International Business Studies*, 45, 643–648.

Fernhaber, S. A., Gilbert, B. A., and McDougall, P. P. (2008). International entrepreneurship and geographic location: an empirical examination of new venture internationalization. *Journal of International Business Studies*, 39(2), 267–290.

McDougall, P. P. (1989). International versus domestic entrepreneurship: new venture strategic behavior and industry structure. *Journal of Business Venturing*, 4(6), 387–400.

McDougall, P. and Oviatt, B. M. (2000). International entrepreneurship: the intersection of two research paths. *Academy of Management Journal*, 43(5), 902–906.

Oviatt, B. M. and McDougall, P. (1994). Toward a theory of international new ventures. *Journal of International Business Studies*, 25(1), 45–64.

Oviatt, B. M. and McDougall, P. P. (2005). The internationalization of entrepreneurship. *Journal of International Business Studies*, 36(1), 2–8.

Prashantham, S. and Dhanaraj, C. (in press). MNE ties and new venture internationalization: exploratory insights from India. *Asia Pacific Journal of Management*, forthcoming.

Prashantham, S. and Young, S. (2011). Post-entry speed of international new ventures. *Entrepreneurship Theory and Practice*, 35(2), 275–292.

Sarasvathy, S., Kumar, K. K., York, J. G., and Bhagavatula, S. (2014). An effectual approach to international entrepreneurship: overlaps, challenges, and provocative possibilities. *Entrepreneurship: Theory and Practice*, 38(1), 71–93.

Schweizer, R., Vahlne, J-E. and Johanson, J. (2010). Internationalization as an entrepreneurial process. *Journal of International Entrepreneurship*, 8(4), 343–370.

Sleuwaegen, L. and Onkelinx, J. (2014). International commitment, post-entry growth and survival of international new ventures. *Journal of Business Venturing*, 29(1), 106–120.

Teece, D. J. (2014). A dynamic capabilities-based entrepreneurial theory of the multinational enterprise. *Journal of International Business Studies*, 45, 8–37.

Zahra, S. A., Newey, L. R. and Li, Y. (2014). On the frontier: the implications of social entrepreneurship for international entrepreneurship. *Entrepreneurship, Theory and Practice*, 38(1), 137–158.

Part I

The emergence of international entrepreneurship

1

International entrepreneurship

A review and future directions

Alex Rialp, Josep Rialp and Gary A. Knight

Introduction

Business internationalization, generally understood as the process of increasing involvement in international operations across borders (Welch and Loustarinen, 1988) and of adapting firms' operations to such international environments (Calof and Beamish, 1995) has become a core part of the strategy-driven process of many contemporary firms (Welch and Welch, 1996). Accordingly, the internationalization of the firm has received much academic interest in the last four decades (Rialp and Rialp, 2001; Werner, 2002). For a long time, a large portion of scientific research on internationalization had focused on empirically testing the behavioral-based sequential or gradualist approach earlier postulated by the Internationalization Process Model or Uppsala-Model (Cavusgil, 1980; Johanson and Vahlne, 1977, 1990). This model views firm internationalization as a lengthy process that develops in stages, assuming that market knowledge is acquired primarily through experience from current business activities in increasingly psychologically distant target foreign markets. This gradualist approach, however, has been criticized and lately revisited (Andersen, 1993; Johanson and Vahlne, 2006, 2009) due largely to the emergence of early internationalization perspectives (Knight and Cavusgil, 1996; Madsen and Servais, 1997; Oviatt and McDougall, 1997).

Indeed, the salient features of early and rapid business internationalization from inception are best captured at the intersection of the entrepreneurship and internationalization perspectives (McDougall and Oviatt, 2000; Mathews and Zander, 2007). International entrepreneurship (IE) has emerged as a distinctive and interdisciplinary field of research at the interface between internationalization and entrepreneurship (McDougall and Oviatt, 2000; Oviatt and McDougall, 1999, 2005a, b; Dimitratos and Jones, 2005; Hessels, 2008; Fernhaber et al., 2009) and focusing primarily, but not exclusively, on the challenging phenomenon of infant firms that operate internationally early after inception. While the two most commonly used terms to label these firms are international new ventures (INVs) (Oviatt and McDougall, 1994, 1997; McDougall et al., 1994, 2003; Prashantham and Young, 2011; Spence et al., 2011) and born global firms (BGFs) (Rennie, 1993; Knight and Cavusgil, 1996, 2004; Madsen and Servais, 1997; Andersson and Wictor, 2003; Sharma and Blomstermo, 2003; Chetty and Campbell-Hunt, 2004; Hashai and Almor, 2004; Nordman and Melén, 2008; Cavusgil and Knight, 2009), scholars use other terms such as global start-ups (Jolly et al., 1992; Oviatt and McDougall, 1995); born international SMEs (Kundu and Katz, 2003), early internationalizing firms (Rialp et al., 2005a; Schwens and Kabst, 2009) or rapidly internationalizing ventures (Cesinger et al., 2012). This disparity in terminology can create confusion, especially when used interchangeably (Svensson, 2006; Svensson and Payan, 2009; Crick, 2009; Baum et al., 2011). Nonetheless these terms all refer to essentially the same phenomenon, i.e., new or young and independent ventures internationalizing at inception or very shortly thereafter (typically within three years of foundation). Such businesses have come of age during the current era of globalization and advanced technology. For brevity's sake, we will collectively refer to such young companies as born global firms (BGFs).

Since the early 1990s, numerous researchers have focused on explaining the particularly early and accelerated internationalization of "born globals" mostly in high-technology sectors (Jolly et al., 1992; Bell, 1995; Knight and Cavusgil, 1996; Crick and Jones, 2000), but also in more traditional, mature industries (McAuley, 1999; Fillis, 2004). Regardless of the context of empirical investigation, much scholarly research has described these firms and attempted to advance theoretical perspectives, especially given the inability of extant international business theories and models to fully account for them (McDougall et al., 1994; Oviatt and McDougall, 1997; Bell et al., 2004).

Given the widespread appearance of born global firms, researchers have devoted much scholarly attention to this phenomenon, which is very frequently considered in comprehensive reviews of the contemporary literature (Coviello and McAuley, 1999; Fillis, 2001; Fletcher, 2004; Ruzzier et al., 2006; Rialp and Rialp, 2007; Wright et al., 2007; Jones et al., 2011). However, despite its growing significance as a current research issue, mostly documented at the empirical level so far, some authors believe that more advanced and comprehensive explanations of this phenomenon are still lacking (Oviatt and McDougall, 1999, 2005a; Knight and Cavusgil, 2004; Jones and Coviello, 2005; Zahra, 2005; Coviello, 2006; Mathews and Zander, 2007; Weerawardena et al., 2007; Gabrielsson et al., 2008a). Thus, more dedicated research efforts are needed to enrich existing knowledge on the born global phenomenon (Zahra and George, 2002; Bell et al., 2001, 2004; Melén and Nordman, 2009; Rialp et al., 2010).

The born global phenomenon was first reviewed by Rialp et al. (2005a) and, more recently, by others (Aspelund et al., 2007; Jones et al., 2011; Cesinger et al., 2012; and Madsen, 2013). However, it is one mainstream topic, although perhaps the most developed and consolidated one, of the different streams of research belonging to IE (Oviatt and McDougall, 2005a, b; Jones et al., 2011). Accordingly, in this chapter we focus our review effort specifically on examining contemporary studies of BGFs.

We aim to provide an updated and integrated review of the contemporary international business and entrepreneurship literatures focused on smaller born global firms (BGFs)[1] (including both conceptual contributions and empirical studies) with the twofold objective of (a) examining the current state of knowledge on the born global phenomenon as a contemporary research issue, and (b) identifying future research directions from which to promote further conceptual and empirical progress in the field.

We structure our chapter as follows: first, an overview of international entrepreneurship as a field of research is provided in which BGFs are positioned as a very relevant category of international entrepreneurial ventures, followed by an integrative overview of the past and current literature focused on this challenging born global phenomenon. Then, based upon our literature review, we critically assess the current status of this field and propose new directions for future research. We close with concluding remarks.

International entrepreneurship as a field of research

Since its earliest origin in the late 1980s until nowadays, research in international entrepreneurship (IE) (Wright and Ricks, 1994; McDougall and Oviatt, 2000; Dimitratos and Jones, 2005) is characterized by a multiplicity of evolving definitions, approaches, frameworks, methods, and even gaps (McDougall, 1989; McDougall et al., 1994; Oviatt and McDougall, 1994, 1997, 1999; 2005a, b; Zahra and George, 2002; Coviello and Jones, 2004; Autio, 2005; Jones and Coviello, 2005; Zahra, 2005; Coombs et al., 2009; Keupp and Gassmann, 2009; Szyliowicz and Galvin, 2010; Jones et al., 2011; Reuber and Fischer, 2011; de Clercq et al., 2012; Kiss et al., 2012; Peiris et al., 2012; Covin and Miller, 2013; Mainela et al., 2014).

Numerous scholars have sought to define the boundaries of IE (cf. Jones and Nummela, 2008; Jones et al., 2011), some focusing mainly on BGFs (Rialp et al., 2005a, b; Aspelund et al., 2007; Gabrielsson and Kirpalani, 2004, 2012) and others noting that older, established companies, not only new or young ones, can also show international entrepreneurial behavior (Wright and Ricks, 1994; McDougall and Oviatt, 2000; Zahra, 2005). Actually, the most updated, well accepted, and broadest definition of IE "the discovery, enactment, evaluation, and exploitation of opportunities across national borders to create future goods and services" (Oviatt and McDougall, 2005a: 539) fosters both international opportunity (Mainela et al., 2014) and international entrepreneurial orientation (Covin and Miller, 2013) as key constructs, and applies to all firm sizes, large and small, and types of firms, young and old. Over time, the IE field has tended to shift from its early focus on firm age (new), size (small) and industry (hi-tech) to increasingly emphasize the role of firm resources, capabilities, processes, and (international) opportunities. The above definition accommodates such an evolution in the born global literature.

Although some authors claim IE research has not yet attained the necessary theoretical rigour and external theoretical legitimization (Keupp and Gassmann, 2009), others believe that IE research is progressing well, achieving consistency and gradually developing unifying paradigms and theoretical perspectives (Jones et al., 2011). Thus, while still in an emergent status, IE can be considered an integrative, coherent, and highly promising scholarly field whose domain encompasses at least three main research avenues, branches or thematic areas: (a) entrepreneurial internationalization (cross-national-border behavior of entrepreneurial actors); (b) international comparisons of entrepreneurship (cross-national comparisons of domestic entrepreneurship); and (c) comparative entrepreneurial internationalization (cross-country comparisons of new venture internationalization) (Hessels, 2008; Jones et al., 2011; Terjesen et al., 2013).

Accordingly, IE currently covers a wide array of international entrepreneurial activities (Wright and Ricks, 1994; Jones and Coviello, 2005; Zahra, 2005; Mathews and Zander, 2007) due mostly to the fact that international entrepreneurial behavior may simultaneously concern both new and established firms irrespective of age, size or industry (Dimitratos and Jones, 2005). Diverse classifications, typologies and/or archetypes of international entrepreneurial ventures are emerging in the growing body of IE literature (Zucchella and Scabini, 2007; Gabrielsson et al., 2008b; Bell at al., 2004, 2011; Kuivalainen et al., 2012; Madsen, 2013).

Within this general IE domain, born global firms (Madsen and Servais, 1997; Madsen et al., 2000; Moen, 2002; Moen and Servais, 2002; Knight and Cavusgil, 2004; Rialp et al., 2005b) undoubtedly constitute the most distinctive type of new organizational form in IE research with a comparatively much higher level of presence than any other type of venture in the specialized literature in the last two decades. However, other smaller but more long-established ventures (SMEs) can be also detected in the contemporary IE field that may also exhibit international entrepreneurial behavior like born globals, such as born again global firms (Bell et al., 2001, 2004, 2011; Jantunen et al., 2008; Tuppura et al., 2008), global entrepreneurial SMEs or globalizing internationals (Gabrielsson and Gabrielsson, 2003, 2004; Dimitratos et al., 2010; Kalinic and Forza, 2012), and even micro-multinationals (Dimitratos et al., 2003), apart from smaller foreign subsidiaries linked to a larger MNE and new emerging market multinationals (Mathews, 2006; Guillén and García-Canal, 2009, 2010; Cuervo-Cazurra, 2011). However, due to the fact that better understanding the earlier and usually faster or accelerated internationalization process from inception of entrepreneurial new ventures like BG firms is a mainstream topic within IE research (Hurmerinta-Peltomäki, 2003; Oviatt and McDougall, 2005a, b; Jones et al., 2011), the remaining sections of this chapter address the literature examining BGFs as a main typology of international and entrepreneurial new ventures.

Integrating past and contemporary literature on born global firms

A brief look at the origins: pioneering studies on INVs/BGFs[2]

While for several decades research in international business had emphasized large, established multinational corporations, with entrepreneurial SMEs receiving much less research attention; since the late 1970s some scholars in international business turned their attention to the incremental process through which smaller exporting firms gradually internationalize to psychically distant markets (Johanson and Vahlne, 1977; Cavusgil, 1980; Welch and Luostarinen, 1988).

However, a few scholars began identifying companies that undertake early internationalization from inception through more flexible managerial attitudes and practices (Hedlund and Kverneland, 1985; Morrow, 1988; Ganitsky, 1989). In her seminal work on new ventures' international sales, entrepreneurship scholar McDougall (1989) defined international entrepreneurship (IE) as the emergence of new companies that, from their inception, engage in international business thus viewing their operating domain as international from the initial stages of the firm's operation, and termed "International New Ventures or Start ups (INVs)" those firms emphasizing aggressive foreign market entry, with management taking an international perspective from the firm's earliest days. They pursued broad strategies serving numerous customers in diverse market segments, developing high market or product visibility, and developing and controlling numerous distribution channels (McDougall, 1989).

In 1993, Rennie introduced the term "born global" to describe companies that internationalize at or near their founding, based on his research on exporting firms from Australia. Rennie (1993) found that a large proportion of new Australian firms targeted foreign markets from inception, in large part because of the relatively small size of Australia's domestic market. Like McDougall, Rennie was a pioneer in the born global literature. In his study of 300 firms, Rennie (1993) found that Australian born globals began exporting, on average, only two years after founding and obtained some three-quarters of their revenues from abroad. These small firms successfully competed against larger established players worldwide. Remarkably, Rennie (1993) found that born globals accounted for some 20 percent of Australia's high-value-added manufacturing exports. He argued that the emergence of born globals reveals how SMEs can power a nation's economic growth.

In 1994, McDougall et al. compared five generally accepted IB perspectives—Monopolistic Advantage Theory, Product Cycle Theory, Stage Theory of Internationalization, Oligopolistic Reaction Theory, and Internalization Theory—and concluded that some aspects of born global firms are not well explained by extant international business theories.

In a related and highly acclaimed work, Oviatt and McDougall (1994: 49) provided the first substantive conceptual explanation in the academic literature of INVs, these being defined as "business organizations that, from inception, seek to derive significant competitive advantage from the use of resources and the sale of outputs in multiple countries." By examining value chain activities and the number of countries entered, the authors identified four types of INVs:

1 Export/import start-ups (with few international activities in few countries).
2 Multinational traders (with few international activities in many countries).
3 Geographically focused start-ups (with many international activities in few counties).
4 Global start-ups (with many international activities in many countries).

They presented an explanatory framework of early internationalizing firms by integrating accepted MNE and international business theories with developments in entrepreneurship research. They noted that many such firms succeed by controlling rather than owning unique resources, especially knowledge.

Although Oviatt's and McDougall's (1994) early typology of INVs has been widely accepted in the literature, empirical testing of the determinants of INV types remains incomplete. Zahra (2005), Crick (2009), Baum et al. (2011), and Madsen (2013) perceive that the original INV typology merits additional scholarly attention to examine, for example, sources of competitive advantages, market scope, and strategies that affect their performance.

In the mid 1990s, Knight and Cavusgil (1996: 11) and Knight (1997) defined born global firms (BGFs) as "small, technology-oriented companies that operate in international markets from the earliest days of their establishment." These authors argued that the born global phenomenon challenged traditional views of company internationalization (e.g. Johanson and Vahlne, 1977), and described the factors and implications associated with the arrival of born global firms, and the limitations posed for conventional internationalization views.

Contemporary research on the born global phenomenon: an integrated overview

Since its origins in the late 1980s, the academic literature on born global firms has largely increased, almost exponentially year after year in the current century, to become one of the main and more consolidated research issues in the emerging and interdisciplinary field of International Entrepreneurship (IE).

In Table 1.1, a review of existing research developed on the born global phenomenon in the last decades is presented and organized according to a number of key research topics typically addressed by international business and entrepreneurship academics alike, including both conceptual and empirical studies and also literature reviews. We have classified studies based on their dominant focus, although some works address two or more topical areas. Because we include only exemplary works, the table does not represent an exhaustive collection of available studies in the field. We, however, alert the reader that we only collectively refer to these studies here, without specifically citing authors (who appear carefully noted in Table 1.1).

From the international business discipline numerous topics have been analyzed, with varying depth, in research focused on the emergence and further development of BGFs. Many authors have identified both internal and external/environmental factors that drive early and rapid internationalization. Also, the key role played by knowledge-based resources and (dynamic) capabilities in the early internationalization process is highlighted. We note that scholars have given less emphasis, by contrast, to examining how knowledge-based organizational learning processes impact information seeking and foreign market research by these firms. Also, relevant managerial decision-making processes regarding foreign country market/segment selection (especially dealing with higher or lower geographic and psychic distance between home and foreign markets) and entry mode choice in born global firms have been perhaps lesser examined to date mostly

Table 1.1 Extant research on born global firms*

Core discipline	*Key research topic*	*Example studies in past research*
International business	Determinants of early and rapid internationalization (internal and environmental driving factors)	Rennie (1993); Roberts and Senturia (1996); Knight and Cavusgil (1996, 2004, 2005); Knight (1997); Autio et al. (2000); Crick and Jones (2000); Shrader et al. (2000); Moen (2002); Moen and Servais (2002); Andersson and Wictor (2003); McDougall et al. (2003); Bell et al. (2003, 2004); Etemad (2004); Andersson (2004); Rialp et al. (2005a, b); Fernhaber et al. (2007); Fan and Phan (2007); Zucchella et al. (2007); Kudina et al. (2008); Cavusgil and Knight (2009); Kuivalainen et al. (2012); Nowinski and Rialp (2013)
	Organizational resources and (dynamic) capabilities	McDougall et al. (1994); Liesch and Knight (1999); Bloodgood et al. (1996); Knight and Cavusgil (2004); Autio et al. (2000); Zahra et al. (2000); Moen and Servais (2002); Kuemmerle (2002); McDougall et al. (2003); Zahra et al. (2003); Kundu and Katz (2003); Lostarinen and Gabrielsson (2006); Rialp and Rialp (2006); Zhang and Tansuhaj (2007); Laanti et al. (2007); Mudambi and Zahra (2007); Weerawardena et al. (2007); Zucchella and Scabini (2007); Karra et al. (2008); Autio et al. (2011)
	Foreign market research, information seeking and organizational learning/knowledge	Liesch and Knight (1999); Autio et al. (2000); Zahra et al. (2000); Yeoh (2000, 2004); Kuemmerle (2002); Michailova and Wilson (2008); Weerawardena et al. (2007); Zhou (2007); Gassmann and Keupp (2007); Jantunen et al.(2008); Nordman and Melén (2008); Fernhaber et al. (2009); Schewns and Kabst (2009); Prashantham and Young (2011)
	Foreign country market/segment selection (niche focus)	Jolly et al. (1992); Bell (1995); Bloodgood et al. (1996); Madsen et al. (2000); Yip et al. (2000); Shrader et al. (2000); Crick and Jones (2000); Aspelund and Moen (2001); Moen (2002); McNaughton (2003); Knight and Cavusgil (2004); Knight et al. (2004)
	Entry mode selection	McDougall et al. (1994); Burgel and Murray (1998); Zahra et al. (2000); Shrader et al. (2000); Crick and Jones (2000); Yip et al. (2000); Gabrielsson and Kirpalani (2004); Freeman et al. (2006); Servais et al. (2006); Taylor and Jack (2012); Ripollés and Blesa (2012)
	Global vs. regional/ local approach	Moen (2002); Kuemmerle (2005); Svensson (2006); Svensson and Payan (2009); Acs and Terjesen (2012)
	International (marketing) strategy/ international marketing orientation and competence	McDougall and Oviatt (1996); Knight (2000); Aspelund and Moen (2001); McDougall et al. (2003); Knight et al. (2004); Chetty and Campbell-Hunt (2004); Bell et al. (2004); Knight and Cavusgil (2004, 2005); Gabrielsson (2003, 2005); Loustarinen and Gabrielsson (2006); Aspelund et al. (2007); Harstfield et al. (2009)
	Psychic distance	Bell (1995); Crick and Jones (2000); Madsen et al. (2000); Moen and Servais (2002); Arenius (2003) Andersson (2004); Yamin and Sinkovics (2006); Ojala (2009); Taylor and Jack (2012)

Table 1.1 Extant research on born global firms* (Continued)

Core discipline	*Key research topic*	*Example studies in past research*
	Internet-enabled internationalization	Sinkovics and Bell (2006); Yamin and Sinkovics (2006); Arenius et al. (2006) Loane (2006); Servais et al. (2007); Zhang and Tansuhaj (2007); Gabrielsson and Gabrielsson (2011); Reuber and Fischer (2011)
	Post-international entry and expansion	Yip et al. (2000); Luostarinen and Gabrielsson (2006); Morgan-Thomas and Jones (2009); Melén and Nordman (2009); Prashantham and Young (2011); Efrat and Shoham (2012); Sleuwaegen and Onkelinx (2013)
(International) Entrepreneurship	International enterpreneurial networks (business, social, personal)	Johanson and Vahlne (1990, 2009); Bell (1995); Coviello and Munro (1995, 1997); Yeoh (2000); McDougall et al. (2003); Andersson and Wictor (2003); Sharma and Blomstermo (2003); Harris and Wheeler (2005); Freeman et al. (2006); Mort and Weerawardena (2006); Coviello (2006); Coviello and Cox (2006); Angdal and Chetty (2007); Zhou et al. (2007); Ojala (2009); Parshantham and Dhanaraj (2010); Vasilchenko and Morris (2011); Fernhaber and Li (2012)
	International entrepreneurial orientation/culture/ dynamics	McDougall et al. (1994); Oviatt and McDougall (1995); Knight (2000); Knight and Cavusgil (2004); Mathews and Zander (2007) ; Zhang and Tansuhaj (2007); Kuivalainen et al. (2007); Jantunen et al. (2008); Covin and Miller (2013)
	Founding process	Oviatt and McDougall (1995); Moen and Servais (2002); Kuemmerle (2002); McDougall et al. (2003); Rasmussen et al. (2001); Andersson and Wictor (2003)
	Entrepreneur-managers' characteristics (global mindset, international vision and orientation, cognition, risk taking, and proactivity)	Jolly et al. (1992); Oviatt and McDougall (1995); Knight and Cavusgil (1996); Bloodgood et al. (1996); Reuber and Fischer (1997, 2002); Kundu and Katz (2001); Moen (2002); Moen and Servais (2002); McDougall et al. (2003); Andersson (2004); Etemad (2004); Knight et al. (2004); Chetty and Campbell-Hunt (2004), Nummela et al. (2004); Gabrielsson and Kirpalani (2004); Zahra et al. (2005); Zhou (2007); Acedo and Jones (2007); Freeman and Cavusgil (2007); Federico et al. (2009)
	International opportunity recognition, evaluation and exploitation	McDougall, Shane and Oviatt (1994); Crick and Spence (2005); Zahra et al. (2005); Mort and Weerawardena (2006); Di Gregorio et al. (2008), Karra et al. (2008); Chandra et al. (2009, 2012); Butler et al. (2010); Kontinen and Ojala (2011); Mainela et al. (2014)
	Causation vs. effectuation	Andersson (2011); Evers and O'Gorman (2011); Fisher and Reuber (2011); Harms and Schiele (2012); Nowinski and Rialp (2013)
	Public policy implications	Bell and McNaughton (2000); Bell et al. (2003, 2004)
(International) Marketing/ entrepreneurship interface/ entrepreneurial marketing		Knight (2000), Kokac and Abimbola (2009); Mort et al. (2012); Hallbäck and Gabrielsson (2013)

(continued)

Table 1.1 Extant research on born global firms* (Continued)

Core discipline	*Key research topic*	*Example studies in past research*
Conceptual developments		Oviatt and McDougall (1994, 1997, 1999, 2005a, b); Madsen and Servais (1997); McDougall et al. (1994); McDougall and Oviatt (2000, 2005a); Zahra and George (2002); Bell et al. (2003); Hurmerinta-Peltomäki (2003, 2004); Etemad (2004); Rialp et al. (1995a); Jones and Coviello (2005); Prashantham (2005); Sapienza et al. (2006); Weerawardena et al. (2007); Zucchella and Scabini (2007); Gabrielsson et al. (2008a, b); Johanson and Vahlne (2003, 2006, 2009); Rialp et al. (2010)
Literature reviews/ comments on BGFs/INVs and IE		Coviello and McAuley (1999); Zahra and George (2002); Coviello and Jones (2004); Rialp et al. (2005a); McDougall and Oviatt (2005b); Autio (2005); Zahra (2005), Aspelund et al. (2007); Cavusgil and Knight (2009); Keupp and Gassman (2009); Coombs et al. (2009); Szyliowicz and Galvin (2010); Reuber and Fischer (2011); Jones et al. (2011); Cesinger et al. (2012); de Clercq et al. (2012); Kiss et al. (2012); Peiris et al. (2012); Casillas and Acedo (2012); Covin and Miller (2013); Madsen (2013); Mainela et al. (2014); Terjesen et al. (2013)

*:Due to space concerns, only those references also included in the body of this chapter are listed in the chapter's References section. The full list of references cited in this Table is, however, available upon request.

because most studies focus on born global exporters sometimes in comparison with more traditional exporting firms and, with some exceptions, do not generally deal with other foreign entry modes also available to these firms. Several authors have exhaustively examined a range of international competitive and marketing strategies adopted by born global firms. For example, born globals are often seen to exhibit high levels of international marketing orientation, capability, and competence. Further scholars have investigated the key role of the internet and communications technologies in born global firms for improving communication and for managing customer relationships, distribution channels and intermediaries, sales transactions and fulfillment activities (internet-enabled internationalization). There is, also, increased interest in investigating post international entry and global expansion determinants of these firms.

Applying a more entrepreneurial perspective, scholars have also investigated the key role of networks (either business, social and/or personal ones both in the domestic and international context) and the entrepreneur-manager's characteristics underlying early and rapid internationalization processes (especially, global mindset, international vision and orientation, cognition, risk-taking, and proactiveness). Also, the notion of (international) entrepreneurial orientation has become a key construct in contemporary research on BGFs and international entrepreneurship. More recently, some current research on BGFs has focused on causation vs. effectuation processes within these firms which is derived from their current consideration in the general entrepreneurship field nowadays.[3] There is also increased interest in investigating international opportunity identification, evaluation, and exploitation processes undoubtedly linked to the latest and broadest definition of IE concerning "the discovery, enactment, evaluation, and exploitation of opportunities across national borders to create future goods and services" (Oviatt and McDougall, 2005a: 539). Some works have also dealt with the pre-founding and founding processes of BGFs, and public policy implications related to their emergence and further development. Both aspects, however, are still highly underdeveloped and require further attention in future research in this field.

Also, important conceptual and empirical progress in the IE field in the last decades is clearly observable in the growing number of both theoretical works and literature reviews on BGFs and IE research in general which have recently emerged. Interestingly, however, other seemingly important research issues such as the (international) marketing/entrepreneurship nexus and entrepreneurial marketing in BGFs, which seem clearly to be at the intersection of entrepreneurship- and internationalization-oriented researchers' interests, are still underrepresented topics in contemporary research on IE.

Taking stock and looking ahead: main gaps and directions for future research on born global firms

Despite substantial advances made in recent decades in the scholarly domain of born global firms regarding how and why BGFs are able to internationalize so early and even succeed in international business, much more work remains to be done. In this section, we discuss some challenging research opportunities in the field.

Taking stock: theoretical and methodological lessons from past research

From our perspective, future researchers should aim first at unifying and improving operational definitions of "born-globalness," which remain heterogeneous (Aspelund et al. 2007; Gabrielsson et al., 2008b; Svensson and Payan, 2009). For example, operational definitions of born globals should consider the fact that some are in fact spin-offs from larger, long-established firms and, therefore, potentially may access substantial resources of the parent firm. More broadly, further work is also needed in improving and clarifying international entrepreneurship definition and domain (Zahra, 2005; Coviello et al., 2011). The development of more standardized and unifying definitions and conceptualizations will help make future research efforts more understandable and comparable. Likewise, despite increased theoretical and empirical rigor in the field, more research is needed to develop and refine theoretical explanations and causal models regarding the born global phenomenon (Knight and Cavusgil, 1996; Oviatt and McDougall, 1999; Bell et al., 2003). Future studies also should aim to advance the methodological domain of international entrepreneurship research (Coviello and Jones, 2004).

We note that much extant research relies on a single theoretical framework, such as the Uppsala Internationalization Model or the network theory perspective, to investigate born global firms (Rialp et al., 2005a). More work is needed to extend or integrate internationalization models and the network view with more recent developments, such as the resource-, dynamic capabilities, and knowledge-based views of the firm, to explain internationalization in small, entrepreneurial firms. In addition, the sometimes forgotten time-based dimension still has a crucial role to play in current and future internationalization process research (Hurmerita-Peltomäki, 2003; Jones and Coviello, 2005) and, more particular, in better understanding of the born global firm phenomenon. Such a dynamic conception would perceive time rather as a flow of events. For example, we conjecture that timing of internationalization is likely dependent on industry-level characteristics such as the need for large scale, industry structure, the nature of global competition, and the dispersion of requisite external resources around the world. Moreover, there is much contrast between time-dependent theories and the traditional stage-based models of internationalization which cannot fully describe early internationalization

(Hurmerita-Peltomäki, 2003). By focusing on states or positions (stages), rather than on those events or change of events which probably caused them, the Uppsala Model and other gradualist views have substantially failed to capture the dynamics of internationalization (Morgan-Thomas and Jones, 2009).

Coviello and McAuley (1999) argued that future research should integrate major perspectives, particularly foreign direct investment theory, the stages models, and the network approach. They concluded that born global internationalization can be best understood by integrating these major theoretical frameworks. Accordingly, from a theoretical standpoint several insightfully integrated conceptual frameworks and models can already be found in the born global-related literature (see Table 1.2).

More recently, Aspelund et al. (2007) recommend examining concepts of variation, selection, and retention offered by evolutionary economics because they might prove to be relevant theoretical

Table 1.2 Some useful theoretical frameworks on the born global phenomenon

Author/s	*Conceptual contribution model*
Oviatt and McDougall (1994)	A theory and a classification of small firms with a proactive international strategy from inception, based upon existing internationalization theories and recent developments in the fields of strategic management and entrepreneurship. Four main conditions for explaining their sustainable existence are: (1) organizational formation through internalization of some transactions; (2) strong reliance on alternative, hybrid governance structures to access resources; (3) establishment of foreign location advantages; and (4) control over unique resources. Four different types of international new ventures emerge according to the number of countries involved and the level of co-ordination of value chain activities: export/import start-ups; multinational traders, geographically focused start-ups and global start-ups.
Oviatt and McDougall (1999)	A more dynamic theory explaining accelerated internationalization according to which, while rapidly changing technology is taken as the foundation of this process, a number of political, economic, and industrial conditions together with some firm-specific effects and the management team also constitute key building blocks.
Coviello and Munro (1995, 1997)	A network theory perspective is adopted to examine the impact of network relationships on international market development and marketing-related activities among entrepreneurial firms.
Madsen and Servais (1997)	The propensity of born global firms to emerge and their further development are likely to be affected by the characteristics of the environment itself (market internationalization, technology level and specialization), and those of the organization (competences, routines, governance, structures and business networks) and the founder/entrepreneur (past experience, ambition level, motivation, and personal networks), simultaneously. Born global firms' international behavior seems to develop in a way that may to a certain degree be in accordance with the sequential internationalization process model (the Uppsala-Model), evolutionary thinking, and the (international) network theory.
Knight and Cavusgil (1996)	Born global firms pose a relevant challenge to the most traditional internationalization theories mostly because these fail to explain why some small companies are currently able to operate abroad very soon after their birth. Born global firms are, among other specific characteristics, most usually managed by highly visionary entrepreneurs and business people that seem to perceive the entire world as their natural marketplace.

Table 1.2 Some useful theoretical frameworks on the born global phenomenon (Continued)

Author/s	*Conceptual contribution model*
Zahra and George (2002)	A general theoretical model on international entrepreneurship, understood as a major and interdisciplinary research field, which basically connects its main antecedents with several types of activities and outcomes, together with other strategic and environmental influencing factors.
Jones and Coviello (2005)	Drawing upon classic approaches to internationalization and importing insights from entrepreneurship theory, three potential models of firm internationalization, evolving from the simple through general to precise levels of conceptualization, are presented as a time-based process of entrepreneurial behavior. Entrepreneurial internationalization is both time-based and time-dependent and the cyclical effect of time in respect of how the environment, firm, and entrepreneur interact and learn to impact on internationalization is highlighted. The relationships existing among the internationalization process, experiential knowledge, and the time and behavior dimensions are considered to be critical in this model.
Rialp et al. (2005a)	A resource-based model of early internationalizing firms in which three key issues are basically highlighted: a firm's intangible resource base (1) would be of the highest importance in generating a critical level of that firm's early internationalization capability (2), which contributes, although moderated by external environmental conditions, to the development of the highly particular strategic behavior exhibited by born global firms abroad (3).
Weerawardena et al. (2007)	Building on the extant literature and drawing on the dynamic capabilities view of competitive strategy, the authors present a conceptual model of born global firm internationalization in which a set of dynamic capabilities that are built and nurtured by internationally oriented entrepreneurial founders enable these firms to develop cutting-edge, knowledge-intensive products, paving the way for their accelerated market entry.
Gabrielsson et al. (2008a, b)	The BG phenomenon is conceptualized by establishing three main phases of successful development: (1) introductory; (2) growth and resource accumulation; and (3) break-out to independent growth as a major global player. A number of events and incidents concerning key aspects such as financing, channel/network choice, and learning are singled out in each phase.
Rialp et al. (2010)	A deeper conceptual understanding of the early and rapid internationalization process of born global firms is offered by means of applying the lens of the strategy-making process. In other words, this paper offers an integrated strategic management perspective to explain the so-called born global phenomenon. Born global firms' strategy-making processes can be aligned with different schools of strategic thought depending mostly upon the nature of the specific factor/s triggering their particular international strategic behavior and also the specific phase in which they may find themselves along their international development process from inception.

constructs, applicable in future research in the attempt to analyze which firms will survive and generate earnings under the currently turbulent market conditions. Therefore, future research might leverage multiple theoretical frameworks, the resource/knowledge-based view of the firm, transaction cost theory, the organizational capability perspective and the organizational learning and organizational theories, among others, in order to advance knowledge on born global firms. Incorporating insights from such contemporary perspectives can help future researchers to address issues raised about the ability of born global firms to develop and retain competitive advantage over time. Such perspectives will bring a degree of dynamism to analyses on the evolution of these firms (Zahra, 2005).

Most theoretical and empirical research on born global firms and international entrepreneurship in general has been developed either by international business researchers or entrepreneurship-oriented researchers acting rather separately. Consequently, the full potential of combining diverse strategic management and marketing-oriented approaches with entrepreneurship developments for better understanding strategy-making processes associated with born global firms' emergence and international development is yet unrealized (Rialp et al., 2010). There remains substantial scope for developing improved theoretical frameworks of reference on the born global phenomenon by linking entrepreneurial and strategic management-oriented approaches more closely. Only in this way will more holistic theoretical frameworks assist in the development of better explanations, new research hypotheses, and propositions in this field.

Focusing now on methodological aspects, much research on born global firms is dominated by a positivist, hypothetic-deductive perspective. That is, the research is very much focused on deductively confirming or disproving hypotheses and research questions without benefit of prior exploratory research. Studies use quantitative surveys and sophisticated analytical methods such as regression analysis or structural equation modeling. Advanced empirical studies that test hypotheses should be reserved for research in relatively advanced fields. Scholarship in a relatively young field like international entrepreneurship, by contrast, should emphasize exploratory research aimed at defining, identifying, and explaining key concepts and basic phenomena. Research should aim to develop constructs and theory that lay the foundation for subsequent empirical research. In this early phase of inquiry, extensive use of confirmatory research methods may be premature. In numerous areas, more exploratory research is needed to formulate and enhance underdeveloped concepts, constructs, relationships, and theory (Marschan-Piekkäri and Welch, 2004). Studies that utilize qualitative and inductive research methods, such as exploratory and explanatory case studies, can provide rich, context-specific description and explanation of born global firms. For example, the case-based approach led Bell et al. (2001) to uncover the so-called "born-again global firm" which actually became a very surprising discovery in their research. Ultimately, the best research combines exploratory and confirmatory approaches, by mixing both qualitative and quantitative research methods and data sources. For instance, a methodological research strategy initially based on a number of case studies of born global (and even non born global) firms together with further longitudinal surveys of large-scale, statistically representative samples of born global and other types of firms would prove very useful and promising in this field. Therefore, future research will benefit from skillfully combining quantitative and qualitative approaches.

In addition, regarding data collection processes in born global firm-oriented research, numerous past empirical studies focused on just one country or sector (usually a well-developed Western economy and/or a high-tech industry). Future scholars should obtain data from various contexts, including developed and less-developed economies (Kiss et al., 2012), diverse industries (such as traditional and hi-tech manufacturing and service sectors), in order to produce findings with substantial external validity. Drawing data from various research settings and countries ensures external validity of findings and/or uncovers differences in born global firms around the world. External validity is important because it shows how findings from the study can be generalized to other countries, industries, and populations of firms.

Likewise, future research would largely benefit from a perspective that recognizes internationalization as a dynamic, time-sensitive process. Longitudinal research facilitates deeper understanding of how born globals evolve over time. In the long run, some born global firms flourish, some flounder, and a proportion of them likely will merge with large companies as smaller firms often do. Empirical research that attempts to provide a more insightful understanding of how, why, and when a new/young firm's international growth pattern reflects clear development stages, relates to surrounding domestic and/or international networks, or exhibits advanced foreign entry modes beyond exports, such as international co-operation agreements and/or foreign direct investments, would be welcome to further understand complex organizational behavior such as that shown by born global firms.

Future research in this field should be more pluralistic and "triangulated" than before, employing a variety of conceptual frameworks, suitable research methods, and analytical techniques to examine this challenging born global phenomenon more sophistically which will allow researchers to optimize the likelihood of generating meaningful knowledge (Coviello and McAuley, 1999; Coviello et al., 2011).

Looking ahead: key topics and research questions for the future

From our systematic and integrative review of this literature, we also believe that future research on born global firms should aim at better clarifying the key sources of their international precocity and dynamics by means of examining their performance antecedents and consequences, environmental conditions, internal and external resources or capabilities, and strategic marketing strategies typically associated with these firms, as well as the highly influential characteristics of the entrepreneur-managers who found them and drive their early and typically accelerated internationalization process.

A primary topic of interest resides in providing more refined and plausible explanations that help examine better the type of technological and/or market-related strategies that are currently enabling an increasing number of young firms to internationalize early. Future research should seek to deepen knowledge about the current environmental/institutional and internal factors that drive early internationalization (Szyliowicz and Galvin, 2010; Zucchella et al., 2007; Fernhaber et al., 2009). In this sense, possible relevant differences could be identified between early internationalizing firms in manufacturing vs. service sectors (are they indeed different?). Even more intriguing is how resource-poor born global firms are able to reconcile the usually costly customized product needs of unique foreign markets segments spread all over the world with the parallel need to achieve cost economies through product, price, distribution and/or communication standardization practices (i.e., the globalization vs. localization of the international marketing strategy dilemma). For example, what accounts for the early international success of born globals in light of the resource constraints they typically face? According to Zahra (2005), even the born global firm's organizational form itself could be a key source of competitive advantage, so opportunities need not be found only in its external environment. While numerous studies have attempted to portray characteristics and behaviors typically observed in born global firms, as well as the factors determining their performance in international markets (Rialp et al., 2005a), we are still largely unaware of the specific characteristics or conditions, both internal and external to the firm, that give rise to early internationalization, consolidated international growth, and superior international performance.

Another interesting research question centers on the role of personal, social, and business network relationships associated with early and substantial internationalization. In particular, how and why do both domestic and mostly international networks support early internationalization and what types of network contacts and ties are most beneficial to achieve higher market space?

Likewise, how and under what circumstances does the behavior of born globals parallel or differ from the international behavior of long-established SMEs and large multinational firms? In particular, future research investigating how organizational culture orientations and innovative, entrepreneurial strategies being currently applied by born global firms might be leveraged to improve international performance in larger and long-established firms as well would be an important contribution to knowledge in various areas, including general internationalization views and international strategy (Coviello et al., 2011). Very likely, older and larger companies can also benefit from sophisticated technological and marketing-oriented strategies found among born global firms thus adopting the resources, capabilities, and postures that help these smaller new ventures succeed internationally. As mentioned above, future research about born global firms would benefit from comparative investigations across various levels in regard to industry and/or national setting, and organizational resource base, including firm size. Resultant information would be useful for advancing theory about the different strategies that born global firms apply to reach their internationalization goals.

As reviewed before, past born global firm-oriented research also highlights the role of the entrepreneur/s in the founding and even pre-founding process of early and rapidly internationalizing firms. Managerial vision, international orientation, high-level of personal competences, and awareness of growth opportunities abroad allow some entrepreneurs to aggressively pursue international opportunities almost from their firms' inception. This perspective contrasts with the traditional view of internationalization, earlier advanced by the stages models, which emphasize the firm as the unit of analysis. It is likely that international entrepreneurship arises at multiple levels, including the industry, firm, and individual. We surmise there are even numerous governments worldwide that possess a relatively strong entrepreneurial orientation; for example, Chile and South Korea have advanced national strategies intended to support the internationalization of their indigenous firms. Investigating the extent to which the international entrepreneurship perspective is at least partly shifting the relevant unit of analysis from the firm itself to the individual (founder entrepreneur-manager or even a founding team) gives rise to very interesting research questions such as, for example, what is the role of international managerial vision and global mindset in early and dedicated internationalization? How does the nexus between the individual and the foreign business opportunity (new product/process discoveries) take place? How do the international entrepreneurial orientation and international marketing orientation of these firms' decision-makers translate into specific strategies, tactics, and performance outcomes? What is the role of cognitive processes at the managerial level? Some authors have remarked on the role of the managerial cognitions in defining born global firms' identity, strategies, and organizational cultures (McDougall et al., 2003; Knight and Cavusgil, 2004; Zahra et al., 2005). These cognitions evolve over time and shape managers' ability to foresee opportunities in foreign markets, thereby influencing the various decisions to be made and how they are executed. More research is needed to reveal how these cognitions contribute to the success or failure of born global firms.

Knowledge on born globals also would benefit from research that distinguishes the underlying causes of these firms' long-term performance (success vs. failure). To date, researchers have hardly examined the longer-term survival of born global firms and very little is known about their survival relative to other types of young companies or organizational forms. Thus, future research should investigate what happens with or what becomes of born global firms in the long run. More research is needed to examine the extent to which born globals remain small companies, what proportion become large or very successful firms, how many merge with other firms, and how many go out of business. Another issue centers on how born globals overcome the inertia and "bottle necks" of evolving from small to large companies. As they grow, small firms frequently encounter rising, substantial competition, intense growth, and resource gaps that constrain development into large companies, and can even threaten survival of the firm. Scholars might investigate how resource-intensive internationalization and growing exposure to international competitors endanger born global survival and prosperity over time. By the same token, youth and small size tend to confer flexibility and agility that can help born globals compete more effectively than larger rivals (Autio et al., 2000). Further research is needed to examine how age, size, international experience, and other demographic characteristics influence the international success and sustainability of born global firms.

Scholars might also examine much more how, what, and when new ventures learn, and how such learning, characterized by numerous dimensions (Weerawardena et al., 2007) facilitates early internationalization and superior international performance (Autio et al., 2000; Zahra et al., 2000; Autio, 2005; Zahra, 2005; Schwens and Kabst, 2009). Learning capabilities are important sources of vital knowledge that enable born global firms to prosper and succeed in international markets. Research might investigate how different types of learning processes influence the various dimensions of internationalization and firm performance.

On the other hand, it has been also pointed out that early internationalization might also carry important disadvantages (Zahra, 2005). There are likely numerous cases of born globals that failed at internationalizing or went bankrupt because they could not overcome the risks of early foreign market entry, the challenges of competing against larger and longer-established rivals, or other limitations that encumber young, resource-poor firms. Thus, instead of being aimed at providing advantages, early internationalization might have sometimes very opposite and negative effects for survival and growth for some young firms. In this sense, another potential contribution would be to identify resource gaps and establish ways to overcome resource constraints faced by young firms that might impede their successful development abroad.

Finally, once the nature and success factors of born global firms become more significantly understood, further research should also investigate which public policy initiatives can facilitate and promote the development and progress of this distinctive breed of firms. Born global firms are often drivers of national economic development and innovativeness. However, national export promotion organizations often focus on large firms, to the detriment of young ventures. Public policy often is designed to support incremental or gradual internationalization, characteristic of more traditional firms. The earlier internationalization process of born global firms also represents an important challenge to governmental export promotion agencies: that of defining the nature of support and assistance that best supports young firms' needs (Bell and McNaughton, 2000). Government agencies should, in general terms, emphasize policies and programs that are tailor-made to addressing firms' changing specific needs. Export and/or internationally oriented public policy should be reconsidered to better address the specific gaps and support needs of born global firms. Given the limited financial and tangible resources that characterize many of them, public policy might aim at supporting the success of such businesses in their international endeavors by focusing on promoting intangible, human- and/or knowledge-based assets as well as developing better infrastructures. Accordingly, research that assists policy-makers to better understand what types of public policies can best support the emergence and successful sustainability of these firms is absolutely welcome.

Table 1.3 summarizes the topics and research questions raised above. Addressing these and other similar research questions will further elucidate their nature and specific needs.

Table 1.3 Key topics and questions for further research on born global firms

Key future research topics	*Research questions*
External factors driving early internationalization	Which are the current external factors facilitating and promoting the early internationalization of the firms? Does early internationalization also occur among firms that specialize in services? If so, how do they differ from early internationalizing manufacturers?
Internal resources, networks, and strategies of born global firms	What specific conditions within the firm give rise to early internationalization? How do networks advance early internationalization goals and international performance? What types of network contacts are most beneficial? How do resource-poor born global firms reconcile the costly customized product needs of unique foreign markets with the need to achieve economies through product standardization? How and in what circumstances does the behavior of born global firms truly differ from larger firms?
Roles of founding entrepreneurs	What is the role of managerial vision and drive, product/process discoveries, and other such factors in the internationalization process of the born global firms?
Learning, development, successful performance, and failure determinants	What is the role of the firm's age in the international success of born global firms? How, what, and when do new ventures learn? What accounts for the early international success of born global firms, particularly in light of the resource constraints they typically face? To what extent do born global firms go out of business? To what extent do born global firms remain small companies? What proportion become big, successful firms? How many merge with other firms? How do born globals overcome the "growing pains" of evolving from small to large firms?
Public policies tailored to born global firms	Which public policy initiatives can facilitate and promote the development and progress of this distinctive breed of enterprise?

Concluding remarks

BGFs, as well as other types of international entrepreneurial ventures, represent a multifaceted phenomenon that requires interdisciplinary research both at the conceptual and empirical levels. Scholars in entrepreneurship and international business, with few exceptions, have tended to work relatively independent of each other. As McDougall and Oviatt (2000) already recommended several years ago, collaborative scholarship is needed that more effectively integrates and leverages the perspectives of these and other fields, to support higher-level research on born global firms.

Due largely to their distinct disciplinary origin, IB researchers have mostly contributed in examining, usually by means of increasingly sophisticated quantitative data analysis, key issues of born global firms' international management mostly related to their strong international marketing orientation, technological and marketing-related capabilities, foreign market research activities, country market/segment and entry mode selection decision-making processes, global vs. local approaches of their international marketing strategies (product, price, distribution, and communication at the international level) and, more recently, internet-enabled internationalization. Entrepreneurship researchers also interested in born global firms have, however, mainly contributed to this literature by focusing perhaps on the earliest stages of BGFs' emergence (pre- and founding process), the founding entrepreneur's (or founding team) characteristics and cognition, international entrepreneurial orientation, the nexus individual (international) opportunity and its recognition, evaluation, and exploitation in a new business format, the role of entrepreneurial networks in the constitution and development of born global firms, and so on, very often by means of qualitative-oriented (case-based) research methods.

However, born global firms in particular and international entrepreneurship in general, as emergent streams of research, link both disciplinary traditions: IB more traditionally focused on investigating established firms' internationalization processes and entrepreneurship much more focused on new business creation and its determining factors. Future endeavors in this field point to closer collaboration between IB and entrepreneurship-oriented researchers aimed at better combining their specific and unique research capabilities thus generating positive synergies. Such collaborations will engender mutual benefits aimed at integrating and jointly redefining key constructs, theoretical frameworks, measurement scales, and research methods. Only in this way a more holistic view of the phenomenon of "born globalness" of common interest for both disciplines can be reached. The emerging research field of international entrepreneurship opens new and large windows of opportunities for more advanced contributions by international business researchers (Styles and Seymour, 2006), and exactly the same applies for entrepreneurship scholars. Actually, even new entrants to the field coming from other different disciplines who may contribute new insights on this complex phenomenon would be highly welcome as well (Coviello et al., 2011).

Notes

1 It is worth mentioning here, by the way, that traditionally IB researchers investigating internationalizing new ventures – like BGFs – vs. long-established SMEs, have still put greater emphasis on their smaller size condition as compared to larger, long-established international firms than entrepreneurship scholars in this IE field, who tend to largely emphasize earliness in a venture's life rather than size (SME). We particularly thank the co-editors of this book for this pertinent comment.
2 In this particular section, we make use of the original name given by different authors to this type of early internationalizing new firm, though we collectively refer to them as born global firms throughout the chapter as mentioned earlier in the introduction section.
3 See Saravasthy (2001) for a more general discussion of effectuation and causation in entrepreneurship research.

References

Andersen, O. (1993): "On the internationalization process of the firm: a critical analysis," *Journal of International Business Studies*, 24 (2), 209–231.
Andersson, S. and Wictor, I. (2003): "Innovative internationalization in new firms: born globals, the Swedish case," *Journal of International Entrepreneurship*, 1 (3), 249–276.
Aspelund, A., Madsen, T., and Moen, O. (2007): "A review of the foundation, international marketing strategies, and performance of international new ventures," *European Journal of Marketing*, 41 (11/12), 1423–1448.
Autio, E. (2005): "Creative tension: 'The significance of Ben Oviatt's and Patricia McDougall's article? Toward a theory of international new ventures,'" *Journal of International Business Studies*, 36, 9–19.
Autio, E., Sapienza, H., and Almeida, J. (2000): "Effects of age at entry, knowledge intensity, and imitability on international growth," *Academy of Management Journal*, 43 (5), 909–924.

Baum, M., Schwens, C., and Kabst, R. (2011): "A typology of international new ventures: empirical evidence from high-technology industries," *Journal of Small Business Management*, 49 (3), 305–330.

Bell, J. (1995): "The internationalization of small computer software firms: a further challenge to 'stage' theories," *European Journal of Marketing*, 29 (8), 60–75.

Bell, J., Crick, D., and Young, S. (2004): "Small firm internationalization and business strategy: an explanatory study of 'knowledge-intensive' and 'traditional' manufacturing firms in the UK," *International Small Business Journal*, 22 (1), 23–56.

Bell, J., Loane, S., McNaughton, R., and Servais, P. (2011): "Toward a typology of rapidly internationalizing SMEs." In N. Nummela (ed.), *International Growth of Small and Medium Enterprises*, NY: Routledge, pp. 177–190.

Bell, J. and McNaughton, R. (2000): "Born global firms: a challenge to public policy in support of internationalization," *Marketing in a Global Economy Proceedings*, 176–185.

Bell, J., McNaughton, R., and Young, S. (2001): "'Born-again' global firms: an extension to the 'born global' phenomenon," *Journal of International Management*, 7, 173–189.

Bell, J., McNaughton, J., Young, R., and Crick, D. (2003): "Towards an integrative model of small firm internationalization," *Journal of International Entrepreneurship*, 1, 339–362.

Calof, J.L. and Beamish, P.W. (1995): "Adapting to foreign markets: explaining internationalization," *International Business Review*, 4 (2), 115–131.

Cavusgil, S.T. (1980): "On the internationalization process of firms," *European Research*, 8 (6), 273–281.

Cavusgil, S.T. and Knight, G.A. (2009): *Born Global Firms: A New International Enterprise*. NY: Business Experts Press.

Cesinger, B., Fink, M., Madsen, T.K. and Kraus, S. (2012): "Rapidly internationalizing ventures: How definitions can bridge the gap across contexts," *Management Decision*, 50 (10), 1816–1842.

Chetty, S. and Campbell-Hunt, C. (2004): "A strategic approach to internationalization: a traditional versus a 'born global' approach," *Journal of International Marketing*, 12 (1), 57–81.

Coombs, J.E., Sadrieh, F., and Annavarjula, M. (2009): "Two decades of international entrepreneurship research: what have we learned – where do we go from here?" *International Journal of Entrepreneurship*, 13, 23–64.

Coviello, N.E. (2006): "The network dynamics of international new ventures," *Journal of International Business Studies*, 37 (5), 713–731.

Coviello, N.E. and Jones, M.V. (2004): "Methodological issues in international entrepreneurship research," *Journal of Business Venturing*, 19 (4), 485–508.

Coviello, N.E. and McAuley, A. (1999): "Internationalisation and the smaller firm: a review of contemporary empirical research," *Management International Review*, 39 (3), 223–256.

Coviello, N.E., McDougall, P.P., and Oviatt, B.M. (2011): "The emergences, advance and future of international entrepreneurship research – an introduction to the special forum," *Journal of Business Venturing*, 26: 625–631.

Coviello, N.E. and Munro, H. (1995): "Growing the entrepreneurial firm: Networking for international market development," *European Journal of Marketing*, 29 (7), 49–61.

Coviello, N.E. and Munro, H. (1997): "Network relationships and the internationalization process of small software firms," *International Business Review*, 6 (4), 361–386.

Covin, J.G. and Miller, D. (2013): "International entrepreneurial orientation: conceptual considerations, research themes, measurement issues, and future research directions," *Entrepreneurship Theory and Practice*, Special issue (February), 1–34.

Crick, D. (2009): "The internationalisation of born global and international new venture SMEs," *International Marketing Review*, 26 (4/5), 453–476.

Crick, D. and Jones, M.V. (2000): "Small high technology firms and international high technology markets," *Journal of International Marketing*, 8 (2), 63–85.

Cuervo-Cazurra, A. (2011): "Selecting the country in which to start internationalization: the non-sequential internationalization model," *Journal of World Business*, 46 (4), 426–437.

de Clercq, D., Sapienza, H.J., Yavuz, R.I., and Zhou, L. (2012): "Learning and knowledge in internationalization research: past accomplishments and future directions," *Journal of Business Venturing*, 27 (1), 143–165.

Dimitratos, P., Johnson, J., Slow, J., and Young, S. (2003): "Micromultinationals: new types of firms for the global competitive landscape," *European Management Journal*, 21 (2), 164–174.

Dimitratos, P. and Jones, M.V. (2005): "Future directions for international entrepreneurship research," *International Business Review*, 14 (2), 119–128.

Dimitratos, P., Plakoyiannaki, E., Pitsoulaki, A., and Tüselmann, H. (2010): "The global smaller firm in international entrepreneurship," *International Business Review*, 19, 589–606.
Fernhaber, S.A., McDougall, P.P., and Shepherd, D.A. (2009): "International entrepreneurship: leveraging internal and external knowledge sources," *Strategic Entrepreneurship Journal*, 3, 297–320.
Fillis, I. (2001): "Small firm internationalisation: an investigative survey and future research directions," *Management Decision*, 39 (9), 767–783.
Fillis, I. (2004): "The internationalizing smaller craft firm," *International Small Business Journal*, 22 (1), 57–82.
Fletcher, D. (2004): "International entrepreneurship and the small business," *Entrepreneurship and Regional Development*, 16 (July), 289–305.
Gabrielsson, M. and Gabrielsson, P. (2003): "Global marketing strategies of born globals and globalizing internationals in the ICT field," *Journal of Euromarketing*, 12 (3/4), 123–145.
Gabrielsson, M. and Kirpalani, M.V.H. (2004): "Born globals: how to reach new business space rapidly," *International Business Review*, 13, 555–571.
Gabrielsson, M. and Kirpalani, M.V.H. (eds) (2012): *Handbook of Research on Born Globals*. Cheltenham, UK: Edward Elgar.
Gabrielsson, M., Kirpalani, M.V.H., Dimitratos, P., Solberg, C.A., and Zucchella, A. (2008a): "Born globals: propositions to help advance the theory," *International Business Review*, 17 (4), 385–401.
Gabrielsson, M., Kirpalani, M.V.H., Dimitratos, P., Solberg, C.A., and Zucchella, A. (2008b): "Conceptualizations to advance born global definition: a research note," *Global Business Review*, 9 (1), 45–50.
Gabrielsson P. and Gabrielsson, M. (2004): "Globalizing internationals: portfolio and marketing strategies in the ICT field," *International Business Review*, 13, 661–684.
Ganitsky, J. (1989): "Strategies for innate and adoptive exporters: lessons from Israel's case," *International Marketing Review*, 6(5), 50–65.
Guillén, M.F. and García-Canal, E. (2009): "The American model of the multinational firm and the new multinationals from emerging economies," *Academy of Management Perspectives*, 23 (2), 23–35.
Guillén, M.F. and García-Canal, E. (2010): *The New Multinationals. Spanish Firms in a Global Context*. Cambridge, UK: Cambridge University Press.
Hashai, N. and Almor, T. (2004): "Gradually internationalizing 'born global' firms: an oxymoron?" *International Business Review*, 13 (4), 465–483.
Hedlund, G., and Kverneland, A. (1985): "Are strategies for foreign markets changing? The case of Swedish investment in Japan," *International Studies of Management and Organization*, 15 (2), 41–59.
Hessels, J. (2008): *International Entrepreneurship: Value Creation Across National Borders*. Erasmus Research Institute of Management (ERIM), Rotterdam, NL: Erasmus University Rotterdam.
Hurmerinta-Peltomäki, L. (2003): "Time and internationalization: theoretical challenges set by rapid internationalization," *Journal of International Entrepreneurship*, 1, 217–236.
Jantunen, A., Nummela, N., Puumalainen, K., and Saarenketo, S. (2008): "Strategic orientations of born globals: do they really matter?" *Journal of World Business*, 43 (2), 158–170.
Johanson, J. and Vahlne, J.E. (1977): "The internationalization process of the firm: a model of knowledge development and increasing foreign market commitments," *Journal of International Business Studies*, 8 (1), 23–32.
Johanson, J. and Vahlne, J.E. (1990): "The mechanism of internationalization," *International Marketing Review*, 7 (4), 11–24.
Johanson, J and Vahlne, J.E. (2006): "Commitment and opportunity development in the internationalization process: a note on the Uppsala internationalization process model," *Management International Review*, 46 (2), 165–178.
Johanson, J. and Vahlne, J.E. (2009): "The Uppsala internationalization process model revisited: from liability of foreignness to liability of outsidership," *Journal of International Business Studies*, 40 (9), 1411–1431.
Jolly, V., Alahuhta, M., and Jeannet, J.P. (1992): "Challenging the incumbents: how high-technoloy start-ups compete globally," *Journal of Strategic Change*, 1, 71–82.
Jones, M.V. and Coviello, N.E. (2005): "Internationalisation: conceptualising an entrepreneurial process of behaviour in time," *Journal of International Business Studies*, 36 (3), 284–303.
Jones, M.V., Coviello, N.E., and Tang, Y.K. (2011): "International entrepreneurship research (1989–2009): a domain ontology and thematic analysis," *Journal of Business Venturing*, 26, 632–659.
Jones, M.V. and Nummela, N. (2008): "International entrepreneurship: expanding the domain and extending our research questions," *European Management Journal*, 26 (6), 349–353.

Kalinic, I. and Forza, C. (2012): "Rapid internationalization of traditional SMEs: between gradualist models and born globals," *International Business Review*, 21 (4), 694–707.
Keupp, M.M. and Gassmann, O. (2009): "The past and the future of international entrepreneurship: a review and suggestions for developing the field," *Journal of Management*, 35 (3), 600–633.
Kiss, A.N., Danis, W.M., and Cavusgil, S.T. (2012): "International entrepreneurship research in emerging economies: a critical review and research agenda," *Journal of Business Venturing*, 27, 266–290.
Knight, G.A. (1997): *Emerging Paradigm for International Marketing: The Born Global Firm*. Unpublished doctoral dissertation, Michigan State University: East Lansing.
Knight, G.A. and Cavusgil, S.T. (1996): "The born global firm: a challenge to traditional internationalization theory." In S.T. Cavusgil and T.K. Madsen (eds), *Export Internationalizing Research: Enrichment and Challenges, Advances in International Marketing* 8. Greenwich, CT: JAI Press, pp. 11–26.
Knight, G., and Cavusgil, S.T. (2004): "Innovation, organizational capabilities, and the born global firm," *Journal of International Business Studies*, 35 (2), 124–141.
Kuivalainen, O., Saarenketo, S., and Puumalainen, K. (2012): "Start-up patterns of internationalization: a framework and its application in the context of knowledge-intensive SMEs," *European Management Journal*, 30, 372–385.
Kundu, S.K. and Katz, J.A. (2003): "Born-internationals SMEs: BI-level impacts of resources and intentions," *Small Business Economics*, 20, 25–47.
Madsen, T.K. (2013): "Early and rapidly internationalizing ventures: similarities and differences between classifications based on the original international new venture and born global literatures," *Journal of International Entrepreneurship*, 11 (1), 65–79.
Madsen, T.K., Rasmussen, E.S., and Servais, P. (2000): "Differences and similarities between born globals and other types of exporters." In A. Yaprak and J. Tutek (eds) *Globalization, the Multinational Firm, and Emerging Economies* (*Advances in International Marketing*, 10). Amsterdam: JAI/Elsevier Inc, pp. 247–265.
Madsen T. and Servais, P. (1997): "The internationalization of born globals: an evolutionary process?" *International Business Review*, 6 (6), 561–583.
Mainela, T. Puhakka, V., and Servais, P. (2014): "The concept of international opportunity in international entrepreneurship: a review and a research agenda," *International Journal of Management Reviews*, 16 (1), 105–129.
Marschan-Pickkäri, R. and Welch, C. (2004) (eds): *Handbook of Qualitative Research Methods for International Business*. Cheltenham, UK: Edward Elgar.
Mathews, J.A. (2006): "Dragon multinationals: new players in 21st-century globalization," *Asia Pacific Journal of Management*, 23, 5–27.
Mathews, J. and Zander, I. (2007): "The international entrepreneurial dynamics of accelerated internationalisation," *Journal of International Business Studies*, 38 (3), 387–403.
McAuley, A. (1999): "Entrepreneurial instant exporters in the Scottish arts and crafts sector," *Journal of International Marketing*, 7 (4), 67–82.
McDougall, P.P. (1989): "International versus domestic entrepreneurship: new venture strategic behavior and industry structure," *Journal of Business Venturing*, 4 (6), 387–399.
McDougall, P.P. and Oviatt, B.M. (2000): "International entrepreneurship: the intersection of two research paths," *Academy of Management Journal*, 43 (5), 902–906.
McDougall, P.P., Oviatt, B.M. and Shrader, R.C. (2003): "A comparison of international and domestic new ventures," *Journal of International Entrepreneurship*, 1 (1), 59–82.
McDougall, P.P., Shane, S., and Oviatt, B.M. (1994): "Explaining the formation of international new ventures: the limits of theories from international business research," *Journal of Business Venturing*, 9 (6), 469–487.
Melén, S. and Nordman, E.R. (2009): "The internationalization modes of born globals: a longitudinal study," *European Management Journal*, 27 (4), 243–254.
Moen, O. (2002): "The born globals: a new generation of small European exporters," *International Marketing Review*, 19 (2), 156–175.
Moen, O. and Servais, P. (2002): "Born global or gradual global? Examining the export behavior of small and medium-sized enterprises," *Journal of International Marketing*, 10 (3), 49–72.
Morgan-Thomas, A. and Jones, M.V. (2009): "Post-entry internationalization dynamics: differences between SMEs in the development speed of their international sales," *International Small Business Journal*, 27 (1), 71–97.
Morrow, J.F. (1988): "International entrepreneurship: a new growth opportunity," *New Management*, 3, 59–61.

Nordman, E.R. and Melén, S. (2008): "The impact of different kinds of knowledge for the internationalization process of born globals in the biotech industry," *Journal of World Business*, 43 (2), 171–185.
Oviatt, B.M. and McDougall, P.P. (1994): "Toward a theory of international new ventures," *Journal of International Business Studies*, 25 (1), 45–64.
Oviatt, B.M. and McDougall, P.P. (1995): "Global start-ups: entrepreneurs on a worldwide stage," *Academy of Management Executive*, 9 (2), 30–43.
Oviatt, B.M. and McDougall, P.P. (1997): "Challenges for internationalization process theory: the case of international new ventures," *Management International Review*, 37 (2), 85–99.
Oviatt, B.M and McDougall, P.P. (1999): "A framework for understanding accelerated international entrepreneurship." In A.M. Rugman and R.W. Wright (eds), *Research in Global Strategic Management: International Entrepreneurship*. Stamford, CT: JAI Press, pp. 23–40.
Oviatt, B.M. and McDougall, P.P. (2005a): "Defining international entrepreneurship and modeling the speed of internationalization," *Entrepreneurship Theory and Practice*, 29 (5), 537–553.
Oviatt, B.M. and McDougall, P.P. (2005b): "The internationalization of entrepreneurship," *Journal of International Business Studies*, 36 (1), 2–8.
Peiris, I.K., Akoorie, M.E.M., and Sinha, P. (2012): "International entrepreneurship: a critical analysis of studies in the past two decades and future directions for research," *Journal of International Entrepreneurship*, 10, 279–234.
Prashantham, S. and Young, S. (2011): "Post-entry speed of international new ventures," *Entrepreneurship Theory and Practice*, 35 (2), 275–292.
Rennie, M. (1993): "Born global," *McKinsey Quarterly*, 4, 45–52.
Reuber, A.R. and Fischer, E. (2011): "International entrepreneurship in internet-enabled markets," *Journal of Business Venturing*, 26, 660–679.
Rialp, A., Galván, I., and Suárez, S. (2010): "A configuration-holistic approach to born-global firms' strategy formation process," *European Management Journal*, 28 (2), 108–123.
Rialp, A. and Rialp, J. (2001): "Conceptual frameworks on SMEs' internationalisation: past, present, and future trends of research," in C.N. Axinn and P. Matthyssens (eds), *Reassessing the Internationalisation of the Firm* (*Advances in International Marketing*, 11), Amsterdam: JAI/Elsevier Inc., pp. 49–78.
Rialp, A. and Rialp, J. (eds) (2007): "International marketing research: opportunities and challenges in the 21st century," *Advances in International Marketing*, 17, 1–13.
Rialp, A., Rialp, J., and Knight, G.A. (2005a): "The phenomenon of early internationalizing firms: what do we know after a decade (1993–2003) of scientific inquiry?" *International Business Review*, 14 (2), 147–166.
Rialp, A., Rialp, J., Urbano, D., and Vaillant, Y. (2005b): "The born-global phenomenon: a comparative case study research," *Journal of International Entrepreneurship*, 3 (2), 133–171.
Ruzzier, M., Hisrich, R.D., and Antoncic, B. (2006): "SME internationalization research: past, present, and future," *Journal of Small Business and Enterprise Development*, 13 (4), 476–497.
Saravasthy, S.D. (2001): "Causation and effectuation: toward a theoretical shift from economic inevitability to entrepreneurial contingency," *Academy of Management Review*, 26 (2), 243–263.
Schwens, C. and Kabst, R. (2009): "How early opposed to late internationalizers learn: experience of others and paradigms of interpretation," *International Business Review*, 18 (5), 509–522.
Sharma, D.D. and Blomstermo, A. (2003): "The internationalization process of born globals: a network view," *International Business Review*, 12 (6), 739–753.
Spence, M., Orser, B., and Riding, A. (2011): "A comparative study of international and domestic new ventures," *Management International Review*, 51, 3–21.
Styles, C. and Seymour, R.G. (2006): "Opportunities for marketing researchers in international entrepreneurship," *International Marketing Review*, 23 (2), 126–145.
Svensson, G. (2006): "A quest for a common terminology: the concept of born globals," *Management Decision*, 44 (9), 1311–1317.
Svensson, G. and Payan, J.M. (2009): "Organizations that are international from inception," *Journal of Small Business and Enterprise Development*, 16 (3), 406–417.
Szyliowicz, D. and Galvin, T. (2010): "Applying broader strokes: extending institutional perspectives and agendas for international entrepreneurship research," *International Business Review*, 19, 317–332.
Terjesen, S., Hessels, J., and Li, D. (2013): "Comparative international entrepreneurship: A review and research agenda," *Journal of Management* (forthcoming), DOI: 10.1177/0149206313486259.
Tuppura, A., Saarenketo, S., Puumalainen, K., Jantunen, A., and Kyläheiko, K. (2008): "Linking knowledge, entry timing and internationalization strategy," *International Business Review*, 17 (4), 473–487.

Weerawardena, J., Mort, G.S., Liesch, P.W., and Knight, G.A. (2007): "Conceptualizing accelerated internationalization in the born global firm: a dynamic capabilities perspective," *Journal of World Business*, 42 (3), 294–306.

Welch, D.E. and Welch, L.S. (1996): "The internationalisation process and networks: a strategic management perspective," *Journal of International Marketing*, 4 (3), 11–28.

Welch, L.S. and Luostarinen, R. (1988): "Internationalization: evolution of a concept," *Journal of General Management*, 14 (2), 34–55.

Werner, S. (2002): "Recent developments in international management research: a review of 20 top management journals," *Journal of Management*, 28 (3), 277–305.

Wright, M., Westhead, P., and Ucbasaran, D. (2007): "Internationalization of small and medium-sized enterprises (SMEs) and international entrepreneurship: a critique and policy implications," *Regional Studies*, 41 (7), 1013–1030.

Wright, R.W. and Ricks, D.A. (1994): "Trends in international business research: twenty-five years later," *Journal of International Business Studies*, 25, 687–701.

Zahra, S.A. (2005): "Theory on international new ventures: a decade of research," *Journal of International Business Studies*, 36 (1), 20–28.

Zahra, S.A. and George, G. (2002): "International entrepreneurship: the current status of the field and future research agenda." In M. Hitt, R. Ireland, M. Camp, and D. Sexton (eds), *Strategic Leadership: Creating a New Mindset*. London, UK: Blackwell, pp. 255–288.

Zahra, S.A., Ireland, R.D., and Hitt, M.A. (2000): "International expansion by new venture firms: international diversity, mode of market entry, technological learning and performance," *Academy of Management Journal*, 43, 925–950.

Zahra, S.A., Korri, J.S., and Yu, J. (2005): "Cognition and international entrepreneurship: implications for research on international opportunity recognition and exploitation," *International Business Review*, 14 (2), 129–146.

Zucchella, A., Palamara, G., and Denicolai, S. (2007): "The drivers of the early internationalization of the firm," *Journal of World Business*, 42 (3), 268–280.

Zucchella, A. and Scabini, P. (2007): *International Entrepreneurship: Theoretical Foundations and Practices*. Houndmills, UK: Palgrave.

2

"Where to" international entrepreneurship?

An exploration of seminal articles

Pavlos Dimitratos and Nicolas Li

Introduction

The international entrepreneurship (IE) field has been gaining significant momentum since the publication of Patricia McDougall's (1989) article that has paved the way to the development of a fascinating research stream. The IE field has been benefiting greatly from advances in its two "parental" areas, that is, entrepreneurship and international business (IB) (McDougall and Oviatt, 2000). While researchers in the former field have paid attention primarily to venture creation and the management of small and medium-sized enterprises (SMEs) within the domestic context, the latter research has focused mostly on established, large multinational companies (MNCs). The evolvement of IE is devoted to addressing the trend that "the demarcation segregating international business and entrepreneurship has begun to erode" (McDougall and Oviatt, 2000, p. 902).

In order to fully appreciate where IE stands in the literature, it is crucial to summarize landmark development of the field as well as of its parental areas in retrospect. Such an investigation is important since, although the IE area has seemingly been entering a maturity era, it is still in search of solid theoretical frameworks that could guide further investigations. The examination of seminal articles can thus assist researchers to take stock of the present inspiring papers of the three areas; show how key entrepreneurship and IB papers assist the growth of the IE field; and finally, possibly illuminate the "where to" of IE research. The goal of this chapter is to explore the influential articles of the three fields in order to illuminate how the current development of IE can benefit from citing and extending those germane studies. In doing so, we aim to illustrate how IE research has been assisted by the developments in its parental fields; as well as where this leaves the field in terms of potential future scholarly directions.

This chapter is structured as follows. The following section explores the methodology employed to find out the seminal articles of the entrepreneurship, IB and IE fields; and presents the associated findings. The final section summarizes the key trends of investigation as revealed from our analysis; and suggests six directions for future research in the IE field.

Methodology and results

We adopted the following criteria when selecting seminal articles in each field, including both subjective and objective considerations. We initially performed keyword search queries for published journal articles ranked by citation counts in the *ISI Web of Science (WOS)* database for the period 1960–2013 (inclusive). Those most-cited papers form the basis for identifying the seminal works. In particular, we used the terms "entrepreneur," "entrepreneurship," and "entrepreneurial opportunity" for entrepreneurship articles; "international business," "globalization," and "internationalization" for IB articles; and, "international entrepreneurship," "born-global," and "international new venture" for IE articles. We excluded all the articles from journals that published fewer than 26 topical papers in the timeframe (for example, *Economic Journal, Journal of Monetary Economics* as they did not publish more than 26 related papers in the last 53 years) because an average rate of one thematic paper every two years "was the minimum needed to consider the construct a part of the journal's research domain" (Lane et al., 2006, p. 839). In addition, the research domain was limited to "social sciences," the research area to "business economics" in English language.

At the same time, we also cross-checked the citation record using *Google Scholar* because although *Google Scholar* cannot rank articles by citation counts, it may provide a less biased result than the *WOS* (Harzing, 2013). We observed nevertheless that the ranking of article citations in both sources is highly consistent. Further, ranking articles by citation counts only is not comprehensively fair to recent prominent works as they do not have sufficient time for citations. Thus, we only considered articles published prior to 2004 (inclusive). In each section, we listed our selection of seminal articles chronologically; also, subjectively added major books that we considered to be of influential importance in each area.

The majority of IE scholars agree that it was McDougall (1989) that signalled IE as an independent domain[1]. In order to get an overview of the three fields since then, we present the bar charts on the number of published articles in each year since then in Figure 2.1. One limitation is that not all relevant journals are *WOS*-indexed. For example, the *Journal of International Entrepreneurship*, which was first published in 2001, is not being included in the *WOS* database. In general, all three fields seemed to show a sustainable speed of growth, the trend of which is more prominent in the twenty-first century. IB is the most prolific field in terms of the total volume of journal publication (although there is oftentimes a difficulty figuring out whether a publication falls within the boundaries of IB or IE). While the development of entrepreneurship follows a similar pattern to that of IB, IE seems to have a stepwise trend in four periods, namely 1989–1999, 2000–2003, 2004–2009, and 2010 onwards (an evident "leap forward" in terms of publication volume was observed in 2000, 2004, and 2010, compared to the average annual volume of the previous periods). As a relatively new field, this may indicate IE is still struggling to grow itself in terms of scholarship.

Seminal articles in entrepreneurship

Entrepreneurship can act as a "soft power" of a country, facilitating economic and societal development throughout the world. Following the common idea of classical economists (e.g. Smith, Richardo, Knight, Schumpeter, Hayek, and Kirzner) that entrepreneurs explore and exploit opportunities to create economic gain, entrepreneurship is an interaction between enacting individuals (the entrepreneurs) and entrepreneurial opportunities (Eckhardt and Shane, 2003; Shane, 2000). Entrepreneurship research has become more theory driven and coalesced around a dominant core of themes, issues, methodologies, and debates (Wiklund et al., 2011). A recent interesting academic debate in the *Academy of Management Review* was observed on Shane's recent commentary (2012) on the most cited entrepreneurship paper, namely Shane and Venkataraman (2000) (Alvarez and Barney, 2013; Garud and Giuliani, 2013; Eckhardt and Shane, 2013).

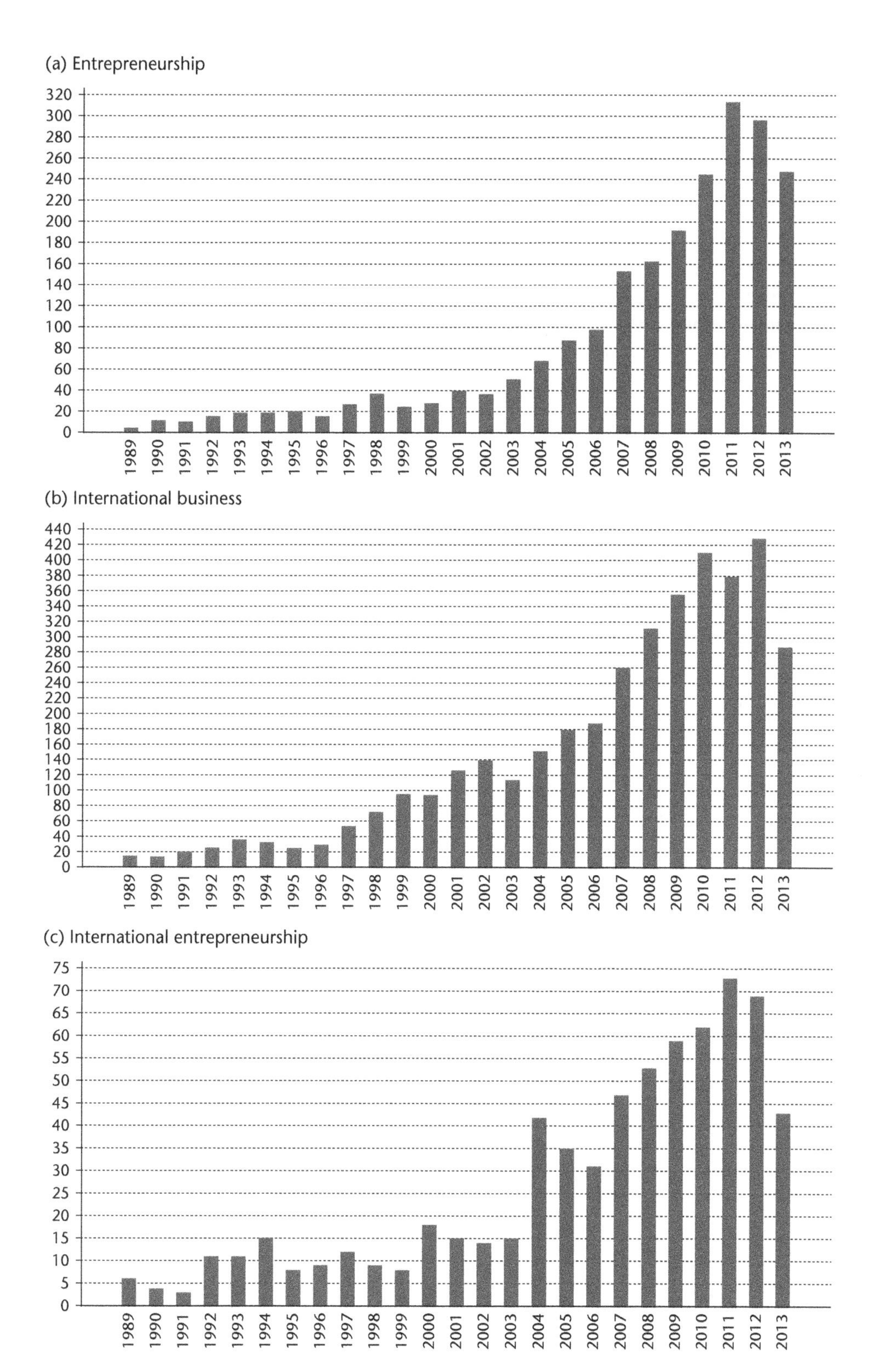

Figure 2.1 Published articles in three fields in each year 1989–2013

(Source: *WOS*)

Entrepreneurs are those economic actors who seek to exploit opportunities in pursuit of wealth creation (Alvarez et al., 2013). What makes an entrepreneur is the capability to precisely appraise the potential of a particular opportunity (Baron, 1998). Being distinct from managers, entrepreneurs establish a business in order to gain profit and growth by employing strategic management practices and an innovative behaviour (Carland et al., 1984). Economies in all geographic regions showed that the highest entrepreneurship rates usually occur among 25–34 year olds. Together with 35–44 year olds, the two age groups could make nearly 50 percent of all entrepreneurs (GEM, 2012). GEM findings have also consistently reported greater involvement in entrepreneurship among men than women in most economies (some exceptions are Nigeria, Panama, Ecuador, Thailand etc.).

Scholarly discussion on opportunity has popularized in the new century. In the by-far best-cited paper in entrepreneurship (see Table 2.1), Shane and Venkataraman (2000) argue that opportunity is intersubjective. The assumption of the objective existence of market opportunities is warranted by Kirznerian entrepreneurs; meanwhile, Schumpeterian entrepreneurs subjectively create opportunities and bring them to the market (Kirzner, 1973; Schumpeter, 1934). Thus, an opportunity may be first formed by exogenous shocks to the firm's industry or market and then proactively enacted by entrepreneurs themselves (Alvarez and Barney, 2007). Opportunities are not considered products, business models, or organizations; rather they are economic situations where profits are sought through correct, suitable, and service combinations, and proper strategies (Eckhardt and Shane, 2003). Such executions can be done either by technological innovation (Schumpeter, 1934) or by balancing the demand and supply of the market (Kirzner, 1973). However, an opportunity is meaningless unless an entrepreneur takes actions upon it in the real world. So Alvarez and Barney (2007) emphasize more the subjectivity of opportunity, such as "social constructions that do not exist independent of entrepreneur's perception" (2007, p. 15). In a similar stance, Sarasvathy (2009) suggests the idea of effectuation, adopting an instrumental view of the firm. In contrast to predictive reasoning, an effectual entrepreneur makes rather than discovers opportunities. Sarasvathy's (2001) theoretical innovation is laudable as she centers entrepreneurs in her entrepreneurship effectuation theory (the firm exists because the entrepreneur exists).

The sub-fields of entrepreneurship have also flourished in recent years. While IE is discussed later, to begin with, "social entrepreneurship" is a process of creating values by combining existing resources in new ways in order to stimulate social change or by meeting social needs (Mair and Marti, 2006). Moreover, "corporate entrepreneurship" (including MNC subsidiary entrepreneurship) consists of innovation aimed at business creation and venturing, and strategic renewal (Zahra and Covin, 1995; Ireland et al., 2009). Also, related to strategic management, "strategic entrepreneurship" emphasizes the entrepreneur's influence on firm growth and wealth creation, involving simultaneous advantage-seeking and opportunity-seeking behaviours that lead to superior firm performance (Ireland et al., 2003; Wright and Stigliani, 2013). The idea of "institutional entrepreneurship" further highlights the ways in which entrepreneurs work toward their strategic objectives by proactively leveraging resources in order to manipulate the structures in which they are embedded (Garud et al., 2002; Tracey et al., 2011).

Although GEM surveys attitudes, activities, and growth expectations in order to capture the level of entrepreneurship, a more scholarly acknowledged measure is using entrepreneurial orientation (EO). EO, touted as the best established empirical instrument for assessing a firm's degree of entrepreneurship (Brown et al., 2001), has become a central concept in the domain of entrepreneurship; and, has received a substantial amount of theoretical and empirical attention (Covin et al., 2006), prompting a recent meta-analysis (Rauch et al., 2009), literature reviews (e.g. Edmond and Wiklund, 2010; Wales et al., 2012), and a recent *Entrepreneurship Theory and*

Practice special issue (e.g. Covin and Lumpkin, 2011). Sometimes referred to as the M/C&S scale (Miller, 1983; Covin and Slevin, 1989), an EO construct includes innovativeness, proactiveness, and risk attitude. Lumpkin and Dess (1996) additionally suggest two more EO dimensions, competitive aggressiveness and autonomy. Besides, Stevenson's (1983) conceptualization of entrepreneurial management, that is a set of opportunity-based management practices that can help firms remain competitive and contribute to the value creation of firm and societal levels, partially overlaps with EO. None the less, the dimensions of EO may occur in different combinations, representing the multidimensional concept of EO (George, 2011).

We present 10 seminal journal articles on entrepreneurship in Table 2.1. The paper by Shane and Venkataraman (2000) is undoubtedly the most influential work recognized by both citation count sources. The three sets of research questions (*why, when, and how opportunities for the creation of goods and services come into existence*) they asked in this paper have guided many subsequent studies. Other papers related to entrepreneurial opportunities are those of Busenitz and Barney (1997) and Shane (2000). Another important stream is on entrepreneurial orientation as aforementioned (Covin and Slevin, 1989; Miller, 1983; Lumpkin and Dess, 1996). These works are widely cited whenever a study needs to quantitatively evaluate entrepreneurship or probe the entrepreneurship–performance relationship. The last group of seminal papers investigates an important question: what makes an entrepreneur? From different perspectives such as resource-based view or strategy management, these scholars define entrepreneurship and lay important theoretical foundation works for the field (Alvarez and Busenitz, 2001; Baron, 1998; Busenitz and Barney, 1997; Eisenhardt and Schoonhoven, 1996; Stevenson and Jarillo, 1990).

Table 2.1 Ten seminal journal articles in entrepreneurship[2]

Year of Publication	*Author(s)*	*Number of times cited in* ISI	*Number of times cited in* Google Scholar	*Journal*	*Key theme(s)*
1983	Miller	666	2151	MS	Determinants of entrepreneurship
1989	Covin and Slevin	595	2268	SMJ	Opportunity formation
1990	Stevenson and Jarillo	470	1927	SMJ	Corporate entrepreneurship
1996	Eisenhardt and Schoonhoven	598	1728	OS	Strategic alliance; innovation; resource-based view
1996	Lumpkin and Dess	1069	3534	AMR	Entrepreneurial orientation; performance
1997	Busenitz and Barney	436	1389	JBV	Opportunity; entrepreneurial decisions
1998	Baron	239	837	JBV	Characteristics of entrepreneurs
2001	Alvarez and Busenitz	278	926	JM	Resource-based view; domain of entrepreneurship
2000	Shane	733	2250	OS	Opportunity discovery
2000	Shane and Venkataraman	1530	5093	AMR	Existence, discovery, and exploitation of entrepreneurial opportunities

Note: The citation record was checked on January 10, 2014.

Seminal articles in international business (IB)

IB can be simply seen as the study of the firm's cross-border activities (internationalization). Internationalization can be viewed as an entrepreneurial activity. As the world's economies have become more interconnected than ever before, firms, regardless of size or age, often need to go beyond their home country in order to seek survival, productivity, growth, competitive advantage, optimal combination of resources and capabilities, and so on. Empirical evidence has also confirmed that a firm's exposure to internationalization leads to a higher chance of survival and success (Ganotakis and Love, 2012; Ojala, 2009). Although IB scholars have seemingly studied the discipline exhaustively over the last few decades (for a discussion see Buckley, 2002), we posit that IB remains robust in terms of research themes and theory building as new forms of internationalization patterns and processes evolve in the new century.

Prior to the substantial development of IB research in the 1970s (e.g. Buckley and Casson, 1976; Johanson and Vahlne, 1977; Knickerbocker, 1973), economists have attempted to explain economic activities across national borders, such as Coase's transnational cost analysis, Penrose's firm growth theory, and Heckscher and Ohlin's H-O model. However, IB research was largely initiated when scholars realized that they did not have proper analytical tools for explaining the increasing international trade and investment activities in the post-war period (Vernon, 1966). A review of the IB scholarship reveals that the field gained its momentum by studying multinationals in the 1970s. Several IB-contextual frameworks were developed. The two most influential ones are Johanson and Vahlne's Uppsala/Stage model (1977) and Buckley and Casson's (1976) internationalisation theory of multinational enterprises (MNEs). The Uppsala model is a knowledge-based internationalization process theory developed in the context of developed economies with the assumption that a firm's decision makers have incomplete and imperfect knowledge about foreign markets. The model proposes a positive relationship between market knowledge and market commitment in a firm's internationalization process. Internationalization is an incremental process in which organizational knowledge for international markets and operations expands, reducing the risk of international activities. On the other hand, employing a transaction cost perspective, Buckley and Casson (1976) maintain that a firm grows by internalizing imperfect external markets until bounded by markets in which the transaction benefits of further internalization are outweighed by the costs. These theories have built a solid foundation for the evolvement of the IB research agenda.

The popularity of studying MNEs continued in the 1980s (Rugman, 1981; Hennart, 1982; 1988; Porter, 1980). However, due to the increasing phenomenon of exporting small firms, the focus of research also shifted to the study of international SMEs. One of the most prominent theories in this period is Dunning's eclectic paradigm (1980, 1988). The eclectic paradigm explains three types of advantages a firm may possess on foreign entry mode selection, namely ownership, location, and internalization advantages (also known as the OLI-model). A key contribution is that its strong grounding in economic theory provided a basis for further development and the integration of strategic models based on similar theories, while its focus on firm-level characteristics provided opportunities to incorporate new ideas from organizational studies into the study of international strategy (Tallman, 2003). In particular, ownership advantage adopts a resource-based view which supports the works of Barney and Peng; equivalently, location and internalization advantage are influenced by the transaction cost analysis. In short, this school of thought has been proven powerful and, over time, stimulated academic exchange in the last 30 years.

In the 1990s, while the theory of MNEs and international SMEs continued to develop concurrently, IE, or the international new venture approach, emerged and attracted a number of scholars (Oviatt and McDougall, 1994; Wright and Ricks 1994; Zahra, 1993). IB also imported concepts from other theories such as dynamic capabilities (Teece et al., 1997), institutional theory (DiMaggio and Powell, 1991), network perspective (Coviello and Munro, 1997), and the resource-based view of the firm (Barney, 2001).

In the first decade of the new century, IB scholarship continued to grow strongly (see Figure 2.1). Interestingly, many "traditional" IB theories were extended or further explained by the theorists themselves (Buckley and Casson, 2003; 2009; Hennart, 2009; Johanson and Vahlne, 2003; 2009; Rugman and Verbeke, 2003; 2004; Vahlne and Johanson, 2013). On the other hand, these IB theories, mostly evolved within the developed country setting, have been further examined in the context of emerging economies. IB research associated with emerging economies (especially BRIC countries) has become the latest trend.

To review some important journal articles in IB (Table 2.2), first of all, it is notable that Johanson and Vahlne's work (1977) on the Uppsala model is a "must-cite" paper, with a far greater number of citations than any other work. Other important works on internationalization process include Andersen (1993) and Johanson and Wiedersheim-Paul (1975). In a similar vein, Hennart (1988) is a pivotal work on the transaction cost perspective of internationalization, while Peng (2003) adopts a resource-based view in a context of emerging economies. In addition, Dunning (1998) and Rugman and Verbeke (2004) mainly investigate the firm behaviour of MNEs; however, Cavusgil and Zou (1994) and Lu and Beamish (2001) focus on smaller firms, especially their performance-related aspects. Finally, Hagedoorn (1993) contributes to the research orientation of contractual arrangements and organizationally complex alliances.

Seminal articles in international entrepreneurship (IE)

The first decade of the twenty-first century has witnessed a "golden era" for the development of the IE field. As a hybrid of entrepreneurship and IB, IE first gained its recognition as a

Table 2.2 Ten seminal journal articles in international business (IB)

Year of Publication	*Author(s)*	*Number of times cited in* ISI	*Number of times cited in* Google Scholar	*Journal*	*Key theme(s)*
1975	Johanson and Wiedersheim-Paul	543	2274	JMS	Internationalization process
1977	Johanson and Vahlne	1599	6169	JIBS	Internationalization process
1988	Hennart	529	1764	SMJ	Transaction cost theory
1993	Andersen	249	1237	JIBS	Internationalization process
1993	Hagedoorn	617	1988	SMJ	Strategic alliance
1994	Cavusgil and Zou	398	1298	JoM	Exporting firms; first strategy and performance
1998	Dunning	588	1398	JIBS	FDI theory; MNE activities
2001	Lu and Beamish	308	976	SMJ	Firm performance; SME activities
2003	Peng	427	1080	AMR	Institutional influences; emerging economies
2004	Rugman and Verbeke	269	658	JIBS	Global/regional strategy; localization; value chain

Note: The citation record was checked on January 10, 2014.

distinct field following McDougall's milestone paper (1989), which gives an early definition of the term "IE" focusing on new ventures that engaged in IB. As a young field, IE has grown rapidly (Coviello et al., 2011). Although there have been various versions on the definition of IE, based on Shane and Venkataraman (2000), Oviatt and McDougall offered a refined IE definition as "the discovery, enactment, evaluation, and exploitation of opportunities – across national borders – to create future goods and services" (2005, p. 540). They argue that the most critical distinction between international entrepreneurs and domestic ones is the intentional pursuit of international opportunity. In their review paper which examined 323 IE articles between 1989 and 2009 (excluding review papers), Jones et al. (2011) have identified three major areas of IE research (entrepreneurial internationalization; international comparisons of entrepreneurship; and, international comparisons of entrepreneurial internationalization) and then thematic areas within each. They developed research agendas for each area and critically pointed out important operational issues for research in IE.

Nearly half of the IE literature focuses on early internationals (Jones et al., 2011). They are normally called international new ventures or born globals, which may be used interchangeably in a broad sense (for a detailed classification for the two terms, see Madsen, 2013). Coviello et al. (2011) argue that, however, the most distinctive difference of the two terms is the commonality between "new" and "born." Firms being studied in the IE paradigm should be new and young, but firm size is less of a concern. That being said, the study of larger firms is still under-developed in IE research (Coviello et al., 2011). Notably, Birkinshaw (2000) made a key contribution by studying how subsidiaries contribute to entrepreneurship in MNEs. Some of the issues he raised still need further investigations a decade later, such as the relationship of subsidiary initiatives and entrepreneurship from a network perspective of the multinational; and, the impact of subsidiary level initiative input to corporate strategy. However, Birkinshaw does not seem to position his work within the IE domain even though he has widely been cited in IE studies.

There are also other ways of classifying IE-type small firms. To highlight SMEs that adopt advanced (non-exporting) entry modes, Dimitratos et al. (2003) coined the term micromultinationals (mMNEs). In addition, in contrast to born globals, born regionals are firms that only internationalize to regional neighbouring countries, even if their most strategic market is rather distant (Lopez et al., 2009). The last example addresses an emerging phenomenon of transnational entrepreneurs. They are first-generation immigrants operating entrepreneurial firms with an international presence at least in their home and host countries (Drori et al., 2009).

At the intersection of entrepreneurship and IB, on the one hand, IE requires to be studied using multi-theoretical perspectives. Careful considerations are needed to choose which theories may be useful in explaining various aspects of IE phenomena (Autio, 2005). On the other hand, as IE research is highly flexible to fit itself into the theoretical frameworks in entrepreneurship and IB and also bridges the two subjects, the maturing field of IE can start to pay back to more established strands of research. In other words, IE may be utilized to integrate the fields of entrepreneurship (e.g. Covin and Miller, 2014; Dimitratos et al., 2014) and IB (e.g. Ellis, 2011; Jones and Coviello, 2005). As such, IE research may still be fragmented, inconsistent, and under-developed as a relatively new field. Jones et al. (2011, p. 684) comment that

> due to the multi-disciplinary and multi-theoretical nature of IE, the continuance of debate and theorizing is appropriate and healthy.... It is perhaps unlikely that theories unique to IE will be produced. Instead, it will continue to develop theory that spans the domains of international business and entrepreneurship, as well as beyond.

McDougall and Oviatt are not only two of the founding scholars in the field, but they are by far the most influential authors in IE because of their inclusion of their IE works into the seminal article list (Table 2.3). In these articles, they set the boundary of the IE domain, define and refine what IE is, and lay theoretical foundations for the field. Following their discussion of international new ventures and born globals, Jones (1999), Knight and Cavusgil (2004), and Zahra et al. (2000) advance the theory of early internationals. As IE gains momentum as a significant and relevant field of research, methodological issues should be addressed (Coviello and Jones, 2004), such as using comparative entrepreneurship to triangulate research results (Thomas and Mueller, 2000). Finally, the study of Autio et al. (2000) was comprehensive in the sense that they included and tested a few contingent factors on firm growth (though, to a significant extent, falling within the realm of IB as well). Employing the knowledge-based theory, Autio et al. suggest that early initiation of internationalization, more imitable technologies, and greater knowledge intensity associate with faster international growth.

To sum up, these selected IE papers demonstrate the theoretical foundation of the field. However, they cannot reflect the fast expansion of the field after 2004. Quality review papers on IE have emerged (e.g. Jones et al., 2011; Keupp and Gassman, 2009; Rialp et al., 2005; Zahra, 2005) and the field is thus being integrated to grow as an independent discipline. In addition, closely tied to IE research, Covin and Miller (2014) manifest the contribution of the international entrepreneurial orientation construct to IE. Further, to connect with IB perspectives, while Coviello (2006) illustrates the network dynamics of international new ventures, Jones and Coviello (2005) significantly contribute to the discussion of entrepreneurial internationalization in temporal and other dimensions. Similarly, Ellis (2011) interlinks IE with entrepreneurship through his conceptual and empirical treatment on international opportunity.

Table 2.3 Ten seminal journal articles in international entrepreneurship (IE)

Year of Publication	*Author(s)*	*Number of times cited in* ISI	*Number of times cited in* Google Scholar	*Journal*	*Key theme(s)*
1989	McDougall	112	356	JBV	IE definition and conceptualization
1994	Oviatt and McDougall	587	2122	JIBS	International new venture
1994	McDougall, Shane and Oviatt	332	1168	JBV	International new venture
1999	Jones	129	453	JIM	Early internationalization
2000	Autio et al.	457	1385	AMJ	Strategic planning; knowledge management; early internationalization
2000	McDougall and Oviatt	257	844	AMJ	Conceptualization of international entrepreneurship
2000	Thomas and Mueller	125	460	JIBS	Comparative entrepreneurship; firm performance
2000	Zahra, Ireland and Hitt	502	1396	AMJ	Early internationalization
2004	Coviello and Jones	112	337	JBV	Methodology
2004	Knight and Cavusgil	269	870	JIBS	Born global; innovation

Note: The citation record was checked on January 10, 2014.

A synopsis and future research directions

In this chapter, we presented the seminal works on IE and its two parental fields. It appears that the influential papers in the entrepreneurship area refer to (a) the opportunity theme, (b) the conceptualisation of EO, and (c) the issue of "what makes an entrepreneur." In relation to the IB field, these ground-breaking writings concern (a) MNE activities, (b) exporting aspects, (c) the Uppsala model, (d) the transaction-cost framework, and (e) themes around emerging economies. As regards the IE area, seminal works pertain to (a) early internationalisation, (b) innovation and entrepreneurial process, (c) networking aspects, (d) conceptualisation of international EO, and (e) mature born globals.

We argue therefore that the IE field has significantly been influenced by the developments in the other two fields; and, may continue to be. We outline our ideas regarding six future research directions now. To elaborate, recently, there is some debate in the IE field (e.g. Mainela et al., 2014) on (1) the unit of analysis (whether the firm, the entrepreneur or the opportunity), which follows the key issues identified in entrepreneurship. It may be that IE research has to go beyond customary units of study, which include the entrepreneurial firm or the agent whose actions can account for the entrepreneurial acts of the enterprise. Likewise there is some reflection on (2) how international EO can be appropriately captured, which has led to suggestions to operationalize IE more holistically (e.g. Covin and Miller, 2014; Dimitratos et al., 2012); and, echoes the consideration to this issue given in entrepreneurship. The situation is similar when one takes into account the development of the IB field. If IE is to become truly international it has to highlight what are the aspects of entrepreneurial disposition, which refer to activities abroad and are different to domestic activities. In doing so, it will stress its unique character and demarcate the boundaries of the IE field. Considerable IE emphasis has been given, and is likely to continue to be given to (3) either newly internationalized firms or "mature born globals" to challenge the Uppsala model and/or the transaction-cost framework; arguing in favour of the networking perspective or other resource-based views espousing innovation and entrepreneurial processes. We may need more fine-tuning on the variables and methodologies in this particular area as these challenges have entered an obsolescence era. Sophisticated inductive approach studies and longitudinal examinations can be of paramount importance to this effect.

However, if one follows this matching between the themes identified in the seminal works in the two parental fields and IE, it appears that there are three additional issues that we may also see more IE articles in the years to come. These are (4) the increasing realization that large firms, and big MNEs and their subsidiaries can behave entrepreneurially. We claim that this is one of the most under-investigated fields whose exploration can emphasize how important entrepreneurial agents and initiatives may be to the performance of the MNE and the prosperity of host regions. (5) Entrepreneurship of firms into and from emerging economies that have unique institutional characteristics. With the emergence of these economies as important home and host FDI countries, research has to pinpoint their unique institutional aspects that allow the entrepreneurial spirit of firms to flourish. Also, (6) the identification of opportunities and associated decision-making processes by entrepreneurs and their firms. In other words, how rational or intuitive is this process throughout the identification, evaluation, and exploitation of international opportunities.

Investigation into international entrepreneurial behaviour of the firm is likely to keep on being a fascinating field of study. We posit that the IE area will continue to benefit from advances in its two parental fields. It appears that influential authors in IE have realized that the understanding of both the "I" and the "E" aspects is necessary in order to add to the comprehension of the uniqueness of these activities that pertain to an increasingly larger number of internationalized firms worldwide.

Abbreviations for journals in the tables of this chapter:

AMJ – *Academy of Management Journal*; AMR – *Academy of Management Review*; JBV – *Journal of Business Venturing*; JIBS – *Journal of International Business Studies*; JM – *Journal of Management*; JIM – *Journal of International Marketing*; JoM – *Journal of Marketing*; JMS – *Journal of Management Studies*; MS – *Management Science*; OS – *Organization Science*; SMJ – *Strategic Management Journal*.

Notes

1 For example, Jones et al.'s (2011) comprehensive review on IE used 1989 as the starting point.
2 For Tables 2.1–2.3, please refer to the endnote for journal abbreviations.

References

Andersen, O. (1993) On the internationalization process of firms: A critical analysis. *Journal of International Business Studies*, 24(2), 209–231.

Alvarez, S. A. and Barney, J. B. (2007) Discovery and creation: Alternative theories of entrepreneurial action. *Strategic Entrepreneurship Journal*, 1(1–2), 11–26.

Alvarez, S. A. and Barney, J. B. (2013) Epistemology, opportunities, and entrepreneurship: Comments on Venkataraman et al. (2012) and Shane (2012). *Academy of Management Review*, 38, 154–157.

Alvarez, S. A., Barney, J. B. and Anderson, P. (2013) Forming and exploiting opportunities: The implications of discovery and creation processes for entrepreneurial and organizational research. *Organization Science*, 24(1), 301–317.

Alvarez, S. A. and Busenitz, L. W. (2001) The entrepreneurship of resource-based theory. *Journal of Management*, 27(6), 755–775.

Autio, E. (2005) Creative tension: The significance of Ben Oviatt's and Patricia McDougall's article "toward a theory of international new ventures". *Journal of International Business Studies*, 36(1), 9–19.

Autio, E., Sapienza, H. J. and Almeida, J. G. (2000) Effects of age at entry, knowledge intensity, and imitability on international growth. *Academy of Management Journal*, 43(5), 909–924.

Barney, J. B. (2001) Resource-based theories of competitive advantage. *Journal of Management*, 27, 643–650.

Baron, R. A. (1998) Cognitive mechanisms in entrepreneurship: Why and when entrepreneurs think differently than other people. *Journal of Business Venturing*, 13(4), 275–294.

Birkinshaw, J. M. (2000) *Entrepreneurship in the Global Firm*. London, Sage Publishing.

Brown, T. E., Davidsson, P. and Wiklund, J. (2001) An operationalization of Stevenson's conceptualization of entrepreneurship as opportunity-based firm behavior. *Strategy Management Journal*, 22, 953–968.

Buckley, P. J. (2002) Is the international business research agenda running out of steam? *Journal of International Business Studies*, 33(2), 365–373.

Buckley, P. J. and Casson, M. C. (1976) *The Future of the Multinational Enterprise*. London, Macmillan.

Buckley, P. J. and Casson, M. C. (2003) The future of the multinational enterprise in retrospect and in prospect. *Journal of International Business Studies*, 34(2), 219–222.

Buckley, P. J. and Casson, M. C. (2009) The internalisation theory of the multinational enterprise: A review of the progress of a research agenda after 30 years. *Journal of International Business Studies*, 40(9), 1563–1580.

Busenitz, L. W. and Barney, J. B. (1997) Differences between entrepreneurs and managers in large organizations: Biases and heuristics in strategic decision-making. *Journal of Business Venturing*, 12(1), 9–30.

Carland, J. W., Hoy, F., Boulton, W. R. and Carland, J. A. (1984) Differentiating entrepreneurs from small business owners. *Academy of Management Review*, 9(2), 354–359.

Cavusgil, S. T. and Zou, S. (1994) Marketing strategy-performance relationship: An investigation of the empirical link in export. *Journal of Marketing*, 58(1), 1–21.

Coviello, N. E. (2006) The network dynamics of international new ventures. *Journal of International Business Studies*, 37(5), 713–731.

Coviello, N. E. and Jones, M. V. (2004) Methodological issues in international entrepreneurship research. *Journal of Business Venturing*, 19(4), 485–508.

Coviello, N. E., McDougall, P. P. and Oviatt, B. M. (2011) The emergence, advance and future of international entrepreneurship research. *Journal of Business Venturing*, 26(6), 625–631.
Coviello, N. E. and Munro, H. (1997) Network relationships and the small software firms. *International Business Review*, 6(4), 361–386.
Covin, J. G., Green, K. M. and Slevin, D. P. (2006) Strategic process effects on the entrepreneurial orientation-sales growth rate relationship. *Entrepreneurship Theory and Practice*, 30(1), 57–81.
Covin, J. G. and Lumpkin, G. T. (2011) Entrepreneurial orientation theory and research: Reflections on a needed construct. *Entrepreneurship Theory and Practice*, 35(5), 855–872.
Covin, J. G. and Miller, D. (2014) International entrepreneurial orientation: Conceptual considerations, research themes, measurement issues, and future research directions. *Entrepreneurship Theory and Practice*, 38(1), 11–44.
Covin, J. G. and Slevin, D. P. (1989) Strategic management of small firms in hostile and benign environments. *Strategic Management Journal*, 10(1), 75–87.
DiMaggio, P. J. and Powell, W. W. (1991) *The New Institutionalism in Organizational Analysis*. Chicago, University of Chicago Press.
Dimitratos, P., Johnson, J., Slow, J. and Young, S. (2003) Micromultinationals: New types of firms for the global competitive landscape, *European Management Journal*, 21(2), 164–174.
Dimitratos, P., Liouka, I. and Young, S. (2014) A missing operationalization: Entrepreneurial competencies in multinational enterprise subsidiaries. *Long Range Planning*, 47(1), 64–75.
Dimitratos, P., Voudouris, I., Plakoyiannaki, E. and Nakos, G. (2012) International entrepreneurial culture: Toward a comprehensive opportunity-based operationalization of international entrepreneurship. *International Business Review*, 21(4), 708–721.
Drori, I., Honig, B. and Wright, M. (2009) Transnational entrepreneurship: An emergent field of study. *Entrepreneurship Theory and Practice*, 33, 1001–1022.
Dunning, J. H. (1980) Toward an eclectic theory of international production: Some empirical tests. *Journal of International Business Studies*, 11, 9–31.
Dunning, J. H. (1988) The eclectic paradigm of international production: A restatement and some possible extensions. *Journal of International Business Studies*, 19, 1–31.
Dunning, J. H. (1998) Location and the multinational enterprise: A neglected factor? *Journal of International Business Studies*, 29(1), 45–66.
Eckhardt, J. T. and Shane, S. A. (2003) Opportunities and entrepreneurship. *Journal of Management*, 29(3), 333–349.
Eckhardt, J. T. and Shane, S. A. (2013) Response to the commentaries: The individual-opportunity (IO) nexus integrates objective and subjective aspects of entrepreneurship. *Academy of Management Review*, 38 (1), 160–163.
Edmond, V. and Wiklund, J. (2010) The historic roots of entrepreneurial orientation research. In: Landström, H. and Lohrke, F. (eds) *The Historical Foundations of Entrepreneurship Research*. Cheltenham, Edward Elgar Publishing, pp. 142–160.
Eisenhardt, K. M. and Schoonhoven, C. B. (1996) Resource-based view of strategic alliance formation: Strategic and social effects in entrepreneurial firms, *Organization Science*, 7(2), 136–150.
Ellis, P. D. (2011) Social ties and international entrepreneurship: Opportunities and constraints affecting firm internationalization. *Journal of International Business Studies*, 42(1), 99–127.
Ganotakis, P. and Love, J. H. (2012) Export propensity, export intensity and firm performance: The role of the entrepreneurial founding team. *Journal of International Business Studies*, 43(8), 693–718.
Garud, R. and Giuliani, A. P. (2013) A narrative perspective on entrepreneurial opportunities. *Academy of Management Review*, 38(1), 157–160.
Garud, R., Jain, S. and Kumaraswamy, A. (2002) Institutional entrepreneurship in the sponsorship of common technological standards: The case of Sun Microsystems and Java. *Academy Management Journal*, 45, 196–214.
George, B. A. (2011) Entrepreneurial orientation: A theoretical and empirical examination of the consequences of differing construct representations. *Journal of Management Studies*, 48(6), 1291–1313.
Global Entrepreneurship Monitor (2012) *2012 Global Report* [online]. Available from: www.gemconsortium.org/docs/download/2645 [accessed 23 July 2013].
Hagedoorn, J. (1993) Understanding the rationale of strategic technology partnering: Nterorganizational modes of cooperation and sectoral differences. *Strategic Management Journal*, 14(5), 371–385.
Harzing, A. W. (2013) A preliminary test of Google Scholar as a source for citation data: A longitudinal study of Nobel prize winners. *Scientometrics*, 94(3), 1057–1075.

Hennart, J-F. (1982) *A Theory of Multinational Enterprise.* Ann Arbour, University of Michigan Press.
Hennart, J-F. (1988) A transaction costs theory of equity joint ventures. *Strategic Management Journal*, 9(4), 361–374.
Hennart, J-F. (2009) Down with MNE-centric theories! Market entry and expansion as the bundling of MNE and local assets. *Journal of International Business Studies*, 40(9), 1432–1454.
Ireland, R. D., Covin, J. G. and Kuratko, D. F. (2009) Conceptualizing corporate entrepreneurship strategy. *Entrepreneurship Theory and Practice*, 33, 19–46.
Ireland, R. D., Hitt, M. A. and Sirmon, D. G. (2003) A model of strategic entrepreneurship: The construct and its dimensions. *Journal of Management*, 29(6), 963–989.
Johanson, J. and Vahlne, J.-E. (1977) The internationalization process of the firm: A model of knowledge development and increasing foreign market commitments. *Journal of International Business Studies*, 8(1), 23–32.
Johanson, J. and Vahlne, J.-E. (2003) Business relationship learning and commitment in the internationalization process. *Journal of International Entrepreneurship*, 1(1), 83–101.
Johanson, J. and Vahlne, J.-E. (2009) The Uppsala internationalization process model revisited: From liability of foreignness to liability of outsidership. *Journal of International Business Studies*, 40(9), 1411–1431.
Johanson, J. and Wiedersheim-Paul, F. (1975) The internationalization of the firm: Four Swedish cases. *Journal of Management Studies*, 12, 305–323.
Jones, M. V. (1999) The internationalization of small high-technology firms. *Journal of International Marketing*, 15–41.
Jones, M. V. and Coviello, N. E. (2005) Internationalisation: Conceptualising an entrepreneurial process of behaviour in time. *Journal of International Business Studies*, 36(3), 284–303.
Jones, M., Coviello, N. and Tang, Y. K. (2011) International entrepreneurship research (1989–2009): A domain ontology and thematic analysis. *Journal of Business Venturing*, 26, 632–659.
Keupp, M. M. and Gassmann, O. (2009) The past and the future of international entrepreneurship: A review and suggestions for developing the field. *Journal of Management*, 35(3), 600–633.
Kirzner, I. M. (1973) *Competition and Entrepreneurship.* Chicago, University of Chicago Press.
Knickerbocker, F. T. (1973) *Oligopolistic Reaction and Multinational Enterprise Division of Research*, Cambridge, Harvard Graduate School of Business Administration.
Knight, G. A. and Cavusgil, S. T. (2004) Innovation, organizational capabilities, and the born-global firm. *Journal of International Business Studies*, 35(2), 124–141.
Lane, P. J., Koka, B. R. and Pathak, S. (2006) The reification of absorptive capacity: A critical review and rejuvenation of the construct. *Academy of Management Review*, 31(4), 833–863.
Lopez, L. E., Kundu, S. K. and Ciravegna, L. (2009) Born global or born regional: Evidence from an exploratory study in the Costa Rican software industry. *Journal of International Business Studies*, 40(7), 1228–1238.
Lu, J. W. and Beamish, P. W. (2001) The internationalization and performance of SMEs. *Strategic Management Journal*, 22(6–7), 565–586.
Lumpkin, G. T. and Dess, G. G. (1996) Clarifying the entrepreneurial orientation construct and linking it to performance. *Academy of Management Review*, 21(1), 135–172.
Madsen, T. K. (2013) Early and rapidly internationalising ventures: Similarities and differences between classifications based on the original international new venture and born global literatures. *Journal of International Entrepreneurship*, 11, 65–79.
Mainela, T., Puhakka, V. and Servais, P. (2014) The concept of international opportunity in international entrepreneurship: A review and a research agenda. *International Journal of Management Reviews*, 16(1), 105–129.
Mair, J. and Marti, I. (2006) Social entrepreneurship research: A source of explanation, prediction, and delight. *Journal of World Business*, 41(1), 36–44.
McDougall, P. P. (1989) International versus domestic entrepreneurship: New venture strategic behavior and industry structure. *Journal of Business Venturing*, 4(6), 387–400.
McDougall, P. P. and Oviatt, B. M. (2000) International Entrepreneurship: The intersection of two paths. *Academy of Management Journal*, 43(5), 902–906.
Miller, D. (1983) The correlates of entrepreneurship in three types of firms. *Management Science*, 29(7), 770–791.
Ojala, A. (2009) Internationalisation of knowledge-intensive SMEs: The role of network relationships in the entry to a psychically distant market. *International Business Review*, 18(1), 50–59.
Oviatt, B. M. and McDougall, P. P. (1994) Toward a theory of international new ventures. *Journal of International Business Studies*, 36(1), 29–41.

Oviatt, B. M. and McDougall, P. P. (2005) Defining international entrepreneurship and modelling the speed of internationalization. *Entrepreneurship Theory and Practice*, 29, 537–554.

Peng, M. W. (2003) Institutional transitions and strategic choices. *Academy of Management Review*, 28(2), 275–296.

Porter, M. E. (1980) *Competitive Strategy: Techniques for Analyzing Industries and Competitors*, New York, Free Press.

Rauch, A., Wiklund, J., Lumpkin, G. T. et al. (2009) Entrepreneurial orientation and business performance: An assessment of past research and suggestions for the future. *Entrepreneurship Theory and Practice*, 33(3), 761–787.

Rialp, A., Rialp, J. and Knight, G. A. (2005) The phenomenon of early internationalizing firms: what do we know after a decade (1993–2003) of scientific inquiry? *International Business Review*, 14(2), 147–166.

Rugman, A. M. (1981) *Inside the multinationals: The economics of internal markets*. New York: Columbia Press. Reissued by Palgrave Macmillan in 2006 as *Inside the Multinationals*, (25th Anniversary Edition), Basingstoke, Palgrave Macmillan.

Rugman, A. M. and Verbeke, A. (2003) Extending the theory of the multinational enterprise: Internalization and strategic management perspectives. *Journal of International Business Studies*, 34(2), 125–137.

Rugman, A. M. and Verbeke, A. (2004) A perspective on regional and global strategies of multinational enterprises. *Journal of International Business Studies*, 35(1), 3–18.

Sarasvathy, S. D. (2001) Causation and effectuation: Toward a theoretical shift from economic inevitability to entrepreneurial contingency. *Academy of Management Review*, 26(2), 243–263.

Sarasvathy, S. D. (2009) *Effectuation: Elements of entrepreneurial expertise*. Cheltenham, Edward Elgar Publishing.

Schumpeter, J. A. (1934) *The Theory of Economic Development*. Cambridge, Harvard University Press.

Shane, S. (2000) Prior knowledge and the discovery of entrepreneurial opportunities. *Organization Science*, 11(4), 448–469.

Shane, S. (2012) Reflections on the 2010 AMR Decade Award: Delivering on the promise of entrepreneurship as a field of research. *Academy of Management Review*, 37(1), 10–20.

Shane, S. and Venkataraman, S. (2000) The promise of entrepreneurship as a field of research. *Academy of Management Review*, 25(1), 217–226.

Stevenson, H. H. (1983) A perspective on entrepreneurship. *Harvard Business School Working Paper* 9, 384–131.

Stevenson, H. H. and Jarillo, J. C. (1990) A paradigm of entrepreneurship: Entrepreneurial management. *Strategic Management Journal*, 11(5), 17–27.

Tallman, S. (2003) John Dunning's eclectic model and the beginnings of global strategy. In: Cheng, J. and Hitt, M. A. (eds) *Managing Multinationals in a Knowledge Economy: Economics, Culture, and Human Resources*. Amsterdam, Emerald Group Publishing Limited, pp. 43–55.

Teece, D. J., Pisano, G. and Shuen, A. (1997) Dynamic capabilities and strategic management. *Strategic Management Journal*, 18(7), 509–533.

Thomas, A. S. and Mueller, S. L. (2000) A case for comparative entrepreneurship: Assessing the relevance of culture. *Journal of International Business Studies*, 31(2), 287–301.

Tracey, P., Phillips, N. and Jarvis, O. (2011) Bridging institutional entrepreneurship and the creation of new organizational forms: A multilevel model. *Organization Science*, 22(1), 60–80.

Vahlne, J.-E. and Johanson, J. (2013) The Uppsala model on evolution of the multinational business enterprise: From internalization to coordination of networks, *International Marketing Review*, 30(3), 189–210.

Vernon, R. (1966) International investment and international trade in the product cycle. *The Quarterly Journal of Economics*, 80(2), 190–207.

Wales, W. J., Parida, V. and Patel, P. C. (2012) Too much of a good thing? Absorptive capacity, firm performance, and the moderating role of entrepreneurial orientation. *Strategic Management Journal*, 34(5), 622–633.

Wiklund, J., Davidsson, P., Audretsch, D. B. et al. (2011) The future of entrepreneurship research. *Entrepreneurship Theory and Practice*, 35, 1–9.

Wright, M. and Stigliani, I. (2013) Entrepreneurship and growth. *International Small Business Journal*, 31(1), 3–22.

Wright, R. W. and Ricks, D. A. (1994) Trends in international business research: twenty-five years later. *Journal of International Business Studies*, 25(4), 687–701.

Zahra, S. A. (1993) A conceptual model of entrepreneurship as firm behavior: A critique and extension. *Entrepreneurship Theory and Practice*, 17(4), 5–21.

Zahra, S. A. (2005) A theory of international new ventures: A decade of research. *Journal of International Business Studies*, 36(1), 20–28.

Zahra, S. A. and Covin, J. (1995) Contextual influences on the corporate entrepreneurship–company performance relationship in established firms: A longitudinal analysis. *Journal of Business Venturing*, 10, 43–58.

Zahra, S. A., Ireland, R. D. and Hitt, M. A. (2000) International expansion by new venture firms: International diversity, mode of market entry, technological learning, and performance. *Academy of Management Journal*, 43(5), 925–950.

Part II
The international entrepreneur

3
Cognition in international entrepreneurship

Hana Milanov and Benedikt Maissenhälter

Introduction

The role of cognition in advancing the understanding of entrepreneurship-related phenomena has grown in importance in the last two decades and remains significant for future scholarly inquiry in entrepreneurship (Busenitz et al., 2003; Grégoire et al., 2011; Mitchell et al., 2007). While cognition research is still fairly underrepresented in the literature seeking to understand internationalisation decisions and processes (Acedo and Jones, 2007; Jones et al. 2011), we are witnessing calls to enrich current internationalisation models with this perspective (e.g. Zahra, et al., 2005). In particular, the extant internationalisation literature including established theories of internationalisation such as the Uppsala model (Johanson and Vahlne, 1977, 1990, 2009), the network view (Johanson and Mattsson, 1988; Johanson and Vahlne, 2003, 2009) or the OLI (Ownership, Location, Internalisation) framework (Dunning, 1980, 1988, 1998) – which focus on predicting internationalisation behaviour only *after* the international opportunity has been identified and evaluated – could be greatly enriched by explaining the very origin of international opportunity identification (Chandra et al. 2009) and the processes that underpin early internationalisation (Mathews and Zander, 2007).[1]

Incorporating cognition into international entrepreneurship (IE) shifts the research focus from firm-level phenomena to the process of opportunity identification and evaluation thereby emphasising the central role of entrepreneurs and their thinking patterns. This line of thought can contribute both to IE scholarship, and more broadly, help extend existing international business (IB) frameworks. For IE scholars, even beyond understanding the origin of international opportunity identification, studying founders' cognitions may also help us understand the origin of international new ventures' competitive advantage to the extent that these facilitate both the speed of opportunity identification in international markets (Jones and Casulli, 2014) as well as new ways of exploiting such opportunities (Zahra, 2005). At the same time, the cognitive perspective aids in balancing the current emphasis on firm-level research in IE (Coviello and Jones, 2004) with insights from individual-level research, which ultimately may lay fertile grounds for building rich, multilevel research. For IB scholars, focus on the cognition of entrepreneurial individuals could enrich existing IB frameworks, as their treatment of the international firms' sources of advantage often does not fully account for the range of born-global behaviours we are witnessing today (Mathews and Zander, 2007).

The purpose of this chapter is to survey the extant entrepreneurial cognition literature to the extent that it can inform important research questions in the IE field. This overview assists us in offering a definition of international entrepreneurial cognition, which in turn informs suggested future research directions that can enrich our understanding of IE phenomena as they relate to international entrepreneurial opportunity identification and evaluation.[2] In doing so, we also survey extant methodological approaches and advances that can aid scholars in pursuing suggested research directions.

Entrepreneurial cognition

Cognition can be defined as composed of 'all the processes by which sensory input is transformed, reduced, elaborated, stored, recovered, and used' (Neisser, 1967, p. 4). Building on this definition and early work recognising the importance of cognition in the context of entrepreneurship, Mitchell, Busenitz et al. (2002, p. 97) further define *entrepreneurial* cognition as the 'knowledge structures that people use to make assessments, judgments, or decisions involving opportunity evaluation, venture creation, and growth'.[3] In the context of general entrepreneurship research development, the cognitive perspective has been proven as a valuable research avenue to build entrepreneurship theory, especially in the light of understanding the mechanisms that bridge the 'thinking–doing' link (Mitchell et al., 2007, p. 2). Specifically, the cognitive perspective not only provides a rigorous theoretical lens for understanding how entrepreneurs think (Baron, 1998; Mitchell et al., 2007), but also more generally welcomes back the individual entrepreneur's role into the research focus. In that sense, the cognitive perspective holds promise to understand the uniqueness that may surround entrepreneurial actions, where personality and trait-based approaches have not yielded as many theoretically rigorous explanations on what makes entrepreneurs distinctive from others (e.g. Baron, 1998; Mitchell, Busenitz et al., 2002). Given that entrepreneurship as a field is largely concerned with researching the 'sources of opportunities', the 'processes of discovery, evaluation, and exploitation', as well as addressing the 'who, why, when and how' behind these processes (Shane and Venkataraman, 2000, p. 218), the consideration of cognitive resources provides a powerful theoretical perspective in the identification (e.g. Ucbasaran et al., 2009) and evaluation (e.g. Keh et al., 2002) of entrepreneurial opportunities.

Despite the fairly recent emergence of cognition in entrepreneurship research (Mitchell, Busenitz et al., 2002) a plethora of phenomena capturing characteristics of thinking processes has already been studied. These include, for example, *scripts* as schematic knowledge structures (Gioia and Poole, 1984; Grégoire and Shepherd, 2012), *heuristics* as shortcuts in decision-making (Mitchell et al., 2007; Wright et al., 2000), and *pattern recognition, counterfactual thinking*, and *schemas* in opportunity identification (Baron and Ensley, 2006; Gaglio, 2004; Ucbasaran et al., 2009). In addition, *cognitive biases* (i.e. 'decision processes that lead to alternative perceptions of entrepreneurial opportunities', De Carolis and Saparito, 2006, p.45) such as overconfidence, self-serving bias, illusion of control, the belief in the law of small numbers, or opportunity overload (Baron, 1998; De Carolis and Saparito, 2006; Hmieleski and Baron, 2009; Keh et al., 2002) have been argued to play a pivotal role in opportunity evaluation given their influence on the way individuals perceive and make sense of opportunities. Moreover, while many cognitive processes occur unconsciously (Gioia and Poole, 1984) having been automatised through experience (Kihlstrom, 1987), individuals have a certain control over the cognitive strategies that are being used or avoided in a given situation. This ability – *metacognition* (Haynie et al., 2010) – represents an important area of inquiry in itself.

While the individual's cognition represents a central building block of most entrepreneurial cognition studies, the role of internal as well as external factors should not be neglected when building theory using the cognitive perspective. In terms of internal factors, individual experience has been recognised as a key antecedent to cognition given its role in the process of knowledge accumulation (Kaplan, 2008). At the same time, internal factors such as entrepreneurial passion (Cardon et al., 2009) and affect (Baron, 2008; Hayton and Cholakova, 2012) have been conceptualised as important antecedents and moderators for cognition, decision making, and entrepreneurial behaviour. In terms of external factors, culture and society are argued to importantly shape individual cognition (Busenitz and Lau, 1996; Leung et al., 2005). Similarly, an entire stream of effectuation-based perspective (Sarasvathy, 2001) studies how situations and their uncertainty influence entrepreneurial thinking and in that sense represent an important aspect of entrepreneurial cognition research (Mitchell et al., 2007). In summary, both internal and external factors have an important role in entrepreneurial cognition models: they can be influential predictors of cognitive processes, but their influence can also moderate the effect of cognitive structures and processes on opportunity identification and evaluation.

The remainder of this chapter reviews the extant literature on cognition in the context of IE and IB research and emphasises the relevance of findings in the broader entrepreneurship literature on cognition for IE where appropriate. While the extant literature on entrepreneurial cognition frequently explores its role in other types of opportunities – such as the opportunities around new technologies (Grégoire et al., 2010) – our discussion incorporates this research to the extent that its findings carry relevance for studying identification and evaluation of international opportunities.

Cognition and the international opportunity

The evolution of IE literature in many ways increasingly welcomes the application of the cognitive perspective as a fruitful way to advance our understanding of internationalisation. From the early days, when the focus of inquiry in IE was on firm-level phenomena – as inspired by the definition of international new ventures (Oviatt and McDougall, 1994) – the scholarly interest has broadened to investigate a range of behavioural phenomena as formalised by defining IE as 'a combination of innovative, proactive, and risk-seeking behaviour that crosses national borders and is intended to create value in organizations' (McDougall and Oviatt, 2000, p. 903). Although the transition to a behavioural focus already comes closer to recognising the importance of the individual entrepreneur – it is the most recent definition of IE as consisting of 'discovery, enactment, evaluation, and exploitation of opportunities – across national borders – to create future goods and services' (Oviatt and McDougall, 2005, p. 540) that truly uncovers the potential of the cognitive perspective in exploring in-depth mechanisms behind international opportunity identification and evaluation. Indeed, in offering this definition (and the accompanying model of internationalisation speed) it is suggested that international entrepreneurial behaviour can only be explained 'by understanding how the opportunity, the enabling forces, and the motivating forces are interpreted, or mediated, by the entrepreneurial actor' (Oviatt and McDougall, 2005, p. 542). The field's evolution from a primary interest in firm-level phenomena to studying thought processes surrounding emergence and enactment of cross-border opportunities, together with the acknowledgement of entrepreneurial perceptions as a key mediating mechanism, correspond intimately in their domain of inquiry to the question central to the domain of entrepreneurial cognition – or succinctly put, understanding how entrepreneurs think (Mitchell et al., 2007).

In encouraging IE scholars to include the cognitive perspective in their investigation of international entrepreneurship phenomena, we also offer a definition of international entrepreneurial cognition. While new definitions should only be included with care, providing a definition can help in moving the field forward and garnering an internally consistent conversation around an important set of phenomena. We were aided in the rigour of this effort by (1) a long tradition of cognitive psychology literature, (2) the thorough scholarly efforts that stand behind the refinements of the definition of international entrepreneurship, (3) examples of best practices of other important concepts that have 'crossed borders' from general entrepreneurship to the IE literature (cf. Covin and Miller, 2013, on entrepreneurial and international entrepreneurial orientation).

Accordingly, in defining international entrepreneurial cognition, we were careful to build on original definitions of cognition (Neisser, 1967), entrepreneurial cognition (Mitchell, Busenitz et al., 2002), and international entrepreneurship (Oviatt and McDougall, 2005) in order to define both essential elements of its conceptual space, as well as its boundaries. We define international entrepreneurial cognition as *the mental models and thought processes that people use in identifying, evaluating, and exploiting opportunities across national borders.*

This definition is true to the entrepreneurial cognition and IE fields to the extent that it centres on the individual entrepreneur whose mental models and thought processes are being investigated. Moreover, we embrace the notion that entrepreneurship is fundamentally a field that investigates the processes involved in the identification, evaluation, and exploitation of opportunities (Oviatt and McDougall, 2005; Shane and Venkataraman, 2000). Lastly, in limiting the mental models and thought processes to cross-border opportunities, we honour the definition of IE and also allow for it to encompass extant (and future) efforts of IE scholars, which developed in at least two ways. First, much like with international entrepreneurial orientation (cf. Covin and Miller, 2013), some aspects of current international entrepreneurial cognition research employ traditional entrepreneurial cognition concepts and explore them as antecedents to illuminate IE-context-specific phenomena, such as international opportunity identification or evaluation. Second, such a definition still permits developments (and operationalisations) of distinct international cognitive constructs (such as an international alertness that we describe below), which could be conceptualised as subcategories of traditional cognitive concepts with an international emphasis.

Cognitive aspects of international opportunity identification

Understanding international opportunity identification is an important area of interest for IE scholars studying both young born-globals and more mature companies (Zahra et al., 2005). The cognitive perspective can shed light on the current model of international speed, which so far implicitly assumes that 'an entrepreneurial actor *somehow* discovers or enacts such an opportunity' (Oviatt and McDougall, 2005, p. 542, emphasis added). While prior research extensively recognised the entrepreneurs' international experience as an antecedent of their ventures' internationalisation (Bloodgood et al., 1996; Carpenter et al., 2003; Milanov and Fernhaber, 2014; Reuber and Fischer, 1997), the cognitive perspective is likely to add refinement and layers of complexity to the mechanisms that mediate how founders' personal international experience informs subsequent firm internationalisation behaviour (Jones and Casulli, 2014), to finally inform IE theory on the who, why, when, and how behind international opportunities.

Our review of the literature evidences an emergence of work that has begun to address above-mentioned calls to include the cognitive perspective in IE research (Zahra et al., 2005). For example, seeking to refresh traditional IB perspectives, Mathews and Zander (2007) introduce the 'international entrepreneurial dynamics' framework, situated at the intersection of entrepreneurial and internationalisation perspectives, and point towards discovery of opportunities as the initial milestone that has the potential to highlight the international dimension in an entrepreneurial process. Authors indirectly build on the cognitive perspective in entrepreneurship (Krueger, 2000; Ward, 2004) and IE (Zahra et al., 2005) literatures and emphasise the importance of 'starting with the subjective, creative, and proactive strategizing that underlies the recognition of new business opportunities' (Mathews and Zander, 2007, p. 392). In that sense, we can think of international opportunity identification as an active cognitive process (Chandra et al., 2009) that is critical in the combination and recombination of existing knowledge (Shane and Venkataraman, 2000).

In studying opportunity identification from the cognitive perspective, the core assumption is that 'entrepreneurship concerns itself with distinctive ways of thinking' (Mitchell et al., 2007, p. 3). Following this baseline assumption and applying it to international opportunity identification, we surveyed the literature and found it helpful to present the extant contributions in terms of two related, yet distinct streams that in some ways share commonalities in terms of their emphasis on exploring the distinctiveness of entrepreneurial thinking, yet at the same time differ in terms of the theoretical legacy they draw upon.[4] Tracing its roots to early theories of the entrepreneurship field, one set of IE studies conceptualises these 'distinctive ways of thinking' through some aspect of entrepreneurial alertness (Kirzner, 1979), which was explored specific to the international opportunity context. Another set of studies finds its theoretical roots closer to traditional cognitive psychology, and explores the 'distinctive ways of thinking' in the international context through understanding patterns and characteristics of thought processes. We proceed to review each in the text below.

Cognitive alertness

The entrepreneurship literature has long been interested in a set of cognitive phenomena that could broadly be referred to as cognitive alertness due to their importance for understanding opportunity identification. The concept of alertness – 'attitude of receptiveness to available (but hitherto overlooked) opportunities' (Kirzner, 1997, p. 72) was a central construct in Kirzner's theory of entrepreneurship that distinguishes entrepreneurs from others, and is still influential in directing academic thought in both entrepreneurship and IB fields – for example, entrepreneurial alertness is recognised in the revisited Uppsala internationalisation process model (Johanson and Vahlne, 2009). In the entrepreneurship literature, alertness has been broadly viewed as a 'unique preparedness' (Kaish and Gilad, 1991, p. 48) 'in consistently scanning the environment ready to discover opportunities' (Tang et al., 2012, p. 78); as a 'distinctive set of perceptual and cognitive processing skills that direct the opportunity identification process' (Gaglio and Katz, 2001, p. 96); a concept that captures individuals' general willingness to search for opportunities (Hohenthal et al., 2003), and a mind-set that is alert to them (Harper, 2008). While the literature is mixed in highlighting attitudinal (Kirzner, 1997), schematic (Gaglio and Katz, 2001) and action-based (Tang et al., 2012) aspects of alertness, it is still largely conceptualised as a fairly enduring cognitive characteristic, which as such also carries importance for understanding the identification of international opportunities (Chandra et al., 2009).

In the IE domain, recent studies started exploring aspects of such cognitive alertness. For example, Acedo and Florin (2006) build on previous research in entrepreneurship, cognition, and international business, with the objective to bridge the connection between individuals' attitudes towards internationalisation and firm-level internationalisation behaviour. To this end, authors introduce a new construct, 'individual international posture' (IIP) that 'encompasses the cognitive elements entrepreneurs possess to both identify and exploit international opportunities' (Acedo and Florin, 2006, p. 52). These elements consist of proactive disposition, intuitive cognitive style, tolerance for ambiguity, and international orientation. In their study, authors empirically demonstrate that IIP is significantly related to the degree of firm internationalisation. Finding that successful international entrepreneurs have higher intuitive cognitive style conforms to findings from general entrepreneurship literature, where intuitive individuals were found to display more entrepreneurial behaviour (Allinson et al., 2000). Echoing the calls for cognition literature in IE (Zahra et al., 2005), authors conclude that 'focus on the individual, and the integration of general attitudes with those specific to the international context, provides a rich explanation of the central role played by the entrepreneur's cognitive dimensions' (Acedo and Florin, 2006, p. 61).

In another IE study, Sommer (2010) seeks to explain the impact of SME managers' cognition characteristics on their intention to internationalise. Sommer (2010) examines how attitudes relevant for internationalisation (toward risk, globalisation, international partners, and competing internationally) relate to the SME managers' intentions to participate in international markets. Results confirm findings from related research in finding a strong positive impact of managers' experiences abroad (Bloodgood et al., 1996; Carpenter et al., 2003; Milanov and Fernhaber, 2014; Reuber and Fischer, 1997) and attitudes for the intention to internationalise. However, authors also find that how managers think about their own international business skills – also termed self-efficacy – influences internationalisation intent. In that respect, self-efficacy may not only be 'a particular relevant cognitive construct for entrepreneurship (cf. Krueger and Dickson, 1994), but also for IE' (Sommer, 2010, p. 309) in the sense that it may enhance current models of entrepreneurial alertness and its role in international opportunity identification.

Collectively, this line of work demonstrates that conceptualising aspects of international cognitive alertness is one way to characterise distinctiveness of thinking relevant for international entrepreneurs. In studying alertness as capturing the thinking distinctiveness of entrepreneurs, we would like to point out that such models could also benefit from acknowledging the importance of affect – or – 'the feelings and moods individuals experience' (Baron, 2008, p. 328). In general entrepreneurial cognition literature, affect is argued to be an important source of attitudes and perceptions (Hayton and Cholakova, 2012) because it has a strong impact on how information is stored, memorised and retrieved at a later time (Baron, 2008). For example, we know that positive affect may increase alertness towards the external environment such that individuals perceive a wider spectrum of external stimuli (Baron, 2008; Isen, 2002). Similarly, positive affect is theorised to increase the likelihood of perceiving, storing, accessing and recombining idea-stimulating information, whereas negative affect would result in opposite consequences (Hayton and Cholakova, 2012). In the context of IE, affect has not received as much attention, yet such theorising could (at least in part) help explain the mechanisms behind findings that negative experiences with internationalisation result in entrepreneurs' refusal to re-engage with cross border activities (Crick, 2004). While necessarily speculative, it might be that part of the explanation for these findings lies in the emotional reactions that decrease international entrepreneurial alertness (through reduced perceptions and recombination of information) for these entrepreneurs. In that sense, affect may be an important factor to consider in refining models of cognitive alertness for the discovery of international opportunities.

Pattern recognition

One critique of the described approaches that focus on attitudinal aspects of entrepreneurial intentions is that these still fail to capture the micro-processes that underlie the 'birth' of the idea as such. In that sense, an important line of cognitive entrepreneurship work examines specific characteristics of thinking processes as important antecedents to opportunity identification. Indeed, this line of research holds promise to unpack the mechanisms through which various aspects of entrepreneurs' past experiences shape opportunity identification. In the context of IE, an entrepreneur's prior international experience is one of the most recognised and empirically supported antecedents of internationalisation, yet the arguments that such experience helps with international opportunity identification often remain implicit and somewhat under-specified. In that sense, this line of inquiry can help us to 'open the "black box" of the *logic* of experience to understand the *reasoning* with which it is applied' (Jones and Casulli, 2014, p. 46, emphasis added).

Drawing upon earlier cognition (Kahneman and Tversky, 1973) and entrepreneurial cognition work (Baron and Ensley, 2006; Grégoire et al., 2010) two types of reasoning are juxtaposed as relevant in international opportunity discovery: heuristic and analogical reasoning. Heuristic reasoning is characterised by the use of cognitive shortcuts under conditions of uncertainty, whereas analogical reasoning 'relies on the cognitive capability of the person to recognize patterns, or to join the dots across knowledge domains' (Jones and Casulli, 2014, p. 55). While analogical reasoning is proposed to be less efficient when entrepreneurs are faced with the choice of many international opportunities due to the complexities that are likely to arise in drawing multiple analogies, this type of reasoning has been suggested as especially relevant in identifying new international opportunities (Jones and Casulli, 2014).

Although still lacking empirical support in the IE context, the proposition that 'joining the dots' or analogical reasoning is important for international opportunity identification echoes several findings in the broader entrepreneurial cognition literature. For example, Baron and Ensley (2006) suggest that the mechanism of opportunity identification consists of individuals connecting seemingly unrelated trends and information to their existing opportunity prototypes – 'connecting the dots' this way results in ideas for new opportunities. In contrasting novice and expert entrepreneurs, Baron and Ensley's (2006) empirical test reveals that experienced entrepreneurs possess better-defined and more detailed opportunity prototypes. Later studies echoed and refined these findings. The cognitive process behind opportunity identification is described as consisting of similarity comparison and structural alignment mechanisms (Grégoire et al., 2010), thus highlighting the relevance of pattern recognition in opportunity identification by way of looking for and comparing similarities.

In the context of IE, such analogical reasoning has been theorised to help entrepreneurs in internationalisation. For example, if entrepreneurs are able to draw analogies between their foreign partners' behaviour in own (domestic) markets to own firms' behaviour in international markets – then analogical reasoning might help in international opportunity identification and exploitation (Zheng et al., 2012). Hence, entrepreneurs might rely on identifying similarities to previous experiences or previously identified opportunities in identifying and pursuing international opportunities. Indeed, it is suggested that application of such analogical reasoning might be one explanation for why most international new ventures are observed in knowledge-intensive industries: given that scientists are trained in analogical information processing, these entrepreneurs might be primed towards analogical reasoning, theorised to aid in international opportunity identification (Jones and Casulli, 2014).

Further investigations on the use of similarity comparisons in opportunity identification pointed to an entrepreneur's prior knowledge as an important boundary condition (Grégoire and Shepherd, 2012). In the context of IE, it has been proposed that the entrepreneur's prior international knowledge has important interactions with types of reasoning. Specifically, entrepreneurs lacking prior international experience, or where prior experience was superficial but very recent, are more likely to engage in heuristical reasoning (Jones and Casulli, 2014). In this regard, it is worthwhile to point out that scholars in the entrepreneurial cognition literature (e.g. Ucbasaran et al., 2009) also examined the relationship between the outcome of prior entrepreneurs' experiences and opportunity identification and uncovered interesting complexities. While experiencing low rates of failure can be beneficial for repeat entrepreneurs' opportunity identification because such experiences contribute to diversity in their cognitive schema, beyond a certain rate (20 per cent) prior failures can negatively impact opportunity identification due to a reduced cognitive effectiveness stemming from over-attentiveness to failure. Moreover, this study points to the diminishing returns of entrepreneurial experience in opportunity identification: while experienced entrepreneurs identify a higher number of opportunities, the effect eventually may become checked by a development of cognitive entrenchment. Extending this line of study to the IE context, scholars could investigate how the success (or failure) of previous internationalisation efforts influence further recognition of new international opportunities in the same and/or other countries. Moreover, it would be important to understand whether the successes of frequent and fast international entries of born-globals are at some point checked by cognitive entrenchment that may result from such prior experiences.

Cognitive aspects of international opportunity evaluation

Beyond opportunity identification, understanding the cognitive mechanisms behind international opportunity evaluation can help us in refining the theory of international new ventures (Zahra et al., 2005). Given the lack of information and unknown outcomes surrounding most entrepreneurial opportunities (Alvarez and Barney, 2005) and especially those located abroad (Autio et al., 2011), a central construct in understanding the evaluation process is that of uncertainty. From the cognitive perspective, high levels of uncertainty can be highly consequential because in very ambiguous situations any previously learned schemas or procedures likely lack applicability (Baron and Ward, 2004). Recognising the importance of dealing with uncertainty, early entrepreneurship research focused on studying the general risk propensity of entrepreneurs (e.g. Sitkin and Pablo, 1992). However, due to the inability to distinguish entrepreneurs as having a higher risk-taking propensity than other individuals, such line of inquiry was later refined with examinations of uncertainty perceptions as they apply to specific opportunities (Palich and Bagby, 1995). In that sense, in order to better understand the opportunity evaluation process, we first provide an overview of the cognitive aspects that characterise dealing with uncertainty.

In studying uncertainty that surrounds international opportunity evaluation, a special topic concerns the understanding of cognitive biases – i.e. the 'decision processes that lead to alternative perceptions of entrepreneurial opportunities' (De Carolis and Saparito, 2006, p. 45). While discussion of cognitive biases is as of now not empirically examined in the IE literature, scholars started appreciating the importance of a related concept of heuristic reasoning – or applying cognitive shortcuts and the biases that may result from them – as one that is especially likely to occur in situations filled with uncertainty (Jones and Casulli, 2014). We turn to understand the role of biases in international opportunity evaluation in the section (page 56) following the role of uncertainty that gives rise to them.

Uncertainty and international opportunity evaluation

IE scholars are increasingly trying to understand how relevant cognitive characteristics (e.g. 'connecting the dots', meta-cognition, decision-making styles) and their important correlates (e.g. optimism, attitudes, prior experience) interact with different aspects of uncertainty that characterise internationalisation decisions. In terms of cognitive characteristics, one study suggests that the 'connecting the dots' mechanism described earlier can also have important implications in perceptions of uncertainty. Specifically, it is suggested that 'the culturally contextually specific learning allows opportunistic international entrepreneurs of one culture to see in the uncertain situations *certain connections and associations* that are unseen by the citizens of the second culture' (Butler et al., 2010, p. 127) – where such connections make the opportunity evaluation decisions much less uncertain than for other entrepreneurs lacking these connections. While such cognitive mechanisms are postulated to allow entrepreneurs to absorb uncertainty in opportunity evaluation, authors also emphasise the importance to bear the uncertainty inherent in implementing opportunities in the international context. They attribute international entrepreneurs with the ability to reduce uncertainty by consciously using mental schemas. Such ability resembles the notion of metacognition (Haynie et al., 2010), and given the extensive uncertainties surrounding early internationalisation, deserves more attention in IE literature.

Important strides towards understanding the impact of uncertainty and cognition within the entrepreneurship and internationalisation context have been made in the effectuation literature (Sarasvathy, 2001), which as a 'composite of several different cognitive processes and behaviours' (Perry et al., 2012, p. 852) studies 'heuristics specifically intended for uncertainty' (Read et al., 2009, p. 576). In the IE context several studies explored effectuation. For example, Harms and Schiele (2012) find that entrepreneurs with more international experience (time spent abroad) and with more internationalisation experience (number of international market entries) prefer effectuation principles to causation. In another study, Andersson (2011) follows four born-global firms, and finds evidence of effectuation logic as results pointed to a 'development that is controlled by a growth vision but ... the entrepreneur is able to see opportunities that are not in line with the plan' (p. 638). Similarly, Kalinic et al. (2013) offer qualitative evidence that uncertainty of the internationalisation process makes entrepreneurs more likely to adopt an effectuation logic. Interestingly, authors find that the decision-making logic is not an a priori characteristic of the internationalising entrepreneur – rather, it emerges as a property of the nature of the internationalisation decision (and the uncertainty surrounding it). In that sense, the effectuation literature can contribute towards understanding how entrepreneurs cope with the uncertainty of internationalisation, and more interestingly how international entrepreneurial cognitive characteristics evolve over time and with experience.

An important correlate of cognitive processes is entrepreneurs' optimism. In that regard, entrepreneurial cognition research warns that uncertainty stemming from environmental dynamism can be particularly harmful for highly optimistic entrepreneurs because they do not pay sufficient attention to negative information, or more generally to information that conflicts with previously held beliefs (Hmieleski and Baron, 2009). Hence, future IE research would benefit from understanding the interplay between above-mentioned metacognitive abilities and entrepreneurs' optimism. The two mechanisms would likely align in their effects in the opportunity evaluation stage (or one could imagine a reinforced effect where optimism enhances the ability to bear uncertainty). However, it is unclear whether metacognitive abilities could curb the potentially negative effects of optimism on decision-making noted in the entrepreneurship literature, or whether optimism would reduce entrepreneurs' abilities to control their own cognitive strategies when it comes to bearing uncertainty related to internationalisation.

Several IE studies also explore antecedents of risk perception in their cognition models. For example, Acedo and Florin (2006) find that entrepreneurs' 'individual international posture' (IIP) is an important antecedent of individual risk perception. In a related paper, Acedo and Jones (2007) build on this model and find that cognitive influences such as international orientation, proactivity, and tolerance for ambiguity reduce risk perceptions. In addition, recent entrepreneurship literature argues that individuals also perceive less risk in states of positive affect (Hayton and Cholakova, 2012), which might make for an interesting contribution to existing models of international opportunity evaluation.

Finally, an important aspect of dealing with uncertainty in IE relates to prior internationalisation experience. For example, in dealing with uncertainties specific to international markets (e.g. language barriers, different legal and regulatory environments, customer preferences, employee qualifications), Grégoire et al. (2008), find that a firm's internationalisation experience differentiates how managers think about distinct evaluation factors in internationalisation opportunities. Specifically, authors find that decision makers from already internationalised firms consider the combination of both market *and* opportunity characteristics in opportunity evaluation, while their counterparts that have not previously internationalised predominantly focus on the characteristics of international markets (and do not take into account opportunity-related ones), thereby likely priming concerns about the inherent uncertainty of these markets. In that regard, Prashantham and Floyd (2012) find that the international experience of decision makers is a determinant of their cognitive learning style, which is also consequential in the development of new firm-level capabilities.

These findings echo the importance of experiential learning abroad and its role in dealing with internationalisation uncertainty already espoused by the Uppsala model, where much of the uncertainty is embedded in the concept of 'psychic distance' (Johanson and Vahlne, 1977, 1990)[5] or 'the individual's perception of the differences between the home country and the foreign country' (Sousa and Bradley, 2008, p. 470).[6] Interestingly, while according to the original Uppsala model, international expansion starts with psychically proximate markets that allow the firm to deal with the uncertainty of internationalisation (Johanson and Vahlne, 1977, 1990), later IB research challenged the very definition of what determines such 'distance'. O'Grady and Lane (1996) highlight the importance of a management team's direct experience in a foreign market as the factor that importantly influences the perception of that country's psychic distance over more established country-level indicators of cultural distance. Accordingly, the authors conclude 'the paradox that a close market can be distant, and that a seemingly distant market can be close, ought to be recognized' (O'Grady and Lane, 1996, p. 321), and in that sense, open an interesting area of inquiry of how uncertainty of foreign markets should be conceptualised. Indeed, despite decades of use, empirical evidence for the direct relevance of psychic distance 'remains elusive' (Ellis, 2008, p. 353; Tihanyi et al., 2005). Hence, advances in IE scholars' investigations into how entrepreneurs' international experience and cognitive models of dealing with internationalisation uncertainty shape perceptions and final evaluation of foreign market attractiveness could also shed light on the equivocal findings in the psychic distance, and more generally, IB literature.

Cognitive biases

Given the uncertainty that surrounds many aspects of the entrepreneurial process, entrepreneurship scholars observed that entrepreneurs are likely to be particularly prone to biases (Busenitz and Barney, 1997), and international opportunities are not likely to be exceptions in this regard (Jones and Casulli, 2014). Indeed, the entrepreneurial cognition literature provides important evidence that biases can alter entrepreneurs' risk perceptions, which either partially (Simon et al., 2000) or fully (Keh et al., 2002) mediate the relationship between biases and final opportunity evaluation.

While a comprehensive review of biases is beyond the scope of this chapter, we selectively present cognitive biases following the lead of earlier studies (Simon et al., 2000), thereby focusing on those biases that have been explicitly connected to reducing risk perceptions, or found otherwise relevant in the stage of opportunity evaluation. To that end, much of our discussion revolves around three types of commonly examined biases: (1) overconfidence – which is reflected in the 'failure to know the limits of one's knowledge' (Simon et al., 2000, p. 117); (2) belief in the law of small numbers, which describes situations in which individuals infer conclusions from small, non-representative samples (Tversky and Kahneman, 1971); and (3) illusion of control, which describes situations in which chance (rather than skill) may play a strong role i.e. individuals believe that they personally have higher influence on outcomes than they should realistically expect (Langer, 1975). While each of these biases has been theorised or found to affect opportunity evaluation in entrepreneurial cognition literature, their influence has not as of yet been significantly covered in IE literature to understand their impact on international opportunity assessment. In discussing the findings from the entrepreneurial cognition literature, we address potential implications for international opportunity evaluation.

In a model that aims to understand the impact of biases in risk perceptions and final opportunity evaluation, De Carolis and Saparito (2006) connect three cognitive biases (illusion of control, representativeness or belief in the law of small numbers, and overconfidence) to entrepreneurs' risk perceptions. Authors argue that biases lead individuals to assess risky situations more favourably because they do not account for the full information (overconfidence and representativeness) or because they believe that they can control the situation (illusion of control). A lower risk perception, in turn, increases the likelihood of opportunity exploitation because the chance of failure is evaluated to be lower. Similar propositions have been confirmed in empirical studies that report full (Keh et al., 2002) or partial (Simon et al., 2000) mediation of risk perception in the relationship between two biases (illusion of control and belief in the law of small numbers) and opportunity evaluation (Keh et al., 2002).

An interesting extension of understanding biases is to account for conditions under which they are more likely to emerge. In that sense, De Carolis and Saparito (2006) identify various characteristics of social networks as potential antecedents to cognitive biases. For example, a network filled with strong ties or structural holes might induce individuals to infer representative information from a small number of information sources, or with the latter, overestimate the value of information accessible via their network. In IE literature, this line of reasoning might interestingly extend earlier findings in which weak ties were found to be more important for international new venture knowledge acquisition (Presutti et al., 2007) – indeed, it may be that the role of weak ties in internationalisation success was underestimated to the extent that these types of ties reduce the biases that might influence international opportunity evaluation in the first place.

Individual optimism has also been identified as an important source of cognitive biases (Hmieleski and Baron, 2009), which was empirically shown to negatively impact the performance of optimistic founders' new ventures. Interestingly, it was also found that past entrepreneurial experience – despite more developed cognitive schemas – does not offset the negative effects of optimism on performance – quite the opposite. Indeed, authors argue and find that entrepreneurial experience can further exacerbate confirmation bias and overconfidence, because highly optimistic entrepreneurs learn less from their past and are thus more prone to cognitive biases.

In light of the above findings, IE scholars could find particularly interesting how the consideration of biases informs the link between entrepreneurs' prior experiences and international opportunity evaluation. Indeed, the extant literature predominantly reports positive effects of founders' prior international experiences for their international efforts and final performance abroad. In this regard, scholars could inquire more deeply into the relevance of the recency of founders' international experience for their perceived ability to successfully overcome the challenges inherent in entering a new international market – it may be that drawing on outdated prior international experiences results in overconfidence bias to tackle current challenges. Similarly, knowing that familiarity with the home country's institutional context might prime the location choice and speed of internationalisation (Coeurderoy and Murray, 2008), it would be interesting to observe whether the nature of domestic experience activates possible illusion of control bias in evaluating the opportunity to internationalise to psychically close countries.

Other types of biases, such as belief in the law of small numbers, could be relevant in international opportunity evaluation as well. For example, it would be important to understand whether entrepreneurs are prone to generalising feedback from the first few international customers to the entire foreign market, which could – depending on the nature of the feedback – either prematurely encourage commitment of significant resources abroad, or on the contrary, prematurely discourage international expansion.

Methodological approaches

In this section, we present a review of extant methodological approaches in entrepreneurship cognition research, highlighting both key challenges and progress made in the empirical toolbox of a cognitive entrepreneurship scholar. Empirical investigation of entrepreneurial cognition involves several significant issues stemming from the complexity and fluidity of cognitive processes. One of the key issues scholars face in study design is the ability of the chosen method to consistently measure variables of interest across entities (Kaplan, 2008). In that sense, an important part of cognitive research development in entrepreneurship revolves around evolution of methodological rigour (Baron and Ward, 2004). In efforts to maximise the reliability of measured variables across respondents, our reading of the literature suggests that scholars predominantly address this issue in one of two ways: (1) relying on post-hoc methods to capture relevant proxies of cognitive processes and/or (2) by using (at least partly) real-time techniques that aspire to capture the process itself.

Building on seminal work by Hambrick and Mason (1984), much of the entrepreneurship literature makes the assumption that cognitive characteristics are reflections of individuals' accumulated experiences (Markoczy, 1997), which in turn can be captured by observable characteristics such as education, age or functional background. Indeed, international entrepreneurship literature extensively studied entrepreneurs' international experience, and while not explicitly capturing cognitive arguments, still made implicit claims for their role in the internationalisation process (Jones and Casulli, 2014). For example, De Clercq et al. (2012) summarise the arguments regarding how internationally experienced entrepreneurs influence internationalisation of ventures: (1) they are argued to have a *greater awareness of and receptivity for* international opportunities, which resembles the construct of general cognitive alertness; (2) they have greater *capability of assessing* international opportunities – which suggests patterns for 'connecting the dots' and advanced cognitive patterns in assessing opportunities invoked by the cognitive perspective; and (3) they have a *reduced fear* of international opportunities, which clearly belongs to the affect domain (De Clercq et al., 2012). Hence, IE literature has often used various proxies of founders' prior international experience to capture cognitive mechanisms that drive various aspects of internationalisation.

In terms of future methodological improvements for using post-hoc proxies, scholars suggest refining experience-based measures by explicitly accounting for the depth and diversity in addition to the breadth of e.g. international exposure (Mathews and Zander, 2007; Zahra et al., 2000). Moreover, a recent meta-analysis by Unger et al. (2011) on human capital in entrepreneurship shows that human capital is particularly relevant for entrepreneurial success if it is task related and conceptualised as knowledge/skills rather than education/experience. Such efforts could help disentangle some of the mixed results found in prior literature for differential effects of prior international education vs. prior international operating experience (cf. Bloodgood et al., 1996). Another technique to advance the use of demographic or experience-based proxies is usage of causal maps, which were applied by Markoczy (1997) to study managers' beliefs and their correspondence to managers' background experience. According to the author, the benefit of using causal maps is that these 'capture beliefs on the relevance of constructs and causal relations among them in a given domain' (Markoczy, 1997, p. 1232) and thus their ability to explicitly test assumptions a scholar makes regarding cognitive properties of individuals with certain types of experience in a context-relevant setting. Causal maps are also being used in the entrepreneurship literature. Jenkins and Johnson (1997) for example show that causal maps can illustrate differences in entrepreneurial intentions between entrepreneurs and non-entrepreneurs. The essence of using the causal maps technique is to first develop a pool of relevant constructs (e.g. market size, technology development, opportunity attractiveness), and then engage each respondent in identification, strength, and polarity of influence relationships (which construct influences another, how strongly, positively or negatively). In this way, thinking patterns and knowledge structures of interest to cognition scholars can be captured by proxies in a more refined manner and compared across individuals.

A key criticism of using proxies and post-hoc methods in the empirical realm of cognition research is that they might not reflect key ex-ante considerations (Grégoire et al., 2008). Recently, advancements were made to capture cognition by a combination of post-hoc methods with real-time methods (Busenitz et al., 2003), which allows the scholar to better understand processes underlying opportunity identification but also particular underlying structures of the opportunity evaluation processes. Regarding opportunity identification, *protocol* analysis can be particularly helpful. This method relies on content-analysing the verbalisation of study participants' reactions to specific open-ended questions (Baron and Ensley, 2006) or to the description of a specific context (Grégoire et al., 2010). As such, this technique allows inquiry into a broad range of research questions, and was used to study respondents' level of structural reasoning underlying opportunity identification (Grégoire et al., 2010), thinking processes behind new product ideation (e.g. Dahl and Moreau, 2002), to understanding the properties of entrepreneurs' decision-making logic (e.g. Sarasvathy, 2001).

While protocol analysis is well suited to understand the opportunity identification processes, several methods were also used to better understand opportunity evaluation processes. For example, *conjoint analysis* is a real-time method, which is extensively used to capture respondents' decision-making strategies, thus allowing the scholar to understand how respondents process contingency relationships without relying on their introspection (individuals' self-assessed criteria of their decision making – which is generally inaccurate) (Choi and Shepherd, 2004). In that sense, it is particularly well suited to understand attributes underlying the structure of respondents' decisions. The *policy capturing* method aims to build decision models around the utilisation of individuals' assessments of hypothetical scenarios (West, 2007). The technique allows identification of respondents' theories-in-use where the dependent variable is the respondents' overall assessment of the scenario. Finally, the *socio-cognitive grid* technique extends the policy-capturing method and relies on creating a matrix consisting of dimensions of relevance to participants who subsequently rate the importance of each dimension. To that end, it allows the scholar to capture 'dimensions considered relevant by individuals *and the team to which the individuals belong*' (West, 2007, p. 90, emphasis added).

Beyond the outlined methodological approaches, there are a number of techniques that could be used to further advance our understanding of emerging research questions on entrepreneurial cognition. Baron and Ward's (2004) work is particularly informative to the extent that the authors suggest a number of research techniques from the psychology domain that could allow explorations of new research questions. While covering the broad range of methods that Baron and Ward suggest is beyond the scope of this chapter, scholars interested in understanding the following types of research questions could certainly benefit from a more detailed reading of their work: (1) Do entrepreneurs prefer heuristic to systematic thinking? (2) Do entrepreneurs possess different knowledge structures than others and do they apply them more effectively in a range of situations? (3) Are entrepreneurs better than others in 'connecting the dots' and recognising complex patterns behind opportunities? Finally, leveraging technological aids, researchers may record data on *eye direction and movement*, and on *brain functioning* (e.g. using EEG or MRI technologies) (Baron and Ward, 2004). Indeed, initial attempts to bridge techniques employed in neuroscience within an entrepreneurial context are already yielding interesting results (e.g. Ortiz-Terán et al., 2013).

While some methodological concerns pertain to specific techniques more than others, there are two key limitations that scholars should be especially aware of. First, a potential endogeneity issue poses a conceptual concern: can we differentiate whether it is the individuals' cognitive properties that impact outcomes such as opportunity identification – or whether these cognitive properties are in fact shaped by the initial exposure to the opportunity itself (Grégoire et al., 2011; Sarasvathy, 2008)? A second challenge for scholars that rely on observations of participants' real-time or past actions (behaviour, verbalisation, etc.) is the extent to which individuals' actions directly reflect assumed underlying cognitive processes and, moreover, the extent to which the action–cognition link might have been misinterpreted by the researchers (Zahra et al., 2005). Both of these limitations might be at least partly remedied by using laboratory experiments, given that use of treatment and control groups can help in establishing causality, and a rigorous experiment design can help in removing scholars' misinterpretation of the action–cognition mechanism. To that end, Hayton and Cholakova (2012) encourage experimental designs for studies of affect because researchers can both design specific rewards or tasks that are theorised to prime affective states and through manipulation checks validate the effectiveness of such design across randomly assigned participants to control and treatment groups. An experimental setting would also allow the scholar to carefully operationalise (and simplify) the outcomes of interest, which are otherwise often complex in nature, such as memory, creativity or attention.

In summary, the methodologies applied in extant entrepreneurial cognition research mirror the complexity and heterogeneity of the field. Research in this area necessitates careful planning and selection of the appropriate methods, which is fortunately facilitated by the emergence of literature that focuses on methodological choices in researching entrepreneurial cognition (e.g. Baron and Ward, 2004; Hindle, 2004). This is particularly true in the context of international entrepreneurship research due to the inherent multilevel nature of research questions that try to address the impact of cognition on venture-level outcomes such as speed of internationalisation or internationalisation intensity.

Future research directions

The cognitive perspective has importantly enriched our understanding of entrepreneurial opportunity identification and evaluation. As the reading of the literature review on cognition in international entrepreneurship demonstrates, this line of inquiry can serve to provide theory that illuminates intermediating mechanisms surrounding the recognised role of prior knowledge in early internationalisation (Jones and Casulli, 2014; Oviatt and McDougall, 1994). To that extent, it has the potential to deepen the understanding of why and how international new ventures challenge existing stage-based models of internationalisation (Johanson and Vahlne, 1977, 1990), the essence of which may be – beyond founders' prior experience – deeply embedded in their thinking processes and structures. Indeed, given the central role of entrepreneurial perceptions in Oviatt and McDougall's (2005) model of early internationalisation, the cognitive perspective is a natural backdrop to refine our understanding of 'how the opportunity, the enabling forces, and the motivating forces are interpreted, or mediated, by the entrepreneurial actor' (p. 542).

At the same time, despite contributions spanning several separate aspects of cognition, the literature on cognition in IE is still in its early emergence, and there has been an uneven degree of research attention given to specific topics. Accordingly, to help advance the literature, we take inspiration from the broader cognition literature in entrepreneurship and suggest four broad areas for future inquiry:

(1) What is the role of affect and cognitive biases in international opportunity identification and evaluation?
(2) How can the cognitive perspective help illuminate the role of prior knowledge and experience in internationalisation?
(3) How can we take findings from individual cognition to understand team behaviour and firm-level outcomes?
(4) How can the uses of advanced methods help further research efforts?

While these are by no means meant to be exhaustive of future research questions worth pursuing, we hope that this initial selection will inspire scholars to push our collective research agenda further.

The role of affect and cognitive biases in internationalisation

Following IB research that in some ways recognised the role of managers' cognition in making internationalisation choices (Buckley, 1993), much of the IE research on cognitive antecedents of opportunity identification has in one way or another examined various aspects of general alertness to international opportunities (e.g. Acedo and Florin, 2006). However, we have found no studies that theoretically focus on the role of affect in international opportunity identification. Given the role of affect in shaping the extent of perception of stimuli in the environment (Baron, 2008), IE scholars could investigate not only the role of prior exposure to international contexts, but also the valence of the resulting experience in shaping entrepreneurs' affect – whether this is happiness, anger or fear. Arguably such affectual states could influence entrepreneurs' alertness to international opportunities and subsequent opportunity identification. Indeed, it may be that the positive (or negative) affect regarding the internationalisation *process* as such, or regarding certain *countries* and *cultures*, may be relevant for both receptiveness to information on foreign opportunities, but also in shaping cognitive biases that play a role in evaluating them (cf. Hayton and Cholakova, 2012). Relatedly, the findings on the impact of cognitive biases in general entrepreneurship seem highly interesting for IE scholars as internationalisation represents a highly uncertain process which is fertile for emergence of biases. It is essential that we understand how and when sources of information (such as social networks), information content (availability of positive vs. negative information) and individual cognitive resources (including experiences) might activate specific cognitive biases and potentially even interact in shaping opportunity evaluation and the ultimate success of internationalisation endeavours (Oviatt and McDougall, 2005). Given the argued importance of social capital and networks in entrepreneurial internationalisation and internationalisation in general (Coviello and Munro, 1997; Johanson and Vahlne, 2009; Oviatt and McDougall, 2005; Prashantham, 2008) scholars could further investigate the role of network characteristics (e.g. composition, strength of ties, or structure) both in reducing perceived cognitive uncertainty surrounding evaluation of international opportunities through bias activation, but likewise examine potential negative consequences of network-induced biases such as overconfidence in international opportunity execution. Moreover, while affect and cognition are considered independent, yet intertwined analytical processing systems, there is a lot of potential to examine the nature of their interactions in opportunity identification and evaluation. In that sense, it would be worthwhile to understand the trade-offs that might emerge from antecedents of cognition: for example, some network properties might induce positive affect and contribute to internationalisation intent, yet backfire later in terms of inducing overconfidence in executing on international opportunities. Qualitative methods as well as longitudinal designs would be welcome to uncover such complexities for different internationalisation outcomes over time.

Cognition and the role of knowledge and experience in internationalisation

The role of prior knowledge and experience was extensively recognised in various studies examined in this chapter. Future research could build on these findings and advance the literature by concomitantly accounting for several cognitive elements (Grégoire et al., 2011). Such investigation would offer the potential for understanding their interactions and interdependencies in opportunity identification and evaluation. For example, in the context of entrepreneurial opportunity identification, we can refine our understanding of the mechanisms through which entrepreneurs' past experiences abroad and particularly past experiences in previous internationalisation individually or collectively impact each part of the process through formation of schemas. On the one hand, it may well be that founders of born-globals are quicker to form schemas and accordingly recognise patterns similar to their early internationalisation experiences, which might ultimately make them more efficient in making sense of the available information – indeed, this may be the mechanism underlying the unique competitive advantage suggested by Zahra et al. (2005). On the other hand, extensive experience may result in development of cognitive biases such as overconfidence or familiarity bias, which hinder opportunity identification and decision making (Ucbasaran et al., 2009). A worthwhile research effort would be to investigate theoretical mechanisms that reconcile such apparently opposing effects of experience on internationalisation. More generally, this setting invites a number of future research questions to consider – for example, what is the role of prior internationalisation failure in the formation of schema that are relevant for future international opportunity assessment? Reiterating the importance of examining trade-offs, it might be that building up international expertise leads to cognitive entrenchment which limits flexibility (Dane, 2010) with regard to, for example, international opportunity identification. Likewise, the same types of experience might be helpful in early internationalisation phases, yet activate cognitive biases that stifle later opportunity identification. To that end, comparisons of serial entrepreneurs and novices might be interesting in understanding differential thinking patterns that inform internationalisation (cf. Baron and Ward, 2004).

Crossing levels: from individual cognition to team and firm-level outcomes

While the review of cognition literature in this chapter focused on the role of the individual, thus reflecting the tendency of entrepreneurship scholars to focus their analysis on this level (Davidsson and Wiklund, 2001) entrepreneurship is – especially among the high potential ventures – more often than not a team activity (West, 2007). Given that one cannot assume to understand team decision making by merely summing individual cognitions (Shepherd and Krueger, 2002), this area of inquiry deserves special mention. Reflecting the reasoning that 'by forming a team, entrepreneurs can create a socially extended cognitive nexus whose computational and problem-solving features are distinct from those of its members' (Harper, 2008, p. 617), multiple calls have been made to move beyond individual-level research in cognition to understand cognitive layers of team dynamics (e.g. Busenitz et al., 2003; Grégoire et al., 2011).

Given the importance of a team's collective knowledge and experiences in internationalisation (e.g. Bloodgood et al., 1996; Chandra et al., 2009; Milanov and Fernhaber, 2014; Reuber and Fischer, 1997; Shrader et al., 2000), IE scholars could follow the lead of studies inquiring into team-level cognition performed in other contexts, such as corporate teams (Shepherd and Krueger, 2002), TMTs of universities (Ensley and Hmieleski, 2005) or *Inc 500* start-ups (Ensley and Pearce, 2001) and understand, for example, whether social or shared team cognition can lead to higher international opportunity identification or faster international opportunity evaluation, and to what extent outcomes might depend on the cognitive diversity of team members.

Yet another level to consider in enriching the current understanding of IE phenomena is the firm level. Specifically, while IB literature acknowledged that it is vital for the discipline's advancement to 'embrace frameworks that incorporate entrepreneurial dynamics in their international dimensions, including issues such as discovery of opportunities' (Mathews and Zander, 2007, p. 399), further potential exists in crossing levels between individuals, teams and firms. As stated by Keupp and Gassmann (2009) in offering guidelines for the development of the IE field, it would be valuable to understand how individual and firm-level characteristics interact and what their joint impact on internationalisation outcomes are. Specifically, might individual cognitive characteristics play a more or less prominent role given firm-level characteristics? We know from prior literature that founders' experience lessens in impact on internationalisation as firms accumulate experiential learning abroad (Bruneel et al., 2010), and indeed, that individual mechanisms of dealing with internationalisation uncertainty can contribute to the development of firm-dynamic capabilities, which might be at the core of a venture's international competitive advantage (Autio et al., 2011). Adding the cognitive perspective to such cross-level interactions also leads to research questions on the dynamic process in which individual cognition shapes the organisation but, in turn, organisational learning and the establishment and refinement of an organisational culture in turn shape individuals' cognition.

Advancing research design and measurement

We addressed methodological approaches and already pointed to a range of tools that scholars are encouraged to use in studying cognition in the international entrepreneurship context. Here, we push that agenda further in three directions. First, research at the intersection of cognition and IE provides a principal challenge in that cognition is primarily an individual-level phenomenon, yet the phenomena of interest often include capturing outcomes on the new venture (firm) level. While several papers discussed in this chapter (e.g. Acedo and Jones, 2007; Butler et al., 2010) already combine both levels of analyses, they do not yet leverage the possibilities of employing multilevel empirical models. In that sense, future IE research might employ such advanced models to explicitly account for the nested nature of individual cognitions in new ventures' internationalisation outcomes and hence possibly derive more refined findings. Indeed, a wider call for the use of multilevel models that allow simultaneous testing of hypotheses on multiple levels of analyses (e.g. team-level characteristics and organisational-level outcomes) has been recently made in the IB literature (Peterson et al., 2012). Second, we see interesting potential in combining laboratory experiments with technological monitoring of participants (e.g. eye direction and brain monitoring) as these techniques allow research to circumvent methodological difficulties such as endogeneity and enable a real-time capture of participants' cognition. Third, given the argued heterogeneity of the field of international entrepreneurial cognition and its inherent research challenges, we invite scholars to rely on recent methodological advances to create research designs that tailor the method in use to the underlying complexity and fluidity of entrepreneurial cognitions.

Concluding remarks

In conclusion, the international entrepreneurship field is ripe for extending its insights by employing the cognitive perspective. The rich tradition of cognition research in general and the emergence of entrepreneurial cognition in particular provide a wealth of theoretical mechanisms that are relevant to understanding opportunity identification and evaluation in the international context. Moreover, our methodological overview suggests a range of interesting methods that may aid scholars in answering research questions. We look forward to seeing exciting research that will push the boundaries of our understanding of international entrepreneurship.

Acknowledgements

We would like to thank Nicola Breugst and Anne Domurath for their helpful comments on earlier versions of this manuscript.

Notes

1 Johanson and Vahlne's (1977) framework also accounts for 'opportunities' but rather sees them as part of the 'incremental decisions' (p. 23) in the gradual internationalisation process: 'the model assumes that the state of internationalization affects perceived opportunities and risks which in turn influence commitment decisions and current activities' (p. 27).

2 While we recognise the importance of cross-country comparisons for the domain of IE scholarship (Jones et al., 2011; Terjesen et al., 2013), we do not incorporate this literature in the chapter given our focus on the process of opportunity identification and evaluation across national borders (Oviatt and McDougall, 2005). Still, we point the interested reader to a selection of interesting studies that use a cognitive perspective in cross-cultural or cross-country comparisons (e.g. Mitchell et al., 2000; Mitchell, Smith et al., 2002; Siu and Lo, 2013).

3 The term knowledge structure is defined as: 'mental models (cognitions) that are ordered in such a way as to optimize personal effectiveness within given situations' (Mitchell, Busenitz et al., 2002, p. 97).

4 We acknowledge that other scholars have proposed a different categorisation of subdomains of cognitive research (e.g. Krueger, 2005). However, such subdomains were identified *within* a traditional cognitive perspective, rather than taking international entrepreneurship as the starting point in the organisation of the literature. Given that the focus of this chapter is on the phenomenon of international opportunity as central to the IE field's definition, we hope that our classification aids IE scholars in developing research questions from our grouping of dominant themes in extant entrepreneurial cognition and international entrepreneurship research.

5 In their 2009 update of the Uppsala model, Johanson and Vahlne emphasise the importance of business networks and accordingly see uncertainty predominantly as a liability of outsidership relative to existing networks rather than psychic distance (Johanson and Vahlne, 2009).

6 Psychic distance was originally defined as 'factors preventing or disturbing the flows of information between firm and market' (Johanson and Wiedersheim-Paul, 1975, pp. 307–308) – thus emphasising country-level characteristics. However, the definition was recently adapted to emphasise the role of the individual in perceiving psychic distance and as such is more relevant in the cognitive perspective of IE.

References

Acedo, F. J. and Florin, J. (2006). 'An Entrepreneurial Cognition Perspective on the Internationalization of SMEs'. *Journal of International Entrepreneurship*, 4(1), pp. 49–67.

Acedo, F. J. and Jones, M. V. (2007). 'Speed of Internationalization and Entrepreneurial Cognition: Insights and a Comparison Between International New Ventures, Exporters and Domestic Firms'. *Journal of World Business*, 42(3), pp. 236–252.

Allinson, C. W., Chell, E., and Hayes, J. (2000). 'Intuition and Entrepreneurial Behaviour'. *European Journal of Work and Organizational Psychology*, 9(1), pp. 31–43.

Alvarez, S. A. and Barney, J. B. (2005). 'How Do Entrepreneurs Organize Firms Under Conditions of Uncertainty?'. *Journal of Management*, 31(5), pp. 776–793.

Andersson, S. (2011). 'International Entrepreneurship, Born Globals and the Theory of Effectuation'. *Journal of Small Business and Enterprise Development*, 18(3), pp. 627–643.

Autio, E., George, G., and Alexy, O. (2011). 'International Entrepreneurship and Capability Development: Qualitative Evidence and Future Research Directions'. *Entrepreneurship Theory and Practice*, 35(1), pp. 11–37.

Baron, R. A. (1998). 'Cognitive Mechanisms in Entrepreneurship: Why and When Enterpreneurs Think Differently than Other People'. *Journal of Business Venturing*, 13(3), pp. 275–294.

Baron, R. A. (2008). 'The Role of Affect in the Entrepreneurial Process'. *Academy of Management Review*, 33(2), pp. 328–340.

Baron, R. A. and Ensley, M. D. (2006). 'Opportunity Recognition as the Detection of Meaningful Patterns: Evidence from Comparisons of Novice and Experienced Entrepreneurs'. *Management Science*, 52(9), pp. 1331–1344.

Baron, R. A. and Ward, T. B. (2004). 'Expanding Entrepreneurial Cognition's Toolbox: Potential Contributions from the Field of Cognitive Science'. *Entrepreneurship Theory and Practice*, 28(6), pp. 553–573.

Bloodgood, J. M., Sapienza, H. J., and Almeida, J. G. (1996). 'The Internationalization of New High-potential US Ventures: Antecedents and Outcomes'. *Entrepreneurship Theory and Practice*, 20, pp. 61–76.

Bruneel, J., Yli-Renko, H., and Clarysse, B. (2010). 'Learning from Experience and Learning From Others: How Congenital and Interorganizational Learning Substitute for Experiential Learning in Young Firm Internationalization'. *Strategic Entrepreneurship Journal*, 4(2), pp. 164–182.

Buckley, P. J. (1993). 'The Role of Management in Internalisation Theory'. *Management International Review*, 33(3), pp. 197–207.

Busenitz, L. W. and Barney, J. B. (1997). 'Differences Between Entrepreneurs and Managers in Large Organizations: Biases and Heuristics in Strategic Decision-making'. *Journal of Business Venturing*, 12(1), pp. 9–30.

Busenitz, L. W. and Lau, C.-M. (1996). 'A Cross-Cultural Cognitive Model of New Venture Creation'. *Entrepreneurship Theory and Practice*, 20(4), pp. 25–39.

Busenitz, L. W., West, G. P. I., Shepherd, D., Nelson, T., Chandler, G. N., and Zacharakis, A. (2003). 'Entrepreneurship Research in Emergence: Past Trends and Future Directions'. *Journal of Management*, 29(3), pp. 285–308.

Butler, J. E., Doktor, R., and Lins, F. A. (2010). 'Linking International Entrepreneurship to Uncertainty, Opportunity Discovery, and Cognition'. *Journal of International Entrepreneurship*, 8(2), pp. 121–134.

Cardon, M. S., Wincent, J., Singh, J., and Drnovsek, M. (2009). 'The Nature and Experience of Entrepreneurial Passion'. *Academy of Management Review*, 34(3), pp. 511–532.

Carpenter, M. A., Pollock, T. G., and Leary, M. M. (2003). 'Testing a Model of Reasoned Risk-taking: Governance, the Experience of Principals and Agents, and Global Strategy in High-technology IPO Firms'. *Strategic Management Journal*, 24(9), pp. 803–820.

Chandra, Y., Styles, C., and Wilkinson, I. (2009). 'The Recognition of First Time International Entrepreneurial Opportunities: Evidence from Firms in Knowledge-based Industries'. *International Marketing Review*, 26(1), pp. 30–61.

Choi, Y. R. and Shepherd, D. A. (2004). 'Entrepreneurs' Decisions to Exploit Opportunities'. *Journal of Management*, 30(3), pp. 377–395.

Coeurderoy, R. and Murray, G. (2008). 'Regulatory Environments and the Location Decision: Evidence from the Early Foreign Market Entries of New-technology-based Firms'. *Journal of International Business Studies*, 39(4), pp. 670–687.

Coviello, N. E. and Jones, M. V. (2004). 'Methodological Issues in International Entrepreneurship Research'. *Journal of Business Venturing*, 19(4), pp. 485–508.

Coviello, N. and Munro, H. (1997). 'Network Relationships and the Internationalisation Process of Small Software Firms'. *International Business Review*, 6(4), pp. 361–386.

Covin, J. G. and Miller, D. (2013). 'International Entrepreneurial Orientation: Conceptual Considerations, Research Themes, Measurement Issues, and Future Research Directions'. *Entrepreneurship Theory and Practice*, pp. 1–34.

Crick, D. (2004). 'UK SMEs' Decision to Discontinue Exporting: An Exploratory Investigation into Practices Within the Clothing Industry'. *Journal of Business Venturing*, 19(4), pp. 561–587.

Dahl, D. W. and Moreau, P. (2002). 'The Influence and Value of Analogical Thinking During New Product Ideation'. *Journal of Marketing Research*, 39(1), pp. 47–60.

Dane, E. (2010). 'Reconsidering the Trade-Off Between Expertise and Flexibility: A Cognitive Entrenchment Perspective'. *Academy of Management Review*, 35(4), pp. 579–603.
Davidsson, P. and Wiklund, J. (2001). 'Levels of Analysis in Entrepreneurship Research: Current Research Practice and Suggestions for the Future'. *Entrepreneurship Theory and Practice*, 25(4), pp. 81–100.
De Carolis, D. M. and Saparito, P. (2006). 'Social Capital, Cognition, and Entrepreneurial Opportunities: A Theoretical Framework'. *Entrepreneurship Theory and Practice*, 30(1), pp. 41–57.
De Clercq, D., Sapienza, H. J., Yavuz, R. I., and Zhou, L. (2012). 'Learning and Knowledge in Early Internationalization Research: Past Accomplishments and Future Directions'. *Journal of Business Venturing*, 27(1), pp. 143–165.
Dunning, J. H. (1980). 'Toward an Eclectic Theory of International Production: Some Empirical Tests'. *Journal of International Business Studies*, 11(1), pp. 9–31.
Dunning, J. H. (1988). 'The Eclectic Paradigm of International Production: A Restatement and Some Possible Extensions'. *Journal of International Business Studies*, 19(1), pp. 1–31.
Dunning, J. H. (1998). 'Location and the Multinational Enterprise: A Neglected Factor'. *Journal of International Business Studies*, 29(1), pp. 45–66.
Ellis, P. D. (2008). 'Does Psychic Distance Moderate the Market Size–Entry Sequence Relationship?'. *Journal of International Business Studies*, 39(3), pp. 351–369.
Ensley, M. D., and Hmieleski, K. M. (2005). 'A Comparative Study of New Venture Top Management Team Composition, Dynamics and Performance Between University-based and Independent Start-ups'. *Research Policy*, 34(7), pp. 1091–1105.
Ensley, M. D. and Pearce, C. L. (2001). 'Shared Cognition in Top Management Teams: Implications for New Venture Performance'. *Journal of Organizational Behavior*, 22(2), pp. 145–160.
Gaglio, C. M. (2004). 'The Role of Mental Simulations and Counterfactual Thinking in the Opportunity Identification Process'. *Entrepreneurship Theory and Practice*, 28(6), pp. 533–552.
Gaglio, C. M. and Katz, J. A. (2001). 'The Psychological Basis of Opportunity Identification: Entrepreneurial Alertness'. *Small Business Economics*, 16(2), pp. 95–111.
Gioia, D. A. and Poole, P. P. (1984). 'Scripts in Organizational Behavior'. *The Academy of Management Review*, 9(3), pp. 449–459.
Grégoire, D. A., Barr, P. S., and Shepherd, D. A. (2010). 'Cognitive Processes of Opportunity Recognition: The Role of Structural Alignment'. *Organization Science*, 21(2), pp. 413–431.
Grégoire, D. A., Corbett, A. C., and McMullen, J. S. (2011). 'The Cognitive Perspective in Entrepreneurship: An Agenda for Future Research'. *Journal of Management Studies*, 48(6), pp. 1443–1477.
Grégoire, D. A. and Shepherd, D. A. (2012). 'Technology-market Combinations and the Identification of Entrepreneurial Opportunities: An Investigation of the Opportunity–Individual Nexus'. *Academy of Management Journal*, 55(4), pp. 753–785.
Grégoire, D. A., Williams, D. W., and Oviatt, B. M. (2008). 'Early Internationalization Decisions for New Ventures: What Matters?'. *Frontiers of Entrepreneurship Research*, 28(18), Article 2.
Hambrick, D. C. and Mason, P. A. (1984). 'Upper Echelons: The Organization as a Reflection of Its Top Managers'. *Academy of Management Review*, 9(2), pp. 193–206.
Harms, R. and Schiele, H. (2012). 'Antecedents and Consequences of Effectuation and Causation in the International New Venture Creation Process'. *Journal of International Entrepreneurship*, 10(2), pp. 95–116.
Harper, D. A. (2008). 'Towards a Theory of Entrepreneurial Teams'. *Journal of Business Venturing*, 23(6), pp. 613–626.
Haynie, J. M., Shepherd, D., Mosakowski, E., and Earley, P. C. (2010). 'A Situated Metacognitive Model of the Entrepreneurial Mindset'. *Journal of Business Venturing*, 25(2), pp. 217–229.
Hayton, J. C. and Cholakova, M. (2012). 'The Role of Affect in the Creation and Intentional Pursuit of Entrepreneurial Ideas'. *Entrepreneurship Theory and Practice*, 36(1), pp. 41–68.
Hindle, K. (2004). 'Choosing Qualitative Methods for Entrepreneurial Cognition Research: A Canonical Development Approach'. *Entrepreneurship Theory and Practice*, 28(6), pp. 575–607.
Hmieleski, K. M. and Baron, R. A. (2009). 'Entrepreneurs' Optimism and New Venture Performance: A Social Cognitive Perspective'. *Academy of Management Journal*, 52(3), pp. 473–488.
Hohenthal, J., Johanson, J., and Johanson, M. (2003). 'Market Discovery and the International Expansion of the Firm'. *International Business Review*, 12(6), pp. 659–672.
Isen, A. M. (2002). 'Missing in Action in the AIM: Positive Affect's Facilitation of Cognitive Flexibility, Innovation, and Problem Solving'. *Psychological Inquiry*, 13(1), pp. 57–65.
Jenkins, M. and Johnson, G. (1997). 'Entrepreneurial Intentions and Outcomes: A Comparative Causal Mapping Study'. *Journal of Management Studies*, 34(6), pp. 895–920.

Johanson, J. and Mattsson, L.-G. (1988). 'Internationalization in Industrial Systems: A Network Approach'. In Hood, N. and Vahlne, J.-E. (Eds), *Strategies in Global Competition* (pp. 287–314). New York: Croom-Helm.
Johanson, J. and Vahlne, J.-E. (1977). 'The Internationalization Process of the Firm: A Model of Knowledge Development and Increasing Foreign Market Commitments'. *Journal of International Business Studies*, 8(1), pp. 23–32.
Johanson, J. and Vahlne, J.-E. (1990). 'The Mechanism of Internationalisation'. *International Marketing Review*, 7(4), pp. 11–24.
Johanson, J. and Vahlne, J.-E. (2003). 'Business Relationship Learning and Commitment in the Internationalization Process'. *Journal of International Entrepreneurship*, 1(1), pp. 83–101.
Johanson, J. and Vahlne, J.-E. (2009). 'The Uppsala Internationalization Process Model Revisited: From Liability of Foreignness to Liability of Outsidership'. *Journal of International Business Studies*, 40(9), pp. 1411–1431.
Johanson, J. and Wiedersheim-Paul, F. (1975). 'The Internationalization of the Firm: Four Swedish Cases'. *Journal of Management Studies*, 12(3), pp. 305–323.
Jones, M. V. and Casulli, L. (2014). 'International Entrepreneurship: Exploring the Logic and Utility of Individual Experience Through Comparative Reasoning Approaches'. *Entrepreneurship Theory and Practice*, 38(1), pp. 1–25.
Jones, M. V., Coviello, N., and Tang, Y. K. (2011). 'International Entrepreneurship Research (1989–2009): A Domain Ontology and Thematic Analysis'. *Journal of Business Venturing*, 26(6), pp. 632–659.
Kahneman, D. and Tversky, A. (1973). 'On the Psychology of Prediction'. *Psychological Review*, 80(4), pp. 237–251.
Kaish, S. and Gilad, B. (1991). 'Characteristics of Opportunities Search of Entrepreneurs Versus Executives: Sources, Interests, General Alertness'. *Journal of Business Venturing*, 6(1), pp. 45–61.
Kalinic, I., Sarasvathy, S. D., and Forza, C. (2013). 'Internationalization and Effectuation: Explaining Entrepreneurial Decision-making in Uncertain International Environment'. *International Business Review*, 23(3), 635–647.
Kaplan, S. (2008). 'Cognition, Capabilities, and Incentives: Assessing Firm Response to the Fiber-Optic Revolution And Hypotheses'. *Academy of Management Journal*, 51(4), pp. 672–695.
Keh, H. T., Foo, M. Der, and Lim, B. C. (2002). 'Opportunity Evaluation under Risky Conditions: The Cognitive Processes of Entrepreneurs'. *Entrepreneurship Theory and Practice*, 27(2), pp. 125–148.
Keupp, M. M. and Gassmann, O. (2009). 'The Past and the Future of International Entrepreneurship: A Review and Suggestions for Developing the Field'. *Journal of Management*, 35(3), pp. 600–633.
Kihlstrom, J. (1987). 'The Cognitive Unconscious'. *Science*, 237(4821), pp. 1445–1452.
Kirzner, I. M. (1979). *Perception, Opportunity, and Profit: Studies in the Theory of Entrepreneurship*. Chicago: University of Chicago Press.
Kirzner, I. M. (1997). 'Entrepreneurial Discovery and the Competitive Market Process: An Austrian Approach'. *Journal of Economic Literature*, XXXV(March), pp. 60–85.
Krueger, N. F. (2000). 'The Cognitive Infrastructure of Opportunity Emergence'. *Entrepreneurship Theory and Practice*, 24(3), pp. 5–23.
Krueger, N. F. (2005). 'The Cognitive Psychology of Entrepreneurship'. In Acs, Z. J. and Audretsch, D. B. (Eds), *Handbook of Entrepreneurship Research* (pp. 105–140). Springer.
Krueger, N. and Dickson, P. R. (1994). 'How Believing in Ourselves Increases Risk Taking: Perceived Self-efficacy and Opportunity Recognition'. *Decision Sciences*, 25(3), pp. 385–400.
Langer, E. J. (1975). 'The Illusion of Control'. *Journal of Personality and Social Psychology*, 32(2), pp. 311–328.
Leung, K., Bhagat, R. S., Buchan, N. R., Erez, M., and Gibson, C. B. (2005). 'Culture and International Business: Recent Advances and their Implications for Future Research'. *Journal of International Business Studies*, 36(4), pp. 357–378.
Markoczy, L. (1997). 'Measuring Beliefs: Accept No Substitutes'. *Academy of Management Journal*, 40(5), pp. 1228–1242.
Mathews, J. A. and Zander, I. (2007). 'The International Entrepreneurial Dynamics of Accelerated Internationalisation'. *Journal of International Business Studies*, 38(3), pp. 387–403.
McDougall, P. and Oviatt, B. M. (2000). 'International Entrepreneurship: The Intersection of Two Research Paths'. *Academy of Management Journal*, 43(5), pp. 902–906.
Milanov, H. and Fernhaber, S. A. (2014). 'When do Domestic Alliances Help Ventures Abroad? Direct and Moderating Effects from a Learning Perspective'. *Journal of Business Venturing*, 29(3), pp. 377–391.

Mitchell, R. K., Busenitz, L. W., Bird, B., Gaglio, C. M., McMullen, J. S., Morse, E. A., and Smith, J. B. (2007). 'The Central Question in Entrepreneurial Cognition Research 2007'. *Entrepreneurship Theory and Practice*, 31(1), pp. 1–27.

Mitchell, R. K., Busenitz, L., Lant, T., McDougall, P. P., Morse, E. A., and Smith, J. B. (2002). 'Toward a Theory of Entrepreneurial Cognition: Rethinking the People Side of Entrepreneurship Research'. *Entrepreneurship Theory and Practice*, 27(2), pp. 93–104.

Mitchell, R. K., Smith, J. B., Morse, E. A., Seawright, K. W., Peredo, A. M., and McKenzie, B. (2002). 'Are Entrepreneurial Cognitions Universal? Assessing Entrepreneurial Cognitions across Cultures'. *Entrepreneurship Theory and Practice*, 26(4), pp. 9–32.

Mitchell, R. K., Smith, B., Seawright, K. W., and Morse, E. A. (2000). 'Cross-cultural Cognitions and the Venture Creation Decision'. *Academy of Management Journal*, 43(5), pp. 974–993.

Neisser, U. (1967). *Cognitive Psychology*. New York: Appleton-Century-Crofts.

O'Grady, S. and Lane, H. W. (1996). 'The Psychic Distance Paradox'. *Journal of International Business Studies*, 27(2), pp. 309–333.

Ortiz-Terán, E., Turrero, A., Santos, J. M., Bryant, P. T., and Ortiz, T. (2013). 'Brain Cortical Organization in Entrepreneurs During a Visual Stroop Decision Task'. *Neuroscience and Neuroeconomics*, 2, pp. 33–49.

Oviatt, B. M. and McDougall, P. (1994). 'Toward a Theory of International New Ventures'. *Journal of International Business Studies*, 25(1), pp. 45–64.

Oviatt, B. M. and McDougall, P. P. (2005). 'Defining International Entrepreneurship and Modeling the Speed of Internationalization'. *Entrepreneurship Theory and Practice*, 29(5), pp. 537–553.

Palich, L. E. and Bagby, D. R. (1995). 'Using Cognitive Theory to Explain Entrepreneurial Risk-taking: Challenging Conventional Wisdom'. *Journal of Business Venturing*, 10(6), pp. 425–438.

Perry, J. T., Chandler, G. N., and Markova, G. (2012). 'Entrepreneurial Effectuation: A Review and Suggestions for Future Research'. *Entrepreneurship Theory and Practice*, 36(4), pp. 837–861.

Peterson, M. F., Arregle, J.-L., and Martin, X. (2012). 'Multilevel Models in International Business Research'. *Journal of International Business Studies*, 43(5), pp. 451–457.

Prashantham, S. (2008). 'New Venture Internationalization as Strategic Renewal'. *European Management Journal*, 26(6), pp. 378–387.

Prashantham, S. and Floyd, S. W. (2012). 'Routine Microprocesses and Capability Learning in International New Ventures'. *Journal of International Business Studies*, 43(6), pp. 544–562.

Presutti, M., Boari, C., and Fratocchi, L. (2007). 'Knowledge Acquisition and the Foreign Development of High-tech Start-ups: A Social Capital Approach'. *International Business Review*, 16(1), pp. 23–46.

Read, S., Song, M., and Smit, W. (2009). 'A Meta-analytic Review of Effectuation and Venture Performance'. *Journal of Business Venturing*, 24(6), pp. 573–587.

Reuber, A. R. and Fischer, E. (1997). 'The Influence of the Management Team's International Experience on the Internationalization Behaviors of SMEs'. *Journal of International Business Studies*, pp. 807–825.

Sarasvathy, S. D. (2001). 'Causation and Effectuation: Toward a Theoretical Shift from Economic Inevitability to Entrepreneurial Contingency'. *The Academy of Management Review*, 26(2), pp. 243–263.

Sarasvathy, S. D. (2008). *Effectuation: Elements of Entrepreneurial Expertise*. Northampton, MA: Edward Elgar Publishing.

Shane, S. and Venkataraman, S. (2000). 'The Promise of Entrepreneurship as a Field of Research'. *The Academy of Management Review*, 25(1), pp. 217–226.

Shepherd, D. A. and Krueger, N. F. (2002). 'An Intentions-Based Model of Entrepreneurial Teams' Social Cognition'. *Entrepreneurship Theory and Practice*, 27(2), pp. 167–185.

Shrader, R. C., Oviatt, B. M., and McDougall, P. (2000). 'How New Ventures Exploit Trade-offs Among International Risk Factors: Lessons for the Accelerated Internationization of the 21st Century'. *Academy of Management Journal*, 43(6), pp. 1227–1247.

Simon, M., Houghton, S. M., and Aquino, K. (2000). 'Cognitive Biases, Risk Perception, And Venture Formation: How Individuals Decide to Start Companies'. *Journal of Banking and Finance*, 15(2), pp. 113–134.

Sitkin, S. B. and Pablo, A. L. (1992). 'Reconceptualizing the Determinants of Risk Behavior'. *Academy of Management Journal*, 17(1), pp. 9–38.

Siu, W. and Lo, E. S. (2013). 'Cultural Contingency in the Cognitive Model of Entrepreneurial Intention'. *Entrepreneurship Theory and Practice*, 37(2), pp. 147–173.

Sommer, L. (2010). 'Internationalization Processes of Small- and Medium-sized Enterprises: A Matter of Attitude?'. *Journal of International Entrepreneurship*, 8(3), pp. 288–317.

Sousa, C. M. P. and Bradley, F. (2008). 'Cultural Distance and Psychic Distance: Refinements in Conceptualisation and Measurement'. *Journal of Marketing Management*, 24(5–6), pp. 467–488.

Tang, J., Kacmar, K. M. M., and Busenitz, L. (2012). 'Entrepreneurial Alertness in the Pursuit of New Opportunities'. *Journal of Business Venturing*, 27(1), pp. 77–94.

Terjesen, S., Hessels, J., and Li, D. (2013). 'Comparative International Entrepreneurship: A Review and Research Agenda'. *Journal of Management*. Published online before print May 1, 2013, doi: 10.1177/0149206313486259.

Tihanyi, L., Griffith, D. A, and Russell, C. J. (2005). 'The Effect of Cultural Distance on Entry Mode Choice, International Diversification, and MNE Performance: A Meta-analysis'. *Journal of International Business Studies*, 36(3), pp. 270–283.

Tversky, A. and Kahneman, D. (1971). 'Belief in the Law of Small Numbers'. *Psychological Bulletin*, 76(2), pp. 105–110.

Ucbasaran, D., Westhead, P., and Wright, M. (2009). 'The Extent and Nature of Opportunity Identification by Experienced Entrepreneurs'. *Journal of Business Venturing*, 24(2), pp. 99–115.

Unger, J. M., Rauch, A., Frese, M., and Rosenbusch, N. (2011). 'Human Capital and Entrepreneurial Success: A Meta-analytical Review'. *Journal of Business Venturing*, 26(3), pp. 341–358.

Ward, T. B. (2004). 'Cognition, Creativity, and Entrepreneurship'. *Journal of Business Venturing*, 19(2), pp. 173–188.

West, G. P. I. (2007). 'Collective Cognition: When Entrepreneurial Teams, Not Individuals, Make Decisions'. *Entrepreneurship Theory and Practice*, 31(1), pp. 77–102.

Wright, M., Hoskisson, R. E., Busenitz, L. W., and Dial, J. (2000). 'Entrepreneurial Growth through Privatization: The Upside of Management Buyouts'. *The Academy of Management Review*, 25(3), pp. 591–601.

Zahra, S. A. (2005). 'A Theory of International New Ventures: A Decade of Research'. *Journal of International Business Studies*, 36(1), pp. 20–28.

Zahra, S. A., Ireland, R. D., and Hitt, M. A. (2000). 'International Expansion by New Venture Firms: International Diversity, Mode of Market Entry, Technological Learning, and Performance'. *Academy of Management Journal*, 43(5), pp. 925–950.

Zahra, S. A., Korri, J. S., and Yu, J. (2005). 'Cognition and International Entrepreneurship: Implications for Research on International Opportunity Recognition and Exploitation'. *International Business Review*, 14(2), pp. 129–146.

Zheng, C., Khavul, S., and Crockett, D. (2012). 'Does it Transfer? The Effects of Pre-internationalization Experience on Post-entry Organizational Learning in Entrepreneurial Chinese Firms'. *Journal of International Entrepreneurship*, 10(3), pp. 232–254.

4

The international entrepreneur

From experience to action

Svante Andersson

Introduction

International entrepreneurship has emerged as a growing independent field in the interface between entrepreneurship and international business research areas. One reason for the emergence of the field is that international business theories and entrepreneurship theories independent and alone do not seem able to explain phenomena such as international new ventures, that is "business organisations that from inception seek to derive significant competitive advantage from the use of resources and the sale of outputs in multiple countries" (Oviatt and McDougall, 1994, p. 49). These firms grow rapidly in foreign markets from inception. Despite significant research output in recent decades on international new ventures (also referred to as "born globals") (for reviews, see Jones et al., 2011; Keupp and Gassman, 2009; Rialp et al., 2005), there still remains a deficit on research focusing on the individual entrepreneur's influence on the international new venture's (INV's) international development. Research has shown that entrepreneurs' capabilities and personal networks are crucial for rapid international expansion in INVs (Andersson and Wictor, 2003; Evers et al., 2012; Madsen and Servais, 1997). This contradicts mainstream international business research, which does not focus on the entrepreneur/manager as a strategic actor affecting international performance and behavior. The eclectic paradigm explains international business in terms of ownership advantages, location advantages, and internalization (Dunning, 1988), while the Uppsala school focuses on organizational learning (Johanson and Vahlne, 1977, 1990). These theories assume that managers are either rational maximizers or behaviorally oriented individuals who are part of strong networks and/or strong firm or industry cultures.

Some of the international entrepreneurship research argues that entrepreneurs/managers greatly affect their firms' international development, however also here the focus is not on the individual entrepreneurs but on the group or firm level. For example, research has found that some managers adopt an international strategy from inception while others focus on their home market (Andersson and Wictor, 2003; Madsen and Servais, 1997; McDougall et al., 2003). Research in international entrepreneurship has also shown that some managers are interested in international growth while others are not (Andersson, 2000; Nummela et al., 2004). This strand of research shows that liabilities of newness and foreignness in international new ventures (INVs) can be compensated by the founding entrepreneurs' capabilities and resources, such as knowledge, experiences, and networks from past activities.

Although already early works in the international entrepreneurship area such as Oviatt and McDougall (1994), Knight and Cavusgil (1996), and Madsen and Servais (1997) acknowledge the importance of the entrepreneur, other factors than the entrepreneur himself/herself have been dominant in international entrepreneurship research. One reason for the exclusion of the entrepreneur in many studies might be that some of the definitions of international entrepreneurship do not focus on the individual entrepreneur. For example, one of the most frequently used definitions of international entrepreneurship is: "international entrepreneurship is a combination of innovative, proactive, and risk-seeking behavior that crosses national borders and is intended to create value in organizations" (McDougall and Oviatt, 2000, p. 903). This definition is heavily influenced by Covin and Slevin (1989) and does not explicitly focus on the individual entrepreneurs within a firm but on entrepreneurial behavior at company level.

Another reason for the exclusion of the entrepreneurs might be the definition of entrepreneur. Many researchers focus on start-up of a firm as the activity that distinguishes entrepreneurs from others. However, this is a one-time event and it has been disputed that this one-time action is a suitable definition of an entrepreneur, and that other entrepreneurial activities than a start-up of a firm can distinguish individual entrepreneurs. In international entrepreneurship literature, starting a new firm is not the main aspect that distinguishes an entrepreneur. Here the entering of foreign markets is in focus. The international entrepreneur is in this chapter defined as an individual that carries out entrepreneurial actions across borders. This definition is strongly influenced by Schumpeter (1934), where the opening of a new market is one example of entrepreneurial innovation. For international entrepreneurs, rapid internationalization is the entrepreneurial action that characterizes them as entrepreneurs. In small new firms, such as international new ventures, decision power is often concentrated in the hands of one person or a few people, and the CEO has a unique and influential role in the organization.

This chapter continues with a discussion on earlier research on entrepreneurs in international new ventures. It can be concluded that research has shown that the entrepreneur is an important factor to understand the inception and development of INVs. It can also be concluded that the research, so far, has came up with somewhat different conclusions and focused on different aspects on how entrepreneurs influence firms' international behavior. Following the above discussion the effects of the international entrepreneur's background and experience on firms' international development is further treated. It is discussed how entrepreneurs' background and experience including their knowledge base, networks, mindset and behavior influence new venture internationalization. In the next section a model is developed dealing with how the entrepreneur creates an INV and how this is done via a process focusing on the entrepreneur's action. The entrepreneur learns and creates knowledge and gets new contacts, which expand the network, through his/her actions. The chapter concludes with some practical implications.

Earlier research on entrepreneurs in international new ventures

In Jones's et al.'s (2011) review of international entrepreneurship research only three articles were classified as articles which focused on the entrepreneur (McGaughey, 2007; Ruzzier et al., 2007; Perks and Hughes, 2008). This section starts with a review of these influential articles.

McGaughey studied portfolio entrepreneurship. She discussed how a portfolio of small firms controlled by three entrepreneurs could transfer knowledge among the portfolio firms. In line with Autio et al. (2000) she expected that the small new firms should have learning advantages of newness, that is that the firms have not over time built structures and cultures that hindered the adoption of new ideas. However, she found that "Rather than demonstrating a 'collective mind-set,' the history of the group of small firms in Tasmania portrays an inter- and intra-firm environment that was often fragmented, comprising coalitions of shifting interest groups and individual motivations" (McGaughey, 2007, p 318). She concludes that even information that may be considered largely objective is transformed into highly personal knowledge as individuals pass the same information through different cognitive filters based on unique personal histories (McGaughey, 2002). This is also in line with Andersson (2000) and Ghannad and Andersson's (2012) discussions about how different types of entrepreneurs develop different cognitive filters, through their personal background, interest, and experience. The roles of entrepreneurs can become set, inducing rigidities which determine the entrepreneurs' firms' development: "some entrepreneurs are notoriously dogmatic" (Zahra, 2003, p. 26). She concludes that INVs are different and to understand the diversity of INV development it is important to include the entrepreneurs in the analysis.

Ruzzier et al. (2007) identified four indicators of the human capital of an SME's entrepreneur that could influence internationalization of the firms: international business skills, international orientation, environmental perception, and management know-how. Through an empirical study they could conclude that international orientation and environmental perception is the most predictive of a SME's internationalization. Ruzzier at al. (2004) also found that entrepreneurs who are exposed to foreign markets and cultures, for example through work experience, travel, or residence are likely to accumulate experiential knowledge of different cultures and international market characteristics which benefits them when internationalizing their firms. Ruzzier et al. (2004) also concluded that entrepreneurs who see less risk when competing in international markets are more likely to respond to international opportunities.

Perks and Hughes (2008) found that industry environment, cultural context, and resource constraints did not influence an entrepreneurial manager's decision to internationalize. Instead the entrepreneurial manager's connection with the customer, tacit knowledge and vision, and product-service complexity were the factors that influenced the decision to internationalize, which is moderated by the strength of the business case and resource-based risk tolerance.

Although Jones et al. (2011) only classified the above three articles, in the international entrepreneurship area, as ones with a main focus on the entrepreneur, many other researchers also have included the entrepreneur as an important influence on firms' international behavior. Reuber and Fisher (1997) discussed how an international, experienced top management team is more likely to have foreign strategic partners which lead to a higher degree of internationalization. Andersson (2000), inspired by literature on strategic choice (Child, 1972), the upper echelons of firms (Hambrick and Mason, 1984), and entrepreneurial theory (Schumpeter, 1934; Feezer and Willard, 1990), argues that it is important to focus on the individual entrepreneurs/managers to explain international development in firms. Oviatt and McDougall (1995) point out that a global vision dating from a firm's inception is probably the most important characteristic associated with born global entrepreneurs. This is connected with the entrepreneurs' levels of ambition and general motivation. Another important characteristic is the international experience of top management. Bloodgood et al. (1996) found that international work experience among top managers was strongly associated with the internationalization of new high-potential ventures in the US. Oviatt and McDougall (1994) and Madsen and Servais (1997) conclude that the entrepreneurs' history had considerable influence on the emergence of born globals. Nummela et al. (2004) conclude that there exist many concepts such as global orientation, international entrepreneurial orientation, global outlook, and global mindset that are used and defined differently in different studies. This chapter will try to shed some light and give a better structure to how the entrepreneurs' experience and attitudes, through their actions, affect the entrepreneurs' behavior.

Many researchers have found that international experience is an important factor explaining why some entrepreneurs choose a rapid international growth strategy in their firms. However, some recent research has shown that some international new ventures are started and run by entrepreneurs without international experience (Evers, 2011; Ghannad and Andersson, 2012). International experience alone cannot explain the INV phenomenon.

Politis (2005) discusses how experience needs to be transformed to knowledge to be useful for entrepreneurs. She maintains that learning and knowledge creation are central to the understanding of entrepreneurial firms (Politis, 2005). She also argues that cognitive ability is necessary. Research has also shown how relationships and networks are crucial for firms' international development. However, most studies on international networks are based on established firms and focus on processes, routines and systems at company level (e.g. Håkansson, 1982; Johanson and Vahlne, 1990). These studies have mainly regarded international networks as rather stable relationships, which were hard for individual decision-makers to influence (Johanson and Vahlne, 1990). Reuber and Fischer (1997) showed how international experienced top managers used more foreign strategic partners and more recently, the importance of a proactive developing of personal networks for firms' international development has been pointed out (Andersson and Wictor, 2003; Frishammar and Andersson, 2009).

In the foregoing discussion earlier research on the entrepreneurs' influence on INV development has been discussed. It can be concluded that there is a lot of research that has shown that the entrepreneur is an important factor for understanding INV. It can also be concluded that the research, so far, has come up with somewhat different conclusions. Some researchers have pointed out the importance of the entrepreneurs' international experience while others have found that this is not a crucial factor (Evers, 2011; Ghannad and Andersson, 2012). The importance of personal networks has also been pointed out (Andersson and Wictor, 2003), while others have found that INV can grow internationally without these networks (Rasmussen et al., 2001). International mindsets and knowledge seem to be factors that researchers agree on to have a positive influence on firms' internationalization. Andersson and Evangelista (2006) maintain that the entrepreneur should be in focus when analyzing new firms' potential to expand abroad. Entrepreneurs can use their international experience, visions, ambitions, and networks as crucial competencies in an international expansion. While industries and countries have contextual limitations, entrepreneurial competencies are crucial factors for the newly established firm and its international development. In the next section a deeper discussion follows on how these different entrepreneurial attributes affect INV internationalization.

Effects of the international entrepreneur

The international entrepreneur's background and experience

For international entrepreneurs, rapid internationalization is the entrepreneurial action that characterizes them as entrepreneurs. Although there is an extensive research stream that tries to find traits that differentiate entrepreneurs from non-entrepreneurs, this has also met with extensive critique (e.g. Gartner, 1988). The international entrepreneurs described in the study of Andersson and Wictor (2003) display both common traits and significant differences. Two out of three entrepreneurs have an academic degree, and one entrepreneur has embarked on doctoral studies. Another entrepreneur has no academic degree, however. Furthermore, in most cases their parents cannot be characterized as entrepreneurs. Some of the entrepreneurs had previous experience of the industry in which they had created their business, while others had no prior experience. Entrepreneurs are hard to characterize as a single group, as they are individuals with their own ideas and an ability to implement those ideas, even if they do not always receive much encouragement from their environment. Where other people see problems, they interpret the problem as an opportunity and a challenge. These opportunities can also include ventures abroad. For these entrepreneurs a global strategy is the most natural, although most others would have chosen a different strategy.

An interest in and motivation to do business abroad distinguishes the entrepreneurs in "born globals." All the international entrepreneurs included in the Andersson and Wictor (2003) study had extensive international experience. This experience had been gained in different ways, such as earlier work experience, informal networks or studies abroad. In most cases it was a combination of the above-mentioned activities. This concurs with earlier research in this area (Bloodgood et al., 1996; Oviatt and McDougall, 1994; Madsen and Servais, 1997).

Andersson and Evangelista (2006) carried out a study in which they explored the influence of entrepreneurs on early internationalizing firms. They compared companies in Australia and Sweden and found many similarities among entrepreneurs in the two countries. Different types of entrepreneur were identified. One type of international entrepreneur is the experienced employee, who works in a large organization and has ambitions and ideas that are difficult to fulfil in a large organization. He/she is keen on starting a new business on his own or together with others who share his ideas and ambitions. The other is the younger, not so experienced entrepreneur, who is nevertheless ambitious and has new ideas. He/she doesn't want to be a part of a large organization, but would rather realize his ideas in his own organization. Both these types of entrepreneurs have a global mindset and have acquired this in different ways.

However, some recent studies have found that international experience or work experience is not the critical factor that can explain a firm's international growth. All individuals have experiences but other types of experience might be more important. For example, Evers and O'Gorman (2011) argue that past experience may influence and shape the information an INV manager is alert to, though the information does not need to pertain directly to international markets, nor does the manager need to have a deep understanding of sector or international markets. Similarly, Ghannad and Andersson (2012) assert that managers' childhood experiences are important in their firms' development and that managerial capabilities do not need to be created through past professional or international experiences.

The international entrepreneur's knowledge base

How firms can gain the knowledge required for successful international expansion is a main question in research dealing with firms' internationalization (Bruneel et al., 2010; Johanson and Vahlne, 1977, 1990).

Eriksson et al. (1997) find that liability of foreignness hinders a firm's international development and that institutional market knowledge (e.g., knowledge about language, laws, and rules) is necessary for successful international development. They also conclude that business market knowledge is related to a firm's business network. In line with this discussion, Johanson and Vahlne (2009) coined the concept of the "liability of outsidership." They argue that market-specific knowledge is necessary for firms to enter a market/network. The above discussion on knowledge is based on the behavioral theory of the firm, that is an organization's behaviors and actions are viewed as based on past activities and previously developed routines (Cyert and March, 1963). However, in research dealing with new firms there is no knowledge at firm level, but there are individuals with experiences and knowledge. Bruneel et al. show how congenital knowledge (that is knowledge brought in by individuals starting the firm) and also learning from other organizations can compensate for the lack of knowledge at firm level when firms are new. They also show that as the firm becomes older organizational learning becomes more important than congenital and interorganizational learning (Bruneel et al., 2010). However, other researchers have also shown how individual decision makers also strongly influence strategic decisions in old and large firms (Adner and Helfat, 2003).

Andersson (2000) discusses how entrepreneurs with different knowledge bases create firms with different strategic directions. He distinguished between technical entrepreneurs and marketing entrepreneurs, suggesting that marketing entrepreneurs are more proactive in the international marketing process, while technical entrepreneurs focus on technology development and are not very active in international marketing activities. Knowledge refers to learned skills (Adner and Helfat, 2003) and requires investment in training, education, or other types of learning. A technical entrepreneur will continue to develop the direct resources in his/her firm, which will continue to strengthen the firm's technical capabilities. Even if international entrepreneurs might have interests and skills in both technology and marketing, they are often more interested and have knowledge in one specific area. In new high-tech industries, rapid internationalization is possible without the need for active internationalization, as the high-tech product is often very specialized and the home market too small in countries like Sweden and Australia. In a more mature industry, however, active internationalization is necessary if the firm is to expand abroad. This is in line with Andersson's (2004) findings that different industry contexts influence firms' international strategies. In new industries, like the high-tech industry, it is easier for a newcomer to get established. In mature industries, such as the automotive industry, significant resources are necessary to get established in the market. Bruneel et al. (2010) also highlighted the importance of learning from interactions with other actors. This is further discussed in the next section, which deals with networks.

The international entrepreneur's personal networks

The network and social capital literature distinguishes between different categories of relationships and networks, such as strong versus weak (Granovetter, 1973), business versus private, and local versus international (Keeble et al., 1998; Söderqvist, 2011). In this chapter the international entrepreneurs' individual relationships are in focus. These relationships build social capital that is beneficial for the entrepreneur (Nahapiet and Ghoshal, 1998). Many studies have highlighted the role of international networks in firms' internationalization processes. In new firms, networks are crucial resources both at the creation stage and for the further development of the born global firm (Mort and Weerawardena, 2006). A network is not only a way to obtain resources but also a resource itself (Coviello and Cox, 2006). Sharma and Blomstermo (2003) suggest that the internationalization process for born globals includes learning through international networks. They maintain that it is crucial to make early contacts with internationalized firms on the domestic market or abroad. Contacts with a locally based internationalized firm may help new ventures engage in activities abroad as "client followers" (Bell, 1995).

Personal networks are very important for entrepreneurs in born global firms. Entrepreneurs with experience of the industry can use their contacts to expand their own businesses. Reuber and Fischer (1997) show that international experienced top management team members use more foreign strategic partners, which leads to a greater degree of internationalization. Personal networks are also important in the securing of finance and finding partners in other areas. In the early start-up stages born global firms are small with few financial resources. In order to expand abroad they have to cooperate with others. These partners are often found in personal networks.

Andersson et al. (2013) also show how both local and international networks were important for firm's international growth and that international entrepreneurs have the capability to connect international and local networks (Anderson et al., 2012).

The international entrepreneur's global mindset

This sector deals with individuals' cognitive processes, that is individuals' beliefs and mental models that serve as a basis for decision making (Walsh, 1995). Jones and Casulli (2014) discuss cognitive processes in an international entrepreneurship context. They maintain that reasoning by comparison between previously known (experienced) situations and those newly encountered (Holyoak and Morrison, 2012), are especially relevant for international new ventures, in which often-complex decisions are made in conditions of uncertainty, and limited computational capability and information access (Simon, 1972). Such conditions may force entrepreneurs to turn to reasoning by comparison of new international activities with previously experienced domestic or international situations, and their own idiosyncratic life experiences (Casulli, 2011; Jones and Casulli, 2014). An individual's capacity to process new information is limited, and thus people try to minimize cognitive efforts (Baron, 1998). To do so, people develop heuristics (simplified models) that guide them in their decision making. Research in the business literature has discussed these models using different terminology, including mental maps, frames of reference, mindsets, cognitive bases, schemata, cognitive structures, cognitive maps, and ways of thinking (Calori et al., 1994; Hellgren and Melin, 1993). This research stream is developed from March and Simon's (1958) and Cyert and March's (1963) behavioral theory of the firm. These authors argue that the cognitive base for decisions consists of assumptions or knowledge about future events, alternatives, and consequences of the alternatives. According to bounded rationality, decision makers may not have complete information about future events, alternatives, and consequences. Managerial value systems also affect the preferential ordering of alternatives and consequences. The international entrepreneurs' way of thinking is crucial to an understanding of the inception of born global firms. These entrepreneurs interpret their environment in a different way, and see international opportunities where others do not. McGaughey (2007) showed that external information was not decisive for the entrepreneur's decision making. Instead the entrepreneurs had developed cognitive heuristics through their idiosyncratic life experiences that guided their decisions, which led to their firms' different development. International entrepreneurs interact with the environment and change it and create new international strategies (Weick, 1995; Rasmussen et al., 2001). This is in line with earlier findings, which show that although entrepreneurs in born globals are exposed to the same opportunities as others, the difference is that they take advantage of the opportunities (McAuley, 1999). This is exemplified by the following quote:

> We decided that we should start to export this product. We did the opposite to all the advice we got. They told us to start slowly with representatives but we started subsidiaries in Germany, France, the US and England. The first years were very tough, but the subsidiaries in France and the US are very successful.
>
> *(Founder and CEO of a Swedish international new venture)*

A positive attitude towards internationalization is a prerequisite for early internationalization. This was shown in Crick and Jones' (2000) study in which several firms displayed evidence of an international orientation and international strategy from the date of inception. This attitude and way of thinking has been named "global mindset" (Nummela et al., 2004). Nummela et al. (2004, p. 54) further develop this discussion and define the global mindset as "a manager's openness to and awareness of cultural diversity and the ability to handle it." In their study they found a positive relationship between global mindset and "objective" financial indicators of firms' international performances; however, no significant relationship between global mindset and managers' subjective evaluations of performance was found. The positive relationship between entrepreneurs' global mindset and their firms' international growth has been shown in many studies, for example Andersson (2011) shows how a founder already from inception had a global business mission – the whole world as the market. This founder succeeded in expanding his business to over 100 markets within ten years.

The global vision of the born global entrepreneur is an important factor in understanding the firm's global development. But why do some entrepreneurs develop a global vision and succeed in implementing this vision in a growing international firm? Andersson et al. (2004) found that younger entrepreneurs were heads of international firms more often than older ones. This result suggests that the younger generation is being brought up in a more global environment, and as such, they may not consider national borders barriers to business opportunities. However, to have a mindset is one thing, but to succeed with building an international new venture, the entrepreneur needs to create an international venture. To build an international organization and manage and lead personnel are crucial activities for the international entrepreneur. "Leadership must inevitably be performed through action, not cognition" (Denison et al., 1995, p. 524).

The international entrepreneur's behavior

Andersson and Florén (2011) have shown that managers in small international firms do behave differently from managers in small domestic firms: they have a different activity pattern and uphold different roles within their firms. They concluded that international managers are less oriented toward operative work and are more proactive in using their networks. They also concluded that the international entrepreneurs' behavior was an intended behavior to achieve the aim of international growth. Not only is a proactive stance in relation to market opportunities important for international entrepreneurs, but a proactive stance in relation to network contacts is also a key element. The international entrepreneurs had made a strategic decision to grow internationally and to implement an international strategy; they have devoted time that favoured international expansion. They have also implemented a decentralized organization that could deal with operative matters, while the entrepreneurs focus on building relationships with international strategic partners.

This is in line with earlier research, which has shown that proactiveness is important in order to succeed in international markets (Frishammar and Andersson, 2009). This also supports and extends the literature on international entrepreneurship, from which we know that international new ventures are often dominated by proactive entrepreneurs, who use their personal networks to expand abroad (Andersson and Wictor, 2003; Autio, 2005; Rialp et al., 2005).

The above mentioned research is strongly influenced by the managerial work and practice tradition (see Carlson, 1951; Mintzberg, 1973). This research stream focuses on "what managers really are doing" and uses methods such as observation study, where the managers are followed over time. More research in this tradition is recommended to catch how managerial behavior is carried out in international firms in different contexts.

From experience to action: entrepreneurs building INV

In the earlier section we have discussed the entrepreneurs' background and experience, knowledge base, networks, and behavior. To understand the inception and development in INVs these are crucial factors to involve in an analysis. However, these factors are not static. It is important to follow how these factors change over time. The entrepreneurs are acting and experiencing new activities, which create knowledge, relationships, and some experiences that might also change the entrepreneur's mindset. This can be exemplified by the international entrepreneur who started the company Alfa (Andersson, 2011). This international entrepreneur had former international, industrial experience and a strong local and international network when he started his firm. He was internationally oriented and from inception the whole world was regarded as the market for Alfa. The company started in 1990 and the sales turnover in Sweden has never been more than 20 percent of the total turnover. Alfa entered approximately ten markets per year, and in 2001 Alfa was present in 80 countries. This development was strongly influenced by the entrepreneur's earlier international and industry experience that had formed his "mindset." His network was also essential for the firm's development.

However, his mindset also hindered the develpment at one stage. The products the company produced had been targeted toward the off-shore industry. The entrepreneur had developed a heuristic logic that was focused on the off-shore industry and he did not see opportunities in other sectors. However, the entrepreneur learned that other industries (such as construction and electronics) also were suitable for the firm's products. After some years without international growth, the firm acknowledged new opportunities in other sectors and began to grow internationally again.

In the firm's early phases we can see that the decision making follows an effectuation logic (there are no clear goals, the entrepreneur uses his experiences, networks, and knowledge and creates opportunities together with other stakeholders (Sarasvathy, 2001)). The firms' inception was constituted from the entrepreneur's characteristics and experience (who he is), his knowledge about industry and internationalization (knowledge corridors), and who he knows (international and local networks). The entrepreneur worked proactively with different stakeholders in his network to develop marketing capabilities for international development and growth (Evers et al., 2012). Effectuation logic seems to enhance the positive impact of cooperation with network actors for capability development leading to international growth (Gabrielsson and Gabrielsson, 2013). The turbulent context and fast growth in multiple markets made a causation logic less plausible (with opportunity recognition as a planned process where opportunities are recognized after a purposeful, rational, and systematic search process). Kalinic et al. (2013) found a similar behavior in their study. Successful entrepreneurs were able to change between causal and effectual logic and used effectual logic in situations where the context was turbulent and they did not have information and knowledge to use causal logic.

As the INV grows it is also important to include the relationship between the firm and individual in the analysis. The entrepreneur is building an organization and invests in different technologies and markets and these commitments will affect the INV's future development.

In our case firm, Alfa, we could identify that more causation logic was needed when the firm was larger and present on more than 100 markets. The tricky thing for the entrepreneur/manager was to balance the entrepreneurial spirit and still create routines on a firm level to control the larger firm. More research is recommended that deals with how managers can balance effectuation and causation logic in firms to create international growing firms.

> Effective leaders are those who have the cognitive and behavioural complexity to respond appropriately to a wide range of situations that may in fact require contrary or opposing behaviours.
>
> *(Hooijberg and Choi, 2001, p. 526)*

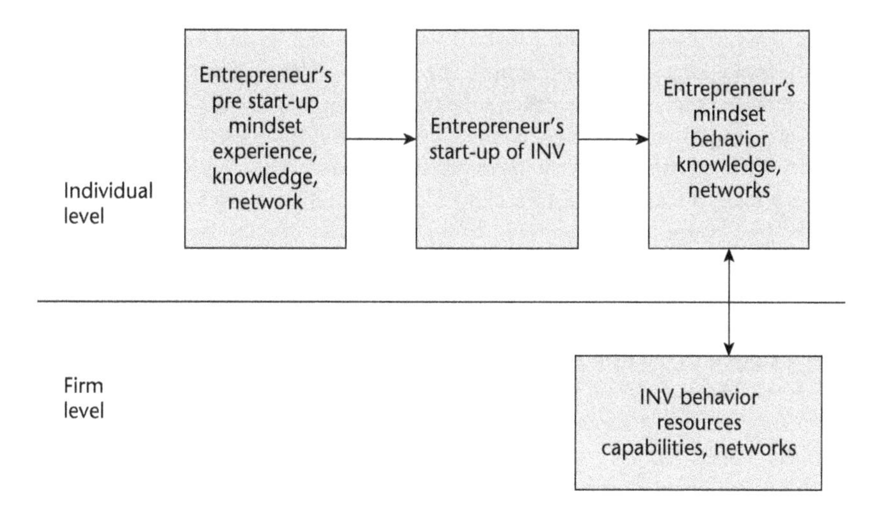

Figure 4.1 From experience to action: entrepreneurs building INVs

To start an INV and to continue to grow the firm internationally, all the above discussed factors are important, however, the action is the crucial part. Experience, knowledge, and networks facilitate the inception of the INV but are not indispensable. Without action no firm will be created, or a firm will not continue to grow (Andersson, 2000). A factor that will strongly influence the direction of the action is the entrepreneur's mindset. McGaughey (2007) showed how the individual's cognitive filters are more important than external information for the entrepreneur's decision making. The entrepreneur interprets external stimuli to create international action. An entrepreneur with a global mindset will acknowledge international and global opportunities and act upon them to increase the entrepreneur's firm's international presence. When the INV is up and running the entrepreneur will gain knowledge and experience through the INV's activities, which will affect the entrepreneur's and firm's behavior. The entrepreneur (but also the firm) will gain international knowledge and the entrepreneur's and firm's international network will grow. This process will further facilitate the firm's international growth (Figure 4.1).

Figure 4.1 gives suggestions for future research. There is a need to further investigate the entrepreneurs' experience, knowledge, and networks before the INV start-up (Ghannad and Andersson, 2012). This is important for gaining knowledge of how education and policy programs can be constructed. How can education be formed to facilitate the creation of more international entrepreneurs and INVs?

Another important suggestion for future research is to deeper investigate the entrepreneur's influence on further growth in the INV. How can the entrepreneur build a global organization? Will the same entrepreneurs be able to start the company and grow it? There are examples of entrepreneurs who have both started companies and been successful with an international growth strategy (e.g. Ingvar Kamprad at IKEA), but also examples of entrepreneurs who have been successful in the start-up and early phases, but unsuccessful with continued international growth.

Practical implications

Further research in the international entrepreneurship area can provide important insights with regard to implications for management. Many small and medium-sized firms do not exploit their international potential. As earlier research and international consultants advocate a cautious incremental strategy, research in international entrepreneurship gives examples of a much faster and more successful international expansion. The strategy is developed on the basis of the company's resources, and the entrepreneur's mindset, knowledge, experience, personal networks, and behavior play an important role. New technology and fewer trade barriers will make it possible for new small firms to compete in the international arena.

Many new firms do not regard international opportunities as a serious growth alternative. Advice given by governmental actors and consultants is also often quite negative towards early internationalization. However, research has shown that early internationalization can be a successful growth strategy for new small firms. The positive effect of an early internationalization is not only that a higher turnover can be reached. Competition in an international environment may create a culture in the firm that makes it possible to learn from international markets and generate knowledge that can be transformed to a competitive edge. Creating an international successful team doesn't just mean taking part in a national competition; you also need to be a part of global competition.

International entrepreneurship research also suggests the need for education. As most business is now influenced by globalization, business education needs to encompass the international and global aspects. Studying abroad has proved to be good preparation both for individuals wanting to start their own business and for those wanting to work in international firms. Even though entrepreneurship education has increased dramatically during the last decade, few entrepreneurship programs deal with international opportunities. In order to prepare for today's global competition, entrepreneurship education also needs to deal with international matters.

References

Adner, R. and Helfat C. E. (2003). Corporate effects and dynamic managerial capabilities. *Strategic Management Journal*, 24, 1011–1025.

Anderson, A., Dodd, D., and Jack, S. S. (2012). Entrepreneurship as connecting: Some implications for theorising and practice. *Management Decision*, 50(5), 958–971.

Andersson, S. (2000). The internationalization of the firm from an entrepreneurial perspective. *International Studies of Management & Organization*, 30(1), 63–92.

Andersson, S. (2004). Internationalization in different industrial contexts, *Journal of Business Venturing*, 19(6), 851–875.

Andersson, S. (2011). International entrepreneurship, born globals and the theory of effectuation. *Journal of Small Business and Enterprise Development*, 18(3), 627–643.

Andersson, S. and Evangelista, F. (2006). The entrepreneur in the born global firm in Australia and Sweden, *Journal of Small Business and Enterprise Development*, 13(4), 642–659.

Andersson, S., Evers, N., and Griot, C. (2013) Local and international networks in small firm internationalisation: Cases from the Rhône-Alpes medical technology regional cluster. *Entrepreneurship and Regional Development*, 25(9–10), 867–888.

Andersson, S. and Florén, H. (2011). Differences in managerial behavior between small international and non-international firms. *Journal of International Entrepreneurship*, 9(3), 233–258.

Andersson, S., Gabrielsson, J., and Wictor, I. (2004). International activities in small firms: Examining factors influencing the internationalization and export growth of small firms. *Canadian Journal of Administrative Science*, 21(1), 22–34.

Andersson, S. and Wictor, I. (2003). Innovative internationalisation in new firms: Born globals—the Swedish case. *Journal of International Entrepreneurship*, 1(3), 249–275.

Autio, E. (2005). Creative tension: The significance of Ben Oviatt's and Patricia McDougall's article "Toward a theory of international new ventures". *Journal of International Business Studies*, 36(1), 9–19.

Autio, E., Sapienza, H. J., and Almeida, J. G. (2000). Effects of age at entry, knowledge intensity, and imitability on international growth. *Academy of Management Journal*, 43(5), 909–924.

Baron, R. A. (1998). Cognitive mechanisms in entrepreneurship: Why and when entrepreneurs think differently than other people. *Journal of Business Venturing*, 13(4), 275–294.

Bell, J. (1995). The internationalization of small computer software firms: A further challenge to 'stage' theories. *European Journal of Marketing*, 29(8), 60–75.
Bloodgood, J. M., Sapienza, H. J., and Almeida, J. G. (1996). The internationalization of new high-potential US ventures: Antecedents and outcomes. *Entrepreneurship Theory and Practice*, 20, 61–76.
Bruneel, J., Yli-Renko, H., and Clarysse, B. (2010). Learning from experience and learning from others: How congenital and interorganizational learning substitute for experiential learning in young firm internationalization, *Strategic Entrepreneurship Journal*, 4, 164–182.
Calori, R., Johnson, G., and Sarnin, P. (1994). CEOs' cognitive maps and the scope of the organization. *Strategic Management Journal*, 15(6), 437–458.
Carlson, S. (1951). *Executive behaviour*. Stockholm: Strömberg.
Casulli, L. (2011). Making internationalisation decisions: How heuristics and biases affect the reasoning processes of leaders of small and medium-sized firms (Doctoral thesis). University of Glasgow, Glasgow, UK.
Child, J. (1972). Organizational structure, environment and performance: The role of strategic choice. *Sociology*, 6, 2–22.
Coviello, N. and Cox, M. (2006). The resource dynamics of international new venture networks. *Journal of International Entrepreneurship*, 4, 113–132.
Covin, J. G. and Slevin, D. P. (1989). Strategic management of small firms in hostile and benign environments. *Strategic Managent Journal*, 10(1), 75–87.
Crick, D. and Jones, M.V. (2000). Small high-technology firms and international high-technology markets. *Journal of International Marketing*, 8(2), 63–85.
Cyert, R. M. and March, J. G. (1963). *A behavioral theory of the firm*. Englewood Cliffs, NJ: Prentice Hall.
Denison, D., Hooijberg, R., and Quinn, R. (1995). Paradox and performance: Toward a theory of behavioral complexity in managerial leadership. *Organization Science*, 6(5), 524–543.
Dunning, J. H. (1988). The eclectic paradigm of international production: A restatement and possible extension. *Journal of International Business Studies*, 19(1), 1–31.
Eriksson, K., Johanson, J., Majkård, A., and Sharma, D. (1997). Experiential knowledge and cost in the internationalization process. *Journal of International Business Studies*, 28, 337–360.
Evers, N. (2011). International new ventures in low-tech sectors: A dynamic capabilities perspective. *Journal of Small Business and Enterprise Development*, 18(3), 502–528.
Evers, N., Andersson, S., and Hannibal, M. (2012). Stakeholders and marketing capabilities in international new ventures: Evidence from Ireland, Sweden, and Denmark. *Journal of International Marketing*, 20(4), 46–71.
Evers, N. and O'Gorman, C. (2011). Improvised internationalization in new ventures: The role of prior knowledge and networks, *Entrepreneurship & Regional Development*, 23(7/8), 549–574.
Feezer, H. R. and Willard, G. E. (1990). Founding strategy and performance: A comparison of high and low growth high-tech firms. *Strategic Management Journal*, 11(2), 87–98.
Frishammar, J. and Andersson, S. (2009). The overestimated role of strategic orientations for international performance in smaller firms. *Journal of International Entrepreneurship*, 7, 57–77.
Gabrielsson, P. and Gabrielsson, M. (2013) A dynamic model of growth phases and survival in international business-to-business new ventures: The moderating effect of decision-making logic. *Industrial Marketing Management*, 42(8), 1357–1373.
Gartner, W. B. (1988). Who is an entrepreneur? Is the wrong question, *American Journal of Small Business*, 13, 11–32.
Ghannad, N. and Andersson, S. (2012). The influence of the entrepreneur's background on the behaviour and development of born globals' internationalisation processes. *International Journal of Entrepreneurship and Small Business*, 15(2), 136–153.
Granovetter, M. S. (1973). The strength of weak ties. *American Journal of Sociology*, 78(6), 1360–1380.
Håkansson, H. (Ed.) (1982). *International marketing and purchasing of industrial goods*. Chichester: Wiley.
Håkansson, H. and Johanson, J. (1992). A model of industrial networks. In B. Axelsson and G. Easton (Eds.), *Industrial networks: a new view of reality* (pp. 28–34). Routledge, Chapman & Hall, Incorporated.
Hambrick, D. C. and Mason, P.A. (1984). Upper echelons: The organization as a reflection of its top managers. *Academy of Management Review*, 9, 193–206.
Hellgren, B. and Melin, L. (1993). The role of strategists' ways-of-thinking in strategic change processes. In Hendry, J. and Johnson, G. (Eds.) *Strategic thinking: leadership and the management of change*. Chichester: Wiley.

Holyoak, K. J. and Morrison, R. G. (2012). Thinking and reasoning: A reader's guide. In Holyoak, K. J. and Morrison, R.G. (Eds.), *The Oxford handbook of thinking and reasoning* (pp. 1–10). New York: Oxford University Press.

Hooijberg, R. and Choi, J. (2001), The impact of organizational characteristics on leadership effectiveness models: An examination of leadership in a private and a public sector organization. *Administration and Society*, 33(4), 403–432.

Johanson, J. and Vahlne, J. E. (1977). The internationalization process of the firm: A model of knowledge development and increasing foreign market commitments. *Journal of International Business Studies*, 8(1), 23–32.

Johanson, J. and Vahlne, J. E. (1990). The mechanism of internationalisation. *International Marketing Review*, 7(4), 11–24.

Johanson, J. and Vahlne, J. E. (2009). The Uppsala internationalization process model revisited: From liability of foreignness to liability of outsidership, *Journal of International Business Studies*, 40(9), 1411–1431.

Jones, M.V. and Casulli, L. (2014). International entrepreneurship: Exploring the logic and utility of individual experience through comparative reasoning approaches. *Entrepreneurship Theory and Practice*, 38: 45–69.

Jones, M. V., Coviello, N., and Tang, Y. K. (2011). International entrepreneurship research (1989–2009): A domain ontology and thematic analysis. *Journal of Business Venturing*, 26(6), 632–659.

Kalinic, I., Sarasvathy, S. D., and Forza, C. (2013). "Expect the unexpected": Implications of effectual logic on the internationalization process. *International Business Review*, 22(3), 635–647.

Keeble, D., Lawson, C., Lawton Smith, H., Moore, B., and Wilkinson, F. (1998). Internationalisation Processes, Networking and Local Embeddedness in Technology-Intensive Small Firms. *Small Business Economics*, 11, 327–342.

Keupp, M. M. and Gassmann, O. (2009). The past and the future of international entrepreneurship: A review and suggestions for developing the field. *Journal of Management*, 35(3), 600–633.

Knight, G. A. and Cavusgil, S. T. (1996). The born global firm: A challenge to traditional internationalization theory. *Advances in International Marketing*, 8, 11–26.

Madsen, T. K. and Servais, P. (1997). The internationalization of born globals: An evolutionary process? *International Business Review*, 6(6), 561–583.

March, J. G. and Simon, H. A. (1958). *Organizations*. New York: Wiley.

McAuley, A. (1999). Entrepreneurial instant exporters in the Scottish arts and crafts sector. *Journal of International Marketing*, 7(4), 67–82.

McDougall, P. P. and Oviatt, B. M. (2000). International entrepreneurship: The intersection of two paths, Guest Editors' Introduction. *Academy of Management Journal*, 43(5), 902–908.

McDougall, P.P., Oviatt, B. M., and Shrader, R.C. (2003). A comparison of international and domestic new ventures. *Journal of International Entrepreneurship*, 1(1), 59–82.

McGaughey, S. L. (2002). Strategic interventions in intellectual asset flows. *Academy of Management Review*, 27(2), 248–274.

McGaughey, S. L. (2007). Hidden ties in international new venturing: The case of portfolio entrepreneurship. *Journal of World Business*, 42(3), 307–321.

Mintzberg, H. (1973). *The nature of managerial work*. New York: Harper & Row.

Mort, G. S. and Weerawardena, J. (2006). Networking capability and international entrepreneurship: How networks function in Australian born global firms, *International Marketing Review*, 23, 549–572.

Nahapiet, J. and Ghoshal, S. (1998). Social capital, intellectual capital, and the organizational advantage. *Academy of Management Review*, 23(2), 242–266.

Nummela, N., Saarenketo, S., and Puumalainen, K. (2004). Global mindset: A prerequisite for successful internationalisation? *Canadian Journal of Administrative Science*, 21(1), 51–64.

Oviatt, B. M. and McDougall, P. P. (1994). Toward a theory of international new ventures. *Journal of International Business Studies*, 25(1), 45–64.

Oviatt, Benjamin M. and McDougall, Patricia (1995). *Academy of Management Executive*, 9(2), 30–43.

Perks, K. J. and Hughes, M. (2008). Entrepreneurial decision-making in internationalization: Propositions from mid-size firms. *International Business Review*, 17(3), 310–330.

Politis, D. (2005) The process of entrepreneurial learning: A conceptual framework. *Entrepreneurship Theory and Practice*, 29(4), 399–424.

Rasmussen, E., Madsen, T. K., and Evangelista, F. (2001). The founding of the born global company in Denmark and Australia: Sense-making and networking. *Asia Pacific Journal of Marketing and Logistics*, 13(3), 75–107.

Reuber, A. R. and Fischer, E. (1997). The influence of the management team's international experience on the internationalization behaviors of SMEs. *Journal of International Business Studies*, 28(4), 807–825.
Rialp, A., Rialp, J., and Knight, G. A. (2005). The phenomenon of early internationalizing firms: What do we know after a decade (1993–2003) of scientific inquiry? *International Business Review*, 14(2), 147–166.
Ruzzier, M., Antoncic, B., Hisrich, R. D., and Konecnik, M., (2007). Human capital and SME internationalization: a structural equation modelling study. *Canadian Journal of Administrative Sciences*, 24(1), 15–29.
Sarasvathy, S. D. (2001). Causation and effectuation: Toward a theoretical shift from economic inevitability to entrepreneurial contingency. *Academy of Management Review*, 26(2), 243–263.
Schumpeter, J. A. (1934). *The theory of economic development*. Cambridge, MA: Harvard University Press.
Sharma, D. D. and Blomstermo, A. (2003). The internationalisation process of born globals: A network view. *The International Business Review*, 12, 739–753.
Simon, H. A. (1972). Theories of bounded rationality. In McGuire, C. B. and Radner, R. (Eds.), *Decision and organization* (pp. 161–176). Amsterdam: North Holland.
Söderqvist, A. (2011). Opportunity exploration and exploitation in INVs: A study of relationships' involvement in early entrepreneurial and internationalisation events. Doctoral dissertation, Hanken School of Economics, Vasa, Finland.
Walsh, J. P. (1995). Managerial and organization cognition: Notes from a trip down memory lane. *Organization Science*, 6(1), 280–321.
Weick, K. E. (1995). *Sensemaking in organizations*. Thousand Oaks, CA: Sage.
Zahra, S. A. (2003). A theory of international new ventures: A decade of research. *Journal of International Business Studies*, 36, 20–28.

5

The international social entrepreneur

R. Scott Marshall, Jude Lieberman and Michelle Pagès

Introduction

Since McDougall (1989) published her seminal article distinguishing domestic and international entrepreneurship, academic scholars have significantly advanced our understanding of international entrepreneurship (e.g. Acs et al., 2003; Giamartino et al., 1993; Oviatt and McDougall, 1994, 1999, 2005). These scholars have employed numerous theoretical frames – including resource-based theory, institutional theory, and network theory – to define what international entrepreneurship is (and is not) (Oviatt andMcDougall, 2005), how entrepreneurs effectively activate international operations (McDonald et al., 2003) and the organizational attributes that enhance international entrepreneurship (Dimitratos et al., 2012).

With Dees' (1998) provocative statement that "(s)ocial entrepreneurs are one species in the genus entrepreneurs," numerous scholars have taken up research into the field of social entrepreneurship (e.g. Leadbetter, 1997; Mair and Marti, 2006; Paredo and McLean, 2006; Weerawardena and Sullivan Mort, 2006; Zahra et al., 2009). These authors have investigated various aspects of social entrepreneurship, including the tensions between for-profit and social mission objectives (Paredo and McLean, 2006), the approaches of social entrepreneurs in opportunity identification (Zahra et al., 2009), and how social entrepreneurs strive to create social value amidst dynamic environments (Weerawerdena and Sullivan Mort, 2006).

However, there is a paucity of research conducted at the intersection of"international entrepreneurship" and "social entrepreneurship" – that is, the concept of"international social entrepreneurship" (Zahra et al., 2014). To that end, the purpose of this chapter is to explore this specific type of entrepreneurship. As the previous chapter focused on international entrepreneurship, we will begin with an overview of the concept of social entrepreneurship, in order to understand how "social" is a distinguishing modifier. The first section will also examine how value creation is viewed from the perspective of social entrepreneurship. Following this section, the second section discusses the "international" dimension of social entrepreneurship. The third section provides three brief case examples of international social enterprise models operating throughout various parts of the world. Looking closely at VisionSpring, Tropical Salvage, and Honey Care Africa provides more concrete understanding of how social challenges are defined, international social enterprises are established, and social value creation is assessed. The final section will discuss recent trends in the field, recommend theoretical frames for further studying this concept, and provide a summary conclusion with a list of sources for further reading.

Social entrepreneurship

Defining social entrepreneurship

The difference between traditional entrepreneurship and social entrepreneurship is at the starting point. Traditional entrepreneurship starts by understanding a market opportunity; whereas social entrepreneurship starts by understanding a social challenge. It is based on this distinction that significant research has been conducted on social entrepreneurship over the last fifteen years (e.g. Austin et al., 2006; Barendsen and Gardner, 2004; Bornstein, 2004; Dees, 2001; Dees et al., 2004; Dimitratos et al., 2012; Leadbetter, 1997; Mair et al., 2012; Marshall, 2011; Mort et al., 2002; Paredo and McLean, 2006; Zahra et al., 2009).

The Ashoka Foundation, founded by Bill Drayton in the early 1980s, defines social entrepreneurs as: "individuals with innovative solutions to society's most pressing social problems. They are ambitious and persistent, tackling major social issues and offering new ideas for wide-scale change"(*What is a social entrepreneur*, n.d.). Social entrepreneurs, similar to conventional entrepreneurs, are engaged in provisioning goods or services; however, they do not view products or services as ends in themselves; rather, they serve as "an integral part of an intervention to achieve social objectives, thereby contributing to social change" (Mair et al., 2012, p. 353).

Just as with a social entrepreneur, there seems to be no commonly agreed upon definition of a traditional entrepreneur; however traits often include risk-taking, innovation, proactivity, and the pursuit of profits (Paredo and McLean, 2006). If we consider what distinguishes a social entrepreneur in particular, Paredo and McLean (2006) argue that while social entrepreneurs display some similar traits with those of traditional entrepreneurs, in fact, "it may well be that the mix of managerial competencies appropriate to successful pursuit of social entrepreneurship differs in significant ways from the mix relevant to success in entrepreneurship without the social component"(57). Dees (2001) outlines the activities of a social entrepreneur: (1) adopting a mission to create and sustain social value (not just private value); (2) recognizing and relentlessly pursuing new opportunities to serve that mission; (3) engaging in a process of continuous innovation, adaptation, and learning; (4) acting boldly without being limited by resources currently in hand; and, (5) exhibiting heightened accountability to the constituencies served and for the outcomes created.

There is much debate over the precise constitution of a social enterprise, particularly around the subject of scale, legal structure, and profit-seeking motives. Some will argue that a for-profit and a social enterprise are mutually exclusive, relegating social entrepreneurship to the idea of nonprofits pursuing revenue-generating activities. For the purposes of this section, we are assuming a broader definition, containing the following components: (1) Social entrepreneurship is a field that merges business tools with social objectives. (2) A social enterprise is an institution acting as a vehicle of social entrepreneurship; a socially driven venture established to create sustainable social benefit. (3) The social mission must be predominant or in parity to profit pursuits. The entity will aim to be economically viable, and direct any revenue profits generated back into the business. (4) A social enterprise organization can be legally structured as a nonprofit, for-profit, or hybrid of the two.

Thus where in the past, a segregated model viewed the work of addressing social problems as the arena of not-for-profits or government, a social entrepreneur recognizes that societal needs can be better met when all three sectors are tackling problems and partnering together, making, "A conscious choice to address a persistent social or environmental problem with market-driven solutions, rather than initiating civil society or governmental-based programs" (Marshall, 2011: 186).

Defining social value

In order to understand the true worth of a social enterprise, we shift our understanding of value creation in the traditional business sense from the concept of shareholder wealth, to that of social or shared value. In his HBR article, Michael Porter defines the principle of shared value as "policies and operating practices that enhance the competitiveness of a company while simultaneously advancing the economic and social conditions in the communities in which it operates" (Porter and Kramer, 2011: 66). Thus in this case, "value" is not just about economic benefits and costs, but also includes societal ones. Economic development investments have shown that when the needs of all people – including those at the lower end of the socio-economic scale – are addressed, the economic value of society increases as a whole (Porter and Kramer, 2011: 65).

Social enterprise lies at the cross-section of traditional business and nonprofit organizations. Table 5.1 shows a continuum, with the social enterprise space indicated in bold, although it should be noted that by definition, a continuum does not have firm boundaries. There are two distinguishing features of significance that differentiate a social enterprise from those enterprises at either end of the spectrum: (1) commercial exchange must be a part of the enterprise model in order to be self-sustaining; (2) social goals must be at parity with or take precedence over profit-making goals.

Social enterprises may pursue a double bottom line (social and economic), or a triple bottom line, accounting for the "three P's: profit, people and planet" (*The Economist, Triple bottom line*, 2009). The choice by the social entrepreneurs of whether to operate as a for-profit or not-for-profit depends on a variety of factors, including the set of social needs, the type, amount and accessibility of necessary resources, and the means for obtaining financial returns (Mair and Marti, 2006). That is, regardless of organizational form, social entrepreneurs seek to earn revenue through offering products or services (economic/profit) while addressing social and/or environmental issues. However, as illustrated in Table 5.1, mission-related impact related to society is held as the primary metric; "wealth is just a means to an end for social entrepreneurs" (Porter and Kramer, 2011: 64).

Table 5.1 Continuum of non-profit to for-profit

Charity / NGO	*NGO with revenue-generating activities*	*Social enterprise*	*Socially-responsible business or B-corporation*	*Corporate social responsibility (CSR)*	*Traditional corporation*
Enterprise has exclusively social goals with no commercial exchange	Profits directly or indirectly support exclusively social goals	Social goals are primary or equal to profit-making goals	Social goals are prominent but secondary to profit-making goals	Social goals exist in support of primary profit-making goals	Enterprise has exclusively profit-making goals

Source: Alter, 2004: 24; Paredo and McLean, 2006: 63.

Understanding revenue models

In terms of the approach to revenue generation, Fowler (2000) refers to two social enterprise models, "integrated" and "complementary" (645). Integrated social entrepreneurs use an income-generating activity that is directly related to the social outcomes. An example of the integrated social enterprise where the revenue-generating product relates directly to the social benefit outcomes is Guayaki, US-based producers of Guayaki Yerba Mate beverages. Commonplace growing and cultivation techniques of the yerba mate plant in Brazil, Argentina, and Paraguay have threatened rainforest land and biodiversity. Guayaki has worked with indigenous farmers in these areas to change cultivation practices to secure sustainable income for fair trade yerba mate while simultaneously restoring and protecting the rainforest (Guayaki, 2013). Thus, the Guayaki model directly integrates the commercial activity associated with selling yerba mate beverages with the achievement of its social mission of preserving indigenous livelihoods and rainforest.

In contrast, complementary social entrepreneurs structure their enterprises so that a revenue-generating source can cross-subsidize their social purpose. An example of a complementary model is provided by Digital Divide Data (DDD). Operating in Cambodia and Laos, the mission of DDD is to provide job skills training to disenfranchised populations in these countries. Its primary revenue-generating activity is the digitization of hardcopy materials for universities and corporations primarily in the US and Europe. Thus, the commercial activity of DDD provides the source of revenue to support its social mission.

Although somewhat simplified in conveying the revenue-generating approaches of social enterprise, the two models presented by Fowler are useful. Both models emphasise that the mission of the social enterprise is the alleviation of one or more specific social issues and that revenue is generated to support the achievement of the mission.

International social entrepreneurship

In today's modern world, information technology, communication, and transportation, all enable potential internationalization faster and easier than ever. The rise of these technologies has run generally in parallel with the expanding scholarship in international entrepreneurship. International entrepreneurship, as a particular phenomenon, has become of interest because operating across national borders and within different cultural contexts calls on unique approaches to opportunity identification and risk-taking (Gupta and Fernandez, 2009; Zahra et al., 2009). The knowledge gained through this scholarship provide insights on how, what, when, and why to internationalize a business activity. Extending this premise to international social entrepreneurship, it is a phenomenon of interest because it brings new perspectives on how, what, when, and why to internationalize a business activity *that is conducted to support the achievement of a social mission*. Because there is limited research investigating international social entrepreneurship, there remain significant scholarly opportunities to lend understanding to this phenomenon.

Table 5.2 provides a simplistic characterization of entrepreneurship based on geographic scope and mission primacy. Where the geographic scope of the firm is international and the social mission obtains primacy, the firm is identified as an international social entrepreneur.

International social enterprises have arisen as business vehicles to augment efforts deployed by foreign aid programs as well as international NGOs (Alter, 2005: 5). This shift in the private sector signals an emerging legitimacy of social value creation, not just economic value creation, as being a new norm of conducting business. "Social entrepreneurs are motivated to address

Table 5.2 Enterprise models

Mission primacy	*Geographic scope*	
	Domestic	*International*
Commercial	All commercial transactions occur within the borders of one country. Success measured primarily by profitability of the firm	Some portion of the commercial transactions occurs between at least two countries. Success measured primarily by the profitability of the firm
Social	All commercial transactions occur within the borders of one country. Mission to alleviate a social and/or environmental challenge considered above or at parity with profitability of the firm	Some portion of the commercial transactions occurs between at least two countries. Mission to alleviate a social and/or environmental challenge considered above or at parity with profitability of the firm

Source: Marshall, 2010: 185.

an issue in which markets ineffectively value social improvements and public goods and/or to which non-market agents are seemingly unable to effect improvements" (Marshall, 2011: 186). Organizations designed in such a way can alleviate geographical limitations of scope and provide scalable solutions across national borders (Dees, 2007: 24). With respect to demand, as put forth by Dr C. K. Prahalad's 'Bottom of the Pyramid' (BOP) strategy, the world's poorest four billion people constitute an enormous untapped market for business – a strong signal for international social entrepreneurs seeking to create social value by way of capitalizing on new markets.

Success as an international social entrepreneur requires a particular mindset around risk, agility, the ability to operate across and within distinct cultures, and the ability to detect opportunities for collaborative partnerships (Leadbetter, 1997). International entrepreneurship research emphasizes the important role of motivations and goals on patterns, speed, and outcomes of the entrepreneur's activities (Fernhaber et al., 2009; Gabrielsson and Kirpalani, 2004; Melén and Nordman, 2009). And some scholars have found that some traits that international entrepreneurs possess, such as self-reliance, need for achievement, and empathy, are common across country contexts (Gupta and Fernandez, 2009). Research in the social entrepreneurship literature emphasizes how the entrepreneur's focus on solving a social challenge will influence the structure of the organization, the impetus to scale impact, and metrics used to measure success (Paredo and McLean, 2006; Zahra et al., 2009). In terms of international social entrepreneurship, there exist important research questions regarding the traits, motivations, and goals of international social entrepreneurs. Further, it is important to gain a better understanding of how these attributes define the limitations on the organization's international opportunities, the learning that can be obtained internationally, and the amount and types of resources committed to utilize the knowledge gained by competing in the market and attempting to ameliorate the focal social problem.

True social entrepreneurs can identify and exploit unrecognized opportunities, utilize innovation, tolerate risk, and refuse to be daunted by the threat of apparently limited resources (Paredo and McLean, 2006: 56). The entrepreneur's ability to react and change course quickly is an advantage over bureaucratic government agencies and NGOs, or large corporations laden with internal policies and politics. Essentially, these entrepreneurs must possess the capability to translate altruistic intentions into measurable impact and performance (Dees, 2007: 29). And, importantly, this capability often derives from tacit knowledge of local circumstances.

It is now commonly asserted that an international entrepreneur's social network in a country contributes importantly to the likelihood of success of an international entrepreneur (Dubini and Aldrich, 1991; Oviatt and McDougall, 2005). Oviatt and McDougall (2005) suggest that network strength, size, and density are key moderating influences on the speed of entrepreneurs' internationalization and Prashantham (2005) finds that social capital is a key resource for international entrepreneurship in the pursuit of innovation and strategic renewal. The international social entrepreneur model operates in a unique, grassroots fashion wherein solution models are not simply retrofitted to address social problems, but rather social problems themselves are perceived as the business opportunity and the basis for which the model is crafted. Social entrepreneurship holds the capacity to flourish internationally when deep consideration for context drives the development of organizations. Leadbetter (1997) states that "(s)ocial entrepreneurs work by bringing people together in partnerships to address problems that appear insurmountable when they are addressed separately...They use networks of support to gain access to buildings and money, to recruit key staff and create an organisation capable of growing" (25). Given the social mission of an international social entrepreneur, it may be that social networks and the development of social capital are essential antecedents in achieving both the social and financial objectives. However, there is yet to be a solid stream of research to lend understanding to the importance of networks and social capital to the success of the international social entrepreneur.

Marshall (2011) points out that the business challenges of spanning national borders are heightened when it comes to addressing social problems: "When [a social enterprise] crosses borders, it confronts unique challenges; cultural and language differences, geographic distance, and economic and educational disparities likely complicate the design and effective management of an international social enterprise"(183). International entrepreneurs similarly need to possess cross-cultural aptitude to conduct operations and form collaborative relationships (Steensma et al., 2000). However, by nature of the inherent focus on social problems, the international social entrepreneur may be further distinguished by a heightened awareness of cross-cultural issues, with the ability to apply limited resources creatively in order to adapt to specific local contexts. Furthermore, armed with an opportunistic yet global mindset and natural cultural sensitivity, they can establish and leverage network ties in foreign contexts in order to overcome barriers such as uncertainty and unfamiliarity of new markets (Marshall, 2010: 187). Again, there exist significant opportunities to explore the cultural aptitude of international social entrepreneurs as they interpret social problems in distinct cultural contexts and develop innovative solutions to these problems.

International social entrepreneurs: three case examples

In this section we discuss three international social enterprises – VisionSpring, Tropical Salvage, and Honey Care Africa. VisionSpring utilizes an integrated model; Tropical Salvage is built on a complementary business model; and, Honey Care Africa uses both complementary and integrated models. While the three case studies operate different business models, we use a common approach to describing each.[1] In order to illustrate the varied models and contexts which can characterize international social entrepreneurship, this section focuses on model type, legal structure, social problem and impact, social networks and partnerships, and the business model (including advantages and challenges).

VisionSpring

Table 5.3 International social enterprise case summary: VisionSpring

Model type	Integrated
Location of social impact	India, Bangladesh, Tibet, Afghanistan, Cambodia, Indonesia, Vanuatu, Ethiopia, Uganda, Kenya, Rwanda, Zambia, South Africa, Congo, Cameroon, Ghana, Paraguay, Bolivia, Peru, Ecuador, Nicaragua, Honduras, El Salvador, Guatemala, Mexico, and Haiti
Location of consumer market	Same as above
Legal structure	Not-for-profit

Introduction

Dr Jordan Kassalow and Scott Berrie founded VisionSpring (VS) in 2001 as a not-for-profit with headquarters in the United States and social impact in India. The enterprise sought to reduce the exclusivity and expense associated with reading glasses and to instead commoditize the product.

Social problem and impact

Eyeglasses are either inaccessible or not affordable for between 500 million and 1 billion impoverished people worldwide (Karnani et al., 2011). Beyond constituting a health problem, this unmet need compromises educational, economic and public safety objectives. Blurry vision compromises ability to work effectively, to read and learn in school, and to navigate surroundings with sufficient alertness and awareness, yet it remains a largely ignored issue in the international realm of public health policy and advocacy (Karnani et al., 2011).

VS's mission is to mitigate poverty while creating opportunities in developing countries by providing a scalable model that delivers affordable eyeglasses to people who would otherwise not have financial or geographic access to them (VisionSpring, *Partnership Overview*, 2013).

In order to succeed, the VS model had to overcome a host of persistent barriers which compound the social problem, most prominent of which are lack of awareness around the benefits of restorative vision, inaccessibility of eyeglasses, and inability to afford eyeglasses. Lack of proximity to screening centers and optical shops as well as customarily expensive product offerings create insurmountable challenges for the rural poor. Even if sold at cost, custom eyeglasses run at approximately $50 per pair, rendering them unattainable for those living below the poverty line of $3 per day. Other compounding factors include a dearth of qualified optometrists in most developing countries, along with negative biases about eyeglasses that make those people in need unwilling to wear them (Karnani et al., 2011).

An assessment of the economic impact of eyeglasses revealed that the average VS customer who works will increase earning potential by $108 per year, a substantial increase in relative terms. This represents 26 times the return on investment of $4 for each customer (VisionSpring, *Why eyeglasses?* 2013). In June of 2012, the enterprise sold its one-millionth pair of eyeglasses. Each pair spawns a minimal 10 percent increase in productivity for the person wearing them, creating approximately $42 million in added economic growth to the developing world. These estimates are conservative, as glasses can instantly increase productivity by as much as 35 percent. VS's impact is made exponential through partnership; for example, through BRAC, over 90 percent of near-vision need will have been met, 75,000 female health volunteers will have been trained, and more than $600 million will have been generated in one of the most impoverished countries on the planet (Skoll Foundation, *Skoll Entrepreneur Jordan Kassalow*, 2013).

Business model

The business premise of VS is the provision of basic screening services and ready-made reading glasses to rural populations in the developing world, delivered through a hub-and-spoke approach that facilitates scalability. Driven by the interest of cost-efficiency, China was selected as the sourcing partner. To both increase reach and foster livelihoods, VS trains and employs local rural women, referred to as "Vision Entrepreneurs," to go to villages and sell glasses for less than $4 each. Armed with both eye care and management training, each commission-based representative carries a toolkit to facilitate screenings, marketing, and sales. These kits are furthermore part of a franchise model in which VS sells them to other organizations. VS also provides partner organizations with the option for a simpler, DIY approach that eliminates the need for Vision Entrepreneurs. With respect to distribution, VS acts as a wholesaler to urban and rural pharmacies (Karnani et al., 2011).

Social networks and partnerships

As part of its franchise approach, VS partners with microfinance and community health organizations to disseminate affordable eyewear more broadly and extensively into the market. Currently, 20 partnerships exist with organizations in Asia, Latin America and Africa, with Bangladeshi microcredit organization BRAC being the most significant (VisionSpring, *Our Reach,* 2013). The enterprise also partners with US retailer Warby Parker in a one-for-one model: for every pair of glasses that it sells, Warby Parker funds the production of a pair of VS glasses (Zax, 2012).

Advantages to the model

VS's model succeeds most notably in its reduction of costs compared to traditional models. Replacing formally educated optometrists with readily available low cost, low skilled labor, adopting a centralized system of purchasing, sourcing its product from China, and providing relatively standardized products, have all contributed to an ability to lower the price point and thus open up accessibility to more impoverished segments of the market. VS's advantages complement its growth strategy: continuing to promote franchise and wholesale methods that leverage substantial existing distribution networks in targeted developing countries (Karnani et al., 2011: 69). Scaling has been a very successful process for VS, as its reach extends to five continents and 26 developing countries. With its one-size-fits-all franchise model, the enterprise issues supplementary "Business in a Bag" toolkits to facilitate screening and sales. With this approach, VS's model is scalable both across borders and among numerous, varying organizations – be they for-profit or non-profit.

Challenges to the model

The largest challenge to the VS model surrounds financing and scaling. Earned revenue covers less than 20 percent of total costs, making the enterprise heavily reliant on outside funding, mostly in the form of charitable donations. In order to accomplish economies of scale substantial enough to ensure financial self-sufficiency, VS must sell roughly 5 million pairs of glasses per year. This reliance on philanthropy prevents the enterprise from scaling to the size of the vastly unmet market, as do the limitations in current available distribution networks for serving the impoverished, particularly in rural regions. Additionally, VS has received critique for its lack of regard to style in its products, which has proven to be a concern even among the poor (Karnani et al., 2011: 70–71).

Externally, competition is growing in the marketplace for affordable eyeglasses, especially with the advent of technological innovations. Various companies, such as AdSpecs, have begun providing self-adjustable products that eliminate the need for screening or trained instruction, thus significantly reducing production costs. Finally, larger economic and social circumstances continue to fuel (1) an inability to pay for even the least expensive eyeglasses, or (2) a persistent lack of perceived value which erodes willingness to pay among those who can afford them (Karnani et al., 2011: 69–70).

Tropical Salvage

Table 5.4 International social enterprise case summary: Tropical Salvage

Model type	Complementary
Location of social impact	Indonesia
Location of consumer market	United States and Canada
Legal structure	For-profit

Introduction

Tropical Salvage was founded in 1998 by Tim O'Brien after an eye-opening trekking expedition through Indonesia. During the course of the trip, O'Brien was shocked by the startling co-location of natural biodiversity with reckless exploitation of those ecosystems. Additionally, he noticed that Javanese craft traditions, particularly in woodworking, were underutilized. With Tropical Salvage, he constructed a solution that sought to mitigate both environmental degradation and the problem of labor underutilization (Marshall, 2011: 2).

Social problem and impact

Tropical Salvage addresses the environmental and social problems associated with the wasteful sourcing of wood products and the large-scale destruction of rainforests due to logging in Indonesia. Logging exposes once pristine areas to subsistence and industrial agriculture, colonization, exploitation of wildlife, and other forms of unsustainable development. In Indonesia, much logging is done illegally, which in addition to forest loss fuels unfortunate social ills such as violent crime. Meanwhile, wood from deconstructed buildings is often discarded as waste or for overly simplistic functions rather than being reused purposefully. Beyond environmental implications, high rates of deforestation also yield destructive social and economic consequences by rendering millions of Indonesians unemployed (Marshall, 2011: 3, 5).

Tropical Salvage seeks to bring finely crafted, competitive and sustainably produced salvage-wood products to the global marketplace in order to (1) heighten consumer awareness and solidarity for the preservation of tropical forest biodiversity, and (2) create a source of stable employment for rural Indonesians (Tropical Salvage, *Mission, vision, values,* 2012).

With respect to impact, as of 2011, Tropical Salvage gainfully employed 85 people, many of whom likely had prior involvement in illegal logging, and supported Jepara Forest Conservancy efforts. Wages are 20 percent above Indonesian standards, and in accompaniment to pay are benefits such as healthcare and paid vacation. Although no metrics are in place to decipher the equivalent number of living trees saved by the enterprise's wood-salvage efforts, non-profit partner Jepara Forest Conservancy protects 36 hectares of biodiverse Indonesian forest and seeks to expand its protection efforts to 700 hectares. The Conservancy also engages in a constant progression of numerous projects aimed at synergizing regional environmental and social goals (Tropical Salvage, *History of projects at the Jepara Forest Conservancy 2008–2011,* 2012).

Business model

Tropical Salvage represents a dual country integrated model of social entrepreneurship, centered around activities which themselves produce beneficial social outcomes. The enterprise consists of a highly vertically integrated structure including operations and production in Indonesia and wholesale and end-use customers in North America (Marshall, 2011: 2).

The business model both enables the fulfillment of social and environmental objectives and, secondarily, delivers products to customers on an international scale. Through adopting an alternative practice to logging for wood sourcing, the use of salvage wood allows for the protection of old-growth tropical forests. Beyond the threat to biodiversity, the improper treatment of these areas holds significant implications for human life, as they are critical for storing vast amounts of carbon and naturally managing water, and directly threaten the livelihoods of roughly 20 million Indonesians. Through its wood salvage efforts, Tropical Salvage spares living trees, fosters fair trade livelihoods, locks carbon into furniture, and delivers rare products with wood grain uniquely imprinted by varied forms of distress (Tropical Salvage, *History of projects at the Jepara Forest Conservancy 2008–2011*, 2012).

Social networks and partnerships

NGO partnerships have been an integral resource for Tropical Salvage. Most notably, in collaboration with non-profit The Institute for Culture and Ecology (IFCAE), TS supports the Jepara Forest Conservancy in order to create a synergy between environmental restoration and the promotion of social and economic opportunities through cooperative, community-level efforts. The enterprise also partners with Fair Trade Canadian retailer Ten Thousand Villages, among other retailers to some degree, in order to grow the brand and drive sales (Marshall, 2011: 6, 8–9).

Advantages to the model

In looking at the value chain, Tropical Salvage's sources of strategic advantage include procurement, logistics, and operations. Cost of goods sold is low, and due to vertical integration margins remain high. The majority of salvage wood is substantially less expensive due to TS's ability to utilize wood from a broad range of species and damage conditions, and without competition from other entities. Such wood previously would not have been considered suitable for building furniture. Skilled labor is abundantly available due to a long-standing tradition of woodworking and building furniture in Java. Finally, the business enjoys an expedient logistics infrastructure due to the close proximity of the sourcing location to a major shipping port (Marshall, 2011: 5–8).

Challenges to the model

Overcoming cultural and language barriers and learning efficient operational techniques have all been crucial elements to address. As with any international social entrepreneur, navigating the local landscape to establish partnerships and recruit employees was critical, requiring O'Brien to learn the Indonesian language. Persistent challenges include first and foremost marketing and a lack of ability (or knowledge of how) to reach the US target market. Scalability is also a major concern. While the model works in Indonesia, one of the most wood-rich countries in the world, uncertainty exists over whether it can scale (1) in the long-term, and (2) for a more broad competitive market. On the demand side, the atypical, distressed grain nature of the products may be too niche or limited in appeal to drive a larger market. Additionally, expenses associated with expansion, erratic shipping schedules, and inventory tracking and quality control, are all issues that continue to surface.

Although upholding fair trade practices is laudable and a critical component of the mission, fair wages and a requisite higher number of employees create higher labor costs than with conventional wood harvesting. In salvage efforts, more employees are needed to deconstruct buildings and haul trees out of rivers, landslides, and piles of debris (Marshall, 2011: 11–13).

In considering strategies for how best to grow, O'Brien may diversify Tropical Salvage products beyond furniture and venture into the realm of branded retail in the United States. However, the enterprise faces some substantial challenges to its pursuit of future growth (Marshall, 2011: 14). The aforementioned scaling matters represent the greatest challenge for the enterprise. Additionally, logistics viability in South America and Africa are questionable as TS's strategies for sourcing wood present more logistical challenges than conventional forest or plantation wood harvesting. Externally, a niche market like the fine furniture industry is more susceptible to widespread economic fluctuations, and an entity such as Tropical Salvage may struggle to become relevant as a brand (Butler, 2008).

Honey Care Africa

Table 5.5 International social enterprise case summary: Honey Care Africa

Model type	Both integrated and complementary
Location of social impact	Kenya; replicated in Tanzania, and partnering in Malawi and Southern Sudan
Location of consumer market	Same as above
Legal structure	For-profit

Introduction

Founded in 2000 by entrepreneur Farouk Jiwa with the backing of fellow local Kenyans Yusef Keshavjee and Husein Bhanji, Honey Care Africa (HCA) has changed beekeeping in Kenya through a triple-bottom-line approach. By partnering with local NGOs and farmers to capitalize on the strengths of the existing players and infrastructure, while applying solutions at critical points in the value chain of honey production and distribution, HCA works to simultaneously improve livelihoods and natural environment conservation in poor rural communities.

Social problem and impact

When the company was founded, approximately two-thirds of Kenyans lived in rural areas, and three-quarters of the country's labor force was employed in the agricultural sector. There were corrupt and inefficient practices in agriculture, resulting in narrow margins and delayed payments for farmers. In the honey supply chain in particular, although conditions were optimal, farmers had few incentives to pursue the practice, and the product quality and quantity was poor due to inefficient harvest practices using log hives and smoke (Branzei and Valente, 2007). HCA seized upon this market failure and addressed the infrastructure of the honey trade. HCA was a founding member of the Kenya Honey Council, through which much progress has been made in partnership with government ministries to improve policies concerning the local beekeeping sector. By providing micro financing for quality hives, ensuring market demand and paying a fair price to farmers for honey, HCA has been successful in raising income levels for rural Kenyan farmers. Beekeeping provides a supplementary source of income for households as it only requires 5–10 hours per week. Thus where previously apiculture was predominated by men, 43 percent of HCA's beneficiaries are women (United Nations Development Programme, *Honey Care Africa, Kenya*, 2012). Surveys show these revenues are invested predominantly in:

- food and medicine (33 percent)
- farming needs such as seeds and fertilizers (25 percent)
- launching micro-enterprise (18 percent)
- school fees (18 percent)
- improved housing (10 percent).

(Honey Care Africa, 2013)

Furthermore, by furthering apiculture as a viable livelihood supplement, HCA is simultaneously increasing pollination and biodiversity while phasing out non-sustainable practices harmful to the natural environment such as deforestation for charcoal production. Not only do bees benefit ecosystems but they carry great economic value in the pollination of agricultural crops. In 2005, the economic valuation of the service provided by insect pollination for main food crops worldwide was estimated at $208 billion (UNDP, *Honey Care Africa, Kenya*, 2012).

Of least importance, although still significant, is the HCA product itself. Honey is a natural sweetener and unlike granulated sugar, offers many health and medicinal benefits and applications. HCA offers high-quality, premium-priced product lines sold in supermarkets, as well as products created to provide a healthy source of carbohydrates to children at the "Bottom of the Pyramid." HCA holds 68 percent of the honey market share in Kenya, where prior to HCA, Kenya was importing honey due to the low quality of local honey (Branzei and Valente, 2007).

Business model

HCA is a highly vertically integrated model with four primary activities: (1) manufacturing and offering high quality Langstroth beehives through a buy-back loan program to farmers; (2) providing beekeeping training and extension services to farmers to ensure successful honey yields; (3) buying the honey produced at a guaranteed fair market price; and (4) processing, packaging, marketing, and distributing the honey for sale throughout urban areas of Kenya and for export abroad (UNDP, *Honey Care Africa, Kenya*, 2012).

Jiwa felt individual hive ownership through purchase, as opposed to the giveaway model typical of NGO development projects, was important to ensure full motivation and buy-in on the part of farmers. The loan program was devised so that HCA would retain 25–50 percent of honey payments each month until the full initial cost of the hive was paid back, at which point farmers could recognize the value of ownership as their payouts would nearly double (Branzei and Valente, 2007).

Social networks and partnerships

HCA operates as a "tripartite model," creating synergies from key players in the development sector, private sector, and rural communities. Having witnessed too many well-meaning but short-term agriculture projects on the part of NGOs that were unsustainable after initial funding dried up, Jiwa knew what HCA could offer them was a source of continuity and financial sustainability. In turn, key to the success of the HCA model was gaining the trust and loyalty of the farmers. Local NGOs who had worked in rural communities over many years had established trust with farmers, and Jiwa knew it was best to capitalize on these existing relationships. Partnering with NGOs did not come without obstacles, as different philosophies and approaches to social impact had to be negotiated. However in the end, all recognized the shared goal of building "long-term self-sufficiency in rural communities" (Branzei and Valente, 2007).

The company has partnered with various governmental and NGO development and funding agencies at the local, national, and international level, such as Africa Now, USAID, Kiva, the Word Economic Forum, and has received awards and recognition from the United Nations Development Programme (UNDP), the World Economic Forum, and Schwab Foundation, among others (Honey Care Africa, 2013; Branzei and Valente, 2007).

Advantages to the model

HCA has proven that sustainable community-based beekeeping can be a viable entity, yielding profit margins of approximately 10 percent after seven years of operations (UNDP, *Honey Care Africa, Kenya,* 2012). In terms of scaling, HCA has successfully replicated the model in neighboring Tanzania, with plans to expand in Eastern Africa. At face value, the prospects for further scaling are positive; "Beekeeping is a very scalable activity once initial capacities are in place, due to the widespread availability of labor, small actual land requirement, and free natural inputs" (UNDP, *Honey Care Africa, Kenya,* 2012). However, a strong foundational infrastructure is needed to be successful with the HCA model. Local policies around beekeeping and establishing strong local partnerships are two key components. Adaptation to local commercialization opportunities and agricultural infrastructure are key, as well as climate and environmental considerations such as use of indigenous species of bees (UNDP, *Honey Care Africa, Kenya,* 2012). Scaling for HCA may also mean expanding to other agricultural products (dried fruit, for example) as well as increasing export opportunities in markets such as the US (Miner, 2010).

Challenges with the model

Any business based on agriculture is inherently risky, and ultimately, HCA's viability depends on its farmers. Competitors have entered the market and attempted to undercut honey prices, offering to pay up to 10 percent more to HCA farmers. Farmers are not contractually bound to sell to HCA, so often an opportunistic bidder can be a tempting prospect. However, overall, loyalty to HCA has remained high due to the consistency and the guaranteed market that they were able to offer farmers. Farmers recognize the direct and indirect long-term sustainable benefits provided by HCA for themselves and their broader communities (Branzei and Valente, 2007).

Future research directions

In thinking about the future of international social entrepreneurship, we see several emerging trends that may indicate a positive outlook, including the trend of partnering and that of organizational hybridization. However, a few substantial questions remain unanswered as well.

Outstanding questions

There are a number of promising areas of research, building primarily from the extant literatures in international entrepreneurship and social entrepreneurship. There are three areas of recommended research in the realm of international social entrepreneurship: (1) traits, motivations and goals; (2) networks and social capital; and (3) cultural competence.

Scholars in both international and social entrepreneurship areas have investigated the traits, motivations, and goals of their focal research populations. However, in consideration of the international social entrepreneur, we cannot simply assume confluence of these findings to understand this specific "species." For example, Weerawardena and Sullivan Mort (2006) found that social entrepreneurs' risk-taking is notably different from both for-profit entrepreneurs and not-for-profit managers. In fact, social entrepreneurs are foremost concerned about sustainability of their enterprise; given the inherent risk of international operations, the risk-taking of international social entrepreneurs may yet again be distinctly different from international entrepreneurs and social entrepreneurs not active internationally.

Furthermore, because of the "social" emphasis of international social entrepreneurs, it may be assumed that they are very similar to (non-international) social entrepreneurs. That is, both sets of entrepreneurs start with a social problem and work towards a solution. However, just as McDougall et al. (2003) found many differences between domestic and international new ventures, such as experience, aggressiveness, and innovation focus, there may be substantive differences between the domestic and international social entrepreneur. Furthemore, as Zahra et al. (2014) suggest, starting from a social enterprise lens "can broaden how IE opportunities are recognized and evaluated" (p. 146). Initiating research into these attributes will elucidate the unique attributes of the international social entrepreneur.

In terms of goals, again a similarity may exist between domestic and international social entrepreneurs. However, measuring a social entrepreneur's degree of impact, whether domestic or international, in a reliable and efficient manner is a challenging feat. "How and when do we know that someone has been moved out of poverty in a sustainable way or that a strategy will slow global warming? Signs, symptoms, and leading indicators often must be used to provide clues to whether an intervention is having its intended impact"(Dees, 2007: 29). This challenge is potentially exacerbated when operations are international; do international social entrepreneurs commit to the same types of social and financial goals as an entrepreneur not working across borders and cultures?

One of the debatable characteristics of a successful international social entrepreneur is scalability. An entity's ability to scale can be viewed in two ways: growth in size or load, or growth by replication. For the international social entrepreneur, it is of particular importance that expanding across new borders is done in a conscientious and sustainable fashion. As Dees (2007) points out, the process of scaling for social entrepreneurs is often a slow process, and any positive growth of the enterprise itself often pales in comparison to the size and growth of the social problems at hand (30). This is compounded by the fact that, as mentioned, social value is intrinsically difficult to measure. And what is the end goal of scalability? Is it to increase profits? To increase impact? Does scaling always make sense, and to what extent? For VisionSpring it became apparent early that the social problem was global and scalability was essential to meet the social and financial goals. But for Tropical Salvage, the focal problem addressed is in Indonesia and scalability and impact may be more limited. These are some of the important research questions that remain outstanding.

Given the social mission of an international social entrepreneur, it may be that social networks and the development of social capital are essential antecedents in achieving both the social and financial objectives. However, there is yet to be a solid stream of research to lend understanding to the importance of networks and social capital to the success of the international social entrepreneur. Zahra et al. (2009) develop the idea of "social bricoleurs," who "because of their localized and oftentimes tacit knowledge…are uniquely positioned to discover local social needs where they can leverage their motivation, expertise and personal resources to create and enhance social wealth" (p. 524). O'Brien from Tropical Salvage may be classified as a social bricoleur; his embeddness in Indonesia has been essential to understanding the local context, building networks, and enhancing social capital; all in service of the Tropical Salvage mission. On the other hand, Kassalow and Berrie ofVisionSpring might be better considered "social constructionists." According to Zahra et al. (2009), social constructionists "seek to remedy broader social problems by planning and developing formalized or systemized scalable solutions to meet growing needs or could be transferred to new and varied social contexts" (p. 525). The consideration of types of international social entrepreneurs generates numerous future research questions in this realm. How might the need for deep cultural understanding and strong social capital be necessary to the success of international social entrepreneurs? Or, perhaps more fundamental, does the social problem itself define the type of international social entrepreneur and the extent of social networks that will best support the development of a socially and financially viable venture?

Future directions

Hybridization

One recent trend is that of organizational hybridization: where once there were clear distinctions between corporations and NGOs, social enterprise is helping to blur the lines. On one hand we see philanthropic organizations turning to commercial activities as they seek new sources of revenue, and on the other hand, corporations are realizing tangible competitive advantage from sustainability pursuits.

As not-for-profits struggle in the face of dwindling public and private funds, many look to revenue-generating activities to fill their budget gaps. Alter (2004) notes the commonplace practice, stating, "More than half of all nonprofits are engaged in some form of income generation, though few have the tools, knowledge, expertise or desire to develop these activities into enterprises, thus realizing their potential social and economic benefit for the organization" (Alter, 2004). As social needs continue to persist and funding continues to be scarce, more organizations will likely transition from mere supplemental income-generating activities to social enterprise activities.

According to Porter and Kramer, it is increasingly in the best interest of businesses to redefine corporate purpose in pursuit of a shared value principle, wherein economic value is created as to simultaneously create social value. Businesses incorporate a shared value proposition into the design of their strategy by "(1) reconceiving products and markets, (2) redefining productivity in the value chain, and/or (3) enabling regional cluster development" (Porter and Kramer, 2011: 64). This concept acknowledges that social – and not solely economic – needs play a role in shaping markets. Furthermore, it recognizes that social ills are often catalysts for internal firm costs, such as squandered resources as well as lack of proper training and education (Porter and Kramer, 2011: 65).

To emphasize this point, consider the rising trend in new types of hybrid enterprises that are rapidly populating the marketplace. Such enterprises are "blurring the boundary between successful for-profits and nonprofits…one of the strong signs that creating shared value is possible"

(Porter and Kramer, 2011: 67). The concept of socially responsible businesses is relatively new, for example, but in recent years companies purporting the "buy one, give one" model, such as TOMS shoes and Warby Parker, have become household names.

Partnering

Public–private partnerships are not a new concept, but persist as an integral vehicle for the advancement of many social sector organizations. In his essay on "The Age of Social Transformation," Peter Drucker envisioned a society in which the public and private sectors would partner extensively through voucher programs (Dees, 2007: 30).

On the other hand, as we have discussed, partnerships between the public sector and private sector are a relatively new phenomenon, as the two have historically been at odds with one another (Porter and Kramer, 2011: 65). The case study examples exemplified how such a joining together of entities can remove otherwise insurmountable barriers to access, increase scalability, and create synergies via international social entrepreneurship. This is achievable because while private sector enterprises are characteristically far more agile and swift to act than inefficient bureaucratic public entities, "government-supported programs can scale rather rapidly, when the political will and funding are present" (Dees, 2007: 30). Not only does the government hold the power to make compliance compulsory, but it can rally resources through the collection of taxes.

Finally, multinational corporations (MNCs) are beginning to view partnerships with the social sector as key strategic actions. One example is the unexpected partnership between the international environmental NGO Greenpeace and Shell Oil: "The role of NGOs has changed as dramatically as the role of businesses has changed…today, you have Greenpeace in England working in deep collaboration with Shell Oil Company not over a few months, but over many years" (Hollander, 2004: 114). Relationships such as these, although undoubtedly challenging at times, are succeeding in delivering positive social and environmental impact. Hollander goes on to name other MNCs such as Starbucks, Nike, and others, saying, "at almost every company I can think of, some significant part of the positive change has come about because of a relationship with a NGO" (114).

Note

1 Each case example is developed using a variety of secondary sources, including academic articles, interviews, popular press, white papers, and websites from the winter and spring of 2013.

References

Acs, Z., Dana, L-P., and Jones, M. 2003, 'Toward new horizons: the internationalization of entrepreneurship', *Journal of International Entrepreneurship*, 1, pp. 5–12.

Alter, K. 2004, *Social enterprise: a typology*, Virtue Ventures, viewed May 7, 2013, <www.4lenses.org/setypology>

Alter, K. 2005, *Social enterprise primer for development professionals*, Virtue Ventures, viewed October 8, 2014, <https://www.microlinks.org/library/social-enterprise-primer-development-professionals>

Austin, J., Stevenson, H., and Wei-Skillern, J. 2006, 'Social and commercial entrepreneurship: same, different or both?' *Entrepreneurship: Theory & Practice*, 30, 1, pp. 1–22.

Barendsen, L. and Gardner, H. 2004, 'Is the social entrepreneur a new type of leader?' *Leader to Leader*, 34, pp. 43–50.

Bornstein, D. 2004, *How to change the world: social entrepreneurship and the power of ideas*. New York: Oxford University Press.

Branzei, O. and Valente, M. 2007, *Honey Care Africa: a tripartite model for sustainable beekeeping*, Ivy Publishing, The University of Western Ontario.
Butler, R. A. 2008, *An interview with Tropical Salvage's Tim O'Brien*, Mongabay, viewed June 2, 2013, <http://news.mongabay.com/2008/1204-interview_tim_brien_tropical_salvage.html)>
Dees, J. G. 1998, 'The meaning of "social entrepreneurship"', Stanford University: Draft Report for the Kauffman Center for Entrepreneurial Leadership, p. 6.
Dees, J. G. 2001, *The meaning of 'social entrepreneurship'*, Center for the Advancement of Social Entrepreneurship, Duke University, pp. 1–5.
Dees, J. G. 2007, 'Taking social entrepreneurship seriously', *Social Science and Modern Society*, 44, 3, pp. 24–31.
Dees, J. G., Anderson, B. B., and Wei-Skillern, J. 2004, 'Scaling social impact', *Stanford Social Innovation Review*, 1, pp. 24–32.
Dimitratos, P., Voudouris, I., Plakoyiannaki, E., and Nakos, G. 2012, 'International entrepreneurial culture: Toward a comprehensive opportunity-based operationalization of international entrepreneurship', *International Business Review*, 21, pp. 708–721.
Dubini, P. and Aldrich, H. 1991, 'Personal and extended networks are central to the entrepreneurial process', *Journal of Business Venturing*, 6, pp. 305–313.
The Economist 2009, *Triple bottom line*, viewed June 3, 2013, <www.economist.com/node/14301663>
Fernhaber, S. A., McDougall-Covin, P. P., and Shepherd, D. A. 2009, 'International entrepreneurship: leveraging internal and external knowledge sources', *Strategic Entrepreneurship Journal*, 3, 4, pp. 297–320.
Fowler, A. 2000, 'NGDOs as a moment in history: beyond aid to social entrepreneurship or civic innovation?', *Third World Quarterly*, 21, 4, pp. 637–654.
Gabrielsson, M. and Kirpalani, V. H. M. 2004, 'Born globals: how to reach new business space rapidly', *International Business Review*, 13, 5, pp. 555–571.
Giamartino, G. A., McDougall, P. P., and Bird, B. J. 1993, 'International entrepreneurship: The state of the field', *Entrepreneurship Theory and Practice*, 18, pp. 37–41.
Guayaki 2013, *About Guayaki*, viewed June 2, 2013, <http://guayaki.com/about.html>
Gupta, V. and Fernandez, C. 2009, 'Cross-cultural similarities and differences in characteristics attributed to entrepreneurs: a three-nation study', *Journal of Leadership & Organizational Studies*, 15, 3, pp. 304–318.
Hollander, J. 2004, 'What matters most: corporate values and social responsibility', *California Management Review*, 46, 4, pp. 111–119.
Honey Care Africa 2013, *Honey Care Africa*, viewed June 2, 2013, <http://honeycareafrica.com>
Karnani A., Garrette B., Kassalow J., and Lee, M. 2011, 'Better vision for the poor', *Stanford Social Innovation Review*, Spring.
Leadbetter, C. 1997. *The rise of the social entrepreneur*. London: Demos.
Mair, J., Battilana, J., and Cardenas, J. 2012, 'Organizing for society: a typology of social entrepreneuring models', *Journal of Business Ethics*, 111, pp. 353–373.
Mair, J. and Marti, I. 2006, 'Social entrepreneurship research: A source of explanation, prediction, and delight', *Journal of World Business*, 41, pp. 36–44.
Marshall, R. S. 2011, 'Conceptualizing the international for-profit social entrepreneur', *Journal of Business Ethics*, 98, 2, pp. 183–198.
McDonald, F., Krause, J., Schmengler, H., and Tuselmann, H.-J. 2003, 'Cautious international entrepreneurs: the case of the Mittelstand', *Journal of International Entrepreneurship*, 1, 4, pp. 363–381.
McDougall, P. P. 1989, 'International versus domestic entrepreneurship: new venture strategic behavior and industry structure', *Journal of Business Venturing*, 4, pp. 387–399.
McDougall, P. P., Oviatt, B. M., and Shrader, R. C. 2003, 'A comparison of international and domestic new ventures', *Journal of International Entrepreneurship*, 1, 1, pp. 59–82.
Melén, S. and Nordman, E. R. 2009, 'The internationalization modes of born globals: a longitudinal study', *European Management Journal*, 27, 4, pp. 253–254.
Miner, T. 2010, *Snapshots of success from developing markets – Honey Care Africa*, Sustainable Brands, viewed June 2, 2013, <www.sustainablebrands.com/news_and_views/articles/snapshots-success-developing-markets-honey-care-africa>
Mort, G., Weerawardena, J., and Carnegie, K. 2002, 'Social entrepreneurship: towards conceptualization and measurement', *American Marketing Association Conference Proceedings*, 13, 5.
Oviatt, B. M. and McDougall, P. P. 1994, 'Toward a theory of international new ventures', *Journal of International Business Studies*, 25, 1, pp. 45–64.
Oviatt, B. M. and McDougall, P. P. 1999, 'A framework for understanding accelerated international entrepreneurship', in R. Wright (Ed.), *Research in Global Strategic Management*, pp. 23–40. Stamford, CT: JAI Press.

Oviatt B. and McDougall P. 2005, 'Defining international entrepreneurship and modeling the speed of internationalization', *Entrepreneurship Theory & Practice Journal*, Baylor University, September, pp. 537–553.

Paredo A. M. and McLean M. 2006, 'Social entrepreneurship: a critical review of the concept', *Journal of World Business*, 41, pp. 56–65.

Porter, M. and Kramer, M. 2011, 'Creating shared value', *Harvard Business Review*, January–February, pp. 62–77.

Prashantham, S. 2005, 'Toward a knowledge-based conceptualization of internationalization', *Journal of International Entrepreneurship*, 3, 1, pp. 37–52

Skoll Foundation 2013, *Skoll Entrepreneur Jordan Kassalow*, viewed June 2, 2013, <www.skollfoundation.org/entrepreneur/jordan-kassalow/>

Steensma, H. K., Marino, L., and Weaver, K. M. 2000, 'Attitudes toward cooperative strategies: a cross-cultural analysis of entrepreneurs', *Journal of International Business Studies*, 31, 4, pp. 591–609.

Tropical Salvage 2012, *History of projects at the Jepara Forest Conservancy 2008–2011*, viewed June 2, 2013, <http://tropicalsalvage.com/history-of-projects-at-the-jepara-forest-conservancy-2008-2011/>

Tropical Salvage 2012, *Mission, vision, values*, viewed June 2, 2013, <http://tropicalsalvage.com/who-we-are/mission-vision-values/>

United Nations Development Programme 2012, *Honey Care Africa, Kenya*, Equator Initiative Case Study Series, New York, NY.

VisionSpring 2013, *Our Reach*, viewed June 2, 2013, <http://visionspring.org/our-reach/)>

VisionSpring 2013, *Partnership Overview*, viewed June 2, 2013, <http://visionspring.org/wp-content/uploads/2013/03/Partnership-Overview-21.pdf>

VisionSpring 2013, *Why eyeglasses?*, viewed June 2, 2013, <http://visionspring.org/why-eyeglasses/>

Weerawardena, J. and Sullivan Mort, G. 2006, 'Investigating social entrepreneurship: a multidimensional model', *Journal of World Business*, 41, pp. 21–35.

Zahra, S. A., Gedajlovic, E., Neubaum, D. O., and Shulman, J. M. 2009, 'A typology of social entrepreneurs: motives, search processes and ethical challenges', *Journal of Business Venturing*, 24, pp. 519–532.

Zahra, S. A., Newey, L. R., and Yong, L. 2014, 'On the frontiers: the implications of social entrepreneurship for international entrepreneurship', *Entrepreneurship Theory and Practice*, 38, 1, pp. 137–158.

Zax, L. 2012, *The VisionSpring model: creating markets and players instead of empty CSR*, Forbes, viewed June 2, 2013, <www.forbes.com/sites/ashoka/2012/10/05/the-visionspring-model-creating-markets-and-players-instead-of-empty-csr/>

6

Inside the transnational entrepreneur

Dave Crick and Shiv Chaudhry

Introduction

The objective of this chapter is to develop researchers' understanding of the term 'transnational entrepreneur' within the academic domain of international entrepreneurship and the wider international business literature. There is a growing body of knowledge involving 'international entrepreneurship' which McDougall and Oviatt (2000: 903) suggest is 'a combination of innovative, proactive and risk-seeking behaviour that crosses national borders and is intended to create value in organisations'. International entrepreneurial strategies have been found to be influenced by a variety of issues such as the resources that are available, networks, and are also contingent on factors associated with environmental conditions plus the perceived associated risk (Calof and Beamish, 1995; Jones, 1999; Bell et al., 2004).

An increasing migration between various countries has influenced entrepreneurial activities from within certain ethnic minority communities (Zhou, 2004). Indeed, the role of networks in trading in overseas markets, not least with their country of origin, has been especially noticeable (Crick et al., 2001; Zhou et al., 2007). Jones and Ram (2007) suggest that a need exists for studies to identify context-specific practices; this might therefore include those practices described in the current investigation involving 'transnational' entrepreneurs. Drori et al. (2007) suggest that the increasing impact of transnational entrepreneurship has been affected by the evolving nature of migration and diasporas, together with the complex nature of international business activities that are involved in dealing with overseas markets (see also Marger, 2006).

The contribution of this chapter within the domain of international entrepreneurship research is to focus on the internationalisation practices and specifically motives of 'transnational entrepreneurs' within one ethnic community. The research question is whether differences exist between the motives for internationalising between two groups of ethnic entrepreneurs that are based in the UK. First, 'internationally oriented entrepreneurs' were those whose UK-based business traded internationally but did not leverage resources from their country of origin; second, 'transnational entrepreneurs' operated a business in the UK but leveraged resources in their country of origin.

No agreement appears to exist in respect of defining transnational entrepreneurs (Bagwell, 2008; Chen and Tan, 2009; Drori et al., 2007; 2009; 2010; Patel and Conklin, 2009; Portes et al., 2002; Sequeira et al., 2009; Terjesen and Elam, 2009). Portes et al. (2002: 287) view them as 'self-employed immigrants whose business activities require frequent travel abroad and who depend for the success of their firms on their contacts and associates in another country, primarily their country of origin'. Nevertheless, one might argue that this definition could be applied to a number of immigrant-owned firms where key entrepreneurs travel frequently overseas and trade with associates in another country, e.g. from their country of origin.

More recently, Drori et al. (2009: 1001) suggest that:

> transnational entrepreneurs (TEs) are individuals that migrate from one country to another, concurrently maintaining business related linkages with their former country of origin, and currently adopted countries and communities. By traveling both physically and virtually, TEs simultaneously engage in two or more socially embedded environments, allowing them to maintain critical global relations that enhance their ability to creatively, dynamically, and logistically maximize their resource base.

This paper's research focus on 'individuals' rather than 'firms' restricts this study to the international entrepreneurship rather than multinational literature. In contextualising this study, the focus involves UK-based entrepreneurs originating from the Indian sub-continent, but that are based in the UK. The term 'Asian' is a commonly used term from a British perspective although there is a realisation that in other parts of the world the same is not true, e.g. Asian can mean originating from South-East Asia. This ethnic minority group was selected due to their propensity to engage in self-employment in comparison to other ethnic groups (Ward, 1991; Ram and Smallbone, 2003). Interestingly, a good deal of earlier studies suggested that Asian entrepreneurs have a propensity to engage in local community businesses, for example, restaurants and grocery (Rafiq, 1988; Patel, 1989; Ram et al., 2000). More recently, studies have found Asian entrepreneurs with more extensive operations and both inward and outward modes of internationalisation (Crick et al., 2001; Chaudhry and Crick, 2004a; b). It is useful to determine whether differences exist between firms owned by particular types of internationalising ethnic entrepreneurs and this forms the basis of this investigation.

Six sections are included in this chapter commencing with this introduction which identified the objective, contribution and context of the study. Subsequently, a review of the literature underpins the investigation within the existing body of knowledge before specifying the hypothesis that is tested. The methodological approach employed follows before the findings are summarised. A discussion of the main issues arising from the study is then presented before the chapter ends with avenues for further research.

Literature review

Ethnic minority-owned firms

Smallbone et al. (2005: 43) point out that:

> most of the existing literature on ethnic minority-owned firms is based, either explicitly or implicitly, on the view that businesses with ethnic minority owners are 'different' from the rest of the population, both in terms of their behavioural characteristics and in terms of the types of problems that they face.

The strategies, both domestic and international, of entrepreneurs from ethnic minority communities have been well documented for some time. This is especially so in countries with relatively high numbers of businesses owned by those outside of the mainstream indigenous communities (Stanton and Lee, 1995; Sanders and Nee, 1996). Various explanations have been put forward. For example, the concentration of ethnic minority businesses in marginal areas of economic activity has been affected by historical disadvantage and utilisation of members of the ethnic community (Light, 1972; Ward et al., 1986; Min, 1987; Aldrich and Waldinger, 1990; Bates, 1994). This observation of concentrations of ethnic minorities has perhaps in part led to a good deal of the existing research into domestic business practices, instead of trading overseas such as this current study.

Studies have found some entrepreneurs move into self-employment due to the need for 'independence' and 'autonomy', but this is irrespective of their ethnic origin (Storey, 1994). Indeed, the broader entrepreneurship literature considers issues such as opportunity recognition and exploitation, plus traits like being proactive, innovative, risk seeking etc., as typical common characteristics of entrepreneurs' practices (Shane and Venkataraman, 2000; Stokes, 2002). However, problems with racism and unequal gender relations have been found to affect self-employment in ethnic minorities (Ram, 1992; Ram and Sparrow, 1993). Problems with finance are a feature of a number of studies (e.g. Blackburn, 1993), but some are business-related (Curran and Blackburn, 1993), or specifically race-related (Deakins et al., 1992; Jones et al., 1992; Ram et al., 2002). As such, due to these identified differences, certain existing studies have identified the need to consider practices in ethnic minority-owned firms as distinct from the wider 'mainstream' population.

This existing body of research gives rise to debates about what constitutes the 'mainstream' population and what are 'indigenous' communities; for example, in the UK, are researchers considering this to mean the white inter-generational population and are they ignoring the 'acculturalisation' of ethnic minority groups over time? This might especially be relevant in the case of some ethnic entrepreneurs' extended families that developed over time which may allow them to utilise social in addition to business networks. In fact Werbner (1990) found that ethnic entrepreneurs' utilisation of 'social networks' are a major influence on their performance. Their specialist cultural knowledge together with the low overheads of employing family and community members has also been found to assist performance (Jones et al., 1993; 2006).

However, their unwillingness or in some cases inability to attract custom from outside the local ethnic community niche can be a key barrier to potential growth if not business sustainability. Ram and Hillin (1994) identify the need to 'break-out' of what they see as local niches and tap into 'majority' markets. In the context of the current study that involves overseas operations, Crick and Chaudhry (1997) found that some ethnic entrepreneurs achieved break-out by being motivated to expand into overseas markets. In fact Iyer and Shapiro (1999) plus Crick et al. (2001) found that some ethnic entrepreneurs utilised networks and cultural resources to exploit the international opportunities they had identified. Chaudhry and Crick (2004, a; b) identified examples of ethnic entrepreneurs that professionalised their businesses and had broken out of cultural niche markets.

In taking small businesses and especially those of an ethnic origin forward, the provision of government assistance has been criticised. Studies have suggested that policy makers have an inability to meet some entrepreneurs' needs; also, there is often poor marketing of support programs, plus there is sometimes a lack of focus and consistency in the provision of support (Marlow, 1992; Oc and Tiesdell, 1999; Ram and Smallbone, 2003; Fallon and Berman Brown, 2004).

Motives for internationalising

Irrespective of the ethnic background of entrepreneurs, in breaking into overseas markets earlier studies found the internationalisation path to be a gradual, staged and largely 'export-oriented' process (Bilkey and Tesar, 1977). However, more recent studies have found that while some entrepreneurs were motivated to take a gradual, staged and export-oriented approach, others were motivated to rapidly internationalise and utilise more committed modes of market entry (Oviatt and McDougall, 1994; Knight and Cavusgil, 1996; Bell et al., 2004).

Specific factors have been found to influence certain entrepreneurs to internationalise, that include: managerial resources including experience and commitment (Westhead et al., 2001), plus the networks in which they participate (Coviello and Munro, 1997; Hayer and Ibeh, 2006). Sometimes strategies can be contingent on particular circumstances including industry factors and even serendipitous events (Crick and Jones, 2000; Bell et al., 2004). In fact Spence and Crick (2006) found that individual decision-makers react in different ways to a similar opportunity based on the particular circumstances they face plus their perceptions of risk. Therefore, a 'holistic' approach needs to be adopted in studies of this nature as strategies such as the speed, scale, scope and entry mode change over time (Ibeh, 2003; Jones and Coviello, 2005; Jones et al., 2011). A range of factors that might be termed proactive or reactive which are both internal and external to the firm need to be considered (Wiedersheim-Paul et al., 1978; Katsikeas and Piercy, 1993).

'Internal' (to the firm) issues have been found to include: differential firm advantages (Westhead et al., 2001); networks (Coviello and Munro, 1997; Hayer and Ibeh, 2006); production capacity (Johnston and Czinkota, 1982); unsold inventory (Sullivan and Bauerschmidt, 1988); plus, economies resulting from additional orders (Kaynak and Kothari, 1984). In contrast, 'external' issues (to the firm) include: foreign country regulations (Bilkey and Tesar, 1977); foreign market information (Albaum, 1983); increased competition (Ursic and Czinkota, 1984); export promotion programs (Kaynak and Erol, 1989); plus serendipitous events including receipt of unsolicited orders (Spence and Crick, 2006). Of course some issues like value chain advantages (Jones, 1999) and profit and growth opportunities (Crick and Spence, 2005) might be viewed as either internal or external depending or the perspective taken; e.g. are they in the entrepreneur's or firm's immediate sphere of influence or direct perceptions rather than in reality influenced by broader macro factors?

In short, studies have identified a number of issues that affect the decision to internationalise in exploiting overseas opportunities (e.g. speed, scale, scope, entry mode, etc.). Studies have also demonstrated that there may be certain common characteristics of entrepreneurs irrespective of their ethnic background; for example, in the recognition and exploitation of opportunities.

However, existing studies have identified characteristics and practices related to entrepreneurs' ethnic origin that do differentiate them, e.g. their cultural background and how the effects of this may manifest themselves in business practices. This extends from reasons for starting in business through to ongoing practices such as markets served and factors influencing this such as the utilisation of cultural networks. Moreover, a limited amount of research exists on 'transnational entrepreneurs'. Consequently, due to the different way they are socially embedded in comparison to other entrepreneurs of an ethnic origin, it can be hypothesised that their practices differ. The context of this study involves entrepreneurs of an Asian origin to reduce the bias from investigating particular ethnic groups and focuses on their current motives for internationalising (albeit in reality, as previously mentioned, a number of practices may differ). These two strands of literature lead to the following testable hypothesis, placed in the conventional null hypothesis format.

> H1: there are no significant differences between internationally oriented entrepreneurs and transnational entrepreneurs in relation to their current motives for engaging in overseas markets.

Methodology

'Internationally oriented entrepreneurs' were classified for sampling purposes as those whose UK-based business traded internationally but did not leverage resources from their country of origin; they employed an exporting strategy. 'Transnational entrepreneurs' operated a business in the UK but leveraged resources in their country of origin via manufacturing facilities.

A questionnaire was constructed in the course of this investigation after undertaking a review of the existing pertinent literature relevant to this area of research and undertaking five exploratory interviews with Asian entrepreneurs, plus two academics deemed knowledgeable about the topic. A sampling frame could not be located that contained Asian-owned firms trading internationally; particularly containing transnational entrepreneurs. An existing database was utilised and this was based on responses to previous studies that were undertaken containing several hundred businesses. It had been constructed using responses to surveys involving various trade directories and members of business associations. This enabled firms to be identified via background characteristics that included ownership and especially ethnic origin, trade sector, plus international involvement. Importantly, respondents were arguably favourably inclined to participate in academic research given that they had previously provided responses to enable their inclusion in the database (for response rate purposes in the current study).

Only independent firms owned by entrepreneurs that originated from an Asian origin with up to 100 UK-based employees were contacted to minimise resource bias. Nevertheless, certain entrepreneurs had outsourced some manufacturing operations to staff based overseas so were technically larger than the categorisation, but did still fit, given they had minimal employment in the UK. Trade sectoral bias was minimised since only technologically oriented firms were contacted (Boter and Holmquist, 1996; Bell et al., 2004). This was based on their specified principal product; their own categorisation of their use of modern technology, also the extent of technological product and process innovation, and finally the level of product complexity.

A questionnaire went to all the firms in the database exhibiting the previously mentioned characteristics and 98 usable replies were received after a reminder was sent. This was a response rate of 52 percent; arguably quite high for a study of this nature (the sample taken from the larger database excluded firms that did not meet the sample parameters e.g. those not internationalising). However, as previously mentioned, the database contained firms that were perhaps favourably disposed to participating in academic studies given that they had responded to studies undertaken in the past.

The potential for bias from using key respondents was recognised in this study (Phillips, 1981). The cover letter was addressed to the lead entrepreneur (owner/manager) named in the database. Responses were received from 21 firms after the second round declining to participate in the study. The reason in all cases provided was lack of time, work pressures, or a similar reason. Five firms were telephoned to establish their reason for non-response and all related to time constraints. Quantitative analysis involving statistical differences between those responding to the first versus second mailing found no statistical differences over selected variables. Non-response bias was considered to be minimal in the study. Of the 98 replies, 40 respondents' firms were characterised as internationally oriented entrepreneurs in comparison to 58 that were categorised as owned by a transnational entrepreneur.

Eight interviews that represented the two groups were subsequently undertaken to supplement the statistical data, that is, to provide in-depth information of a how and why nature. They were primarily selected on their proximity and willingness to be interviewed due to cost implications; consequently, a non-probability sample was utilised in this respect. Semi-structured interviews lasted about one to two hours and enabled entrepreneurs to freely account for their internationalisation path including past and current motives for engaging in international markets. The statistical phase was restricted to current motives given that some respondents may not recall initial motives. The nature, trustworthiness i.e. credibility, confirmability, etc. and authenticity of the research was considered in an attempt to reduce bias in line with Marshall and Rossman (1995) and Guba and Lincoln (1998). Supplementary data such as newspaper reports, company brochures etc were collected where possible.

The procedure adopted by the researchers for analysis was similar to that used by Jamal and Chapman (2000). Specifically, the interviews were recorded and this allowed within and between case analyses to be independently undertaken. One researcher was born in the Asian sub-continent and fluent in several languages, but had lived in the UK for a good deal of their life. In comparison, the other researcher was born and brought up in the UK. Consequently, different cultural perspectives could be applied to the data analysis within this study; as such, to allow commonalities to be agreed. Only summaries of key perceptions are included in this chapter due to the richness of the data. However, the purpose of the qualitative data was to supplement the quantitative analysis which was the main research tool employed. Selected data associated with the interviewees are outlined in Table 6.1.

Findings

A decision had to be made in respect of testing H1, namely: there are no significant differences between internationally oriented entrepreneurs and transnational entrepreneurs in relation to their current motives for engaging in overseas markets. Given that a number of potential current motives were under investigation, a factor analysis might ideally have been undertaken in the first instance given that this is a widely accepted data reduction technique to identify potential commonality between sets of variables. The relatively small sample size did not enable a robust factor analysis to be undertaken (Hair et al., 1995).

As a result of the relatively small number of responses and as the nature of the differences between the two group sizes was not considered large, a decision was made to employ a t-test rather than a non-parametric test (see, for example, Diamantopoulos and Schlegelmilch, 1997). Table 6.1 highlights entrepreneurs' mean responses regarding both 'internationally oriented entrepreneurs' and 'transnational entrepreneurs'; data are provided indicating whether significant differences exist with respect to their current motives for engaging in overseas markets. Data collection was undertaken using a five-point scale ranging from 1 = not at all important, to 5 = extremely important. The analysis determined that eleven statistical differences were found to exist between the two groups of entrepreneurs out of the 24 variables under investigation. Furthermore, the rank ordering of the mean values was somewhat varied making interpretation difficult. Hypothesis 1 was not fully rejected in the course of this study.

Insights were drawn from the interviews that supplemented the statistical analysis in Table 6.1; certain specific issues are worthy of further consideration from the collection of data outside of entrepreneurs' current motives for internationalising in the main survey. From the relatively small sample, it was apparent that internationally oriented entrepreneurs tended to offer unique tailored products and operate in niche markets. One interviewee mentioned 'we have to adapt to each market we sell to'. They had internationalised early due to the restricted nature of the domestic market, but also in an attempt to obtain a competitive advantage in beating the competition into key markets.

In contrast, the relatively small sample of transnational entrepreneurs tended to offer standardised, but not necessarily less sophisticated products. Their manufacturing operations located

Table 6.1 A comparison of entrepreneurs' motives for internationalising

Issue addressed: we are interested in determining motives for engaging in overseas sales. Therefore, please indicate the extent to which each of the following motivate your current effort.

Mean Responses

Motive	*Internationally oriented Asian entrepreneurs*	*Rank*	*Asian transnational entrepreneurs*	*Rank*	*T Value*	*Sig*
Potential for extra growth resulting from serving overseas markets	4.50	1	2.99	10	5.402	0.000*
Profit advantage	4.40	2	3.71	5	2.262	0.026*
Unique products/brands	4.00	=3	3.83	3	0.499	0.619
Economies of scale resulting from additional orders	4.00	=3	2.53	14	4.855	0.000*
Opportunity to increase the number of country markets and reduce the market-related risk	4.00	=3	2.47	=15	3.492	0.001*
Competitive pressures	3.85	6	2.14	20	3.926	0.000*
Historical customer ties	3.84	7	3.77	4	0.207	0.837
Encouragement by agents and distributors	3.83	=8	2.65	12	3.091	0.003*
Marketing advantage	3.83	=8	3.99	2	–0.585	0.560
Reduction in tariffs	3.50	=10	2.85	11	1.914	0.058
Favourable product regulations in target countries	3.50	=10	3.54	6	–0.090	0.929
Managerial aspirations	3.33	=12	2.33	17	2.634	0.010*
Unsolicited orders from overseas	3.33	=12	3.04	9	0.783	0.435
Favourable currency movements	2.83	=14	1.89	21	2.636	0.010*
New information about sales opportunities overseas	2.83	=14	2.22	18	1.472	0.144
Exclusive information	2.67	16	2.47	=15	0.495	0.622
Initiation of overseas business by domestic competitors	2.33	=17	2.60	13	–0.717	0.475
Encouragement from contacts in social networks, i.e. non business	2.33	=17	4.04	1	–4.118	0.000*
Saturated domestic market	2.17	19	1.79	22	1.319	0.190
National export promotion programmes	2.00	20	1.73	23	0.860	0.392
Declining domestic sales	1.67	21	1.55	24	0.451	0.653
Excess capacity	1.50	=22	2.18	19	–1.779	0.078
Attractive government incentives	1.50	=22	3.38	8	–4.309	0.000*
Over production	1.33	24	3.39	7	–5.155	0.000*

1 = not at all important, to 5 = extremely important.

in countries to benefit from low labour rates were assisting their competitive advantage in overseas markets. One interviewee explained, 'I made a decision that it was the only way to keep down costs'.

All internationally oriented entrepreneurs in the interview stage were influenced to internationalise to realise the potential for extra growth from serving overseas markets, plus the subsequent profit and marketing advantage. Furthermore, extra opportunities overseas allowed entrepreneurs to spread their risk because the niche markets in which they traded could often become difficult to operate within because of, for example, competitors' prices, plus new versions of the product being offered. Networks were developed within major markets; however, more limited representation took place in those perceived as peripheral markets. Put simply, the entrepreneurs balanced resources between markets with an emphasis on those with greater perceived potential. However, entrepreneurs were able to benefit from knowledge (of regulations etc.) and orders from historical ties, plus the encouragement from representatives, e.g. agents and distributors. One interviewee commented, 'price is important so we have to be careful where we go to (where to sell overseas) and especially because we are limited with our budget. We have people on the ground over there to do the work for us (meaning agents not employees)'. The transnational entrepreneurs offered what they perceived as somewhat unique (to the competition) products in the markets in which they operated. They then tried to maximise production runs. However, they leveraged resources in their country of origin to gain both marketing and profit advantages. Networks were utilised including social and business networks; importantly, this was based on their portfolio of operations to assist their internationalisation strategies. As one respondent mentioned, 'wages are much lower (meaning versus the UK)'. In effect, the entrepreneurs had taken advantage of incentives to locate production overseas and in turn this had improved competitiveness.

In comparison to the internationally oriented entrepreneurs, over production was recognised as a potential issue resulting from manufacturing operations in the Indian sub-continent not operating efficiently; or certainly as much as they would have liked. Indeed, being UK-based meant that they had not been fully able to maintain control over all of their operations overseas. One interviewee noted: 'I regularly have to go there (to the country in which the factory is located) to sort out problems'.

All internationally oriented entrepreneurs in the interviews were motivated by their respective managerial aspirations rather than issues that may be termed as 'reactive' in nature, e.g. a saturated domestic market, declining domestic sales, over production etc. Nevertheless, governmental export promotion programs and incentives were not perceived as important. The interviewees considered themselves to be experienced in day-to-day overseas business operations and therefore thought that assistance schemes tended to be of a 'how to' nature and this information was already known. One interviewee noted: 'I have years of experience so what use is it to me?' However, when the interviewer asked 'so what do you think about... (program name mentioned)', the same interviewee had not heard of it. Care must therefore be taken in interpreting the results as interviewees may not have been as knowledgeable about support as they claimed and more research might have uncovered schemes that could have assisted efforts. Furthermore, specific assistance such as locating partners (broadly defined to include joint ventures etc., as well as agents and distributors) was however mentioned; it was perceived this type of support was not adequately available. One interviewee mentioned that: 'we really found it hard to find someone to represent us in America'; a common sentiment among interviewees across respective markets served.

In comparison, transnational entrepreneurs were also motivated primarily by proactive rather than reactive factors. These varied from those of their internationally oriented entrepreneurial counterparts. With reference to perceptions of export promotion programs, this was low albeit it was perhaps not surprising because they had in effect exported jobs from the UK to the Indian sub-continent. One interviewee stated: 'what use is that (government export support) when we do not manufacture here?'

Discussion

This paper addressed Drori et al.'s (2009; 2010) observation that relatively limited research exists concerning the practices of transnational entrepreneurs. In contributing to the growing body of knowledge in the international entrepreneurship literature, the study investigated differences between two groups of UK-based ethnic minority entrepreneurs of an Asian origin in relation to their current motives for internationalising. It reported on responses to a survey plus findings from supplementary interviews that added richness to the quantitative data. These two groups were termed 'internationally oriented entrepreneurs' and 'transnational entrepreneurs'. The findings in the study indicated that statistical differences existed between the two groups in 11 out of the 24 motives; plus there was inconsistency between the mean rankings and therefore hypothesis 1 was not fully rejected. However, the aggregated statistical data to a certain extent masked the importance of certain issues. Results from the follow-up interviews were discussed to consider perceptions and explanations to supplement the statistical data.

Perhaps not surprisingly each interview uncovered different perceptions although space limitations restrict the inclusion of case histories. However, certain broad observations can be discussed. Starting with the internationally oriented entrepreneurs that were interviewed, each was operating in respective niche markets and therefore was motivated to internationalise early to facilitate growth (Jones, 1999); also to obtain first mover status (Crick and Jones, 2000), but focused on what were perceived to be 'lead markets' (Spence and Crick, 2006). Moreover, this strategy was important to maintain as they had limited domestic market potential (Bell et al., 2004). These entrepreneurs tried to minimise transaction costs by employing largely an exporting strategy instead of more committed forms of market entry (Crick et al., 2001). Moreover, networks were utilised (Iyer and Shapiro, 1999; Hayer and Ibeh, 2006) and strategies were adapted where necessary and possible to meet changing conditions (Ibeh, 2003).

Interestingly, the strategies did not contradict a number of earlier studies where each owner's ethnicity did not feature in the design of the research. In other words, the strategies discussed might have been just as applicable to a sample of internationally oriented firms irrespective of whether or not they were from an ethnic minority (in this case Asian origin). In fact the findings were also consistent with what has been termed the 'holistic approach' towards internationalisation that has been discussed in recent studies in the domain of international entrepreneurship. Specifically, no single theory by itself could fully account for firms' strategies and in this case their motives for internationalising, e.g. based on resources, networks and contingency factors (Crick and Jones, 2000; Bell et al., 2004; Jones and Coviello, 2005; Jones et al., 2011).

Turning to a discussion on further issues, these entrepreneurs had tended to restrict their respective management teams' experience by internalising knowledge. Specifically, in three of the four internationally oriented firms, the management team comprised of members of the key entrepreneur's extended family. The extent to which they had 'professionalised' operations to assist growth objectives was questionable. However, in firm three experienced people had been recruited to build the management team from outside of the extended family. The firm was able to draw on an experienced manager's networks and it resulted in the formation of several joint venture relationships in addition to the core export strategy based on their initial classification. In fact government assistance had been utilised as a result of recruiting open minded and professional managers to the benefit of the firm unlike the other three.

In contrast, each of the transnational entrepreneurs also provided their own stories. However, a common feature was that they had all been able to leverage resources in their country of origin to assist performance (Drori et al., 2009; 2010); the associated advantages featured in their motives for internationalising. A key point of discussion that is in contrast to internationally oriented entrepreneurs (and hence a majority of the existing literature) was that certain practices differed; this offered a contribution to knowledge. Each had related experience when starting business operations in the UK, but only transnational firm three started a firm in the UK while the remainder took over an existing business. The key point of note was that each firm utilised their manufacturing operation located in the Indian sub-continent to their advantage, that is, principally lower labour costs. They were able to utilise networks arising from their overseas business experience in a different way to their counterparts by operating in the two socially embedded environments (Crick et al., 2001; Hayer and Ibeh, 2006).

Furthermore, while transnational entrepreneurs utilised knowledge as previously mentioned, where necessary they were prepared to professionalise their respective management team by recruiting experienced managers (Chaudhry and Crick 2004, a; b). It must nonetheless be re-emphasised that the majority of their manufacturing operations had been moved to the Indian sub-continent to take advantage of lower labour costs. Transnational entrepreneurs therefore had little need for or perceived entitlement to certain assistance schemes. Consequently, support played a limited role in stimulating their overseas activities (Crick and Chaudhry, 1997).

This study provided a categorisation of ethnic minority entrepreneurs that are inherently international players in a business sense into those that are: dually embedded in the country of origin (Indian sub-continent) and home country (UK) versus those who are embedded only in the home country (UK) yet internationally oriented. This is potentially counterintuitive in the sense that some researchers might think primarily of differences between 'mainstream' local entrepreneurs (albeit this is difficult to classify following generations of immigration) versus those from ethnic minorities, rather than within the latter category; hence this study has provided a contribution to knowledge concerning the practices of internationalising entrepreneurs.

Future research

This study helped develop researchers' understanding of the term 'transnational entrepreneur' and was positioned within the academic domain of international entrepreneurship; a specific part of the wider international business literature. At this point it is worth reconsidering McDougall and Oviatt's (2000: 903) definition of international entrepreneurship: 'a combination of innovative, proactive and risk-seeking behaviour that crosses national borders and is intended to create value in organisations'. In doing so, arguably relatively little work has been undertaken on the practices of internationalising ethnic entrepreneurs either between minority groups or in comparison to mainstream entrepreneurs in respective countries. Indeed, given that transnational entrepreneurs are socially embedded in at least two environments, further research might consider their practices in comparison with work involving mini-multinationals.

Consequently, avenues for future research can build on the current study and include investigations into aspects of the overseas strategies employed within different types of ethnic minority businesses outside of motives for internationalising. This could include mixed method studies to provide aggregated statistical data followed by in-depth how and why type qualitative analysis. This might involve factors associated with specific industry considerations in various countries, the markets served by management teams, plus their resources including the social capital of the key entrepreneurs. A further interesting area that offers potential opportunities for further research, subject to the problem of locating an adequate sample, is to track firms by employing a longitudinal methodology. This might help facilitate a more effective public–private sector interaction. In the meantime, this investigation has offered a contribution to the under researched area of transnational entrepreneurship on which others can build in different contexts.

Acknowledgements

An earlier version of this chapter was presented at a special conference on transnational entrepreneurs in Waterloo, Canada; plus an expanded version of the qualitative aspects of this paper has been accepted in the *Journal of Small Business and Enterprise Development*. The comments of conference attendees and journal referees are respectively appreciated. However, aspects of the underpinning literature and methodological approach followed are acknowledged to be similar between papers.

References

Albaum, G., 'Effectiveness of government export assistance for US smaller-sized manufacturers: some further evidence', *International Marketing Review*, 1 (Autumn), 1983, 68–75.

Aldrich, H. and R. Waldinger, 'Ethnicity and entrepreneurship', *Annual Review of Sociology*, 16, 1990, 111–135.

Bagwell, S., 'Transnational family networks and ethnic minority business development', *International Journal of Entrepreneurial Behaviour & Research*, 14 (6), 2008, 377–394.

Bates, T., 'Social resources generated by group support networks may not be beneficial to Asian immigrant-owned small businesses', *Social Forces*, 72, 1994, 671–689.

Bell, J., Crick, D. and S. Young, 'Small firm internationalisation and business strategy: an exploratory study of "knowledge-intensive" and "traditional" manufacturing firms in the UK', *International Small Business Journal*, 22, 2004, 23–56.

Bilkey, W. J. and G. Tesar, 'The export behavior of smaller sized Wisconsin manufacturing firms', *Journal of International Business Studies*, Spring/Summer, 1977, 93–98.

Blackburn, R., 'Ethnic minority business in Britain: the experience of different business owners', Paper presented at the Helsinki School of Economics, 1993.

Boter, H. and C. Holmquist, 'Industry characteristics and internationalization processes in small firms', *Journal of Business Venturing*, 11, 1996, 471–487.

Calof, J. L. and P. W. Beamish, 'Adapting to foreign markets: explaining internationalization', *International Business Review*, 4, 1995, 115–131.

Chaudhry, S. and D. Crick, 'A case history of a "successful" Asian entrepreneur in the UK: Sir G. K. Noon', *International Journal of Management Cases*, 7, 2004a, 5–12.

Chaudhry, S. and D. Crick, 'Understanding practices at the marketing/entrepreneurship interface: a case study of Mr Kirit Pathak', *Qualitative Market Research: An International Journal*, 7, 2004b, 183–193.

Chen, W. and J. Tan, 'Transnational entrepreneurship through a network lens: theoretical and methodological considerations', *Entrepreneurship Theory & Practice*, 33 (5), 2009, 1079–1091.

Coviello, N. and H. Munro, 'Network relationships and the internationalization process of small software firms', *International Business Review*, 6 (4), 1997, 361–386.

Crick, D. and S. Chaudhry, 'Export problems and government assistance required by UK exporters: an investigation into the effect of ethnicity', *International Journal of Entrepreneurial Behaviour & Research*, 3, 1997, 3–18.

Crick, D., Chaudhry, S. and S. Batstone, 'An investigation into the overseas expansion of Asian-owned SMEs in the UK clothing industry', *Small Business Economics*, 16, 2001, 75–94.

Crick, D. and M. Jones, 'Small high-technology firms and international high technology markets', *Journal of International Marketing*, 8 (2), 2000, 63–85.

Crick, D. and M. Spence, 'The internationalisation of "high performing" UK high-tech SMEs: a study of planned and unplanned strategies', *International Business Review*, 14, 2005, 167–185.

Curran, J. and R. Blackburn, *Ethnic Enterprise and the High Street Bank*. Kingston Business School Report, 1993.

Deakins, D., Hussain, J. G. and M. Ram, *The Finance of Ethnic Minority Small Businesses*. Birmingham: University of Central England, 1992.

Diamantopoulos, A. and B. B. Schlegelmilch, *Taking the Fear Out of Data Analysis*. London: Dryden, 1997.

Drori, I., Honig, B. and A. Ginsberg, 'Transnational entrepreneurship: a conceptual framework for post-international entrepreneurship', Paper presented at the 10th McGill International Entrepreneurship Conference, Los Angeles, 28–29 September, 2007.

Drori, I., Honig, B. and A. Ginsberg, 'Researching transnational entrepreneurship: an approach based on the theory of practice'. In B. Honig, I. Drori, and B. Carmichael, (Eds), *Transnational and Immigrant Entrepreneurship in a Globalized World.* Toronto: University of Toronto Press, 2010, pp. 3–30.

Drori, I, Honig, B. and M. Wright, 'Transnational entrepreneurship: an emergent field of study', *Entrepreneurship Theory & Practice*, 33 (5), 2009, 1001–1022.

Fallon, G. and R. Berman Brown, 'Supporting ethnic community businesses: lessons from a West Midlands support agency', *Regional Studies*, 38, 2004, 137–148.

Guba, E. G. and Y. S. Lincoln, 'Competing paradigms in qualitative research'. In N. S. Denzin and Y. S. Lincoln (Eds), *The Landscape of Qualitative Research: Theories and Issues*, London: Sage Publications, 1998.

Hair, J. F., Anderson, R. E., Tatham, R. L. and W. C. Black, *Multivariate Data Analysis With Readings*, Englewood Cliffs: Prentice Hall, 1995.

Hayer, J. S. and K. I. N. Ibeh, 'Ethnic networks and small firm internationalisation: a study of UK-based Indian enterprises', *International Journal of Entrepreneurship and Innovation Management*, 6, 2006, 508–525.

Ibeh, K. I. N., 'Toward a contingency framework of export entrepreneurship: conceptualizations and empirical evidence', *Small Business Economics*, 20 (1), 2003, 49–68.

Iyer, G. R. and J. M. Shapiro, 'Ethnic entrepreneurial and marketing systems: implications for the global economy', *Journal of International Marketing*, 7, 1999, 83–110.

Jamal, A. and M. Chapman, 'Acculturation and inter-ethnic consumer perceptions: can you feel what we feel', *Journal of Marketing Management*, 16, 2000, 365–391.

Johnston, W. J. and M. R. Czinkota, 'Managerial motivations as determinants of industrial export behaviour'. In M. R. Czinkota and G. Tesar (Eds), *Export Management: An International Context.* New York: Praeger, 1982, pp. 3–17.

Jones, M. V., 'The internationalization of small high technology firms', *Journal of International Marketing*, 7, 1999, 15–41.

Jones, M. V. and N. E. Coviello, 'Internationalization: conceptualising an entrepreneurial process of behavior in time', *Journal of International Business Studies*, 36, 2005, 284–303.

Jones, M. V., Coviello, N. and Y. K. Tang, 'International entrepreneurship research (1989–2009): a domain ontology and thematic analysis', *Journal of Business Venturing*, 26 (6), 2011, 632–659.

Jones, T., McEvoy, D. and J. Barratt, 'Raising capital for the ethnic minority small business'. In A. Hughes and D. Storey (Eds), *Financing the Small Firm.* London: Routledge, 1992.

Jones, T., McEvoy, D. and J. Barratt, 'Labour intensive practices in the ethnic minority firm'. In J. Atkinson and D. Storey (Eds), *Employment, the Small Firm and the Labour Market.* London: Routledge, 1993.

Jones, T., Ram, M. and P. Edwards, 'Ethnic minority business and the employment of illegal immigrants', *Entrepreneurship & Regional Development*, 18, 2006, 133–150.

Jones, T. and M. Ram, 'Re-embedding the ethnic business agenda', *Work, Employment and Society*, 21, 2007, 439–457.

Katsikeas, C. S. and N. F. Piercy, 'Long-term export stimuli and firm characteristics in a European LDC', *Journal of International Marketing*, 1 (3), 1993, 23–47.

Kaynak, E. and C. Erol, 'The export propensity of Turkish manufacturing and trading house firms', *Journal of Marketing Management*, 5 (2), 1989, 211–229.

Kaynak, E. and V. Kothari, 'Export behavior of small manufacturers: a comparative study of American and Canadian firms', *European Management Journal*, 2 (Summer), 1984, 41–47.

Knight, G. and T. S. Cavusgil, 'The born-global firm: a challenge to traditional internationalization theory', *Advances in International Marketing*, 8, 1996, 11–26.

Light, I., *Ethnic Enterprise in America: Business and Welfare Among Chinese, Japanese and Blacks.* Berkeley CA: University of California, 1972.

Marger, M. N., 'Transnationalism or assimilation? Patterns of sociopolitical adaptation among Canadian business immigrants', *Ethnic and Racial Studies*, 29, 2006, 882–900.

Marlow, S., 'The take-up of business growth training schemes in Britain', *International Small Business Journal*, 7, 1992, 34–46.

Marshall, C. and G. B. Rossman, *Designing Qualitative Research.* London: Sage Publications, 1995.

McDougall, P. P. and B. M. Oviatt, 'International entrepreneurship: the intersection of two research paths', *Academy of Management Journal*, 43, 2000, 902–906.

Min, P. G., 'Factors contributing to ethnic business: a comprehensive synthesis', *International Journal of Comparative Sociology*, 28, 1987, 173–193.

Oc, T. and S. Tiesdell, 'Supporting ethnic minority business: a review of business support for ethnic minorities in city challenge areas', *Urban Studies*, 36, 1999, 1723–1746.

Oviatt, B. M and P. P. McDougall, 'Toward a theory of international new ventures', *Journal of International Business Studies*, 25 (1), 1994, 45–64.
Patel, P. C. and B. Conklin, 'The balancing act: the role of transnational habitus and social networks in balancing transnational entrepreneurial activities', *Entrepreneurship Theory & Practice*, 33 (5), 2009, 1045–1078.
Patel, S., *The Nature and Dynamics of Asian Retailing in Britain*. Unpublished PhD, Open University, 1989.
Phillips, L. W., 'Assessing measurement error in key informant reports: a methodological note on organisational analysis in marketing', *Journal of Marketing Research* 18, 1981, 395–415.
Portes, A., Guarnizo, L. E. and W. J. Haller, 'Transnational entrepreneurs: an alternative form of immigrant economic adaptation', *American Sociological Review*, 67 (2), 2002, 278–298.
Rafiq, M., *Asian Businesses in Bradford, West Yorkshire*. Unpublished PhD, University of Bradford, 1988.
Ram, M., 'Coping with racism: Asian employers in the inner city', *Work Employment and Society*, 6, 1992, 601–618.
Ram, M. and G. Hillin, 'Achieving "break-out": developing mainstream ethnic minority businesses', *Small Business and Enterprise Development*, 1, 1994, 15–21.
Ram, M., Sanghera, B., Abbas, T., Barlow, G. and T. Jones, 'Ethnic minority business in comparative perspective: the case of the independent restaurant sector', *Journal of Ethnic and Migration Studies*, 26, 2000, 495–510.
Ram, M. and D. Smallbone, 'Policies to support ethnic minority enterprise: the English experience', *Entrepreneurship & Regional Development*, 15, 2003, 151–166.
Ram, M., Smallbone, D. and D. Deakins, *Ethnic Minority Businesses in the UK: Access to Finance and Business Support*, London: British Bankers Association, 2002.
Ram, M. and J. Sparrow, 'Minority firms, racism and economic development', *Local Economy*, 8, 1993, 117–129.
Sanders, J. and V. Nee, 'Immigrant self-employment: the family as social capital and the value of human capital', *American Sociological Review*, 61, 1996, 231–249.
Sequeira, J. M., Carr, J. C. and A. A. Rasheed, 'Transnational entrepreneurship: determinants of firm type and owner attributions of success', *Entrepreneurship Theory & Practice*, 33 (5), 2009, 1023–1044.
Shane, S. and S. Venkataraman, 'The promise of entrepreneurship as a field of research', *Academy of Management Review*, 25, 2000, 217–226.
Smallbone, D., Bertotti, M. and I. Ekanem, 'Diversification in ethnic minority business: the case of Asians in London's creative industries', *Journal of Small Business and Enterprise Development*, 12, 2005, 41–56.
Spence, M. and D. Crick, 'A comparative investigation into the internationalization of Canadian and UK high-tech SMEs', *International Marketing Review*, 22, 2006, 524–548.
Stanton, P. J. and J. Lee, 'Australian cultural diversity and export growth', *Journal of Multilingual and Multicultural Development*, 16, 1995, 497–511.
Stokes, D., *Small Business Management*. London: CIP, 2002.
Storey, D. J., *Understanding the Small Business Sector*. London: Routledge, 1994.
Sullivan, D. and A. Bauerschmidt, 'Common factors underlying the incentive to export: studies in the European forest products industry', *European Journal of Marketing*, 22 (10), 1988, 41–55.
Terjesen, S. and A. Elam, 'Transnational entrepreneurs' venture internationalization strategies: a practice theory approach', *Entrepreneurship Theory & Practice*, 33 (5), 2009, 1093–1120.
Ursic, M. and M. R. Czinkota, 'An experience curve explanation of export expansion', *Journal of Business Research*, 12, 1984, 159–168.
Ward, R., 'Economic development and ethnic business'. In J. Curran and R. A. Blackburn (Eds), *Paths of Enterprise*. London: Routledge, 1991.
Ward, R., Randall, R. and K. Krcmar, 'Small firms in the clothing industry: the growth of minority enterprise', *International Small Business Journal*, 4, 1986, 46–56.
Werbner, P., 'Renewing an industrial past: British Pakistani entrepreneurship in Manchester', *Migration*, 8, 1990, 7–41.
Westhead, P., Wright, M. and D. Ucbasaran, 'The internationalisation of new and small firms: a resource based view', *Journal of Business Venturing*, 16, 2001, 333–358.
Wiedersheim-Paul, F., Olson, H. C., and L. S. Welch, 'Pre-export activity: the first step in internationalisation', *Journal of International Business Studies*, 9 (Spring/Summer), 1978, 47–58.
Zhou, L., Wu, W. and X. Luo, 'Internationalization and the performance of born-global SMEs: the mediating role of social networks', *Journal of International Business Studies*, 38, 2007, 673–690.
Zhou, M., 'Revisiting ethnic entrepreneurship: convergencies, controversies, and conceptual advancements', *International Migration Review*, 38 (3), 2004, 1040–1074.

Part III

Strategic issues for entrepreneurial internationalization

7

Networks and social capital

An internationalizing entrepreneurial firm's network is its net worth

Sylvie Chetty and Cecilia Pahlberg

Introduction

One of the most cited models about the internationalization of firms often referred to as the "Uppsala model" was developed by Johanson and Vahlne (1977) in their seminal *Journal of International Business Studies* article. This model has also been very influential in the international entrepreneurship literature not least when it comes to comparing and contrasting it with models explaining the phenomenon of international new ventures (INVs) or born globals (cf. Oviatt and McDougall, 1994; McDougall et al., 1994; Madsen and Servais, 1997; Knight and Cavusgil, 2004).

The Uppsala model emphasizes how firms strive to reduce uncertainty by taking small steps and gradually expanding their international activities. Based on empirical observations of Swedish firms, Johanson and Vahlne noted how these firms often increased their international operations by starting with exporting through an agent before establishing their own sales subsidiaries and later production units. They also observed that firms tended to start their internationalization in countries at a low psychic distance (measured by considering factors affecting the ability of exporters to understand foreign markets, such as differences in culture, language, business practices, etc.) before entering countries further away. Building on the behavioural theory of the firm (Cyert and March, 1963), Johanson and Vahlne describe internationalization as a product of incremental decisions, and these decisions are mainly based on experiences from being present in a market and committing resources there while acquiring knowledge. Hence, the two main concepts of the model are knowledge and commitment, and these are to a large extent market-specific and based on experience.

While the manifestations of the model (the sequential stages when it comes to modes of entry and geographical markets) have been criticized by many scholars within the INV or born global literature, others point out that the theoretical reasoning with the emphasis on knowledge and commitment should be put in the forefront (Madsen and Servais, 1997). Uncertainty reduction is often highlighted when the model is discussed by scholars, although Johanson and Vahlne pointed out that firms are also exposed to opportunities. For instance, they disclose that "the model assumes that the state of internationalization affects perceived opportunities and risks which in turn influence commitment decisions and current activities" (1977, p. 27).

They also indicate the importance for a firm to have knowledge of opportunities, and how such knowledge affects the commitment decisions. This resonates with the entrepreneurship literature where opportunity is a central concept. However, in a revised version of the model (2009), Johanson and Vahlne admit that in the 1977 article they probably underestimated the opportunity dimension.

In addition to highlighting opportunities, Johanson and Vahlne in their 2009 article also emphasize the role of relationships and networks. IE scholars should note that this is not a new observation. Johanson and Vahlne base their reasoning on findings from a research project that started in Uppsala in the mid-1970s and evolved into the large IMP project (industrial marketing and purchasing) which involved research groups from five European countries. In this research, the importance of close and long-lasting relationships were identified (see, for example, Håkansson 1982) and that firms often operate in networks of connected relationships (Anderson et al., 1994), indeed, "exchange in one relationship is linked to exchange in another" (Johanson and Vahlne, 2009, p. 15). They label these connected relationships "business networks," and propose that successful internationalization is a matter of becoming an insider in relevant networks.

The importance of networks has also been stressed by IE scholars such as Coviello and Munro (1995, 1997) who focus on foreign market selection and mode of entry, Oviatt and McDougall (1994) who highlight the importance of networks for INVs to internationalize rapidly and Coviello (2006) who focuses on INV network dynamics such as how networks change over time. Hence, the updated Uppsala model (2009) on internationalization has a great deal in common with IE literature and with its focus on opportunities, relationships and networks. Consequently, by integrating the international business and international entrepreneurship literature we can improve our understanding of the internationalization of entrepreneurial firms.

The two main research objectives in this chapter are as follows:

How do IE firms identify and create opportunities within their relationships and networks?

What are the various types and roles of relationships and networks that IE firms use during their internationalization process?

The rest of the chapter is structured according to Figure 7.1. First, it provides an overview of the internationalization process within a network context. Second, it presents the types of relationships in an INV such as business/social, direct/indirect, strong/weak and web-based relationships. Third, it focuses on three different roles of social capital: efficacy, serendipity and liability. Fourth, it presents future research directions which include the context of emerging and transition economies as well as social media. Fifth, the chapter ends with a conclusion.

Internationalization process within a network context

Since it is the liability of being outside a significant network, rather than the liability of foreignness, that creates uncertainty for internationalizing firms, Johanson and Vahlne (2009) argue that opportunity development should be examined in a business network setting. Business networks could be considered as the relationships a firm has with its customers, distributors, suppliers, competitors and supporting institutions and government. The number and strength of the relationships between different parts of the business network increase as the firm internationalizes.

In the network model (Johanson and Mattsson, 1988; Johanson and Vahlne, 2009), internationalization involves developing relationships with firms that belong to networks that extend into foreign countries. Thus, foreign market selection and entry depends on the location of

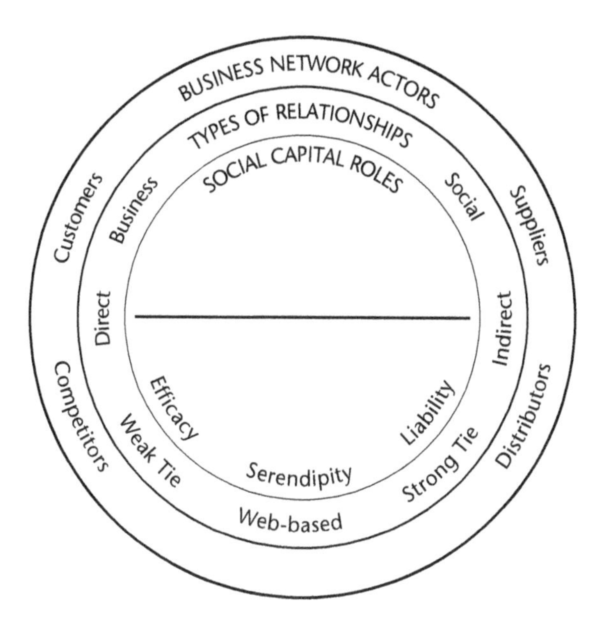

Figure 7.1 Business network actors, relationship types and social capital in international new ventures

existing or possible network partners, and these could be based in the home country and/or foreign markets. These existing relationships tend to drive firms to enter nearby, psychically close markets. One explanation is because when psychic distance becomes greater, it makes network formation more challenging (Johanson and Vahlne, 2009; Ojala, 2009).

Chetty and Blankenburg Holm (2000) use Johanson and Mattsson's (1988) model as a framework to examine four different ways in which firms internationalize, and how this process is influenced by both firm and market characteristics. These four categories are: the Early Starter (the firm has few international relationships but is in a market with a domestic focus); the Lonely International (the firm is highly internationalized but is in a market with a domestic focus); the Late Starter (the firm has domestic focus but the market is highly internationalized); and the International Among Others (the firm and market are highly internationalized). Their study explores the dynamics of how firms utilize their network relationships to extend, penetrate and integrate their international markets. They provide empirical evidence that networks can help internationalizing firms to identify new opportunities, gain knowledge, learn from experiences, and benefit from combining their resources.

Several IE scholars have recognized the importance of social capital and networks. Jones et al.'s (2011) review of the IE literature identifies it as one of five major areas of research within the IE domain. The other areas being venture type, internationalization, organizational issues and entrepreneurship. Other scholars who have contributed towards the IE social capital and networks literature include McNaughton and Bell (1999), Coviello (2006), Coviello and Munro (1997), and Prashantham and Dhanaraj (2010). Slotte-Kock and Coviello (2010) identify three approaches to examine the role of networks and social capital in international entrepreneurship. These include business networks, entrepreneurial networks and the social network perspectives. The business network perspective focuses on inter-organizational networks based on both formal and informal dyadic ties and has no borders. The entrepreneurial network perspective focuses on the individual entrepreneur or firm networks with defined borders.

The social network perspective, however, focuses on individual, intra- and inter-organizational networks with defined borders. This chapter covers the business network perspective to highlight the liability of outsidership (see Johanson and Vahlne, 2009) in the internationalization process and how entrepreneurs recognize and create opportunities through their networks to gain a network position. Furthermore, the chapter covers entrepreneurial network perspective and social network perspective by including strength of ties, web-based relationships and social capital to go deeper into understanding network processes and how entrepreneurs actually create and behave in networks and access resources from them.

The born global or international new venture literature shows that rapid internationalization is often supported by the use of networks or relationships with other organizations (e.g. Chetty and Campbell-Hunt, 2004; Oviatt and McDougall, 1994). These networks allow SMEs to overcome early resource constraints resulting from liabilities of smallness and/or newness (Aldrich and Auster, 1986). The entrepreneurship literature highlights the age of the firm as an important determinant of the types of networks employed. New and early stage ventures tend to rely on resources from social networks, comprising relations with family, friends and colleagues (Ostgaard and Birley, 1994; Ramachandran and Ramnarayan, 1993). This is often attributed to the lack of legitimacy given to new and small firms by more formal or supporting institutions. When the start-up phase of the new venture is completed, organizational needs become more complex and thus require different types of networks to support firm growth. As firms grow they tend to develop more formal relationships with other organizations, for example, suppliers, customers or competitors.

Since a distinguishing feature of entrepreneurial firms is the emphasis on growth, we may find that some entrepreneurs in young firms shun social networks in favour of establishing more strategic networks, such as industry clusters and export networks that support growth immediately (Chetty and Wilson, 2003). In an increasingly globalized world, local networks in the home country provide important sources of information for firms about opportunities in international markets. Local networks are important channels for knowledge transfer, because information and knowledge transfer occurs through frequent personal interaction. Such collaboration allows a firm to acquire essential knowledge quickly at low cost. A supportive institutional environment in the home country, such as business incubators, industry clusters, etc. advances international entrepreneurship by facilitating the development of these networks.

Types of relationships

Relationships can be categorized according to whether they are business or social, or whether they are direct or indirect relationships. While in this chapter we draw on Agndal and Chetty (2007) who provide a detailed explanation for these relationships, we would like to emphasize that there are other typologies in terms of types of relationships in the IE literature. These include international versus domestic relationships (Milanov and Fernhaber, 2014; Yu et al., 2011), internal versus external relationships (Fernhaber et al., 2009; Prashantham and Young, 2011), and informal versus formal relationships (Fernhaber and Li, 2013).

Business and social relationships

Business relationships are referred to as relationships at the level of the organization, in which the actor is an organization. These types of relationship are institutionalized and do not depend on specific individuals. They consist of the long-term relationships that firms have with their customers, distributors, suppliers and competitors (Agndal and Chetty, 2007). It has frequently been reported that these types of relationships influence international market and mode selection

(Johanson and Mattsson, 1988; Zain and Ng, 2006). In social relationships, however, the actor is an individual, and the relationship would not exist without his or her involvement. Indeed, the impact of social networks in the internationalization process has been the focus of an increasing number of studies (Ellis, 2000; Chetty and Patterson, 2002). In a study of Hong Kong toy manufacturers, Ellis (2000) found that the existing social relationships of firms' employees were key drivers in market knowledge acquisition, the identification of market opportunities, and the firms' market entries. Ellis (2011) argues that entrepreneurs identify opportunities though their interpersonal ties, their social networks, instead of through inter-firm networks at a higher level. He found that entrepreneurs in China rated opportunities discovered through social networks to be of higher quality than those discovered through business networks.

Direct and indirect relationships

Direct relationships exist between two parties involved in direct exchange with each other, such as a buyer–seller relationship (Agndal and Chetty, 2007). Indirect relationships are between firms with no direct exchange. Such firms may be referred to as third parties or brokers. Typically, these relationships have been discussed in the literature as "weak ties," which are often considered crucial to firms (Granovetter, 1973). For example, by introducing buyers and sellers, third parties can open up foreign markets for firms. Equally, third parties can create problems, such as when an owner or a powerful customer places pressure on a relationship between two firms, and thereby instigates a strategic change in market or product strategies.

Web-based relationships

Although researchers have discovered the potential for entrepreneurs to enhance networking through web-based communication technologies, this potential remains underexploited (Lewis et al., 2008). In fact, the web has changed "community" and social capital, thus reducing the importance of physical space. Web-based services allow entrepreneurs to (1) design a public or semi-public profile within a bounded structure, (2) present a list of other users who share their connections, and (3) watch and traverse their list of connections and those made by others within the bounded structure (Boyd and Ellison, 2007).

In their study of Icelandic SMEs, Sigfusson and Chetty (2013) examine how software international entrepreneurs use web-based tools, such as online social network sites like LinkedIn, to build and maintain their network relationships. Their data consisted of participant observation on LinkedIn and open-ended face-to-face interviews. They illustrate how entrepreneurs in a small open economy (Iceland), which is distant from its markets, acquire the resources and online social capital that drives their internationalization. Networks formed through LinkedIn have allowed these Icelandic entrepreneurs to gain trust by becoming insiders in foreign networks, and thereby reduce their risk and uncertainty by overcoming the liability of foreignness. They found that entrepreneurs who enjoyed the largest networks typically used online social networks to display their network strength, and to discover opportunities to bridge relationships.

Based on the findings from their study, Sigfusson and Chetty (2013) categorize international entrepreneurs into three types: "responder," "opportunist" and "strategist." First, the responder reacts to requests to form web relationships instead of proactively seeking them. Responders have a well-developed domestic network, but have only a few international relationships. Second, the opportunist considers relationships to be important and is willing to invest the time to actively seek web-based relationships. The opportunist focuses on forming new relationships that can open up new opportunities. Third, the strategist proactively seeks relationships in international markets and receives many requests to connect on LinkedIn, but is very selective about who they accept. The strategist has a large network of relationships, both face-to-face and on the web. They observed that the participants on LinkedIn had a much larger number of relationships than were described during the face-to-face interviews, and most of these relationships were weak. Since LinkedIn provides immense bridging opportunities, participants searched endlessly for the most constructive way to use their networks. Hence, the strategist is especially interesting for other entrepreneurs because they provide the best opportunities for bridging relationships.

Indeed, online social networks provide opportunities for entrepreneurs to form more weak ties, which are especially important for those who are internationalizing. There is a downside, however, as online social networks can absorb time and be unproductive. Entrepreneurs use online social networks to strategically build their networks and gain diverse skills, to build trust and to strengthen network identity for new bridging relationships. Effective online social networks decrease organization costs and benefit business communication.

Strength of ties and internationalization

International entrepreneurship scholars are showing a growing interest in researching the strength of network relationships and ties to determine which is more effective for entrepreneurs. The strength of ties (strong and weak ties) was originally studied within sociology for the purpose of innovation adoption, information transfer and job searches (Granovetter, 1973). Subsequently, this division of strong and weak ties has been adopted by other research disciplines. In economics and business management it has been used for different purposes, such as change management (Krackhardt, 1992) and entrepreneurial processes in venture creation (e.g. Aldrich and Zimmer, 1986; Elfring and Hulsink, 2003).

Some researchers, such as Hite and Hesterly (2001), propose that emerging firms' networks change from consisting mainly of socially embedded dense ties during emergence, towards more calculative networks during early growth stage. Consequently, there is a development from mostly strong ties towards more weak ties, because in the early stages a firm lacks resources. Their network, especially of strong ties, tends to be more willing to assist without any expectations, whereas weak market-based ties expect something (money) in return.

The importance of strength of ties for exploring international market opportunities has been examined by international entrepreneurship researchers. Blomstermo and Sharma (2002) propose that weak ties are important for firms, as they enter international markets based on the information supplied by such ties. Regarding the recognition of international opportunities, Chandra et al. (2009) emphasize that both strong and weak ties are valuable. Weak ties may for example function as bridges between different networks, and strong ties play an important role in disseminating information. Singh (2000) found that entrepreneurs who use a mixture of strong and weak ties recognized more successful new venture opportunities than those who used only strong or only weak ties, or had no contacts at all. The results of these studies are, however, mixed about whether strong or weak ties are more important. According to Chandra et al. (2009, p. 47) it is not the number or type of ties that matter for international opportunity recognition, but if the ties are appropriate they link the "right people and firms at the right time."

The pre-eminence of strong or weak ties, and the dimensions of tie strength, continue to be debated by researchers such as Grabher (1993), Granovetter (1973), and Jack (2005). Söderqvist and Chetty (2013) join this debate by focusing on strength of ties in critical entrepreneurial and internationalization events during the firm's early development. They provide a detailed analysis of the strength of relationships that entrepreneurs use during pre-founding and start-up (entrepreneurial events) as well as early internationalization (internationalization event). They define strong ties as: "close ties based on trust, mutual respect, commitment, deep knowledge and experience of each other." They define weak ties as: "superficial ties not yet based on strong trust, and where the parties do not know each other well and are not emotionally close together. Weak ties are thus considered to be arm's length ties."

Söderqvist and Chetty (2013) use evidence from practice to develop a strength of ties continuum and determine three levels of strength: stronger, equally strong as weak, and weaker. They identify a unique category not yet mentioned in the literature: the equally strong as weak tie, which is so classified when entrepreneurs are unsure about their strength and value. Entrepreneurs experience importance and uncertainty co-existing in such relationships. This continuum is useful because it shows how entrepreneurs actually see their relationships, the complexities of which they must manage. For example, entrepreneurs must deal with the uncertainty inherent in equally strong and weak ties, and in how these ties will evolve as the firm progresses in its internationalization efforts. Such a continuum helps advance understanding of the dynamics of a firm's relationships during its development, and to identify whether stronger relationships are more important than weaker ones during this process. They found that stronger, and equally strong as weak relationships, are used more often than weaker ones during pre-founding, start-up and early internationalization. The entrepreneur's perception that a tie is strong seems to be related to its significance for pre-founding, start-up and early internationalization.

To summarize the chapter up to this point, we have discussed the network setting in which international business takes place, types of relationships and the strength of ties in these relationships. In the next part of this chapter we discuss the resources that firms acquire through these relationships and networks, which start with a discussion on the concept of social capital.

Social capital and international entrepreneurship

The social capital concept first appeared in sociology (e.g. Bourdieu, 1986) and then in economics (e.g. Coleman, 1988). With its transition into management, studies about social capital increasingly focus on the resources available through networks. We draw on Nahapiet and Ghoshal's (1998, p. 243) frequently cited definition of social capital: "the sum of the actual and potential resources embedded within, available through, and derived from the network of relationships possessed by an individual or social unit. Social capital comprises both the network and the assets that may be mobilized through the network." Consequently, social capital includes the network of relationships, which is a structural dimension, as well as the usefulness of the network of relationships, which is an economic dimension. In effect, social capital allows firms to access intangible resources controlled by other firms and individuals, such as knowledge and admittance into new networks. It can also allow access to more tangible resources, such as physical space.

Social capital is not static but highly dynamic, as its structural and economic dimensions change over time. For example, several studies show that during a firm's initial years, entrepreneurs obtain social capital in the shape of supportive resources from family and friends (Birley, 1985; Wilson and Appiah-Kubi, 2002). As the firm starts conducting its business it begins to establish more social capital in the form of relationships with customers, distributors and suppliers. While the number of relationships increases, the diversity and the amount of resources that firms can gain through these relationships also increase. We can, therefore, expect a relationship between years in business and the social capital of a firm, both in terms of the nature of social capital and the extent of social capital accessible.

Prashantham and Dhanaraj (2010) extend social capital theory by focusing on the dynamic influence of social capital on INVs and its contribution to the international growth of the firm.

They found that firms can grow internationally through the beneficial impact of their social capital but when entrepreneurs lose touch with their networks this tie decay will affect their social capital and subsequent international growth. They also highlight the negative aspects of over-embeddedness because it contributes towards the decline in social capital and thus inhibits international growth.

Since small entrepreneurial firms often have limited knowledge and resources to invest in expensive international market research, they may be compelled to proactively draw on external parties to provide the information needed. This helps to reduce uncertainty and guide early decision making about international markets. Such agents may serve as a bridge between the firm and the international market. Other examples include client following (Sharma and Blomstermo, 2003) and piggybacking, which provide important ways for smaller firms to take their first steps internationally. Consequently, such social capital facilitates early internationalization because it helps the internationalizing firm to break away from its domestic market focus.

The key concepts of market knowledge and market commitment in Johanson and Vahlne's (1977) model, as discussed in the introduction of this chapter, can be linked to the literature on social capital. Johanson and Vahlne (2006, p. 1) emphasize that "opportunity development is an important outcome of commitment." They view the concept of social capital that Nahapiet and Ghoshal (1998) propose as being similar to the concept of commitment in the internationalization process model. Johanson and Vahlne (2006) explain that Nahapiet and Ghoshal's claim that social capital encourages cooperative behaviour implies commitment. Thus, Johanson and Vahlne consider the concepts of social capital and mutual commitment to be similar. The existing social capital of a firm determines the opportunities that are available in a particular period (Johanson and Vahlne, 2006).

International entrepreneurship theory emphasizes the dynamic and chaotic aspects of early internationalization where skills, experience, and social networks play a dominant role (e.g. Keupp and Gassmann, 2009; McDougall et al., 1994; Sapienza et al., 2006). Consequently, international entrepreneurship research focuses on how social networks enable the international entrepreneurs to acquire and mobilize resources for early internationalization. International entrepreneurship scholars such as Coviello and Munro (1997), Yli-Renko et al. (2002), McNaughton and Bell (1999), Prashantham and Dhanaraj (2010), Zhou et al. (2007) and Bruneel et al. (2010) highlight the entrepreneur's access to other sources of knowledge as an important resource. In particular, Yli-Renko et al. (2002) state that external social capital in the form of network relationships has a positive influence on the new venture's foreign market knowledge. Increased social capital constitutes improved access to resources and international opportunities, which subsequently surmount the liabilities of newness and foreignness.

In a study on New Zealand and Swedish firms, Agndal and Chetty (2007) illustrate how through interaction with partners in the network, firms get to know each other, develop trust and commit to the relationship. Through this interaction process, partners in the business network begin to see and develop opportunities that others cannot see, as they gain confidential access to information of their own firm and its resources and their counterpart's resources. By understanding how their own idiosyncratic resources may be combined with their partner's idiosyncratic resources, they discover and create new opportunities. Moreover, by developing a strong commitment to their partners, they are able to increase their different knowledge stocks further to exploit new opportunities and to develop capabilities. Hence, it is a process of both exploration and exploitation.

Social capital is a source of strategic change for internationalizing firms. Chetty and Agndal (2007) extend their work on social capital by developing three roles of social capital, and discuss how they influence mode change during the internationalization process. The term "mode" is used to denote the method of doing business, such as exporting, licensing, franchising, joint venture, foreign sales subsidiary, foreign production facilities, etc. The social capital roles include the efficacy role, the serendipity role, and the liability role, which cover both the positive and the negative features of social capital. The liability role appeared most often as the form of social capital to influence mode change.

The efficacy role of social capital

The efficacy role encapsulates the efficacy of the firm's social capital, and how it facilitates mode change in a firm. The usefulness of social capital is inherent in the value of relational assets such as knowledge, information, and access to resources. Firms benefit from regular social interactions with partners to tap into their knowledge. Young and small firms can particularly benefit from access to founding managers' social capital, their customer and supplier relationships. The greater the interaction between network partners, the greater the accumulation of social capital, which opens up new opportunities for the firm. Thus, the efficacy role of social capital enables change. The firm exploits its (and its employees') network to discover new business opportunities or to gain intelligence on new and existing markets. For example, business partners or personal contacts such as family, friends or mentors can point out opportunities for the firm in new foreign markets.

The serendipity role of social capital

This role refers to the unforeseen events that develop from a firm's social capital and cause a mode change. The mode change is therefore serendipitous rather than of the firm's initiative. These unexpected events might take effect through direct or indirect weak ties, such as previous employees, the staff of current business partners, or from third parties making unsolicited contact. While the efficacy role denotes how social capital enables change, the serendipity role denotes how social capital initiates change. Against this background, social capital provides opportunities for a positive change, as perceived by managers. When firms receive this trigger for change, some may possess the social capital to benefit from this information, whereas others might lack the social capital to exploit the opportunity. A study by Prashantham and Dhanaraj (2010) about the dynamics of social capital found that entrepreneurs who are part of a social network are more likely to experience serendipitous opportunities than those who are outside the network.

The liability role of social capital

The liability role refers to the trigger for change that is caused by the time and costs required to manage and maintain social capital and inadequate partnerships that drain the firm's resources. The current social capital literature tends to focus on the advantages of social capital while neglecting its risks. Some exceptions are, for example, Nahapiet and Ghoshal (1998, p. 245), who state that social capital is not a "universally beneficial resource." They maintain that a close network can constrain the group's access to new information and new practices, which can undermine its performance. Moreover, some group norms may discourage collaboration and sharing with others, and be resistant to change. Uzzi (1997) emphasizes the danger of overembeddedness, which he considers a liability because it can exclude the inflow of new information into the network. The investment in social capital may be an inefficient use of resources, as maintaining the relationships might be too costly and the risks might outweigh the benefits. Certainly, the unexpected loss of an important network member can change social capital from an asset into a liability. For example, a firm might become finely tuned at working with a particular supplier, but should this supplier decide to retire, the relationship that initially benefited the firm could become a risky one.

Since the internal accumulation of market knowledge has an important effect on the pace of internationalization, information obtained through social capital may also facilitate a more rapid change of firm modes (Pedersen and Petersen, 1998). Social capital may also reduce a firm's costs of switching between modes. For example, the related costs and risks of establishing or shutting down subsidiaries may be lessened if relationships with reliable partner firms already exist. Many mode change opportunities are triggered serendipitously because social capital can be an important cause for this change. By developing and maintaining relationships, entrepreneurs increase the likelihood of encountering such triggers for change.

The benefits from new relationships are not endless. Agndal et al. (2008) explain that this could be due to an inverted-U curvilinear association between the number of relationships and the efficiency of social capital. As the firm creates more new relationships in more diverse foreign markets in later phases of its internationalization, it may experience information overload whereby maintaining relationships becomes expensive. Consequently, SMEs have to be efficient in building and maintaining relationships that augment their social capital. For example, firms could use social capital effectively to enter several foreign markets simultaneously through a single relationship.

Future research directions

An extended network view

One strategic issue for an entrepreneurial firm is to develop relationships with actors in the network, and as highlighted in this chapter it is essential to be an insider in a relevant business network. Firms are, however, often involved in relationships with non-business actors, such as political actors and actors in the civil society, and in the last decade, these relationships have attained increasing interest. As pointed out by Welch and Wilkinson (2004), the first generation of studies on inter-firm relationships focused on the dyadic relationship between a buyer and a seller, and the second generation focused on business/industrial networks consisting of "systems of interconnected exchange relationships among business actors" (p. 216). By relating to Hadjikhani and Sharma (1999, p. 245) Welch and Wilkinson stress that the focus on inter-firm relationships is too limited, since "business behaviour is explained only by reference to business actors." In order to gain a more realistic picture of a firm's business realities, they introduce a third generation involving a wider set of relationships and focus in particular on the political embeddedness of business networks.

In addition to including relationships with political actors, relationships with other actors in society are currently gaining more interest amongst international business scholars. For instance, Ritvala and Salmi (2011) stress the importance of including non-government organizations (NGOs) in the third generation relationship research. Furthermore, the attention on business activities in emerging markets with less stable institutions calls for a deeper understanding of how firms interact with these non-business actors, for example in order to acquire knowledge and legitimacy.

The above discussion is consistent with Hadjikhani et al. (2008), who describe how multinational corporations (MNCs) are involved in a network of both business and non-business actors (see also Hadjikhani and Ghauri, 2001). These actors are interdependent and the parties involved can all benefit from the interaction. As Hadjikhani et al. (2008, p. 914) state:

> firms depend on the socio-political units because these units, by their legitimate position in the society, can support firms or act against them. At the same time, socio-political units

> depend on MNCs because their investments create jobs that affect the economy as a whole. That, in turn, affects groups like the media and the public at large, on which the social and political actors depend.

Furthermore, they point out that firms undertake strategic actions in order to achieve specific support from their socio-political counterparts. Based on the concepts of commitment and trust, the authors describe how firms behave proactively in the socio-political environment in order to achieve legitimacy. When it comes to relationships with NGOs, it can also be noted that there has been a shift from an earlier more antagonistic view to a more interactive and supportive relationship. This can be related to the present challenges of alleviating global poverty and environmental concerns, which imply that actors from all parts of society need to collaborate.

Internationalizing entrepreneurial firms from emerging and transition economies

The up-and-coming stream of literature on emerging and transition economies now includes the role of networks in building the institutional environment in such economies. This provides opportunity for future researchers to study NGOs and political actors in these economies. Several examples are available of studies on networks and international entrepreneurial firms from emerging economies. First, Li (2013) examines the role of institutional transitions and market opportunities for internationalizing entrepreneurial firms, and how they use their networks. Second, Manolova (2013) studies Czech entrepreneurs and how they use their financial networks to secure the necessary resources for internationalization. Third, Manolova et al. (2010) examine the role of personal and inter-firm networks for new venture internationalization in a transition economy. Fourth, Danis et al. (2011) question whether social networks are more important for international entrepreneurs from emerging than developed economies. Fifth, Shirokova and McDougall-Covin (2012) study the role of networks in Russian internationalizing firms, and find that they play a lesser role than discussed in the literature. Indeed these studies provide the platform for future researchers to build on and to bridge the divide between these different streams of literature from developed and emerging countries. Furthermore, future researchers could identify the idiosyncrasies within emerging and transition economies instead of lumping them into one category.

Social media and network formation

As international entrepreneurs are making huge strides in using social media to build and maintain their networks to reduce uncertainty and explore new opportunities in foreign markets, this needs to be explored further. Furthermore, the technology for social media is changing dramatically, so there is considerable opportunity for new research directions in this area. Social media provides mechanisms for researchers to monitor and analyze networks in real time while international entrepreneurs develop them on the web. It provides opportunities for new methods of doing network research and for scholars to understand network development more than they have ever done before.

Conclusion

This chapter integrates the international business and international entrepreneurship literature to gain deep insight into the internationalization process of entrepreneurial firms. The theoretical framework that is used assumes that the internationalization process of these firms takes place in a network setting. To succeed internationally, a firm needs to position itself inside the network in the relevant foreign market. An internationalizing firm usually develops opportunities in foreign markets through its partners in the network. A business network is composed of a variety of relationships between the various actors in the network, such as customers, suppliers and competitors. The chapter presents new opportunities for future researchers to extend the types of actors in this network. Social media provides new mechanisms for firms to create and maintain networks in their domestic market, as well as worldwide. While the extant literature focuses on strong and weak ties as polar opposites, this chapter introduces the equally strong as weak tie which could be explored further by future researchers. The resources that entrepreneurs or firms acquire from their relationships and networks are referred to as social capital, and this can provide opportunities for firms to internationalize as well as to change their strategy. Future researchers could provide deeper insight into the dynamics of social capital.

References

Agndal, H. and Chetty, S. 2007. The impact of relationships on changes in internationalisation strategies of SMEs. *European Journal of Marketing*, Vol. 41, No. 11/12, 1449–1474.

Agndal, H., Chetty, S. and Wilson, H. 2008. Social capital dynamics and foreign market entry. *International Business Review*, Vol. 17, No. 6, 663–675.

Aldrich, H. and Auster, E. R. 1986. Even dwarfs started small: liabilities of age and size and their strategic implications. *Research in Organizational Behavior*, Vol. 8, 165–198.

Aldrich, H. and Zimmer, C. 1986. Entrepreneurship through social networks. University of Illinois at Urbana-Champaign's Academy for Entrepreneurial Leadership Historical Research Reference in Entrepreneurship.

Anderson, J. C., Håkansson, H. and Johanson, J. 1994. Dyadic business relationships within a business network context. *Journal of Marketing*, Vol. 58, No. 4, 1–15.

Birley, S. J. 1985. The role of networks in the entrepreneurial process. *Journal of Business Venturing*, Vol. 1, No. 1, 107–117.

Blomstermo, A. and Sharma, D. D. 2002. Born globals: a study of learning in networks. 28th EIBA conference, Athens, Greece.

Bourdieu, P. 1986. The forms of capital. In J. G. Richardson (ed.), *Handbook of Theory and Research for the Sociology of Education*. New York, Greenwood, 241–258.

Boyd, D. M. and Ellison, N. B. 2007. Social network sites: Definition, history, and scholarship. *Journal of Computer-Mediated Communication*, Vol. 13, No. 1, 210–230.

Bruneel, J., Yli-Renko, H. and Clarysse, B. 2010. Learning from experience and learning from others: how congenital and interorganizational learning substitute for experiential learning in young firm internationalization. *Strategic Entrepreneurship Journal*, Vol. 4, No. 2, 164–182.

Chandra, Y. Styles, C. and Wilkinson, I. 2009. The recognition of first time international entrepreneurial opportunities: evidence from firms in knowledge-based industries. *International Marketing Review*, Vol. 26, No. 1, 30–61.

Chetty, S. and Agndal, H. 2007. Social capital and its influence on changes in internationalization mode among small and medium-sized enterprises. *Journal of International Marketing*, Vol. 15, No. 1, 1–29.

Chetty, S. and Blankenburg Holm, D. 2000. Internationalisation of small to medium-sized manufacturing firms: a network approach. *International Business Review*, Vol. 9, No. 8, 77–95.

Chetty, S. and Campbell-Hunt, C. 2004. A strategic approach to internationalization: a traditional versus a "born-global" approach. *Journal of International Marketing*, Vol. 12, No. 1, 57–81.

Chetty, S. and Patterson, A. 2002. Developing internationalization capability through industry groups: the experience of a telecommunications joint action group. *Journal of Strategic Marketing*, Vol. 10, No. 1, 69–89.

Chetty, S. and Wilson, H. 2003. Collaborating with competitors to acquire resources. *International Business Review*, Vol. 12, No. 1, 61–81.

Coleman, J. S. 1988. Social capital in the creation of human capital. *American Journal of Sociology*, Vol. 94, No. S1, S95–S120.

Coviello N. E. 2006. Network dynamics of international new ventures. *Journal of International Business Studies*, Vol. 37, 713–731.

Coviello, N. E. and Munro, H. 1995. Growing the entrepreneurial firm: networking for international market development. *European Journal of Marketing*, Vol. 29, No. 7, 49–61.
Coviello N. E. and Munro, H. 1997. Network relationships and the internationalization process of small software firms. *International Business Review*, Vol. 6, No. 4, 361–386.
Cyert, R. M. and March, J. G. 1963. *A Behavioral Theory of the Firm*. Englewood Cliffs, Prentice-Hall.
Danis, W., De Clercq, D. and Petricevic, O. 2011. Are social networks more important for new business activity in emerging than developed economies? An empirical extension. *International Business Review*, Vol. 20, No. 4, 394–408.
Elfring, T. and Hulsink, W. 2003, Networks in entrepreneurship: the case of high-technology firms. *Small Business Economics*, Vol. 21, No. 4, 409–422.
Ellis, P. 2000. Social ties and foreign market entry. *Journal of International Business Studies*, Vol. 31, No. 3, 443–469.
Ellis, P. 2011. Social ties and international entrepreneurship: opportunities and constraints affecting firm internationalization. *Journal of International Business Studies*, 42, 99–127.
Fernhaber, S. A. and Li, D. 2013. International exposure through network relationships: implications for new venture internationalization. *Journal of Business Venturing*, Vol. 28, No. 2, 316–334.
Fernhaber, S. A., McDougall-Covin, P. P. and Shepherd, D. A. 2009. International entrepreneurship: leveraging internal and external knowledge sources. *Strategic Entrepreneurship Journal*, Vol. 3, No. 4, 297–320.
Grabher, G. 1993. The weakness of strong ties: the lock-in of regional development in the Ruhr area. In G. Grabher (ed.), *The Embedded Firm: On Socioeconomics of Industrial Networks*. London: Routledge; 255–277.
Granovetter, M. S. 1973. The strength of weak ties. *American Journal of Sociology*, Vol. 78, No. 6, 1360–1380.
Hadjikhani, A. and Ghauri, P. N. 2001. The internationalization of the firm and political environment in the European Union. *Journal of Business Research*, Vol. 52, No. 3, 263–275.
Hadjikhani, A., Lee, J.-W. and Ghauri, P. N. 2008. Network view of MNCs' socio-political behavior. *Journal of Business Research*, Vol. 61, No. 9, 912–924.
Hadjikhani, A. and Sharma, D. 1999. A view on political and business actors. In Ghauri, P. (ed.), *Advances in International Marketing*, Vol. 9, 243–257.
Håkansson, H. (ed.) 1982. *International Marketing and Purchasing of Industrial Goods: An Interaction Approach*. Cheltenham: Wiley.
Hite, J. M. and Hesterly, W. S. 2001. The evolution of firm networks: from emergence to early growth of the firm. *Strategic Management Journal*, Vol. 22, No. 3, 275–286.
Jack, S. L. 2005. The role, use and activation of strong and weak network ties: a qualitative analysis. *Journal of Management Studies*, Vol. 42, No. 6, 1233–1259.
Johanson, J. and Mattsson, L.-G. 1988. Internationalization in industrial systems: a network approach. In Hood, N. and Vahlne, J.-E. (eds) *Strategies in Global Competition*. New York, NY: Croom Helm.
Johanson, J. and Vahlne, J.-E. 1977. The internationalization process of the firm: a model of knowledge development and increasing foreign market commitments. *Journal of International Business Studies*, Vol. 8, No. 1, 23–32.
Johanson, J. and Vahlne, J.-E. 2006. Commitment and opportunity development in the internationalization process: a note on the Uppsala internationalization process model. *Management International Review*, Vol. 46, No. 2, 165–178.
Johanson, J. and Vahlne, J.-E. 2009. The Uppsala internationalization process model revisited: from liability of foreignness to liability of outsidership. *Journal of International Business Studies*, Vol. 40, No. 9, 1411–1431.
Jones, M. V. Coviello, N. and Tang, Y. K. 2011. International entrepreneurship research (1989–2009): a domain ontology and thematic analysis. *Journal of Business Venturing*, Vol. 26, No. 6, 632–659.
Keupp, M. M. and Gassmann, O. 2009. The past and the future of international entrepreneurship: a review and suggestions for developing the field. *Journal of Management*, Vol. 35, No. 3, 600–633.
Knight, G. A. and Cavusgil, S. T. (2004). Innovation, organizational capabilities, and the born-global firm. *Journal of International Business Studies*, Vol. 35, No. 2, 124–141.
Krackhardt, D., 1992. The strength of strong ties: the importance of philos in organizations. In N. Nohria and R. G. Eccles (eds), *Networks and Organizations: Structure, Form, and Action*. Boston: Harvard Business School Press, 216–239.
Lewis, K., Kaufman, J., Gonzalez, M., Wimmer, A. and Christakis, N. 2008. Tastes, ties, and time: a new social network dataset using facebook.com. *Social Networks*, Vol. 30, No. 4, 330–342.

Li, J. 2013. The internationalization of entrepreneurial firms from emerging economies: the roles of institutional transitions and market opportunities. *Journal of International Entrepreneurship*, Vol. 11, No. 2, 158–171.

Madsen, T. K. and Servais, P. 1997. The internationalization of born globals: an evolutionary process. *International Business Review*, Vol. 6, No. 6, 561–583.

Manolova, T. S. 2013. Friends with money? Owner's financial network and new venture internationalization in a transition economy. *International Small Business Journal*, doi: 10.1177/0266242613482482, 1–23

Manolova, T. S., Manev, I. M. and Gyoshev, B. S. 2010. In good company: the role of personal and inter-firm networks for new-venture internationalization in a transition economy. *Journal of World Business*, Vol. 45, No. 3, 257–265.

McDougall, P., Shane, S. and Oviatt, B. M. 1994. Explaining the formation of international new ventures: the limits of theories from international business research. *Journal of Business Venturing*, Vol. 9, No. 6, 469–487.

McNaughton, R. B. and Bell, J. D. 1999. Brokering networks of small firms to generate social capital for growth and internationalization. *Research in Global Strategic Management*, No. 7, 63–82.

Milanov, H. and Fernhaber, S. A. 2014. When do domestic alliances help ventures abroad? Direct and moderating effects from a learning perspective. *Journal of Business Venturing*, Vol. 29, No. 3, 377–391.

Nahapiet, J. and Ghoshal, S. 1998. Social capital, intellectual capital, and the organizational advantage. *The Academy of Management Review*, Vol. 23, No. 2, 242–266.

Ojala, A. 2009. Internationalization of knowledge-intensive SMEs: the role of network relationships in the entry to a psychically distant market. *International Business Review*, Vol. 18, No. 1, 50–59.

Ostgaard, T. A. and Birley, S. 1994. Personal networks and firm competitive strategy: a strategic or coincidental match? *Journal of Business Venturing*, Vol. 9, No. 4, 281–305.

Oviatt, B. M. and McDougall, P. P. 1994. Toward a theory of international new ventures. *Journal of International Business Studies*, Vol. 25, No. 1, 45–64.

Pedersen, T. and Petersen, B. 1998. Explaining gradually increasing resource commitment to a foreign market. *International Business Review*, Vol. 7, No. 7, 483–501.

Prashantham, S. and Dhanaraj, C. 2010. The dynamic influence of social capital on the international growth of new ventures. *Journal of Management Studies*, Vol. 47, No. 6, 967–994.

Prashantham, S. and Young, S. 2011. Post-entry speed of international new ventures. *Entrepreneurship Theory & Practice*, Vol. 35, No. 2, 275–292.

Ramachandran, K. and Ramnarayan, S. 1993. Entrepreneurial orientation and networking: some Indian evidence. *Journal of Business Venturing*, Vol. 8, No. 6, 513–524.

Ritvala, T. and Salmi, A. 2011. Network mobilizers and target firms: the case of saving the Baltic Sea. *Industrial Marketing Management*, Vol. 40, No. 6, 887–898.

Sapienza, H. J., Autio, E., George, G. and Zahra, S. A. 2006. A capabilities perspective on the effects of early internationalization on firm survival and growth. *The Academy of Management Review*, Vol. 31, No. 4, 914–933.

Sharma D. D. and Blomstermo, A. 2003. The internationalization process of born globals: a network view. *International Business Review*, Vol. 12, No. 6, 739–753.

Shirokova, G. and McDougall-Covin, P. 2012. The role of social networks and institutions in the internationalization of Russian entrepreneurial firms: do they matter? *Journal of International Entrepreneurship*, Vol. 10, No. 3, 177–199.

Sigfusson, T. and Chetty, S. 2013. Building international entrepreneurial virtual networks in cyberspace. *Journal of World Business*, Vol. 48, No. 2, 260–270.

Singh, R. P. 2000. *Entrepreneurial Opportunity Recognition through Social Networks*. New York: Garland Publishing, Inc.

Slotte-Kock, S. and Coviello, N. E. 2010. Entrepreneurship research on network processes: a review and ways forward. *Entrepreneurship Theory & Practice*, Vol. 34, 31–57.

Söderqvist, A. and Chetty, S. 2013. Strength of ties involved in international new ventures, *European Business Review*, Vol. 25, No. 6, 536–552.

Uzzi, B. 1997. Social structure and competition in interfirm networks: the paradox of embeddedness. *Administrative Science Quarterly*, Vol. 42, No. 1, 35–67.

Welch, C. and Wilkinson, I. 2004. The political embeddedness of international business networks. *International Marketing Review*, Vol. 21, No. 2, 216–231.

Wilson, H. I. M. and Appiah-Kubi, K. 2002. Resource leveraging via networks by high-technology entrepreneurial firms. *Journal of High Technology Management Research*, Vol. 13, No. 1, 45–62.

Yli-Renko, H., Autio, E. and Tontti, V. 2002. Social capital, knowledge, and the international growth of technology-based new firms. *International Business Review*, Vol. 11, No. 3, 279–304.
Yu, J., Gilbert, B. A., and Oviatt, B. M. 2011. Effects of alliances, time, and network cohesion on the initiation of foreign sales by new ventures. *Strategic Management Journal*, Vol. 32, No. 4, 424–446.
Zain, M. and Ng, S. I. 2006. The impact of network relationships on SMEs' internationalization process. *Thunderbird International Business Review*, Vol. 48, No. 2, 183–205.
Zhou, L., Wu, W. and Luo, X. 2007. Internationalization and the performance of born-global SMEs: the mediating role of social networks. *Journal of International Business Studies*, Vol. 38, No. 4, 673–690.

8

Is there more to learn?

Knowledge and learning in new venture internationalization research

Harry J. Sapienza, Dirk De Clercq and Liman Zhao

Introduction

Internationalization has been viewed as an important strategy for the sustainable growth of new and young ventures.[1] Indeed, international entrepreneurship emanated out of the dual issues of whether early internationalization is feasible and, if it is feasible, whether it is advisable. Theories prior to the mid-1990s offered only a limited ability to explain why and how such ventures successfully operate across national borders from their inception (McDougall et al., 1994; Oviatt and McDougall, 1994). Oviatt and McDougall (1994) revolutionized thinking about the initiation of the internationalization process by challenging the widely accepted stage-based perspective that conceived of the internationalization process as commencing later in development and proceeding incrementally (Johanson and Vahlne, 1990, 1977; Eriksson et al., 1997). McDougall and colleagues coined the term "international new ventures" to recognize the phenomenon of firms rapidly internationalizing early in their life cycle (McDougall and Oviatt, 2000; McDougall et al., 1994; Oviatt and McDougall, 1994). They observed that many ventures spread internationally early and dramatically, and often successfully (McDougall and Oviatt, 1996).

These ideas paved the way for the field of international entrepreneurship (IE), defined as the "discovery, enactment, evaluation, and exploitation of opportunities across national borders to create future goods and services" (Oviatt and McDougall, 2005). A common thread in this literature is the role of learning and knowledge (De Clercq et al., 2012). While organizational knowledge had played a central role in original stage-based models (Eriksson et al., 1997; Johanson and Vahlne, 1990, 1977), Oviatt and McDougall (1994) pointed to ways in which pre-existing knowledge might enhance rapid and early internationalization.

Thus, in both stage-based and international new venture approaches, knowledge drives received wisdom on internationalization, but it does so in significantly different ways (Prashantham, 2005; Knight and Cavusgil, 2004). The stage-based perspective relies on the behavioral theory of the firm (Cyert and March, 1963) to argue that a lack of organizational foreign knowledge results in organizational uncertainty that impedes early international entry and expansion (Johanson and Vahlne, 1990). The international new venture perspective emphasizes the role of individual knowledge (Oviatt and McDougall, 1994) to argue that ventures may overcome this uncertainty by relying on the experiences, capabilities, and aspirations of the key entrepreneur. In short, the past experiences of founders and other key managers can substitute for organizational deficiencies. Individuals' foreign experience and knowledge thus can help the venture "leapfrog" the incremental processes suggested by the stage-based perspective (Oviatt and McDougall, 2005).

The increasing popularity of this international new venture perspective informed a rich body of literature on the role of knowledge and learning in the internationalization of young ventures. The objective of our chapter is: (1) to highlight aspects of this literature, summarizing salient themes, and (2) to provide guidelines for future research. Before we do so, we provide a brief overview of the general literature on knowledge and learning.

Knowledge and learning in management research

The knowledge-based view (KBV) emphasizes the role of knowledge creation, transfer, and application for explaining firm existence (Grant, 1996; Spender, 1996). It argues that heterogeneity in knowledge is a major explanatory factor for the presence of performance differences across firms. Knowledge is different from information: while information represents the flow of messages or factual statements, knowledge is created as a result of the flow of information (Nonaka, 1994). Further, organizational learning is "the process of assimilating new knowledge into the organization's knowledge base" (Autio et al., 2000). Firm growth, for example, may be the result of the ability to create new knowledge and replicate it to expand the firm's market reach.

Knowledge is a key firm-level resource for entry into new domains (Grant, 1996), such as the entry into new foreign markets by multinational corporations (Kogut and Zander, 1993). According to the KBV, the level of knowledge transfer within firms in particular is important for explaining how firms can extend their existing activity set (Grant, 1996; Szulanski, 1996). Thus, there is a direct connection between the knowledge sharing that takes place within the firm and where the firm allocates its activities. Knowledge transfer brings together complementary knowledge and thus enriches the firm's knowledge base, enhancing its ability to create new knowledge needed to recognize and exploit growth opportunities (Floyd and Lane, 2000; Cohen and Levinthal, 1990). Thus, when firms promote knowledge sharing within their ranks, they are better equipped to act on such opportunities (Floyd and Lane, 2000). Firms can also more *confidently* act on new opportunities when they compare and contrast different decision alternatives in parallel (Eisenhardt, 1989). The breadth of decision alternatives afforded by internal knowledge transfer makes firms more efficient in comparing the relative strengths and weaknesses of different growth pathways, increasing confidence that current knowledge can be effectively applied to the selected alternative (Dimov, 2010). When knowledge transfer is low in intensity, firms likely see few alternatives to their current activities and are unlikely to recognize and exploit new opportunities.

Knowledge can also be accessed externally through inter-firm relationships (Ahuja, 2000; Cohen and Levinthal, 1990). Collaboration with external parties enables access to knowledge through embeddedness in networks (Dyer and Singh, 1998). External knowledge may be scarcer and more difficult to access than internal knowledge (Menon and Pfeffer, 2003). Both internal and external knowledge are important in the foreign operations of young international ventures (De Clercq et al., 2012).

Exploitation and exploration refer to differences in the nature of new knowledge pursued. Exploitation is the incremental updating of existing skills and capabilities and ensures coherence of activities across time (March, 1991). It depends upon a firm's ability to refine its current competencies and resources, and it improves operational efficiency (Ghemawat and Ricart Costa, 1993). Thus, exploitation reflects the firm's ability to undertake its current activities efficiently rather than to invest in new activities that may require the deconstruction of established procedures and rules (Porter, 1996). When referring to knowledge closely related to existing knowledge, exploitation is akin to the firm's absorptive capacity: the extent to which the firm can access, assimilate, transform, and apply new (related) knowledge (Zahra and George, 2002).

In contrast, exploration is the firm's ability to reconfigure its activity set, with a focus on experimentation with radically new activities (March, 1991). Exploration involves challenging existing ideas and markets (Kyriakopoulos and Moorman, 2004). Exploration can reduce the build-up of dysfunctional rigidities (Leonard-Barton, 1992) and reduce the chance of falling into a competency trap when external changes erode the value of the firm's current activities (Teece et al., 1997). Yet neither exploitation nor exploration alone is healthy. Exploitation by itself may tie firms to the past and existing competencies, rendering them defenseless against external changes; exploration on its own leaves the organization unable to replenish its resources or create a stable identity (Levinthal and March, 1993). Thus, to remain competitive, firms may need to be "ambidextrous" and engage in both exploitation and exploration (Gibson and Birkinshaw, 2004).

Knowledge and learning in new venture internationalization research

In the following subsections we highlight several issues that are relevant to the role of knowledge and learning in early internationalization. First, we discuss the role of the *source* of knowledge (internal and external) in the internationalization of new ventures. Second, we attend to the *focus* of ventures' international learning efforts (knowledge exploitation and exploration), as well as to the role of absorptive capacity. Third, we consider *where* the internationalization takes place, addressing the issues of which and how many countries are entered. Fourth, we elaborate on *how* ventures enter foreign markets, and particularly the foreign entry mode used. Finally, we discuss *when* the first internationalization takes place and how the timing may be important in terms of generating learning advantages in foreign markets.

Source of knowledge

Internal knowledge

Research on new venture internationalization points to the critical role of the human capital in ventures' entrepreneurial teams, including knowledge and experiences developed through prior firms (McDougall et al., 1994). Personal international experiences might predispose entrepreneurs to international endeavors, and such prior experience implies relevant managerial skills that may help them identify and exploit international opportunities. Reuber and Fischer (1997) found that ventures that have a management team with greater international experience feature a higher level of internationalization, in terms of their international sales relative to total sales, the geographic scope of their international sales, and their employees' engagement in foreign activities. Similarly, ventures that have more executives with international work or educational experience in their ranks engage in a greater number of primary value chain activities outside of the home country (Bloodgood et al., 1996). Loane et al., (2007) demonstrated that team-based international new ventures, compared with their sole-entrepreneur counterparts, have a greater knowledge base to draw from and accordingly demonstrate a faster pace of internationalization, broader foreign market reach, and higher export ratios.

Thus, the knowledge held by the entrepreneurial team may allow the venture to identify and exploit foreign opportunities unseen by others, which can inform its decision to internationalize early as a possible path to international growth and success (Jones and Coviello, 2005). The venture's foreign market knowledge acquisition can also be enhanced by adding new members to the venture's management team (Loane et al., 2007), a practice known as grafting (Huber, 1991). Michailova and Wilson (2008) showed that internal management practices, such as personal mentoring schemes, can leverage the foreign knowledge that grafted managers bring to the venture.

External knowledge

While internal knowledge embedded in the venture's management team is important, the knowledge sourced from the outside is also of great significance (Fernhaber et al., 2009). Previous research discusses the role of ventures' social capital or embeddedness in social networks (e.g. Zhou et al., 2007; Coviello, 2006). Such networks help new ventures enter international markets, learn new capabilities, gain access to critical foreign resources and knowledge (Keupp and Gassman, 2009; Ellis, 2000), and ultimately enhance international growth (Yli-Renko et al., 2002). Social capital is particularly important for new international ventures because of their resource constraints and need for help in selecting appropriate foreign markets (Zhou et al., 2007; Coviello and Munro, 1997, 1995). While research typically uses a static approach to the roles of networks for foreign market learning, some have investigated dynamic aspects of networks too, such as how networks are developed or experience decay (Prashantham and Dhanaraj, 2010), how changes in network structures enhance the venture's social capital (Coviello, 2006), and how existing networks are leveraged to develop new networks (Loane and Bell, 2006).

Social networks also pose challenges. Some young ventures lack expertise to identify good foreign partners (Wright et al., 2007), and some foreign partners might seek to control the venture or "steal" intellectual property (Wright et al., 2007). A strong asymmetry of interdependence, whereby international ventures depend too much on resources controlled by their foreign partners (O'Farrell et al., 1998), may hamper the realization of the benefits of interdependence. Researchers have also considered the role of domestic networks in the performance outcomes of early internationalization. For example, recent research notes the contribution of local network relationships in the success of ventures' international endeavors (Boethe, 2013; Milanov and Fernhaber, 2013; Zhou et al., 2007). Yet Autio et al., (2000) argued that such domestic social capital could impede or constrain international success, limiting the relational flexibility among ventures that internationalize later in their life time.

Internal and external knowledge combined

Recent research also has started to examine the interaction between internal and external sources of foreign knowledge. For example, Fernhaber et al. (2009) investigated the interplay between the international experience held by a venture's top management team and three external sources of foreign knowledge: alliance partners, venture capital firms, and other firms in close proximity to the focal venture. They found that to the extent that a top management team lacks international knowledge, access to external foreign knowledge is more instrumental to increasing the venture's level of internationalization. Bruneel et al., (2010) also demonstrated that the instrumentality of both internal and external knowledge for increasing the level of internationalization diminishes when the venture has developed extensive experiential knowledge through its foreign activities.

Focus of international learning effort

Knowledge exploitation and exploration

Previous research on new venture internationalization has embraced the aforementioned distinction between knowledge exploitation and exploration, particularly with respect to how ventures allocate their learning efforts when operating in foreign markets. While exploitation of nearby knowledge allows international ventures to deeply develop pre-existing capacities, the exploration of new knowledge encompasses the searching for more distant or lesser known territories. De Clercq et al. (2005) showed that ventures' combined efforts to exploit current foreign knowledge and develop new foreign knowledge increased their expectations of future internationalization. Previous research had typically assumed that knowledge exploitation and exploration operate independently, but it may also be possible that one informs the other. For example, Kuemmerle (2002) examined the sequence between a venture's "home base-augmenting (HBA) activities," which aim at expanding its existing stock of knowledge (mainly through research and development), and its "home base-exploiting (HBE) activities," which attempt to leverage existing firm-specific knowledge (mainly through manufacturing and sales). He found that born-global firms tend to focus on HBA activities first—as these activities can increase profits in the home country—before turning to HBE activities, which are more resource-intensive and therefore benefit from the revenues generated in the home country.

New international ventures may engage in experiential learning through their foreign operations. Huber (1991) defines experiential learning as the acquisition of knowledge through direct experience. This type of learning forms the cornerstone of Johanson and Vahlne's (1990) stage-based models, which postulate that foreign experiential learning informs the incremental nature of the internationalization process. Although such incrementalism seems counter to the premise of early and accelerated internationalization, as advanced by the new venture internalization literature, foreign experiential learning can be useful for new ventures. The greater the time elapsed since first foreign market entry, the more insight young ventures might have gained into which types of foreign market knowledge would be most beneficial (Bruneel et al., 2010).

Knowledge assimilation and absorptive capacity

Previous international entrepreneurship research also emphasizes the importance of ventures' absorptive capacity or the ability to assimilate foreign knowledge into the capacity to grow and prosper (Zahra et al., 2000). Venture performance is driven by the ability not only to exploit nearby knowledge and develop knowledge in new domains but also to integrate knowledge within the venture's boundaries and convert it into value-creating activities (Cohen and Levinthal, 1990). Because "prior knowledge permits the assimilation and exploitation of new knowledge" (Nonaka, 1994), the venture's ability to value, process, integrate, and apply new knowledge to commercial ends relates closely to its ability to link the new knowledge to its existing knowledge base (Cohen and Levinthal, 1990). In line with this argument, Lane et al. (2001) found that international joint ventures with higher absorptive capacity learned more from their foreign parents; their increased ability to understand the value of new knowledge and assimilate it in their current operations was related to higher performance.

Thus, it had been acknowledged that the positive performance outcomes of early internationalization do not emerge automatically. Sapienza et al. (2006) maintained that early internationalization can have negative implications for venture survival. They argued that a lack of resources or reputation can make young international ventures vulnerable to strategic missteps or unexpected downturns in foreign markets, exacerbated by the challenge they face to develop new routines and relationships concurrently in home and foreign markets. Similarly, Carr et al. (2010) argued that younger firms are less likely to survive than older firms after their initial foreign market entry. The relationship between a venture's international activities and performance depends on the extent to which it has the organizational capability to absorb new knowledge gained from such activities. Likewise, Zhou et al. (2010) pointed to the critical role of capabilities in converting an entrepreneurial posture into improved performance in foreign markets. Yet many young international ventures lack such capabilities.

While international entrepreneurship research often refers to the importance of such ability to integrate new foreign knowledge into the existing knowledge and skills set, the presence of knowledge integration is often assumed, not explicitly measured. An exception is Zahra et al. (2000), who demonstrated that the instrumentality of a venture's scope of international activities for its technological learning is greater in the presence of formal knowledge integration mechanisms, such as information-sharing sessions, formal reports that summarize learning effort, and face-to-face discussions by cross-functional teams. Similarly, Zahra and Hayton (2008) demonstrated that a firm's absorptive capacity positively moderates the relationship between international venturing and performance outcomes, such as profitability and revenue growth.

Where to internationalize

Knowledge and multi-country entry

An important facet of the internationalization decision is the number of countries to enter. Oviatt and McDougall's (1994) definition of international new ventures explicitly mentioned the possibility of multi-country entry, though the interplay between the number of countries entered and learning has not received much research attention. Multi-country entry increases the ability to shift resources across country borders, which makes it an effective tool to mitigate risk (Bartlett and Ghoshal, 1998). However, it also creates wider knowledge-related demands, which establish the subsequent possibility of cross-country knowledge spillovers and learning (Shrader et al., 2000).

Thus, multi-country entry might promote a venture's ability to create synergies and organize itself internally to cope with foreign uncertainty (Erikksson et al., 1997). Further, multi-country entry connects the venture with various critical constituencies, thereby increasing its access to a broad range of resources, skills, and technological innovations (Craig and Douglas, 1996; Ghoshal, 1987). Accordingly, because multi-country entry encourages knowledge spillovers and learning across country borders, it can enhance the richness of knowledge absorbed by the venture (Cohen and Levinthal, 1990) and enhance success in foreign markets.

Yet these positive effects of multi-country entry also require increased levels of coordination (Hitt et al., 1995). Knowledge accessed through exposure to multiple countries may be fragmented, which can make its effective use more cumbersome (Bartlett and Ghoshal, 1991), and managers may be limited in their ability to recognize how they might leverage this knowledge gained from different countries to improve venture performance (Simon, 1979). That is, exposure to multiple countries can increase the performance potential of early internationalization, but this positive effect may hold up only to a certain point, after which the multi-country presence creates an information overload, and the effectiveness of learning decreases (Hitt et al., 1997; Huber, 1991). Consistent with the foregoing, Barkema and Vermeulen (1998) found that though multi-country entry provides exposure to diverse experiences and encourages the development of new technological capabilities, these benefits start to diminish when firms go beyond their cognitive capacity to handle increased diversity.

Knowledge and cultural distance

In addition to the number of countries, the *nature* of the countries entered, in relation to the home country, also matters for ventures' international learning. In this regard, previous research has considered the relevance of "psychic distance" and the institutional and cultural differences that exist between the home country and foreign markets entered (Karra et al., 2008; Hofstede, 1991). The greater the difference between the home and target country's institutions or culture, the more challenging the internationalization task is (Shenkar, 2001). However, the extent to which a venture is exposed to a "distant" country can also have a beneficial influence on its establishment of an international competitive advantage (Ghoshal, 1987), because exposure to different cultures, though it increases entry difficulty, can promote learning (Kim, 1997).

Thus, opposing forces may determine the impact of cultural distance on the leveraging of knowledge in foreign markets (Zahra et al., 2000). On the one hand, greater psychic distance increases the complexity and coordination of foreign activities and thus reduces knowledge flows across country borders (Lyles and Salk, 1996). Psychic distance often creates conflict and misunderstanding and impedes cross-country technology transfers (Lyles and Salk, 1996), which may hamper the effective exploitation of knowledge. On the other hand, psychic distance might increase international success because it implies a greater exposure to different stocks of country-specific knowledge (Hitt et al., 1997). Exposure to a "distant" country can enhance the venture's current knowledge base by including new insights and assumptions that increase the potential to combine disparate sources of knowledge in creative ways (Zander and Kogut, 1995). In this regard, future research could draw upon Prashantham and Floyd's (2012) recent theorizing to examine how the psychic distance between home and foreign markets can differently influence the learning capability of international new ventures depending on the learning mode used and whether the learning is planned or unplanned.

How to internationalize

Internationalizing ventures can choose different foreign entry modes, ranging from exporting, importing, and licensing to more committed modes such as joint firms or foreign direct investment (Eriksson et al., 1997; Johanson and Vahlne, 1990). These entry modes vary in the extent to which they enable the venture to learn and integrate new foreign knowledge (Zahra et al., 2000). Low-commitment entry modes (e.g. exporting) typically require fewer interactions with foreign market players; high-commitment modes foster greater exposure to foreign knowledge and experiences (Kim, 1997), such that collaboration with joint firm partners, for example, provides insights into the ins and outs of local new product development and commercialization processes (Zahra et al., 2000).

High levels of commitment enable close observation of foreign companies' strategic moves, promote learning by doing, and facilitate understanding of how foreign market knowledge matches the current knowledge base (Zahra et al., 2000). To the extent that international ventures choose to adopt high-commitment entry modes, their ability to understand how they can apply new foreign knowledge increases (Afuah, 1998); this ability offsets the liabilities of low legitimacy and undeveloped operational routines (Aldrich, 1999). Further, high-commitment entry modes may increase the extent to which the ventures are successful in their foreign markets, because they enhance the intensity of foreign knowledge processing and lead to a quicker understanding of how such knowledge can be absorbed into the venture's existing knowledge base.

Yet the "appropriate" mode of entry may depend on the extent to which the venture's current resource base can be exploited in different foreign markets (Wright et al., 2007). On the one hand, if the venture's current resources are geographically mobile, low-commitment entry modes may allow leveraging knowledge efficiently across countries. On the other hand, if it is costly to distribute the resource base over a broad geographic span, a high-commitment entry mode in a limited number of countries may be better. The effectiveness of a particular entry mode also likely depends on specific, local demands; for example, some customer demands such as after-sales service are best met by high commitment modes (Burgel and Murray, 2000; Crick and Jones, 2000).

When to internationalize

Previous studies show that because ventures that enter foreign markets early in their lifetime are prone to develop an "international identity" (Autio et al., 2000; Boeker, 1989), they attend to understanding the specific conditions that mark a particular foreign market (Sapienza et al., 2003; Ocasio, 1997). This attention is one source of the relative learning advantages of newness (LAN) early internationalizers may have over their older counterparts. The LAN concept suggests that less embedded and fewer organizational routines among young international ventures prompt their relatively greater flexibility; this flexibility increases their learning potential in international markets. Autio et al. (2000), for example, posited that the earlier ventures internationalized, the more rapidly they would learn and, hence, grow. They offered cognitive, political, and relational causes for the existence of LAN. They suggested that, relative to older internationalizers, young internationalizers have few domestic-rooted routines to "unlearn," few relational obligations to meet, and little managerial inclination to protect domestic turf and spurn international opportunities (Autio et al., 2000).

Similarly, Sapienza et al. (2006) theorized that young ventures enjoy advantages over more established ventures, in cognitive and positional terms, when they pursue opportunities in new foreign markets. As ventures grow older, they may develop path-dependent common sense or "dominant logic" and establish long-term relationships with external parties; in turn, these factors decrease their flexibility for acquiring and assimilating new knowledge in foreign markets, relative to younger counterparts. These authors also offer an important structural argument for LAN, in which they suggest that managerial roles for early internationalizers tend to be undifferentiated, so information about international growth opportunities may be exchanged more easily across functions. In contrast, later internationalizers likely are marked by higher levels of functional specialization and thus reduced communication across functions (Sapienza et al., 2006).

Other research that seeks to explain the performance of young international ventures also draws on the LAN concept. Zhou et al. (2010) used the concept to argue that capabilities contribute to the international performance of entrepreneurial firms. Carr et al. (2010) found that younger international firms, with their flexibility and adaptive capability, enjoy higher post-internationalization short-term growth rates than their older counterparts.

Directions for future research

As a branch of international entrepreneurship research, knowledge-focused studies of new venture internationalization have served an essential role. They have begun to explore and explain how and why seemingly disadvantaged young ventures determine to move beyond their domestic borders, and they have explored some of the consequences of such decisions. In our judgment, four broad areas of study appear most ripe for continued advancement and insight:

(1) What can be learned at the individual leader level—as well as at the leader-firm interface—about the role of knowledge in IE?
(2) Given the apparent trade-offs between pre-existing knowledge versus operational flexibility, what can we learn about whether or when newness advantages trump prior knowledge advantages, or vice versa?
(3) What methods and measures might be employed to expand our understanding of the role of knowledge and learning in the internationalization of young ventures?
(4) How might tradeoffs in survival, growth, and profit goals affect strategy formation and internationalizing processes for young ventures?

These four themes do not exhaust the set of plausible and valuable topics for study within this domain, but we discuss these here as potentially useful avenues for future research.

Expand work on individual decision makers and multi-level phenomena

In young ventures, the leader has a much greater role in setting directions and purpose than is the case in established firms. Hence, understanding the knowledge and learning components of the CEOs in such ventures is especially critical to the strategic decision to initiate or to follow an internationalization strategy. Although previous literature pays some attention to the effects of individuals' prior international experience on internationalizing (cf. De Clercq et al., 2012), much more could be examined at the individual or cognitive level (Jones and Casulli, 2014). For example, empirical investigations of the cognitive processes that underlie individual learning in international markets would be useful in predicting both international strategic choice and outcomes. Work on the use of cognitive tools (Gentner and Markman, 1994) and pattern recognition (Grégoire et al., 2010; Williams, 2010), for example, might be especially useful to predict competitive action or inaction.

Given the premise that individual founders or CEOs are especially critical in the trajectories of young ventures, it might well prove fruitful to theorize and test ideas regarding the impact of changing CEOs or removing founders from the top management teams of such ventures (Wasserman, 2003). Some have challenged the conventional wisdom that replacing the founder-CEO is imperative, or even advisable, for the growth of a nascent or high potential venture (e.g. Forbes et al., 2010). In particular, the impact of change may be conditioned upon not only the knowledge, relationships, and networks of the outgoing leader but also by the near- and longer-term target countries the venture seeks to enter. Additional interesting issues abound within this setting, such as:

(1) How do founders or CEOs build their social capital to begin with?
(2) What is the critical social capital and knowledge embedded within the leader?
(3) How can this capital and knowledge be retained in the venture upon departure?

Another underexplored issue at the individual level is the interplay between knowledge, learning, and emotions. Oviatt and McDougall (1994) argued that international networks provide both resources and social context for entrepreneurs, alternately inspiring or constraining their aspirations and their capacities. In her dissertation, Yavuz (2011) noted an unexpected negative relationship between experience in multiple countries and initial survival and growth of young international ventures. She speculated that either overconfidence or social pressure might be behind immigrant entrepreneurs' venturing too widely or too soon in comparison to domestic-only entrepreneurs. As yet, however, these explanations remain under-studied speculation. Johanson and Vahlne (2009) have reformulated their internationalization process model to place inter-firm relationships at its core, placing it alongside knowledge as the mechanism or engine of international expansion; they now depict the process as "the interaction of partners who build knowledge together and come to trust each other as they commit themselves further to the relationship" (Johanson and Vahlne, 2009). Yet herein lies great potential for theory-building and study, as their model provides an initial, skeleton framework for further work. In particular, such research could extend work on entrepreneurial passion (Cardon et al., 2009), and the integration of knowledge-based and passion-based theories might prove especially useful and interesting.

Furthermore, IE research can benefit not only from recent developments in international business literature, but also from consideration of the primary role of individual entrepreneurs' skills and emotions in the drivers, processes, and outcomes of internationalization. Clearly, IE can inform future studies in international business research, which tends to devote less attention to micro-level learning processes (Prashantham and Floyd, 2012). The alignment and synergy between these two literatures is instrumental for ensuring consistency and enrichment across fields.

In short, we see a need to expand our understanding of the interplay between individual level and organization level phenomena. While we called at the outset of this subsection for greater penetration of studies at the individual level, the usefulness of such studies would be limited if no attempts were made to understand how these relate to the organization. Important questions include issues such as when and how are individuals' knowledge incorporated into the organization? When and how does critical knowledge embedded in routines and artifacts of the organization make its way into the thought processes of individuals? How might individual and organizational knowledge best be transformed to match the different challenges of entering very different new markets?

Deepen the study of learning advantages and knowledge disadvantages of newness

Several avenues of study regarding the paradox of advantages and disadvantages for internationalization of young organizations have already been discussed in some depth in De Clercq et al. (2012). The key points in that review include: (1) there have been discrepant theoretical (and empirical) conclusions regarding the efficacy of early internationalization; these have been attributed to conflicting views of the value of prior knowledge; (2) studies of LAN have yet to establish a consistent empirical grounding; and (3) studies have failed to look at the issues facing older small firms that are considering internationalizing for the first time. Of course, too little time has passed since that article to witness any advances on these issues, so we would have to conclude that all of these challenges remain potentially fruitful areas for further study.

In this regard, the paradox of absorptive capacity advantages of older and larger firms versus the flexibility advantages of younger and smaller ventures has been recognized by many scholars (De Clercq et al., 2012). Research has moved beyond the question of when to start the process (Sapienza et al., 2006; Autio et al., 2000) to more nuanced questions such as how quickly to proceed, once begun (Oviatt and McDougall, 2005). One observation we would like to add is that most of the follow-on studies dealing with the paradoxes of learning and knowledge advantages and disadvantages have tended to lump learning and knowledge together. We believe it may be advantageous to conceive of knowledge and learning as two separate but interrelated concepts—knowledge as stock and learning as flow of know-how. Hence, it may then be useful to conduct process studies which examine how the two influence one another and develop. When does a large stock of knowledge result in more effective flows of new knowledge acquisition? When does it impede learning? Is it possible for a venture to learn rapidly in multiple new countries? Can the fruits of such learning be effectively integrated into the existing knowledge base? What kinds of knowledge is lost or wasted during the internationalization process?

Innovate on measurement and methods

Studying the role of knowledge and learning in the internationalization process of young ventures presents a myriad of empirical challenges and barriers. This setting is particularly challenging because of the multiple cultures and languages that are often the topic of study, because of the lack of public data on many of the ventures being studied, because of the threat of survivor bias in panel studies, and because of the complexity and intangibility of many of the core constructs to be measured.

Take, for example, the issue of what it means to "internationalize." Suffice it to say that challenges exist in measuring both the degree of internationalization and the timing or pace of internationalization. In the past, a comprehensive set of dimensions has been used to measure a venture's level or degree of internationalization. Many studies use international sales as a percentage of total sales as the measure of "internationalization." Some have used international sales weighted by the psychic and geographic distance between the home and foreign market, and some have examined the percentage of employees who spend a significant amount of their time in foreign activities (e.g. Bruneel et al., 2010; De Clercq et al., 2005). Yet others have used the number of countries in which sales occur, or the number of value chain activities the company engages in outside its domestic borders (e.g. Bloodgood et al., 1996). Because degree of internationalization is inherently a multi-dimensional construct, some have preferred to create a composite measure that blends many of these measures together in a single measure. This solution offers greater construct coverage but less clarity on what precisely is being studied. Different industries, too, might require different measures to fairly represent the international "quality" of the firm. How, for example, should internet activity and sales be viewed? Researchers should remember to pick their preferred measure based on the question(s) they wish to answer and to be explicit about how these choices bound the inferences they draw.

De Clercq et al. (2012) pointed out that "learning advantages" have not been directly measured. Our observation, however, would be that researchers may not be able to do much better than to measure the outcomes of intangible or semi-tangible constructs as proxies for their existence. Knowledge and learning often defy direct observation or measurement (Huber, 1991). As with the issue of measuring degree and pace of internationalization, researchers wrestling with complex issues of perceived or real learning should make assumptions explicit and continually search for observable artifacts. We recommend the careful use of multiple sources and multiple measures to tackle the complexity of this phenomenon. Artifacts such as company records, press statements, correspondence and the like should be sought to validate and inform the interpretation of company actions and subjective responses to survey questions.

Researchers should aspire to innovate via field experiments, lab experiments, and event studies and whatever other approaches they deem useful. Following Van de Ven's (2007) concept of "engaged scholarship," we believe that the most insightful and revealing research will emerge only through researchers' deep immersion in the phenomenon and the full use of both subjective and objective methods for acquiring and assessing data. It is important for researchers to keep in mind that what we decide to measure and observe plays a large role in what we come to take as "received wisdom." Even the labeling of variables is important in this regard. For example, if we label sales growth, country expansion, survival, and profitability all as "performance," we run the risk of confounding very different cause–effect relationships and detracting from rather than adding to knowledge.

Examine multiple objectives simultaneously

The problem that different types of performance have often been given the same label certainly complicates drawing meaning from studies on new venture internationalization (De Clercq et al., 2012). This labeling issue is common in multiple subfields both within strategy and entrepreneurship literatures. However, perhaps a more important related issue is that ventures actually execute strategies for a variety of reasons and with a variety of objectives in mind (Sapienza et al., 2003). Some ventures internationalize to try to increase survival chances; some to grow rapidly enough to retain personnel; some to try to maximize upon profit opportunities; some to simply establish a foothold in another territory or to accomplish some social good; some for all or a combination of these reasons. Nevertheless, few studies examine more than one outcome of internationalizing (for an exception, see Carr et al., 2010).

We believe that there is an opportunity both in entrepreneurship and strategy literatures on internationalization to contribute to our theories and to the understanding of competitive phenomena by studying the different types of outcomes simultaneously. Such a suggestion, however, is made with the recognition that theoretical, methodological, and practical challenges will ensue—but we believe the potential insights and rewards will be worth the effort. When we acknowledge that, in reality, entrepreneurs and their ventures undertake major strategic initiatives with the hopes of accomplishing multiple purposes, studying how well they do on one particular outcome (whether or not it happens to be their primary goal) yields woefully incomplete understandings. Our understanding of the benefits, costs, and results of internationalizing would be enhanced by looking at several key outcomes at once.

Because an exceedingly large set of possible outcomes may be examined, we recommend that for now survival, growth, and profitability should be the target outcomes. Some of the challenges that face researchers who would like to look at either two or all three outcomes at once are varied. For example, theory would have to be developed to predict the simultaneous and sequential relationships among these dependent variables. Should pursuing growth hinder or help survival in the short run? What about in the long run? If there are tradeoffs, what would we expect these to be and why? Do some efforts have an effect on one outcome but little on the other? It would be interesting to see if long-term patterns emerge among these different variables, patterns that are similar across locales and industries. Do some patterns of internationalizing yield better growth results and others better profitability ones?

One related methodological challenge will be trying to account for and measure differences in the priorities of ventures across the goals. Not only is it difficult to accurately operationalize the strength of ventures' preference for one goal versus another, even comparing the meaning of the outcomes is challenging. What does it mean, for example, to be achieving an annual growth in sales at a mean of 6 percent while at the same time to be reducing the chances of survival by 2 percent every year? What are the prospects for reducing these trends? Can we discover "best mixes" of growth and profitability strategies that are related to the highest likelihood of survival? Do these mixes change over time? How can or should we account for variations in preferences for different outcomes? What theoretical explanations are most likely to be helpful? Canonical correlations and other infrequently used techniques for assessing multiple or simultaneous outcomes will also have to be employed.

Conclusion

IE research started out examining when early internationalization occurs and when it is an advisable strategy to follow. Clearly, empirical evidence has shown that it is certainly possible and even relatively common. Knowledge and learning perspectives have been increasingly central in this quest to understand the processes and outcomes of new ventures' foreign market entry. Yet there is fertile ground remaining to be covered as outlined in the prior sections. We suggest that future researchers can advance this area of study by focusing effort at the individual level and the individual–organization nexus, by disentangling the knowledge–learning advantages paradox, by innovating in measures and methods for studying the phenomenon, and by looking simultaneously at multiple objectives and their interplay. We hope that this chapter can serve as a basis for further addressing these issues.

Note

1 Alternatives of the term "new international venture" are "born global," "young international venture," and "early internationalizer," which we use interchangeably to refer to firms that internationalize early in their life time.

References

Afuah, A. (1998) *Innovation Management: Strategies, Implementation, and Profits*. New York: Oxford University Press.
Ahuja, G. (2000) 'The duality of collaboration: Inducements and opportunities in the formation of interfirm linkages', *Strategic Management Journal*, 21 (3), 317–343.
Aldrich, H. E. (1999) *Organization Evolving*. London: SAGE Publications.
Autio, E., Sapienza, H. J. and Almeida, J. G. (2000) 'Effects of age at entry, knowledge intensity, and imitability on international growth', *Academy of Management Journal*, 43 (5), 909–924.
Barkema, H. G. and Vermeulen, F. (1998) 'International expansion through start-up or acquisition: A learning perspective', *Academy of Management Journal*, 41 (1), 7–26.
Bartlett, C. and Ghoshal, S. (1991) 'Global strategic management: Impact on the new frontiers of strategy research', *Strategic Management Journal*, 12 (S1), 5–16.
Bartlett, C. A. and Ghoshal, S. (1998) *Managing across Borders: The Transnational Solution* 2nd edn. Boston: Harvard Business School Press.
Bloodgood, J. M., Sapienza, H. J. and Almeida, J. G. (1996) 'The internationalization of new high-potential US ventures: Antecedents and outcomes', *Entrepreneurship Theory and Practice*, 20 (4), 61–76.
Boeker, W. (1989) 'Strategic change: The effect of founding and history', *Academy of Management Journal*, 32 (3), 489–515.
Boethe, D. (2013) 'Collaborate at home to win abroad: How does access to local networks influence export behavior', *Journal of Small Business Management*, 51 (2), 167–182.
Bruneel, J., Yli-Renko, H. and Clarysse, B. (2010) 'Learning from experience and learning from others: How congenital and inter organizational learning substitute for experiential learning in young firm internationalization', *Strategic Entrepreneurship Journal*, 4 (2), 164–182.
Burgel, O. and Murray, G. C. (2000) 'The international market entry choices of start-up companies in high-technology industries', *Journal of International Marketing*, 8 (2), 33–62.
Cardon, M. S., Wincent, J., Singh, J. and Drnovsek, M. (2009) 'The nature and experience of entrepreneurial passion', *Academy of Management Review*, 34 (3), 511–532.
Carr, J. C., Haggard, K. S., Hmieleski, K. M. and Zahra, S. A. (2010) 'A study of the moderating effects of firm age at internationalization on firm survival and short-term growth', *Strategic Entrepreneurship Journal*, 4 (2), pp. 183–192.

Cohen, W. and Levinthal, D. (1990) 'Absorptive capacity: A new perspective on learning and innovation', *Administrative Science Quarterly*, 35 (1), 128–152.

Coviello, N. E. (2006) 'The network dynamics of international new ventures', *Journal of International Business Studies*, 37 (5), 713–731.

Coviello, N. E. and Munro, H.J. (1995) 'Growing the entrepreneurial firm: Networking for international market development', *European Journal of Marketing*, 29 (7), 49–61.

Coviello, N. E. and Munro, H. J. (1997) 'Network relationships and the internationalization process of small software firms', *International Business Review*, 6 (4), 361–386.

Craig, C. S. and Douglas, S. P. (1996) 'Developing strategies for global markets: An evolutionary perspective', *The Columbia Journal of World Business*, 31 (1), 70–81.

Crick, D. and Jones, M.V. (2000) 'Small high-technology firms and international high-technology markets', *Journal of International Marketing*, 8 (2), 63–85.

Cyert, R. M. and March, J. (1963) *A behavioral theory of the firm*. Englewood Cliffs, New Jersey: Prentice Hall.

De Clercq, D., Sapienza, H. J. and Crijns, H. (2005) 'The internationalization of small and medium-sized firms: The role of organizational learning effort and entrepreneurial orientation', *Small Business Economics*, 24 (4), 409–419.

De Clercq, D., Sapienza, H. J., Yavuz, R. I. and Zhou, L. (2012) 'Learning and knowledge in early internationalization research: Past accomplishments and future directions', *Journal of Business Venturing*, 27 (1), 143–165.

Dimov, D. (2010) 'Nascent entrepreneurs and venture emergence: Opportunity confidence, human capital, and early planning', *Journal of Management Studies*, 47 (6), 1123–1153.

Dyer, J. H. and Singh, H. (1998) 'The relational view: Cooperative strategy and sources of interorganizational competitive advantage', *Academy of Management Review*, 23 (4), 660–679.

Eisenhardt, K. M. (1989) 'Making fast strategic decisions in high-velocity environments', *Academy of Management Journal*, 32 (3), 543–76.

Ellis, P. (2000) 'Social ties and foreign market entry', *Journal of International Business Studies*, 31 (3), pp. 443–469.

Eriksson, K., Johanson, J., Majkgård, A. and Sharma, D. D. (1997) 'Experiential knowledge and cost in the internationalization process', *Journal of International Business Studies*, 28 (2), 337–60.

Fernhaber, S. A., McDougall-Covin, P. P. and Shepherd, D. A. (2009) 'International entrepreneurship: Leveraging internal and external knowledge sources', *Strategic Entrepreneurship Journal*, 3 (4), 297–320.

Floyd, S. W. and Lane, P. J. (2000) 'Strategizing throughout the organization: Managing role conflict in strategic renewal', *Academy of Management Review*, 25 (1), 154–177.

Forbes, D. F., Korsgaard, M. A. and Sapienza, H. J. (2010) 'Financing decisions as a source of conflict in venture boards', *Journal of Business Venturing*, 25 (6), 579–592.

Gentner, D. and Markman, A. B. (1994) 'Structural alignment in comparison: No difference without similarity', *Psychological Science*, 5 (3), 152–158.

Ghemawat, P. and Ricart Costa, J. E. (1993) 'The organizational tension between static and dynamic efficiency', *Strategic Management Journal*, 14 (S2), 59–73.

Ghoshal, S. (1987) 'Global strategy: An organizing framework', *Strategic Management Journal*, 8 (5), 425–440.

Gibson, C. and Birkinshaw, J. (2004) 'The antecedents, consequences, and mediating role of organizational ambidexterity', *Academy of Management Journal*, 47 (2), 209–226.

Grant, R.M. (1996) 'Toward a knowledge-based theory of the firm', *Strategic Management Journal*, 17 (Winter, Special Issue), pp. 109–122.

Grégoire, D. A., Barr, P. S. and Shepherd, D. A. (2010) 'Cognitive processes of opportunity recognition: The role of structural alignment', *Organization Science*, 21 (2), 413–431.

Hitt, M. A., Hoskisson, R. E. and Kim, H. (1997) 'International diversification: Effects on innovation and firm performance in product-diversified firms', *Academy of Management Journal*, 40 (4), 767–798.

Hitt, M. A., Tyler, B. B., Hardee, C. and Park, D. (1995) 'Understanding strategic intent in the global marketplace', *The Academy of Management Executive*, 9 (2), 12–19.

Hofstede, G. B. (1991) *Cultures and Organizations: Software of the Mind*. London: McGraw-Hill Companies Inc.

Huber, G. P. (1991) 'Organizational learning: The contributing processes and the literatures', *Organization Science*, 2 (1), 88–115.

Johanson, J. and Vahlne, J. E. (1977) 'The internationalization process of the firm: A model of knowledge development and increasing foreign market commitments', *Journal of International Business Studies*, 8 (1), 23–32.

Johanson, J. and Vahlne, J. E. (1990) 'The mechanism of internationalization', *International Marketing Review*, 7 (4), 11–24.

Johanson, J. and Vahlne, J. E. (2009) 'The Uppsala internationalization process model revisited: from liability of foreignness to liability of outsidership', *Journal of International Business Studies*, 40 (9), 1411–1431.
Jones, M. V. and Casulli, L. (2014) 'International entrepreneurship: Exploring the logic and utility of individual experience through comparative reasoning approaches', *Entrepreneurship Theory and Practice*, 38 (1), 45–69.
Jones, M. V. and Coviello, N. E. (2005) 'Internationalization: Conceptualising an entrepreneurial process of behaviour in time', *Journal of International Business Studies*, 36 (3), 284–303.
Karra, N., Phillips, N. and Tracey, P. (2008) 'Building the born global firm: Developing entrepreneurial capabilities for international new venture success', *Long Range Planning*, 41 (4), 440–458.
Keupp, M. M. and Gassmann, O. (2009) 'The past and the future of international entrepreneurship: A review and suggestions for developing the field', *Journal of Management*, 35 (3), 600–633.
Kim, L. (1997) *Imitation to Innovation: The Dynamics of Korea's Technological Learning*. Boston: Harvard Business School Press.
Knight, G. and Cavusgil, S. T. (2004) 'Innovation, organizational capabilities, and the born global firm', *Journal of International Business Studies*, 35 (2), 124–141.
Kogut, B. and Zander, U. (1993) 'Knowledge of the firm and the evolutionary theory of the multinational corporation', *Journal of International Business Studies*, 24 (4), 625–645.
Kuemmerle, W. (2002) 'Home base and knowledge management in international ventures', *Journal of Business Venturing*, 17 (2), 99–122.
Kyriakopoulos, K. and Moorman, C. (2004) 'Tradeoffs in marketing exploitation and exploration strategies: The overlooked role of market orientation', *International Journal of Research in Marketing*, 21 (3), 219–240.
Lane, P. J., Salk, J. E. and Lyles, M. A. (2001) 'Absorptive capacity, learning, and performance in international joint ventures', *Strategic Management Journal*, 22 (12), 1139–1161.
Leonard-Barton, D. (1992) 'Core capabilities and core rigidities: A paradox in managing new product development', *Strategic Management Journal*, 13 (S1), 111–125.
Levinthal, D. A. and March, J. G. (1993) 'The myopia of learning', *Strategic Management Journal*, 14 (S2), 95–112.
Loane, S. and Bell, J. D. (2006) 'Rapid internationalization among entrepreneurial firms in Australia, Canada, Ireland and New Zealand: An extension to the network approach', *International Marketing Review*, 23 (5), 467–485.
Loane, S., Bell, J. D. and McNaughton, R. (2007) 'A cross-national study on the impact of management teams on the rapid internationalization of small firms', *Journal of World Business*, 42 (4), 489–504.
Lyles, M. A. and Salk, J. E. (1996) 'Knowledge acquisition from foreign parents in international joint ventures: An empirical examination in Hungarian context', *Journal of International Business Studies*, 27 (5), 877–903.
March, J. G. (1991) 'Exploration and exploitation in organizational learning', *Organization Science*, 2 (1), 71–87.
McDougall, P. P. and Oviatt, B. M. (1996) 'New venture internationalization, strategic change, and performance: A follow-up study', *Journal of Business Venturing*, 11 (1), 23–40.
McDougall, P. P. and Oviatt, B. M. (2000) 'International entrepreneurship: The intersection of two research paths', *Academy of Management Journal*, 43 (5), 902–906.
McDougall, P. P., Shane, S. and Oviatt, B. M. (1994) 'Explaining the formation of international new ventures: The limits of theories from international business research', *Journal of Business Venturing*, 9 (6), 469–487.
Menon, T. and Pfeffer, J. (2003) 'Valuing internal vs. external knowledge: Explaining the preference for outsiders', *Management Science*, 49 (4), 497–513.
Michailova, S. and Wilson, H. I. M. (2008) 'Small firm internationalization through experiential learning: The moderating role of socialization tactics', *Journal of World Business*, 43 (2), 243–254.
Milanov, H. and Fernhaber, S. A. (2013) 'When do domestic alliances help ventures abroad? Direct and moderating effects from a learning perspective', *Journal of Business Venturing*, 29(3), 377–391.
Nonaka, I. (1994) 'A dynamic theory of organizational knowledge creation', *Organization Science*, 5 (1), 14–37.
Ocasio, W. (1997) 'Towards an attention-based view of the firm', *Strategic Management Journal*, 18 (S1), 187–206.
O'Farrell, P. N., Wood, P. A. and Zheng, J. (1998) 'Regional influences on foreign market development by business service companies: Elements of a strategic context explanation', *Regional Studies*, 32 (1), 31–48.
Oviatt, B. M. and McDougall, P. P. (1994) 'Toward a theory of international new ventures', *Journal of International Business Studies*, 25 (1), 45–64.

Oviatt, B. M. and McDougall, P. P. (2005) 'Global start-ups: Entrepreneurs on a worldwide stage', *Academy of Management Executive*, 9 (2), 30–44.
Prashantham, S. (2005) 'Toward a knowledge-based conceptualization of internationalization', *Journal of International Entrepreneurship*, 3 (1), 37–52.
Prashantham, S. and Dhanaraj, C. (2010) 'The dynamic influence of social capital on the international growth of new ventures', *Journal of Management Studies*, 47, 967–994.
Prashantham, S. and Floyd, S. W. (2012) 'Routine microprocesses and capability learning in international new ventures', *Journal of International Business Studies*, 43, 544–562.
Porter, M. E. (1996) 'What is strategy?', *Harvard Business Review*, 74 (6), 61–78.
Reuber, A. R. and Fischer, E. (1997) 'The influence of the management team's international experience on the internationalization behavior of SMEs', *Journal of International Business Studies*, 28 (4), 807–825.
Sapienza, H. J., Autio, E., George, G. and Zahra, S. A. (2006) 'A capabilities perspective on the effects of early internationalization on firm survival and growth', *Academy of Management Review*, 31 (4), 914–933.
Sapienza, H. J., Korsgaard, M. A. and Forbes, D. (2003) 'The self-determination motive and entrepreneurs' choice of financing', in Katz J. A. and Shepherd D. (ed.), *Advances in Entrepreneurship, Firm Emergence, and Growth: Cognitive Approaches to Entrepreneurship Research*. Oxford: Elsevier JAI, pp. 105–138.
Shenkar, O. (2001) 'Cultural distance revisited: Towards a more rigorous conceptualization and measurement of cultural differences', *Journal of International Business Studies*, 32 (3), 519–535.
Shrader, R. C., Oviatt, B. M. and McDougall, P. P. (2000) 'How new ventures exploit trade-offs among international risk factors: Lessons for the accelerated internationalization of the 21st century', *Academy of Management Journal*, 43 (6), 1227–1247.
Simon, H. A. (1979) *Models of Thought*. New Haven: Yale University Press.
Spender, J. C. (1996) 'Making knowledge the basis of a dynamic theory of the firm', *Strategic Management Journal*, 17 (Winter, Special Issue), 45–62.
Szulanski, G. (1996) 'Exploring internal stickiness: Impediments to the transfer of best practice within the firm', *Strategic Management Journal*, 17 (Winter, Special Issue), 27–43.
Teece, D., Pisano, G. and Shuen, A. (1997) 'Dynamic capabilities and strategic management', *Strategic Management Journal*, 18 (7), 509–533.
Van de Ven, A. H. (2007) *Engaged Scholarship: Creating Knowledge for Science and Practice*. Oxford: Oxford University Press.
Wasserman, N. (2003) 'Founder-CEO succession and the paradox of entrepreneurial success', *Organization Science*, 14 (2), 149–172.
Williams, F. (2010) *Claiming and Framing in the Making of Care Policies: The Recognition and Redistribution of Care*. Switzerland: United Nations Research Institute for Social Development.
Wright, M., Westhead, P. and Ucbasaran, D. (2007) 'Internationalization of small and medium-sized enterprises (SMEs) and international entrepreneurship: A critique and policy implications', *Regional Studies*, 41 (7), 1013–1029.
Yavuz, R. I. (2011) *The 'Outsider' Entrepreneurs: The Role of Founders' Immigrant Status in the Internationalization and Performance of High Technology New Ventures*. Unpublished PhD thesis, University of Minnesota.
Yli-Renko, H., Autio, E. and Tontti, V. (2002) 'Social capital, knowledge and the international growth of technology-based new firms', *International Business Review*, 11, 279–304.
Zahra, S. A. and George, G. (2002) 'Absorptive capacity: A review, reconceptualization, and extension', *Academy of Management Review*, 27 (2), 185–203.
Zahra, S. and Hayton, J. C. (2008) 'The effect of international venturing on firm performance: The moderating influence of absorptive capacity', *Journal of Business Venturing*, 23 (2), 195–220.
Zahra, S. A., Ireland, R. D. and Hitt, M. A. (2000) 'International expansion by new venture firms: International diversity, mode of market entry, technological learning, and performance', *Academy of Management Journal*, 43 (5), 925–950.
Zander, U. and Kogut, B. (1995) 'Knowledge and the speed of the transfer and imitation of organizational capabilities: An empirical test', *Organization Science*, 6 (1), 76–92.
Zhou, L., Barnes, B. and Lu, Y. (2010) 'Entrepreneurial proclivity, capability upgrading and performance advantage of newness among international new ventures', *Journal of International Business Studies*, 41 (5), 882–905.
Zhou, L., Wu, W. and Luo, X. (2007) 'Internationalization and the performance of born-global SMEs: The mediating role of social networks', *Journal of International Business Studies*, 38 (4), 673–690.

9

The role of capabilities in international entrepreneurship

Christiane Prange

Introduction

International entrepreneurship literature is concerned with the study of firms that seek to derive significant competitive advantage from the use of resources, and innovative, pro-active, and risk-seeking behavior that crosses national borders (Oviatt and McDougall, 2000). Earlier definitions of international entrepreneurship focused on small and young firms, later definitions also included the cross-border entrepreneurial behavior of mature firms, opening the field to include corporate entrepreneurship (Oviatt et al., 2003; Keupp and Gassmann, 2009). While it is unanimously accepted that firms – both small and mature – need resources (e.g. finance, human capital), developing and utilizing capabilities to adjust to external contingencies and internal changes helps them to pass the stage from initial idea development to substantial market growth and survival (Macpherson, 2005). Consequently, researchers have expressed an increasing interest into how capabilities develop and impact firm performance in an entrepreneurial context (Autio et al., 2000; Knight and Cavusgil, 2004; Sapienza et al., 2006; Autio et al., 2011).

The dynamic capability view of strategy provides a lens through which this development can be analyzed. Dynamic capabilities (DCs) are the processes, activities, or routines that enable firms to adapt and evolve (Helfat et al., 2007). They emerge when firms try to modify existing capabilities and resources to increase flexibility and competitiveness. Teece (2007) even suggested that successful firms rely on DCs rather than deal with competitive positioning or industry effects. However, limiting DCs to dealing with environmental or competitive changes is too narrow as DCs include the internal ability to generate change and reconfigure existing activities of the firm (Zollo and Winter, 2002). While it is intuitively appealing to apply the concept of DCs to new ventures, or international entrepreneurship in general, such an endeavor entails, at least, three challenges.

First, and despite the broader definition of international entrepreneurship, international new ventures (INVs), that is firms that from inception seek to internationalize their business activities (Oviatt and McDougall, 1994), differ significantly from established multinational firms, notably in terms of resource endowment, strategy processes, and internal structures. For instance, large firms rely on established and often sophisticated processes of analysis and strategic design to prevent losses, whereas entrepreneurial management focuses on opportunity recognition, improvisation, and adaptation in the early stages of company development (Michael et al., 2002).

These differences imply that younger firms in their early development expose higher flexibility to grow in new environments and to rapidly learn about (foreign) market requirements. One of the compelling studies in this regard is that of Autio et al. (2000: 919) who introduce the notion of "learning advantage of newness." In early stages, young firms have not developed routines that potentially lead to inertia. In contrast, more mature firms develop impediments that hamper their abilities to flexibly adapt and grow. Thus, capabilities for learning, change, and growth are likely to differ across different types of firms.

Second, researchers have questioned whether it is the existence of dynamic capabilities or rather their absence that benefits entrepreneurial expansion (Autio et al., 2011). DCs can be understood as routines that change ordinary capabilities; for example, those capabilities that are required to solve day-to-day problems, and to better adapt to the environment (Nelson and Winter, 1982). Entrepreneurial ventures in their early phase of development focus on the entrepreneurial capabilities that brought the venture into existence. Indeed, organizational practices that transform existing capabilities may be less useful for small firms in their post-foundation phase as these may not need to be changed (Zahra et al., 2006). However, at some point in time, even new ventures face the problem that the very capabilities that brought them into being may be the sole reason for their decline. Therefore, new ventures also need dynamic capabilities to update and reconfigure entrepreneurial capabilities to grow the market and increase profitability, though arguably at a later stage of their developement. The distinction between entrepreneurial and dynamic capabilities has only rarely been made (Zahra et al., 2011; Madsen, 2010) but is vital to evaluate the relevance for INVs.

Third, international and domestic new ventures differ significantly from each other (McDougall et al., 2003). INVs pursue a more aggressive and accelerated internationalization trajectory than ventures that expand domestically. In addition, they capitalize on the founder's experiences to attract customers abroad. Authors further suggest that INVs have a distinct attitude to internationalization (Zahra and George, 2002), and that they benefit from relational capabilities expressed in the entrepreneurs' network of contacts (Freeman et al., 2006). This stream of research suggests that although firms may experience a lack of resources in their home country, it may be the availability of resources and opportunities in the international environment that draws INVs into involvement across national borders (Mathews and Zander, 2007). The generation of capabilities needed for internationalization can in fact thrive under conditions of resource scarcity (Gassmann and Keupp, 2007), which can be a driver of, rather than an impediment to internationalization, with both personal and organization network ties helping to overcome initial resource scarcity.

Both these differences and challenges justify a review of the existing literature to identify the role of capabilities in international entrepreneurship, as well as gaps, and further research perspectives. As international entrepreneurship is an interdisciplinary field (McDougall and Oviatt, 2000; Keupp and Gassmann, 2009), insights on capabilities are generated from the intersection between international business, entrepreneurship, and strategic management research. The remainder of this chapter is structured as follows. First, I will provide an overview on capability research, primarily drawing on the dynamic capability view of strategy. Subsequently, I will review the major contributions from entrepreneurship, international business, and international entrepreneurship literature, and discuss how these literatures have dealt with critical issues in capability research. Finally, I suggest avenues for further research.

Dynamic capabilities and their impact on performance

Amit and Schoemaker (1993) refer to capabilities as the capacity of a firm to effectively and efficiently use resources to produce different products and services. This definition regards the dynamic capability view (DCV) of strategy as an extension of the resource-based view (Barney, 1991), acknowledging that competitive landscapes are continually changing and firms have to adapt to varying market requirements. Firms need to possess DCs, which provide them with the potential to continuously develop, align, and reconfigure their firm-specific assets (Eisenhardt and Martin, 2000; Teece et al., 1997). The quest for DCs has further increased due to globally active, dispersed firm activities, and the need to bring innovative products to diverse markets.

DCs are conceptualized in different ways (Teece et al., 1997; Eisenhardt and Martin, 2000; Winter, 2003). For instance, Teece et al. (1997) define DCs as the firm's internal and external competences to address rapidly changing environments. This distinction is particularly important for INVs, which do not only face external challenges, but in the process of growth, also need to reorganize their internal structures, communication systems, functional responsibilities, etc. While some authors consider DCs only in dynamic environments, others (Eisenhardt and Martin, 2000; Ambrosini et al., 2009) suggest that DCs are at play in both dynamic and stable environments. In stable environments, firms focus more on capabilities that help to continuously improve or renew their resource base. In more volatile environments, firms also need to engage in regenerating not only their resource base but also their current set of DCs (Winter, 2003). Accordingly, researchers have proposed a hierarchy, distinguishing between different levels of capabilities. While existing (ordinary or substantive) capabilities are likely to result in improved performance in stable markets, in volatile markets they have to undergo a permanent process of change. It is here that so-called "second-order" capabilities come into play. Second-order capabilities are higher-level DCs that imply the ability to change how the firm solves its problems; "higher-order capabilities alter capabilities" (Zahra et al., 2006: 921).

Entrepreneurial and international entrepreneurial capabilities

A number of authors have discussed DCs in the context of small, entrepreneurial firms with a few of them distinguishing them from entrepreneurial capabilities (ECs) (Woldesenbet et al., 2012; Zahra et al., 2011; see also "Influential readings" section below). Entrepreneurial capabilities enable a company's transformation through sensing and shaping of opportunities as well as providing specific heuristics to evaluate, select, and exploit them (e.g. Bingham et al., 2007). Some scholars proposed that entrepreneurial capabilities are a type of dynamic capability that can bring about change that alters the way the competitive game is played. ECs inform entrepreneurial decision-making on the basis of a noticed opportunity: firms sense changing customer needs, technological opportunities, or competitive developments. Zahra et al. (2011: 6) refer to ECs as having "a special type of dynamic capabilities that extend beyond the change and integration of substantive routines, a capability whose aim is to synchronize and orchestrate the co-incidence of such changes with events and efforts emerging beyond the firm's boundaries." In this sense, ECs are like other DCs in anticipating and realizing organizational change, but differ from them in that their major focus is on the firm's internal ability to induce environmental change rather than relying on external triggers to launch an adaptation process – ECs do from the inside what environmental triggers do from the outside (Madsen, 2010).

ECs also differ from DCs as they gain in prominence during different stages of the corporate life-cycle. Despite their explanatory value for opportunity recognition, venture formation, and the ability to evaluate, select, and exploit (e.g. Bingham et al. 2007; Teece, 2007), ECs may not explain how a venture grows and survives. ECs are crucial to the success at the inception of the venture because they most often are the stellar cause for bringing it into existence. However, they may become less relevant as the venture matures because it operates in an open system of competitors and environmental influences, which increasingly requires changes in ECs, that is the development and deployment of DCs. While the precise relationship between ECs and DCs has remained underresearched (Jantunen et al., 2005) authors argue that both involve exploration (recognition, sensing, selecting, reconfiguring, etc.) and exploitation of opportunities (seizing, consolidating, routinization). Both exploration and exploitation are important but have different performance outcomes (Griffith at al., 2006). ECs further differ from DCs as they are mostly driven by the individual entrepreneur, while dynamic capabilities typically refer to the firm level (Ambrosini et al., 2009), despite recent efforts to investigate their microfoundations (Teece, 2007).

International entrepreneurial capabilities (IECs) are defined as the "ability to leverage resources through a combination of innovative, pro-active, and risk-seeking activities to discover, enact, evaluate, and exploit business opportunities across borders" (Zhang et al., 2009: 293). IECs face the same relationship with DCs as do ECs but are more challenging to develop because they span multiple markets. Authors have tried to depict IECs as a multidimensional construct, which includes international experience and networking, international marketing skills, market orientation and innovativeness, and learning capability (Zhang et al., 2009; Knight and Kim, 2009). With the focus on experience and learning, IECs are considered a constantly evolving construct, that is more of a dynamic capability. Studies on content dimensions advance our knowledge about IEC, but insight into the process side of capabilities is important to understand their performance impact. This is why several authors have increasingly focused on the question of how IECs emerge and change over time (George et al., 2004; Autio et al., 2011; Prashantham and Floyd, 2012).

Capabilities and performance

The output dimension of capabilities is considered one of the most important questions in the field (McEvely and Zaheer, 1999; Barreto, 2010), but only a few studies have investigated the role that DCs play in firms' long-term survival and success (Lampel and Shamsie, 2003; Zahra and George, 2002). Performance itself is something of a black box, given the multiple motivations and objectives that might accompany a firm's strategy. Originally, Penrose (1959) argued that growth depends on the reorganization of resources and routines as well as dynamic capabilities that are at the core of this reorganization. Growth opportunities require the implementation of new routines that rely on actors with the mechanisms and sense-making to act. That is, foreign market growth is contingent on a given portfolio of capabilities and a firm's potential to reconfigure and deploy them for foreign market entry.

Despite the increasing focus on quantifying and measuring the output of DCs (Wilden et al., 2013), authors have also noted that DCs are only those capabilities that result in competitive advantages, which represents an unsatisfying tautology. In fact, DCs create value rather indirectly (Zahra et al., 2006). Consequently, the successful application of DCs manifests itself in the improvement of ordinary capabilities, or given the lack thereof, in the *potential* flexibility and impact of DCs for future action. That is, dynamic capabilities build and reconfigure resource positions (Eisenhardt and Martin, 2000), or operational routines (Zollo and Winter, 2002) and, through them, affect performance. This chain of causality designates an indirect link between dynamic capabilities and performance.

Figure 9.1 summarizes the previous discussion. Taken collectively, research on capabilities involves paradoxes between opposing thoughts or concepts which, however contradictory, are equally necessary to convey a more imposing, illuminating, life-related or provocative insight into truth than either fact can muster in its own right (Smith and Lewis, 2011). As the duality of processes and concepts has inspired researchers to introduce notions of ambidexterity, balance, or

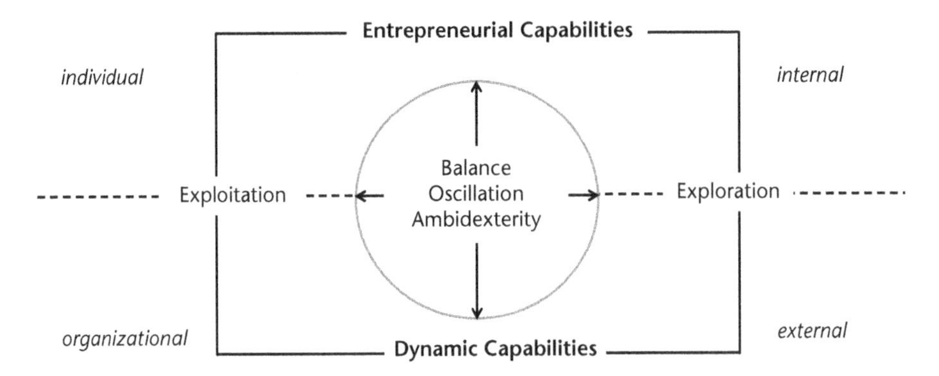

Figure 9.1 The relationship between entrepreneurial and dynamic capabilities

oscillation (Tushman and O'Reilly, 1996; Bingham, 2009), I will highlight these concepts in the discussion part and show how they can further enhance research on capabilities in international entrepreneurship.

Influential readings

International entrepreneurship happens at the intersection of international business, entrepreneurship and strategic management. Thus, researching the role of capabilities in international entrepreneurship is informed by insights from the dynamic capability view of strategy, studies on entrepreneurial capabilities, and research on internationalization capabilities. The following overview on major studies does not aim to be comprehensive but to highlight the major trends that have emerged in the last couple of years.

Capabilities in entrepreneurship research

Entrepreneurial firms use capabilities to explore and exploit opportunities by creating new products or services (Shane, 2000). Until the mid 2000s, research that adopted capabilities at its core mostly focused on more established firms and did not pay much attention to how capabilities develop, emerge, or evolve in small firms that have limited resources, knowledge bases, and expertise (Zahra et al., 2006: 920). The seminal review article by Zahra et al. (2006) provides a systematic overview of the role of capabilities in entrepreneurship and sets the scene for further developments. The authors highlight several inconsistencies in DC research (see again "Dynamic capabilities and their impact on performance" section above), and among other topics, introduce the two central themes that later generated major interest: (1) the role of different capabilities, and (2) the formation of DCs. They also argue that small companies and new ventures need unique capabilities that are different from those of established firms, and that these capabilities need to be actively managed.

More recent research has built on Zahra et al.'s (2006) contribution and discussed different capabilities and their development with an increasing variation in focus (see Table 9.1). Most authors agree on the difference between EC and DC and their vital function for firm survival and growth. However, precise definitions and relationships have remained unclear. For example, Woldesenbet et al. (2012) explicitly focus on small firms and argue that "while it would be difficult to delineate where an entrepreneurial capability ends and a dynamic capability begins, it is important to explore how they combine to drive small firm entry into new product markets"

(p. 495). ECs facilitate a firm's entry into the mainstream market, but it is dynamic capabilities that enable evolution and growth in such a market (p. 494). Aramand and Valliere (2012) show that DCs can be internally and externally driven. Especially ECs are seen to greatly expand the behavioral variety of the firm and thereby better position it for competitive success in the environment. The findings of this study show that DCs have a bidirectional-causal relationship with ECs, whereby the development of DCs leads to the development of ECs – and vice versa – the development of ECs leads to the development of DCs.

The second theme that received major attention is the question of the capability formation process in new ventures. Selected studies, such as Newbert (2005), found evidence that the firm

Table 9.1 Capabilities in entrepreneurship research

Authors (Year)	*Capability definition*	*Major finding*
Alvarez and Busenitz (2001)	Indirectly, capabilities are defined as entrepreneurial recognition, that is the recognition of opportunities and opportunity-seeking behavior as a resource (p. 756)	Resources and cognitive abilities of entrepreneurs facilitate the recognition of new opportunities Early identification of a distinctive domain of entrepreneurship
Newbert (2005)	Dynamic capabilites are the organizational and strategic routines by which firms achieve new resource configurations (Eisenhardt & Martin, 2000: 1107)	Firm formation processes may be considered a dynamic capability Capability is executed at the individual level
Arthurs and Busenitz (2006)	Entrepreneurial capabilities are "the ability to identify opportunities and develop the resource base needed to pursue these opportunities" (p. 199)	Examination and delineation of dynamic capabilities from entrepreneurial capabilities Influence of venture capitalists on DC development in new ventures is high for product / management capabilities
Zahra et al. (2006)	Dynamic capabilities are the "abilities to reconfigure a firm's resource base and routines in a manner envisioned and deemed appropriate by its principal decision maker(s)" (p. 918)	Difference between dynamic and substantial capabilities Unidirectional relationship between ECs and DCs Differences between DCs in new vs. established firms Effects of age / learning style on DC development
Kor et al. (2007)	"[Through] the subjectively perceived multiple uses of a specific resource ... exists a large number of possibilities for entrepreneurial choices and activities, which in turn produces different firm-level economic performance outcomes" (p. 1192)	Subjective focus on entrepreneurship that focuses on individuals' skills, knowledge, resources, and processes of discovery and creativity Knowledge (capabilities) emerge from entrepreneurs' experience
McKelvie and Davidsson (2009)	Dynamic capabilities are idea generation, market disruptiveness, new product development, new process development capabilities	Development of dynamic capabilities in new firms Temporal changes of the resource base affect DCs

(continued)

Table 9.1 Capabilities in entrepreneurship research (Continued)

Authors (Year)	*Capability definition*	*Major finding*
Newey and Zahra (2009) *case study*	A key operating capability within firms is product development, and the corresponding dynamic capability that reconfigures it occurs through product portfolio planning (p. S82)	Interaction of operating and dynamic capabilities through endogeneous change DCs have a critical role in the adaptation of firms
Corner and Wu (2012) *case study*	Dynamic entrepreneurial capabilities are the capacities that entrpreneurs use to identify, amass, integrate, and potentially reconfigure resources as needed in the creation of new ventures (p. 139)	Dynamic capability formation in new ventures Micro-level patterns reflect DCs (prospecting problems and sharing technological features)
Aramand and Valliere (2012) *case study*	Dynamic capabilities are the firm's abilities to purposefully change and improve its substantive capabilities to respond to the changes in the environment (p. 145) Entrepreneurial capabilities are the ... ability to identify and exploit opportunities in a changing environment (p. 145)	Firms need both entrepreneurial and dynamic capabilities Both capabilities are iteratively related; the more iterations, the stronger the capabilities (multidimensional relationship)
Woldesenbet et al. (2012) *case study*	Dynamic capability is a process or a routine that impacts on the resource base of the firm (p. 494) (in addition Zahra et al., 2006: 918) Entrepreneurial capabilities are dynamic, interacting in complex and subtle ways with the environment	Distinction between entrepreneurial and dynamic capabilities Capabilities required for cooperation with large purchase organizations (entrepreneurial, bridging and networking, resource development and integration, strategic service delivery)

formation process in itself can be considered a DC as it is a specifically identifiable organizational processs with a unique set of activities. Increasing market dynamisms seem to reduce the complexity of DCs and learning appears to have an impact on success, which suggests the evolutionary nature of the capability. McKelvie and Davidsson (2009) identified capability development as a largely endogeneously driven process with the founder and the existing resource base exerting major influence on DCs in new firms. However, the impact of the resource base is seen to differ for different types of capabilities, for instance, existing resources positively impact short-term effects such as idea generation and market disruptivenesss capabilities but are negative for the long-term development of new product capabilities. Corner and Wu (2012) also investigate how entrepreneurs develop DCs in the formation process of a new venture. They adopt a "micro-view" focusing on entrepreneurial decision making and behavior, and argue for a new construct of dynamic entrepreneurial capabilities, thereby mixing DCs and ECs, which are both required for endogeneously creating and effectuating opportunities for the new venture. Similarly, Kor et al. (2007) suggest a subjectivist perspective of entrepreneurship focusing on the non-deterministic, evolutionary nature of DCs.

In summary, several questions can be attractive for international entrepreneurship researchers. If DCs and ECs have no clear boundaries, and also overlap with substantial or ordinary capabilites, further classification and operationalization is necessary. Subsequently, central paradoxes of whether capabilities are endogeneously or exogeneously triggered and how they mutually influence each other may be solved (e.g. contradictory insights of Aramand and Valliere, 2012 vs. Zahra et al., 2006). With the focus on individuals as key agents of DC development, which is also a central theme in the IB literature on capabilities in born global firms, researchers may also focus on the role of managerial agency in driving capability development.

Capabilities in international business research

International business (IB) literature has increasingly used insights from the dynamic capability view of strategy (Luo, 2000; Griffith and Harvey, 2001). Researchers analyze success factors as predictors of international performance with one of them being the internationalization capabilities that facilitate the process of expanding abroad by increasing speed, establishing procedures for consolidation, and by fostering new product development (Prange and Verdier, 2011). Internationalization capabilities are also required to increase the flexibility of a firm and avoid inertia resulting from incremental and repetitive market expansion routines (Vermeulen and Barkema, 2001). Other studies have advanced the notion that firms compete with one another based on their ability to learn and apply knowledge to foreign markets, indeed, on the basis of their dynamic capabilities (Chang and Rosenzweig, 2001; Tallman and Fladmore-Lindquist, 2002).

Most studies emphasize a duality of capabilities (Table 9.2). Borrowing from March (1991) the notions of "exploitation" versus "exploration," capabilities have been introduced to IB literature. For instance, Tallman and Fladmore-Lindquist (2002) stress the interplay between capability leverage, or exploitation, and capability building, or exploration, as related to international expansion and global integration. By combining the two processes, firms manage both global expansion and global integration, with the latter being necessary for cross-country synergies. Export researchers focus on DCs by arguing that exploration must be encouraged but within limits that do not exclude exploitation (Knudsen and Madsen, 2002). More generally, exploitation is reflected in the incremental approach to internationalization (Johanson and Vahlne, 1977) and is described as necessarily path-dependent based on prior knowledge acquisition. Thus, internationalization relates to the reduction of uncertainty by accumulating and improving capabilities. In turn, exploration is based on the development of new capabilities through learning and planned experimentation. The trade-off between capabilities has also been related to the age of a firm, introducing a comparison between born globals or international new ventures[1] and more mature firms (Knight and Cavusgil, 2004; Sapienza et al., 2006). Whereas the incremental approach considers international entry at a late stage in the firm's life-cycle to enhance profitability, researchers have proposed the benefits of early internationalization of born global firms, especially as a catalyst for growth.

Both trajectories together can enhance international performance as young firms benefit from imprinting DCs at an early stage but may enhance profitability through slower internationalization, while older firms benefit from resource endowments but require higher speed of internationalization to spur further growth (Verdier et al., 2010). Current research on capabilities in international research hints at the notion of "ambidexterity" to capture these trade-offs. International ambidexterity depicts that a firm needs to combine the seemingly incompatible activities of exploration and exploitation in order to succeed (Prange and Verdier, 2011). However, the conflicting strategies of international exploration and exploitation are not easy to reconcile. This tension is also echoed by the DCV, arguing that switching to new capabilities is difficult, as neither the underlying knowledge nor the social fabric required to support learning processes is well understood (Kogut and Zander, 1992).

Taken collectively, IB literature provides many angles to analyze capabilities though it has mainly focused on large firms in the past (Luo, 2000, 2002). With the recent interest in born

Table 9.2 Capabilities in international business research

Authors (Year)	*Capability definition*	*Major finding*
Griffith and Harvey (2001)	A global DC is the creation of difficult-to-imitate combinations of resources, including effective coordination of inter-organizational relationships, on a global basis that can provide a firm with a competitive advantage	The development of global DC is largely a matter of power Resource-based and market-based assets determine the power of the firm
Luo (2000)	Capability exploitation concerns ... firms' exploits regarding rent-generating resources Capability building involves ... building new capabilities through learning from other organizations, creating new skills, or revitalizing existing skills in a new situation	Capability exploitation and building are inversely associated with environmental complexity and industrial uncertainty Entry mode choice influences capability building
Tallman and Fladmore-Lindquist (2002)	A capability-driven framework of the multinational firm considers the firm's attempts to build, protect, and exploit a set of unique capabilities	Capability development in multinational firms Capability leverage processes and creation of capabilities interact
Knudsen and Madsen (2002)	DCs are the managerial and organizational processes that alter the firm's processes, positions, and paths (based on Teece et al. 2007)	Exporting is tied to the capabilities of the internal actors Firms should balance the exploitation of current capabilities and the exploration of ... future capabilities
Knight and Cavusgil (2004)*	Organizational capabilities reflect the ability to perform repeatedly, or 'replicate', productive tasks that relate to the firms's capacity to create value through the transformation of input into outputs (p. 127)	Born globals are entrepreneurial firms that possess specific capabilities that engender early internationalization Capabilities emerge through the sharing of specialist knowledge among individuals
Sapienza et al. (2006)*	DCs are the organizational and strategic routines by which managers alter their firms' resource base through acquiring, shedding, integrating and recombining resources to generate new value-creating strategies (Eisenhardt & Martin, 2000)	Early and late internationalization affects firms' survival and growth differently Age, managerial experience, and resource fungibility moderate the relationship between capabilities and performance
Weerawardena et al. (2007)*	DCs are the organizational and strategic routines by which firms achieve new resource configurations (Eisenhardt & Martin, 2000)	Entrepreneurial founders build a set of dynamic capabilities to enable born globals to develop cutting-edge knowledge-intensive products A sequence in which capabilities are developed needs to be compiled
Prange and Verdier (2011)	Dynamic exploitative capabilities and dynamic explorative capabilities provide firms with different incentives to address the internationalization process. The former builds on ongoing changes of existing capabilities, while the latter focuses on new capability building (p. 129)	Both young and mature firms need to reconcile dynamic internationalization capabilities International ambidexterity as a capability that balances exploration / exploitation, speed, age, profitability / growth

*Articles also appear in classifications of international entrepreneuship research.

global firms, and their underlying capabilities, a stronger connection to the research domain of international entrepreneurship is built, especially as born globals are seen as intrinsically entrepreneurial firms with the respective capabilities to internationalize early and in an accelerated manner (Knight and Cavusgil, 2004; Weerawardena et al., 2007). With regards to triggers of capability development, IB literature also provides interesting insight with the two dominating approaches focusing on the individual founder (born globals literature) and the firm-level knowledge accumulation process (incremental stage theory).

Capabilities in international entrepreneurship

International entrepreneurship is a particularly complex form of business activity involving even higher degrees of uncertainty than local entrepreneurship. Researchers highlighted the role of capability research for the field (Autio et al., 2011), which falls into the first category of entrepreneurial internationalization as indicated by Jones et al. (2011). However, compared to previous literatures, the amount of articles that explicitly focus on capabilities is still lower and little attention has been devoted to understanding how firms utilize entrepreneurial and dynamic capabilities to become successful in entering foreign markets (see Table 9.3).

Several articles focus on the content dimension of capabilities and regard the role of opportunity recognition as a major capability (Knight and Cavusgil, 2004; Karra et al., 2008; Ellis, 2011). Firms with limited prior international experience tend to discover opportunities in a serendipitous or ad hoc way, rather than search for them deliberately. On the other hand, firms with extensive prior international experience and knowledge utilize a conscious and systematic search for their first international opportunity (Chandra et al., 2009; Bingham, 2009) or create a sequence of capability development (Weerawardena et al., 2007). However, performance implications are contradictory in that improvisation enables flexibility, such that risk-seeking entrepreneurs can seize opportunities faster and more effectively than competitors (Autio et al., 2000). Other authors focus on relational capabilities, both of the founder or the firm, which can substitute for the lack of original resourses, and through cooperation, help to expand internationally (Freeman et al., 2006). Networking as such, is seen as a vital component of internationalization success, but is only rarely analyzed by adopting a capability view (e.g. Oviatt and McDougall, 2005).

The role of experience and knowledge opens up the discussion to considering processes of learning and capability emergence. For instance, George et al. (2004) note trial-and-error and learning-by-doing as the mechanisms through which capabilities are generated, deployed, and changed. These learning processes create, among others, market entry capabilities, and are influenced by organizational factors, resource fit, shared experiences of the management team, and contextual factors, such as product and market uncertainty as important determinants of the variability in capability development across start-ups. While several of these learning processes focus on behavioral learning, Autio et al. (2011) argue that this approach falls short in explaining how new capabilities emerge. Especially, when decision-makers import previous routines from earlier activities, and then only adapt them to new circumstances, they run the risk of reinforcing routines that impede new capability development. Thus, the authors argue that repeated exposure to situational uncertainty compels the firm to expand its set of processes and its awareness of cause–effect relationships (p. 15). Prashantham and Floyd (2012) further explain how capability learning processes build on routine change. While high variability in the ostensive aspects of internationalization routines (abstract patterns) results in trial-and-error processes to inform future action, a larger variety of behavioral patterns (specific actions) leads to improvisatory learning in the course of decision-making. Both learning processes together help to maintain a balance between new capability learning and existing capability improvement.

Table 9.3 Capabilities in international entrepreneurship research

Authors (Year)	*Capability definition*	*Major finding*
Autio et al. (2000)	An organization's knowledge is the capacity to apprehend and use relationships among critical factors in such a way as to achieve intended ends (p. 911)	Firms' age at foreign market entry, their knowledge intensity, and the imitability of their technology impact on international growth Small firms benefit from "learning advantages of newness"
George et al. (2004) *case study*	Firms develop and deploy a capability for entering new markets that is distinct from other organizational or functional capabilities (p. 82)	International market entry capabilities have two distinct subsets: entry-organizing and market intelligence capabilities. Capabilities emerge through trial-and-error learning and learning by doing
Knight and Cavusgil (2004)*	Organizational capabilities reflect the ability to perform repeatedly, or "replicate," productive tasks that relate to the firm's capacity to create value through the transformation of input into outputs (p. 127)	Born globals are entrepreneurial firms that possess specific capabilities that engender early internationalization Capabilities emerge through the integration of specialist knowledge across individuals
Jantunen et al. (2005)	DCs are assets, processes, and structures that enable firms to sense and seize new opportunities and renew their existing asset base (p. 223)	A firm's entrepreneurial orientation and reconfiguration capabilities impact performance International organizational capabilities are important for both small and established firms
Sapienza et al. (2006)*	DCs are the organizational and strategic routines by which managers alter their firms' resource base through acquiring, shedding, integrating and recombining resources to generate new value-creating strategies (Eisenhardt and Martin, 2000)	Early and late internationalization affects firms' survival and growth differently Age, managerial experience, and resource fungibility moderate the relationship between capabilities and performance
Weerawardena et al. (2007)*	DCs are the organizational and strategic routines by which firms achieve new resource configurations (Eisenhardt and Martin, 2000)	Entrepreneurial founders build a set of dynamic capabilities to enable born globals to develop cutting-edge knowledge-intensive products A sequence in which capabilities are developed needs to be compiled
Karra et al. (2008) *case study*	Entrepreneurial capabilities are the skills and competencies that allow the entrepreneur to create international new ventures (p. 440)	Three capabilities are especially important: international opportunity identification, institutional bridging, and a capacity for cross-cultural collaboration

Table 9.3 Capabilities in international entrepreneurship research (Continued)

Authors (Year)	*Capability definition*	*Major finding*
Bingham (2009) *case study*	Improvisation as a capability in opportunity selection and execution	Firms with successful market entry decrease improvisation in opportunity selection but increase improvisation in execution
Autio et al. (2011)	Capabilities are a combination or sequence of processes and their enabling resource commitments that have the potential to reliably achieve outputs congruent with organizational goals (p. 18)	Emergence of new capabilities takes place through the interaction between cognition and behavior Repeated exposure to uncertainty compels firms to reflect on causal relationships
Prashantham and Floyd 2012	Capability learnings are improvements in an organization's ordinary or substantive capabilities, which refer to the set of abilities and resources that go into solving a problem or achieving an outcome (based on Zahra et al., 2006: 921)	Variability in the performance aspects of internationalization routines (specific actions) leads to new capability learning Variability in the ostentative aspects (abstract patterns) of internationalization routines is associated with existing capability improvement

* Articles also appear in classifications of international business research.

In summary, there is agreement that internal firm capabilities are linked to international entrepreneurial capabilities and are embedded in business strategy (Knight and Cavusgil, 2004). This view implies that the ability of certain firms to increase their behavioral variety – often at the expense of discarding old routines – can lead to the development of entrepreneurial capabilities (Autio et al., 2000; Knight and Cavusgil, 2004). The intricate balance between preserving old knowledge and routines and developing new capabilities requires further research, preferably by adopting cognition-based lenses as suggested by Autio et al. (2011). In addition, the variety of mutually complementary or opposing learning processes (e.g. learning through repetition or incremental expansion vs. learning from heterogeneous experiences or non-linear foreign expansion) poses another challenge for international entrepreneurship researchers.

Future research directions

Given the nascent stage of research on capabilities in international entrepreneurship, several topics for future studies exist apart from those mentioned above for the individual literature streams. Several interesting avenues have also been highlighted by others.

For instance, Sapienza et al. (2006) and Autio et al. (2011) stress the importance of investigating capability emergence, including different triggers (internal vs. external), and the role of individuals and the imprints they may leave. For instance, several microprocesses may work together to create organizational routines as a basis for capabilities. How these processes interact and constitute a "grammar of organizing" (Autio et al., 2011: 29) to cope with changes in the internal and external environments is of high importance. Similarly, insight into the firms' repertoire of routine and non-routine-based processes, and their inclination to apply each under certain conditions deserves further attention. These choices may be influenced by past learning and the actual variability in firms' learning activities (e.g. learning by doing, direct experience, social interaction, etc.). For instance, heterogeneous experiences that trigger the emergence of second-order capabilities can be very important for firms changing their international strategy or the rhythm of their international expansion (Vermeulen and Barkema, 2002). Insights into these processes may also help to improve capability learning in the future and to avoid wasteful learning efforts (Prashantham and Floyd, 2012).

Several of these challenges can be understood as trade-offs, starting from incremental vs. accelerated speed, entrepreneurial vs. dynamic capabilities, exploration vs. exploitation capabilities to individual vs. firm behavior. Recent literature has tried to resolve conflicting activities by balancing them. This endeavor seems fruitful in its application to international entrepreneurship research.

Performance improvements through ambidexterity or oscillation

INVs use a portfolio of different capabilities, with some of them being potentially conflicting. The need for an appropriate balance of activities in general has been emphasized by Tushman and O'Reilly's (1996) conceptualization of ambidextrous organizations. Also March (1991) suggested that maintaining an appropriate balance between exploration and exploitation is critical for firms' survival and prosperity. Others argued that organizations need to ensure existing viability and, at the same time, devote enough energy to exploring future possibilities, thereby combining the two capabilities in an ambidextrous manner. More recent research has built on the original arguments by March (1991) that a firm needs to focus on both processes in order to succeed. This may be achieved by a synchronous pursuit of both exploration and exploitation or entrepreneurial and dynamic capabilities via specialized sub-units of a firm, or by sequential pursuit (Gupta et al., 2006). Applied to international entrepreneurship literature, INVs may distinguish between simultaneous and sequential ambidexterity. Simultaneous ambidexterity builds on the idea that firms structurally separate seemingly conflicting activities (Tushman and O'Reilly, 1996), that is, they could allocate responsibilities for capability development or their application to different foreign markets, or to separate business units. In contrast, sequential or temporal ambidexterity relates to seemingly contradictory activities being pursued one after the other (Puranam et al., 2006) – an idea that currently dominates the entrepreneurship literature with ECs being followed by DCs or vice versa. While sequential separation requires the ability to fluidly change organizational attributes and managerial approaches to change, it is supposed to prevent firms from turning inert, especially as cumulative capability development results in being more static, exhibiting structural inertia. How these sequences occur in INVs has remained a major void and requires further research.

Oscillation provides another approach for balancing contradictions that INVs are facing over time. Oscillation can be understood as a dynamic version of ambidexterity, balancing the development and deployment of capabilities at different points in time, where one may be stronger than the other but not necessarily leading to lock-in or path-dependency effects that prevent the development of the other (Luger et al., 2013). Oscillation thus differs from temporal separation, which refers to shifts between discrete periods of either exploration or exploitation, but also from the traditional concept of structural ambidexterity since it captures firms' ability to strive for and operate at a given intermediate point on the exploration–exploitation continuum (Lavie et al., 2010), rather than exploring how they adapt this balance over time (Boumgarden et al., 2012: 588). Future research may explore several questions. For instance, changes in the portfolio of new market entries may require a changing balance of capabilities even more so than penetrating existing markets with new opportunities. Developing capabilities for accelerated market entry may need to be balanced several times with capabilities to consolidate markets.

Or, improvisation capabilities for opportunity discovery may be flexibly adapted during the INVs' life-cycle and reinvigorated after the firm has become older.

Conclusions

This article has provided an overview on capability research in international entrepreneurship drawing on insights from strategic management, entrepreneurship and international business research. Previous research shows that capabilities – in their different forms and occurences – are a vital component of explaining international entrepreneurial behavior. Several definitional and empirical challenges need to be met, while highlighting avenues for research may inspire researchers to travel this road.

Note

1 The term international new venture goes back to the 1994 article by Oviatt and McDougall who define it as a organization that, from inception, seeks to derive significant competitive advantage from the use of resources and the sale of outputs in multiple countries business. I use the term here interchangeably though for selected research purposes a subtle distinction may be required (see also: Coviello et al., 2011: 628).

References

Alvarez, S. A. and Busenitz, L. (2001). The entrepreneurship of resource-based theory. *Journal of Management*, 27(6): 755–775.

Ambrosini, V., Bowman, C., and Collier, N. (2009). Dynamic capabilities as an exploration of how firms renew their resource base. *British Journal of Management*, 20(SI): S9–S24.

Amit, R. and Schoemaker, P. J. (1993). Strategic assets and organizational rent. *Strategic Management Journal*, 14(1): 33–46.

Aramand, M. and Valliere, D. (2012). Dynamic capabilities in entrepreneurial firms: A case study approach. *Journal of International Entrepreneurship*, 10(2): 142–157.

Arthurs, J. D. and Busenitz, L. (2006). Dynamic capabilities and venture performance: The effects of venture capitalists. *Journal of Business Venturing*, 21(2): 195–215.

Autio, E., George, G., and Alexy, O. (2011). International entrepreneurship and capability development: Qualitative evidence and future research directions. *Entrepreneurship, Theory and Practice*, 35(1): 11–37.

Autio, E., Sapienza, H. J., and Almeida, J. G. (2000). Effect of age at entry, knowledge intensity, and imitability on international growth. *Academy of Management Journal*, 43(5): 909–924.

Barney, J. B. (1991). Firm resources and sustained competitive advantage. *Journal of Management*, 17(1): 99–120.

Barreto, I. (2010). Dynamic capabilities: A review of past research and an agenda for the future. *Journal of Management*, 36(1): 256–280.

Bingham, C. B. (2009). Oscillating improvisation: How entrepreneurial firms create success in foreign market entries over time. *Strategic Entrepreneurship Journal*, 3(4): 321–345.

Bingham, C. B., Eisenhardt, K. M., and Furr, N. R. (2007). What makes a process a capability? Heuristics, strategy, and effective capture of opportunities. *Strategic Entrepreneurship Journal*, 1(1–2): 27–47.

Boumgarden, P., Nickerson, J. A., and Zenger, T. R. (2012). Sailing into the wind: Exploring the relationship among ambidexterity, vacilation, and organizational performance. *Strategic Management Journal*, 33(6): 587–610.

Chandra, Y., Styles, C., and Wilkinson, I. (2009). The recognition of first time international entrepreneurial opportunities: Evidence from firms in knowledge-based industries. *International Marketing Review*, 26(1): 30–61.

Chang, S. J. and Rosenzweig, P. (2001). The choice of entry mode in sequential foreign direct investment. *Strategic Management Journal*, 22(8): 747–776.

Corner, P. D. and Wu, S. (2012). Dynamic capability emergence in the venture creation process. *International Small Business Journal*, 30(2): 138–160.

Coviello, N., McDougall, P. P. and Oviatt, B. M. (2011). The emergence, advance and future of international entrepreneurship research: An introduction to the special issue. *Journal of Business Venturing*, 26(6): 625–631.

Eisenhardt, K. M. and Martin, J. A. (2000). Dynamic capabilities: What are they? *Strategic Management Journal*, 21(10/11): 1105–1121.

Ellis, P. D. (2011). Social ties and opportunity recognition. *Journal of International Business Studies*, 42(1): 99–127.

Freeman, S., Edwards, R., and Schroder, B. (2006). How smaller born-global firms use networks and alliances to overcome constraints to rapid internationalization. *Journal of International Marketing*, 14(3): 33–63.

Gassmann, O. and Keupp, M. (2007). The competitive advantage of early and rapidly internationalising SMEs in the biotechnology industry: A knowledge-based view. *Journal of World Business*, 42(3): 350–366.

George, G., Zahra, S. A., Autio, E., and Sapienza, H. (2004). By leaps and rebounds: Learning and the development of international market entry capabilities in start-ups. *Academy of Management Proceedings*, B1–B6.

Griffith, D. A. and Harvey, M. G. (2001). A resource perspective of global dynamic capabilities. *Journal of International Business Studies*, 32(3): 597–606.

Griffith, D. A., Noble, S. M., and Chen, Q. (2006). The performance implications of entrepreneurial proclivity: A dynamic capabilities approach. *Journal of Retailing*, 82(1): 51–62.

Gupta, A. K., Smith, K. G., and Shalley, C. E. (2006). The interplay between exploration and exploitation. *Academy of Management Journal*, 49: 693–706.

Helfat, C., Finkelstein, S., Mitchell, W., Peteraf, M., Singh, H., Teece, D., and Winter, S. (2007). *Dynamic Capabilities: Understanding Strategic Change in Organizations*. Malden, MA: Blackwell.

Jantunen, A., Puumalainen, K., and Saarenketo, S. (2005). Entrepreneurial orientation, dynamic capabilities, and international performance. *Journal of International Entrepreneurship*, 3(3): 223–243.

Johanson, J. and Vahlne, J. E. (1977). The internationalization process of the firm: A model of knowledge development and increasing foreign market commitments. *Journal of International Business Studies*, 8: 23–32.

Jones, M. V., Coviello, N. E., and Tang, Y. K. (2011). International entrepreneurship research (1989–2009): a domain ontology and thematic analysis. *Journal of Business Venturing*, 26(6): 632–659.

Karra, N., Phillips, N., and Tracey, P. (2008). Building the born global firm: Developing entrepreneurial capabilities for international new venture success. *Long Range Planning*, 41(4): 440–458.

Keupp, M. M. and Gassmann, O. (2009). The past and the future of international entrepreneurship: A review and suggestions for developing the field. *Journal of Management*, 35(3): 600–633.

Knight, G. A. and Cavusgil, S. T. (2004). Innovation, organizational capabilities, and the born global firm. *Journal of International Business Studies*, 35: 124–141.

Knight, G. A. and Kim, D. (2009). International business competence and the contemporary firm. *Journal of International Business Studies*, 40: 255–273.

Knudsen, T. and Madsen, T. K. (2002). Export strategy: A dynamic capabilities perspective. *Scandinavian Journal of Management*, 18(4): 475–502.

Kogut, B. and Zander, U. (1992). Knowledge of the firm, combinative capabilities, and the replication of technology. *Organization Science*, 3(3): 383–397.

Kor, Y. Y., Mahoney, J. T., and Michael, S. C. (2007). Resources, capabilities and entrepreneurial perceptions. *Journal of Management Studies*, 44(7): 1187–1212.

Lampel, J. and Shamsie, J. (2003). Capabilities in motion: New organizational forms and the reshaping of the Hollywood movie industry. *Journal of Management Studies*, 40(8): 2189–2210.

Lavie, D., Stettner, U., and Tushman, M. L. (2010). Exploration and exploitation within and across organizations. *Academy of Management Annals*, 4: 109–155.

Luger, J., Raisch, S., and Schimmer, M. (2013). The paradox of static and dynamic ambidexterity. Paper presented at the Academy of Mangement Annual Meeting, Orlando, 2013.

Luo, Y. (2000). Dynamic capabilities in international expansion. *Journal of World Business*, 35(4): 355–378.

Luo, Y. (2002). Capability exploitation and building in a foreign market: Implications for multinational enterprises. *Organization Science*, 13(1): 48–63.

McDougall, P. P. and Oviatt, B. M. (2000). International entrepreneurship: The intersection of two research paths. *Academy of Management Journal*, 43(5): 902–906.

McDougall, P. P., Oviatt, B. M. and Shrader, R. C. (2003). A comparison between international and domestic new ventures. *Journal of International Entrepreneurship*, 1: 59–82.

McEvely, B. and Zaheer, A. (1999). Bridging ties: A source of firm heterogeneity in competitive capabilities. *Strategic Management Journal*, 20(2): 133–156.
McKelvie, A. and Davidsson, P. (2009). From resource base to dynamic capabilities: An investigation of new firms. *British Journal of Management*, 20(SI): S63–S80.
Macpherson A. (2005). Learning to grow: Resolving the crisis of knowing. *Technovation*, 25(10): 1129–1140.
Madsen, E. L. (2010). A dynamic capability framework: Generic types of dynamic capabilities and their relationship to entrepreneurship. In Wall, S., Zimmermann, C., Klingebiel, R., and Lange, D. (Eds.), *Strategic Reconfigurations* (pp. 223–238). Cheltenham, UK: Edward Elgar.
March, J. (1991). Exploration and exploitation in organizational learning. *Organization Science*, 2(1): 71–87.
Mathews, J. A. and Zander, I. (2007). The international entrepreneurial dynamics of accelerated internationalization. *Journal of International Business Studies*, 38(3): 387–403.
Michael, S., Storey, D., and Thomas, H. (2002). Discovery and coordination in strategic management and entrepreneurship. In Hitt, M. A., Ireland, R. D., Camp, S.D., and Sexton, D. L. (eds) *Strategic Entrepreneurship: Creating a New Mindset*,. Oxford: Blackwell Publishers.
Nelson, R. R. and Winter, S. G. (1982). *An Evolutionary Theory of Economic Change*. Cambridge, MA and London: Belknap Press.
Newbert, S. (2005). New firm formation: A dynamic capability perspective. *Journal of Small Business Management*, 43(1): 55–77.
Newey, R. and Zahra, S. (2009). The evolving firm: How dynamic and operating capabilities intract to enable entrepreneurship. *British Journal of Management*, 20(supp.1): S81–S100.
Oviatt, B. M. and McDougall, P. P. (1994). Towards a theory of international new ventures. *Journal of International Business Studies*, 25(1): 45–64.
Oviatt, B. M. and McDougall, P. P. (2000). International entrpreneurship: The intersection of two research paths. *Academy of Management Journal*, 43(5): 902–906.
Oviatt, B. M. and McDougall, P. P. (2005). Defining international entrepreneurship and modeling the speed of internationalization. *Entrepreneurship, Theory and Practice*, 29(5): 537–553.
Oviatt, B. M., McDougal, P. P., and Shrader, R. C. (2003). A comparison of international and domestic ventures. *Journal of International Entrepreneurship*, 1(1): 59–82.
Penrose, E. (1959). *The Theory of the Growth of the Firm*. Oxford: Blackwell.
Prange, C. and Verdier, S. (2011). Dynamic capabilities, internationalization processes and performance. *Journal of World Business*, 46(1): 126–133.
Prashantham, S. and Floyd, S. W. (2012). Routine microprocesses and capability learning in international new ventures. *Journal of International Business Studies*, 43: 544–562.
Puranam, P., Singh, H., and Zollo, M. (2006). Organizing for innovation: Managing the coordination–autonomy dilemma in technology acquisitions. *Academy of Management Journal*, 49(2): 263–280.
Sapienza, H. J., Autio, E., George, G., and Zahra, S. A. (2006). A capability perspective on the effects of early internationalization on firm survival and growth. *Academy of Management Review*, 31(4): 914–933.
Shane, S. (2000). Prior knowledge and the discovery of entrepreneurial opportunities. *Organization Science*, 11(4): 448–469.
Smith, W. K. and Lewis, M. W. (2011). Toward a theory of paradox: A dynamic equilibrium model of organizing. *Academy of Management Journal*, 36(2): 381–403.
Tallman, S. and Fladmore-Lindquist, K. (2002). Internationalization, globalization, and capability-based strategy. *California Management Review*, 45(1): 116–135.
Teece, D. J. (2007). Explicating dynamic capabilities: The nature and microfoundations of (sustainable) enterprise performance. *Strategic Management Journal*, 28(13): 1319–1350.
Teece, D. J., Pisano, G., and Shuen, A. (1997). Dynamic capabilities and strategic management. *Strategic Management Journal*, 18(7): 509–533.
Tushman, M. L. and O'Reilly, C. A. (1996). Ambidextrous organizations: Managing evolutionary and revolutionary change. *California Management Review*, 38(4): 8–30.
Verdier, S., Prange, C., Atamer, T., and Monin, P. (2010). Internationalization performance revisited: The impact of age and speed on sales growth. *Management International*, 15(1): 19–31.
Vermeulen, F. and Barkema, H. (2001). Learning through acquisitions. *Academy of Management Journal*, 44(3): 457–476.
Vermeulen, F. and Barkema, H. G. (2002). Pace, rhythm and scope: Process dependence in building a profitable multinational corporation, *Strategic Management Journal*, 23(7): 637–653.
Weerawardena, J., Sullivan Mort, G., Liesch, P.W., and Knight, G. (2007). Conceptualizing accelerated internationalization in the born global firm: A dynamic capabilities perspective. *Journal of World Business*, 42(3): 294–306.

Wilden, R., Gudergan, S. P., Nielsen, B. B., and Lings, I. (2013). Dynamic capabilities and performance: Strategy, structure, and environment. *Long Range Planning*, 46(1–2): 72–96.
Winter, S. G. (2003). Understanding dynamic capabilities. *Strategic Management Journal*, 24(10): 991–995.
Woldesenbet, K., Ram, M., and Jones, T. (2012). Supplying large firms: The role of entrepreneurial and dynamic capabilities in small businesses. *International Small Business Journal*, 30(5): 493–512.
Zahra, S. A., Abdel-Gawad, S., Svejenova, S., and Sapienza, H. (2011). Entrepreneurial capability: Opportunity pursuit and game changing. Paper presented at the DRUID 2011 conference on Innovation, Strategy, and Structures, Copenhagen Business School, June 15–17, 2011.
Zahra, S. A. and George, G. (2002). Absorptive capacity: A review, reconcepualisation, and extension. *Academy of Management Review*, 27(2): 185–203.
Zahra, S. A., Sapienza, H. J., and Davidsson, P. (2006). Entrepreneurship and dynamic capabilities: A review, model and research agenda. *Journal of Management Studies*, 43(4): 917–955.
Zhang, M., Tansuhai, P., and McCullough, J. (2009). International entrepreneurial capability: The measurement and a comparison between born global firms and traditional exporters in China. *Journal of International Entrepreneurship*, 5: 292–322.
Zollo, M. and Winter, S. (2002). Deliberate learning and the evolution of dynamic capabilities. *Organization Science*, 13(3): S.339–351.

10

Understanding eINVs through the lens of prior research in entrepreneurship, international business and international entrepreneurship

A. Rebecca Reuber, Eileen Fischer and Anna Morgan-Thomas

In this chapter we examine the growing phenomenon of internet-based international new ventures, which we label "eINVs," through the lens of previous research in the fields of entrepreneurship, international business and international entrepreneurship. Our purpose is to identify where these existing bodies of research help us to understand eINVs, and where there are gaps that constitute important questions for future research. We define an eINV by adapting a widely used definition of international new ventures (INVs) (Oviatt and McDougall 2005: 5): an eINV is a venture whose business model is enabled by a digital platform and that, from inception, seeks to derive significant competitive advantage from international growth. With a focus explicitly on how extant research helps us understand eINVs, this review differs from that of Reuber and Fischer (2011b), who focus on firm-level internet-related resources that are related to the internationalization of ventures in general; that of Pezderka and Sinkovics (2011), who focus on risk and the online foreign market entry decisions of small and medium-sized enterprises (SMEs); and that of Chandra and Coviello (2010), who focus on consumers using the internet to pursue international opportunities.

There are both practical and theoretical reasons to study eINVs. From a practice perspective, eINVs are experiencing a significant social and economic impact globally, and are attracting widespread interest from entrepreneurs, investors and policymakers. A recent report by the OECD highlights attractive market conditions for internet firms[1]: within OECD economies, they have constituted the fastest-growing sector for over a decade, and were among the most profitable and R&D-intensive sectors in 2011 (OECD 2012: 45–48). Internet usage is nearly ubiquitous, with roughly 90 percent of businesses and 67 percent of households in OECD economies having a broadband internet connection (OECD 2012: 135, 103), 90 percent of young people accessing the internet from home (OECD 2012: 108), and rapid adoption of internet-connected mobile devices (OECD 2012: 107).

Literature reviews, summarizing the hundreds of studies investigating constructs and relationships relevant to INVs, indicate that technology-intensive organizations tend to become more international, earlier, than organizations in lower technology sectors (e.g. Aspelund et al. 2007;

Coviello and Jones 2004; Dimitratos and Jones 2005; Fischer and Reuber 2008; Jones et al. 2011; Rialp et al. 2005), but little research has focused specifically on eINVs (cf. Reuber and Fischer 2011b). From a theoretical perspective, there is reason to believe that the internationalization of eINVs is enabled by somewhat different factors than those of INVs. INV-related theory and empirical research is based on the resource limitations of young firms and on how factors such as internationally experienced founders and partnerships help to overcome them (e.g. McDougall et al. 1994; Oviatt and McDougall 1994). However, these factors seem to be insufficient to account for the trajectories of many successful eINVs. Those that survive tend not to be poor for long. For example, Airbnb was founded in 2008, received $7.8 million in outside financing within two years (Airbnb 2013a), and, by 2011, supported 16 languages and 17 currencies, operated in 192 countries, and attracted 75 percent of users from outside their domestic market (Airbnb 2013b). Skype was founded in 2003, received $18.8 million in outside financing in its first year (Index Ventures 2004), and by 2005 was operating in 225 countries (eBay Inc. 2005). In both cases, this early funding was explicitly aimed at international expansion. These anecdotal examples suggest that it is valuable to examine eINVs separately from INVs, rather than merely assuming they are a subset of INVs. It is for this reason that we go beyond international entrepreneurship theory in examining the phenomenon, and take into account theoretical developments in the fields of entrepreneurship, focusing on startup processes and choices; and international business, focusing on geographic expansion processes and choices.

In this chapter we focus on capabilities rather than resources, and describe an integrated framework of three "S" capabilities that underlie successful eINVs: sensing, scaling and spreading. These are shown in Figure 10.1. At the core is *sensing*, or the ability for firm managers to perceive how market-related external stimuli can be used to develop international opportunities. Once opportunities are sensed, eINVs need to be capable of exploiting them through *scaling*, which is the rapid expansion of operations in terms of volume, value or scope. Effective scaling is necessary for value creation because it enables economies of scale to be realized and network effects to be capitalized on. Scaling, in turn, creates the need for the capability of *spreading*, or developing awareness of the eINV's existence and appreciation of its offerings across a geographically dispersed base of online stakeholders. This capability is critical because eINVs lack the physical drivers of demand that are sparked by material proximity, yet must develop awareness and attention among distant audiences (Kotha et al. 2001).

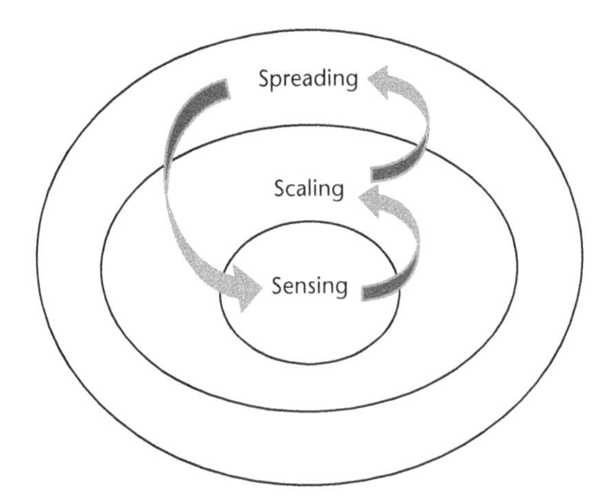

Figure 10.1 Capabilities enabling the success of eINVs

The activities involved in spreading can provide feedback to the sensing function; for example, a firm can analyse the user-generated content of online communities to sense new international opportunities.

In the remainder of this chapter we examine each of these capabilities in turn through the lens of existing theory and empirical research in the fields of entrepreneurship, international business (IB) and international entrepreneurship (IE). There is an extensive body of research on some topics and our aim is to provide a representative, rather than exhaustive, coverage of different perspectives. The key theoretical constructs identified from each perspective, as well as an e-marketing perspective in the case of the spreading capabilities, are shown in Table 10.1. The Discussion Section highlights gaps in our knowledge of eINVs that constitute important questions for future research, and presents the conclusions of this chapter for international entrepreneurship scholars. Table 10.2 summarizes the specific eINVs used as examples in this chapter, and shows that they are not solely a US-based phenomenon. It shows the wide range of eINVs we have examined, in terms of their startup place and time, the first year they received Silicon Valley financing (if any), and the extensiveness of their international presence, in terms of the number of distinct country-related URLs, the number of languages available on their website(s), and the number of countries where they have a physical presence.

Sensing

Sensing refers to the perceptions of market-related external stimuli both at the firm level and at the individual level by firm founders and managers. Although there is some overlap, the entrepreneurship literature and the international business literature tend to emphasize different aspects of sensing. The entrepreneurship literature, for the most part, focuses on the earliest days of the firm and so emphasizes individual-level perceptions relevant to developing an initial opportunity. In contrast, the international business literature tends to take a domestic presence as given, and focuses on the firm-level sensing of new markets that will enable the firm to grow. The international entrepreneurship literature falls somewhere in between, emphasizing network partners and market entries.

Table 10.1 Key concepts relevant to eINVs identified from the literature review

Bodies of literature	*Firm-level capabilities*		
	Sensing	*Scaling*	*Spreading*
Entrepreneurship	Opportunity recognition Opportunity creation	Business models Platform-based markets	Transfer of reputation and status Narratives, symbolic communication
International business	Learning from experience Sequencing market entries	Internalization Standard-setting Replication	Adaptation vs. standardization
International entrepreneurship	Networks Learning from experience Sequencing market entries	Financial resource acquisition	Networks Co-branding International forums
E-marketing			Online communities Data mining Customer relationship management

Table 10.2 The eINVs used as examples in this chapter

Company	*Founding year and place*	*Description*	*Silicon Valley financing*	*Number of URL country domains*	*Number of website languages*	*Number of countries with an office*
Airbnb	2008: San Francisco, USA	Online market for accommodation	2008	12	24	11
Alibaba	1999: Hangzhou, China	Online market for SME trade	2004	1	10	1
Amazon	1995: Seattle, USA	Online retailer	1995	11	8	18
BlueNile	1999: Seattle, USA	Online diamond retailer	1999	1	6	2
DesignCrowd	2008: Sydney, Australia	Crowdsourced design work	–	9	1	1
eBay	1995: San Jose, USA	Online auction site	1997	39	21	27
FreshBooks	2003: Toronto, Canada	Online accounting software	–	1	1	1
Groupon	2008: Chicago, USA	Online deal-of-the-day site	2008	49	22	1
HubSpot	2006: Boston, USA	Online marketing and web analytics	2008	1	1	2
Huddle	2006: London, UK	Document sharing/collaboration platform	2010	1	1	1
Jamba!	2000: Berlin, Germany	Digital content distributor	–	15	9	1
MackieLab	2011: London, UK	Custom-made toys	–	1	1	1
MyMuesli	2007: Berlin, Germany	Online retailer in customized cereal	–	2	2	2
PayPal	1998: Palo Alto, USA	Online payment processing	1998	190	9	22
Pinterest	2010: San Francisco, USA	Online tool for collections	2011	1	8	1
Sellaband	2006: Amsterdam, Netherlands	Crowdsourced music funding	–	3	3	1
Skype	2003: Luxembourg	VoIP software and services	2003	1	23	3
Twitter	2006: San Francisco, USA	Online microblogging service	2007	1	36	1

Date sources: Company websites as of May 2013, press releases from companies, and news articles about companies.

Entrepreneurship literature

Much of the entrepreneurship literature on the sensing of opportunities assumes either that entrepreneurs recognize opportunities that exist exogenously or that entrepreneurs create opportunities endogenously (Alvarez and Barney 2007). A discovery, or opportunity recognition, approach is predominantly cognitive in nature and involves two perceptions on the part of an entrepreneur: first, that an opportunity exists due to changes in the environment, and second, that the firm has the means and motivation to act on it (McMullen and Shepherd 2006). Through experience, individuals develop cognitive frameworks that impact whether and how they perceive opportunities from external stimuli (Baron and Ensley 2006), and as well as cognitive processes that enable them to draw on past market experiences when reasoning about possibilities for new technology (Grégoire et al. 2010).

In contrast, an opportunity creation approach is predominantly action-oriented, in that opportunities are viewed as being created endogenously by the actions and interactions of entrepreneurs in a market. In particular, effectuation theory holds that opportunities are constructed by entrepreneurs increasing their stock of knowledge and resources through commitments from market actors such as partners and early customers (Read et al. 2009; Sarasvathy 2001). Thus, sensing in opportunity creation is closely intertwined with both scaling and spreading, as all three aspects are iteratively involved in building opportunities.

A close embeddedness of sensing, scaling and spreading is characteristic of recent perspectives on opportunity that encompass a duality of recognition and creation. For example, Cornelissen and Clarke (2010) argue that entrepreneurs use experientially based inductive analogical reasoning when starting a venture (the recognition aspect) and that these analogies facilitate comprehension and justification of the venture for resource-providers in the market (the creation aspect). From a practice perspective, the lean startup methodology popular among internet-based startups (Ries 2011) emphasizes the articulation of hypotheses about a venture's target market and value proposition (the recognition aspect) and the empirical testing of these hypotheses in the market aimed at acquiring stakeholder commitment to the venture (the creation aspect). We therefore consider the sensing of the opportunities associated with eINVs as involving both individual-level cognition and firm-level venture development activities associated with scaling and spreading.

Although an individual's experience as a source of information (and cognitive biases) underlies much of the literature on entrepreneurial opportunities, this body of research also highlights other sources of information, particularly social sources, which are relevant to opportunity recognition and creation. Such sources include user communities (e.g. Shah and Tripsas 2007), mentors, industry networks and professional forums (e.g. Ozgen and Baron 2007), and feedback from potential customers and partners (e.g. Read et al. 2009; Ries 2011). This knowledge is often acquired from the internet itself and so may be socially sourced, but at a distance (Prashantham 2005). For eINVs, the sensing of the potential of emerging technologies, both at startup and on an ongoing basis, is expected to be particularly important, given the continual changes in networks, devices, operating systems, application services and cloud computing (OECD 2012: 61–80); however, this aspect of sensing has not been emphasized in the literature.

International business literature

In contrast to the entrepreneurship literature, which focuses on the level of the individual entrepreneur and the founding management team in sensing, the international business literature, in general, focuses more at the level of the firm. This difference in the level of analysis is consistent with the entrepreneurship literature's primary interest in explaining the development of early stage opportunities, and the IB literature's primary interest in explaining foreign market entries subsequent to a domestic presence. A particularly relevant stream of this literature for eINVs is concerned with the sequencing of foreign market entries.

A long-established perspective on internationalization is that expansion into foreign markets requires knowledge accumulation through firm-level experience (Johanson and Vahlne 1977; 2009). Successful internationalization is seen as incremental, from culturally similar to dissimilar markets, and from low commitment entry modes like exporting to higher commitment entry modes like establishing a subsidiary, in order to minimize the uncertainty associated with foreign market entry. This is consistent with a study of early internet-based firms from the US which found that a greater cultural distance between the US and a possible host country is associated with a lower likelihood of entering that country (Rothaermel et al. 2006). It should be noted, however, that the negative relationship found between cultural distance and likelihood of entry was positively moderated by market size, indicating that firms were more motivated to overcome the risk of cultural distance when market returns were expected to be higher.

The impact of learning from experience in other markets is affected by multiple factors. When firms are new to a dissimilar culture, they can draw erroneous conclusions. This "incorrect learning" has been shown to be aggravated by a fast pace of foreign expansion (Zeng et al. 2013), which is typically characteristic of rapidly growing eINVs. However, if a firm has a technological advantage, and sets standards and trends, it has fewer challenges – and therefore lower learning needs – in distant markets (Banalieva and Dhanaraj 2013). This can be an advantage for those eINVs which benefit from herding behaviour, and a concomitant early dominance, in their market (cf. Duan et al. 2009). Nevertheless, there are increasingly complex information-processing demands on a firm as the number of foreign markets increases, which have been found to result in an inverted U-shaped relationship between international diversification and firm performance (Hitt et al. 1997). However, this relationship has not yet been tested in the context of eINVs.

Firms can acquire knowledge about the potential of foreign markets from diverse sources: current customers and domestic competitors (Martin et al., 1998), companies in the host country (Salomon and Wu 2012), and network partners (Johanson and Vahlne 2009). An additional source of knowledge that is expected to be particularly important for eINVs is venture capital firms, which are increasing their international investments (Fernhaber and McDougall-Covin 2009; Guler and Guillén 2010; Humphery-Jenner and Suchard 2013). Indeed, new eINVs that are initially located (or that relocate early on) close to Silicon Valley, with its internet-related expertise and financing power, are likely to enjoy a location-based advantage (cf. Dunning 2009). There is a lower requirement to acquire market-specific knowledge in global industries than in multidomestic industries because there is less pressure to conform to local preferences, practices and regulations (Kobrin 1991; Porter 1986), and a logical implication of this argument is that eINVs operating in global market niches have less need to acquire local information than those operating in multidomestic market niches.

International entrepreneurship literature

Although the international entrepreneurship literature has a wide scope, here we examine two specific aspects of new ventures – network partners and market entries – that have been central to the field since its inception (McDougall et al. 1994; Oviatt and McDougall 1994). Both are relevant to an eINV's sensing capability.

Networks are an important enabler of early and extensive internationalization (Coviello 2006; Coviello and Munro 1997). Bell and Loane (2010) emphasize the importance of partnerships in providing eINVs with both online distribution and physical distribution in distant markets. We contend that establishing such partnerships is part of the opportunity creation process for eINVs. This is consistent with research showing that rapid internationalization involves a path-dependent process of opportunity development encompassing learning through experience and exposure to new information and network ties (Chandra et al. 2012; Mathews and Zander 2007). However, network ties tend to be bounded by geography and cultural distance, which can expand or constrain the opportunities an entrepreneur can perceive (Chandra et al. 2012; Ellis 2011). In addition, the necessity for speed given competitive pressures (cf. Loane et al. 2004) and herding behaviours (cf. Duan et al. 2009) in internet markets can limit the available time and attention that managers can devote to developing the trust required for effective networks (cf. Johanson and Vahlne 2009; Rangan 2000). This suggests that it can be difficult for entrepreneurs founding eINVs to integrate foreign partnerships into the construction of their venture without access to globally connected social capital (cf. Prashantham and Dhanaraj 2010). Indeed, Fernhaber et al. (2009) found that new ventures whose management teams had limited international experience benefitted most from external knowledge sources, such as alliance partners and venture capitalists, and we expect this to be especially true for eINVs.

The international entrepreneurship literature also indicates that the nature of market entries affects the sensing capability of eINVs. Recent literature at the individual level suggests that reasoning about internationalization decisions is based on experientially developed heuristics or analogies (Jones and Casulli 2014). At the firm level, there is evidence to suggest that INVs should enter foreign markets, and diversified foreign markets, quickly after startup to enhance learning capabilities in general (Autio et al. 2000) and technological learning in particular (Zahra et al. 2000). However, it is important to note that these learning advantages of newness have not been studied in the context of eINVs. Yamin and Sinkovics (2006) warn against a 'virtuality trap', the perception 'that the learning generated through virtual interactions obviates the need for learning about the target markets through non-virtual means' (2006: 340). It may be the case that as some eINVs internationalize quickly and widely, they become more reliant on online data and more susceptible to the virtuality trap, which constrains the extent to which they can learn about distant markets. This is expected to be particularly true for eINVs that have only a minimal physical presence outside their home country.

The international entrepreneurship literature also points out that while some foreign market entry is deliberate and intentional, it is often unplanned due to serendipitous encounters (e.g. Crick and Spence 2005). Petersen et al. (2002) point out that setting up a website can render a firm more visible to foreign partners and customers, leading to more unsolicited orders, and more numerous, faster and ad hoc entries. Such serendipity may be dysfunctional: Bingham's research (2009) suggests that a deliberate, coherent selection of markets is preferable, because it enables managers to build their experiential base of knowledge, from more similar markets to less similar markets, and from smaller, less visible markets to larger, more visible markets. We do not yet have an understanding of which eINVs are best served by either approach. The first strategy (expanding as fast as possible) may be advantageous when there is herding in the market and the size of a firm's user base is an important criterion on which a firm's value is based. The second strategy (a planned sequence of entries) may be preferable when there is greater offline activity associated with a firm's business model, such as, for example, a large number of people selling local advertising or attracting local merchants.

Scaling

Scaling refers to an eINV's ability to configurationally enact and manage rapid international growth through expansion of operations in terms of volume, value or scope. Considering that internationalization is a costly pursuit affected by time compression diseconomies (Jiang et al. 2014) and that growth and survival can be competing objectives for young international firms (Sapienza et al. 2006), it might be puzzling that eINVs would pursue rapid growth. Below we draw on the entrepreneurship, IB and IE literatures to address this puzzle and to explain how rapid scaling may be achieved.

Entrepreneurship literature

Having something worth expanding is a necessary prerequisite for effective scaling. By focusing on the question of how an organization may configure itself to best extract value, the entrepreneurship literature draws our attention to the scaling of a firm's business model (Zott and Amit 2007; Bock et al. 2012; George and Bock 2011; Onetti et al. 2010; Teece 2010). Following George and Bock (2011), we define a business model as an 'organization's configurational enactment of a specific opportunity' (2011: 102). The business model literature argues that the process of modelling involves purposeful weaving together of activities into a structure that explains what the firm does and how it extracts value, and that this process begins with the question of the value proposition itself (Zott et al. 2011). Zott and Amit (2007) draw a useful distinction between novelty and efficiency as sources of value. Novelty-centered models exploit new ways of conducting transactions 'by connecting previously unconnected parties, by linking transaction participants in new ways, or by designing new transaction mechanisms' (2007: 184). MackieLab and its business model, which straddles toy and online entertainment categories, represent a case in point. Founded in 2011, the London-based firm exploits a technological capability of converting digital game objects into physical toys to enable its customers to co-create customisable toys on demand, thus offering an innovation in the process of toy production. By contrast, efficiency-centered business models rely on doing things in a more efficient way. For example, BlueNile exploits inefficiencies in the global diamond industry value chain and adopts a made-to-order logic to implement direct online sales of diamond jewellery to consumers. This business model research suggests that, like any other entrepreneurial venture, eINVs need to have either innovative novelty-centered or innovative efficiency-centered business models if they are to be able to scale effectively.

Further, eINVs are distinguished by the complex and unusual ways that value may be extracted and captured (Teece 2010), and an important aspect of this is their digital platform. Research on platform-mediated markets (Adomavicius et al. 2007; Parker and Van Alstyne 2008; West 2003) draws attention to the difference between platform and product strategies, where platforms are technology or service foundations that facilitate interactions between different users (Eisenmann et al. 2011). Gawer and Cusumano (2008) argue that while product strategies rely on value extracted from transactions with end users, platform strategies capitalize on complex arrangements involving a broad range of stakeholders and partners. End users typically expect the service to be free (Teece 2010) and the goal of the platform is to provide an independent ecosystem that enables charging other platform participants (Parker and Van Alstyne 2008). Online search engines like Google, for example, allow non-paying users to access the platform for free because revenues are extracted from fee-paying advertisers. Platforms can display strong network effects and achieving platform status often involves winner-takes-all battles (Lee and Mendelson 2008), whereby a new platform replaces an older one (e.g. Facebook replacing MySpace).

The value of a platform depends on the number of users, and so rapid growth is achieved through envelopment strategies involving complements, substitutes or functionally unrelated products (Eisenmann et al. 2011).

Platform ecosystems are subject not only to ongoing battles for scale, they are also subject to constant change (Lee and Mendelson 2008). Ever-changing technologies, aggressive competitors and contested norms mean that the ability to adjust continuously represents an important strategic capability. Rindova and Kotha (2001) trace the evolution of two eINVs and show that such hypercompetitive environments impose continuous change to firms' business models. They conclude that flexible arrangements of resources and structures are needed for constant readjustment. Their findings seem to support the notion that structural inertia and rigidities are disadvantageous in rapidly changing environments (cf. Sapienza et al. 2006) and that reliance on resources such as partners actually reduces strategic flexibility during business model innovation (Bock et al. 2012). This contrasts with a tenet of the IE literature that emphasizes the benefits of partners to international new ventures. Overall, the research on platforms helps to explain why rapid geographical expansion represents a strategic imperative for at least some eINVs, an imperative that seems to override the concerns of profitability.

International business literature

An effective business model is a necessary but not sufficient condition for scaling: what distinguishes scaling from other forms of opportunity exploitation is the explicit emphasis on rapid expansion and enlargement of the opportunity. The question of how a firm may scale up its operations by entering foreign markets represents the very cornerstone of international business enquiry and so the IB literature offers valuable insights on eINVs pursuing international expansion. There is a rich tradition in IB research concerning the interplay between a firm's technology and the pattern of its international growth (Banalieva and Dhanaraj 2013; Nachum and Zaheer 2005; Rangan and Sengul 2009). The principle of internalization is a dominant theme within this stream of research (Buckley and Casson 1976; Rugman 1981). It holds that large multinational firms exist because alternative means of organizing international transactions such as markets, alliances or partnerships are less desirable, and this is particularly true when proprietary technology is at play (Rugman and Verbeke 2004), as is often the case for eINVs. Moreover, we expect that eINVs use information and communication technologies effectively, which lowers the informational, communication and administrative costs on internalization (Buckley and Casson 2009; Rangan and Sengul 2009). Thus, we expect that greater internalization distinguishes eINVs from other INVs that prioritize control, rather than ownership, of resources (cf. Oviatt and McDougall 1994).

Recent studies on trade theory in IB provide an additional insight into the link between a firm's technological advantage and its internationalization (Melitz 2003; Nocke and Yeaple 2007). A premise of this literature is that when technology is highly sophisticated and valuable, as it is for many eINVs, the technology itself may facilitate rapid international growth. Nocke and Yeaple (2007) argue that as technology becomes more sophisticated, its imitability by competitors decreases, and the firm becomes a standard setter. The establishment of a standard reduces the need to adapt to local markets, which in turn reduces the cost of internationalization (Nocke and Yeaple 2007). It is worth noting that the focus on standards in trade theory complements the research on platforms (Eisenmann et al. 2011; West 2003). If global consumers become locked into a firm's technology because it constitutes a standard (cf. Amit and Zott 2001), it will be easier for that firm to deter local competition in distant markets, thereby accelerating its internationalization.

The final insight from the IB literature concerns replication as a distinct scaling mechanism for international expansion (Jonsson and Foss 2011). Unlike innovation, which involves flexibility and change, replication relies on leveraging existing routines and organizational rigidities (Friesl and Larty 2013). The logic of replication assumes that rather than following a slow process of learning and change in the process of international growth (Vermeulen and Barkema 2002; Johanson and Vahlne 1977; 2009), organizations may standardize, fix and then replicate parts of its value chain (Winter and Szulanski 2001). The German digital content provider Jamba! and its template-based internationalization clearly illustrates this principle (Kaufmann et al. 2006). During its expansion into European markets in 2003, Jamba! developed a 'country launch manual' where each foreign market entry strictly adhered to four detailed steps: linking to an aggregator, preparing content, implementing media plan and administering the launch. The exploitation of the standardized pattern enabled the venture to enter 12 countries and more than quadruple its workforce in the time span of 12 months.

A narrow value proposition, a narrow product line, and a need to mass distribute the end product are characteristics that favour replication (Jonsson and Foss 2011). Huddle, a London-based venture established in 2006, offers an illustration. By concentrating on a narrow set of functionalities (document sharing and collaboration solutions for larger enterprises), the venture was able to standardize and rapidly scale up its operations to span 180 countries by 2012 (*Financial Times* 2012). The example of six-year-old MyMuesli, a German online firm that offers customized cereal boxes, demonstrates that replication may also be beneficial in consumer markets.

Empirical studies on replication show that in order to replicate, routines need to be made explicit and formatted into guidelines or manuals (Jonsson and Foss 2011). In other words, successful replication relies on the ability to effectively code and encode the business format to convert it into practice (Szulanski 1996; 2000). The examples above show that digitization of a firm's offering seems to favour replication. By virtue of being online, eINVs are firms with significant parts of the business process digitized, and therefore already encoded (Kallinikos 2009). We therefore expect replication to be particularly advantageous as a method of scaling for eINVs.

International entrepreneurship literature

The IE literature holds that the rapid internationalization of young firms is possible because access to resources is explicitly differentiated from, and prioritized over, ownership of them (Oviatt and McDougall 1994). Given that scaling requires resources, the resource access mechanisms identified in the IE literature (such as partnerships) are relevant to scaling. For example, many eINVs rely on financial resources provided by external partners, typically venture capitalists. Evidence shows that external financing facilitates international growth by allowing a more aggressive approach to be adopted (McDougall et al. 2003), which enables a broader scale and scope of foreign market entry (George et al. 2005). The knowledge and reputation of external stakeholders can also support scaling (Fernhaber and McDougall-Covin 2009). The role of external stakeholders is yet to be examined specifically for eINVs, but the track records of well-known eINVs provide strong evidence of their need for, and their ability to attract, resources that facilitate the scaling capability.

Spreading

The third capability we consider is 'spreading', which refers to developing awareness of an eINV's existence and appreciation of its offerings across a geographically dispersed base of online stakeholders. Given that eINVs lack the drivers of demand that are sparked by proximity, how can these ventures with limited track records build both awareness and positive affect in short order?

This challenge is particularly difficult given that competition for online attention and affiliation is intense (cf. Humphreys 2013; Wang et al. 2013). In this section, we scan the entrepreneurship, IB, IE and e-marketing literatures to illuminate how eINVs can meet this challenge.

Entrepreneurship literature

Two streams in the entrepreneurship literature offer insights that could apply to eINVs seeking to spread awareness of, and appreciation for, their offerings. The first investigates how startups leverage their affiliations with other parties, such as partners, investors, and customers (e.g. Deutsch and Ross 2003; Reuber and Fischer 2005; Shane and Cable 2002; Stuart et al. 1999). Studies in this stream show that prospective stakeholders exposed to information that links a startup with an established and reputable entity, such as a prestigious investor or a blue-chip customer, are likely to regard that startup as more credible than one that lacks such affiliations (Fischer and Reuber 2007). Reuber and Fischer (2005) also note that when new firms can publicize their affiliations with particular types of customers, they can also create awareness of the range, size and segments of customers they are able to serve. This is relevant to those eINVs that can showcase endorsements from customers based in diverse geographic regions because they can signal to prospective clients that they are capable of serving international markets. Freshbooks, a Toronto-based eINV selling accounting software to small businesses, profiles international clients on its website to convey to non-domestic prospects that it can serve their needs (Reuber and Fischer 2011a).

The second stream in the entrepreneurship literature deals with narratives (Martens et al. 2007) or symbolic communication practices (Zott and Huy 2007) that new firms can use to increase their perceived legitimacy and reputability in the eyes of stakeholders. Aldrich and Fiol (1994) were the first to draw attention to how entrepreneurial firms can deploy selected symbolic practices and narrative tactics to encourage stakeholders to regard them favourably. In a study of narratives in IPO prospectuses, Martens et al. (2007) found that portraying entrepreneurial firms as aspiring leaders with track records had a positive impact on the valuation premiums at IPO, but portraying them as aspiring leaders with social ties or conveying ambiguous identity narratives both had a *negative* impact on valuation premiums. Further, in a study of symbolic practices of new firms, Zott and Huy (2007) found that impactful communications included, for example, those conveying the entrepreneur's personal credibility (e.g. displaying educational credentials), those indicating the organization's capability for professional organizing (e.g. maintaining a highly functional website), and those signifying the organization's achievement (e.g. publicizing awards won). The specific kinds of symbolic communication practices or narratives that will lend credibility to eINVs may differ from those appropriate for other new ventures, given that different genre conventions (cf. Orlikowski and Yates 1994) may dominate in the online communication platforms on which eINVs rely; however, the premise that some narratives are more effective than others for engaging stakeholders appears likely to hold for eINVs.

International business literature

International business scholars have asserted that to gain international awareness and attention, businesses must leverage their home-market reputations (e.g. Kotha et al. 2001: 772). The logic is that firms that are prominent and well-regarded in their home environment can take advantage of their reputational assets because potential stakeholders in foreign markets will already know and be favourably disposed towards the firm. However, eINVs may have no home-market track record to draw on, making this aspect of the international business literature of limited relevance.

A second strand of the international business literature, one that might be more applicable to eINVs, debates the adaptation versus standardization of marketing strategies for communicating with stakeholders in diverse geographic regions (e.g. Cavusgil et al. 1993; Levitt 1983; Samiee and Roth 1992; Wind 1986). This literature has evolved toward a contingency perspective, advocating that the advisability of adaptation depends, for example, on the company, physical product, and targeted export market characteristics. Cavusgil et al. (1993) argue that firms should adapt their positioning, packaging/labelling and promotional approaches when they have high export sales goals and unique products, as is the case with eINVs. However, they also argue that firms should not adapt their positioning, packaging/labelling and promotional approaches when they are selling technology-intensive products and targeting multiple export markets simultaneously, as is also the case with eINVs. Thus at present it remains unclear under what contingent conditions eINVs should adapt rather than standardize the tactics they use to spread awareness and gain positive affect toward their offerings.

International entrepreneurship literature

This body of work overlaps with both of those already reviewed, but studies specifically focused on INVs provide some distinct, and valuable, insights. Several INV articles indicate that leveraging the resources (including, but not limited to, reputation) of international stakeholders with whom the firm is affiliated can help a startup spread its global visibility and credibility (e.g. Altshuler and Tarnovskaya 2010; Coviello and Munro 1997; Gabrielsson 2005; Gabrielsson and Gabrielsson 2003; Gabrielsson and Kirpalani 2004). Co-branding between a startup and multinational is one such type of leveraging. Co-branding is a form of cooperation between firms in which the brand names of both are exposed to their joint customer base (Blackett and Boad 1999). Paypal is an eINV that achieved significant international spread by virtue of its brand alliance with the more established firm, eBay, that featured Paypal as a payment option on its website. So successful did Paypal's "spread" become that eBay ultimately bought the company and shut down development of a competitor (Fischer and Reuber 2007).

The INV literature also highlights that new firms can leverage international forums to achieve spread (e.g. Gabrielsson 2005), as they reach well beyond a domestic audience. International tradeshows are one such type of forum. To illustrate, the eINV Freshbooks takes advantage of the annual SXSW tradeshow to achieve spread among the segment of potential customers who attend this music, film and interactive gaming event. Online markets are another type of international forum of value to some eINVs. For example, the online market download.com provides an international platform for many eINVs selling software (e.g. Reuber and Fischer, 2009). While not every eINV competes in an industry that features such international forums, those that do can accelerate spread by taking advantage of them.

E-marketing literature

A growing body of marketing studies examine how firms can broaden their reach online. Most research thus far on successful online 'spreading' has been conducted for established companies selling consumer goods (e.g. Fournier and Avery 2011), though a few have considered new and/or B2B firms (e.g. Ashworth et al. 2006; Fischer and Reuber 2014). As of yet, none have considered how new online firms can increase awareness and appreciation among international audiences; however, two interrelated threads in this work are useful for understanding eINVs.

The first thread focuses on networks that emerge (or that can be created) among online stakeholders and how these may benefit firms. Numerous studies have discussed online 'communities' or collectives of people who share an interest in product categories (such as smartphones, e.g. Kozinets et al. 2010) or brands (such as Stri-vectin, e.g. Schau et al. 2009). Evidence indicates that, in such online networks, members frequently share information and opinions about specific companies and offerings, since participants derive value from doing so (Schau et al. 2009). Some firms have tried to accelerate communication about their own brand within existing communities, while others have tried to create new online communities by promoting Facebook fan pages or company Twitter accounts (e.g. Dholakia and Durham 2010). Although certain studies indicate that firms can benefit from these efforts, others note that firms may face backlash and hostility from online community members if their efforts are too explicitly sales oriented or if interactions that express negative sentiments are censored (e.g. Fournier and Avery 2011).

Some eINVs have nonetheless managed to achieve spread effectively via online networks. For example, despite initial skepticism about a user-generated innovation, the 'hashtag' symbol (#) that allowed users to assign a topic to their posts to the micro-blogging website Twitter, executives ultimately recognized and harnessed the potential inherent in communities of interest that clustered around hashtags to increase levels of awareness and usage among geographically disparate users. By making it easy to search for and find posts about hashtagged topics on Twitter (for example, during political uprisings such as those in Iran or during natural disasters such as the earthquake in Haiti, both in 2009) Twitter not only enabled existing users to communicate with one another, it also enabled new users to find others who shared similar interests. Twitter's fame and user base also spread because of the publicity that ensued when mainstream media realized the role Twitter could play in facilitating communication among citizens at critical times in critical places (Bilton 2013). While this example is a vivid one, it begs the question for eINVs of less celebrity of what tactics are effective when they attempt to cultivate spread in online communities that include stakeholders from disparate cultures with disparate needs and perceptions.

The second practice highlighted by the e-marketing literature entails harnessing the massive volumes of data that the firm may be able to glean from monitoring online behaviours of its customers. The OECD (2012) refers to this as 'social customer relationship management (social CRM)' and defines it as 'the use of social media services, techniques and technology by organizations to actively engage with customers' (p. 77). One example of such social CRM is 'suggestive selling', which refers to the practice of recommending products to a prospective customer based on perceived similarity with the detected purchase or preference patterns of prior customers. eINVs with the capacity for capturing and analyzing the data that online selling so abundantly affords can develop customized recommendations (Barrutia and Echebarria 2007) and even highly customized product offerings (cf. Bell and Loane 2010). Amazon's practice of recommending books purchased by readers with similar patterns of interest illustrates this suggestive selling approach.

Discussion

Having considered how prior research and theory illuminate the capabilities that matter for eINVs, we now highlight a number of research questions that seem particularly relevant for eINVs and yet are not addressed by prior research. These research questions are not specific to any one capability discussed above, but rather span two or more.

The first research question we identify concerns how eINVs can reconcile the requirements of scale and international diversity, yet retain a competitive advantage over time, given that complexity escalates as firms do business in multiple, increasingly diverse, foreign markets. An approach to addressing this question would be to identify the conditions under which there is an inverted U-shaped relationship between international diversification and firm performance among eINVs, a relationship that has been found for manufacturers (e.g. Hitt et al. 1997). While some eINVs may be able to target an ever wider array of new countries without encountering a point beyond which it becomes decreasingly profitable, we expect that many will face limits to business model scalability given demands for local isomorphism (Salomon and Wu 2012) and local partners (Johanson and Vahlne 2009). Early in their history, eINVs may be able to avoid this variability if their opportunity is constructed around a narrow, homogenous target market and a value proposition that enables scaling and spreading. However, as competitors enter the market and as the management team looks for product diversification opportunities, there may be pressures to widen both the value proposition and the target market in order to expand the functionality of the market offering.

A second research question concerns the differences in the sensing and spreading capabilities required depending upon the eINV's method of customer acquisition and revenue generation. Firms that primarily acquire customers offline (e.g. Groupon's acquisition of merchants and HubSpot's acquisition of customers) may require different sensing and spreading capabilities than those that primarily do so via online 'self-service' (e.g. Twitter). Similarly, the sensing and spreading capabilities required by eINVs that rely primarily on advertising revenue (e.g. Facebook) may differ from those that rely primarily on customer payments (e.g. FreshBooks) because of the local nature of much advertising. eINVs that acquire customers offline, as well as those that rely on customers for revenue, may need to commit to a physical presence in local markets, and so the sensing and spreading functions may need to be isomorphic with companies in those local markets (cf. Salomon and Wu 2012). However, the extent to which this is the case, and the extent to which this affects scalability, are topics that require empirical investigation in the future.

A third research question is: when is it beneficial for an eINV to have an online intended market image (cf. Brown et al. 2006: 103) that is global vs. multi-domestic? There is variation in practice. For example, Pinterest, a multi-billion dollar eINV, makes no mention of its international activities on its website, while Airbnb, another eINV with a valuation exceeding $10 billion, emphasizes them. DesignCrowd has different domain names for different countries, and there is an Australian accent in the 'how it works' video on the '.com.au' website, a British accent on the '.co.uk' website and an American accent on the '.com' website. In contrast, Sellaband, another crowdsourcing eINV, has a single English website. Amazon has 10 country-specific domain names, Skype has websites in over 25 languages available at a single '.com' domain name, and Twitter is available in more than 20 languages by changing user preferences at the single domain name. A related question is: when is it desirable for eINVs to emphasize an image based on their country-of-origin (e.g. Gurhan-Canli and Maheswaran 2000). For example, Alibaba emphasizes its Chinese origins and presence which highlights the vast number of manufacturers that global buyers can connect with. However, it may be desirable for eINVs to hide their country-of-origin if it is associated with negative stereotypes (Reuber and Fischer 2011b). These observations indicate that we require research to understand the contingencies that matter to which kind of spread-related capabilities an eINV should seek to build, and how the types of spreading capabilities impact the sensing and scaling capabilities required. We also point out that scholars should be aware of the variation in practice, and the reasons behind this variation, when using indicators such as website-based languages or the number of country-specific domain names as measures in empirical research.

A fourth potential area for investigation concerns the interplay between the pace of international expansion and firm-level learning. Both the IE and IB literatures maintain that international experience accumulates over time and that time compression (a more rapid pace of internationalization) may inhibit learning (e.g. Zeng et al. 2013) and have a negative impact on performance (e.g. Jiang et al. 2014; Vermeulen and Barkema 2001; 2002). Given this evidence, how do some eINVs manage to internationalize at unprecedented speed, seemingly without the opportunity to learn through experience? A contrasting view is that when a business is radically innovative, prior learning may be of little relevance and there can be a risk of either knowing the wrong thing or learning incorrectly (Zeng et al. 2013). Further, it may be that for the eINVs that are pioneers in homogeneous global markets (for example, DropBox), local conditions may be of little relevance, rendering rapid, profitable internationalization possible. In general, further research is required to understand the factors that may enable eINVs to overcome liabilities of foreignness at unprecedented speed.

Fifth, it is worthwhile to note the similarities and differences between our sensing-scaling-spreading framework of eINV capabilities and Teece's sensing-seizing-reconfiguring framework of dynamic capabilities for sustainable superior performance (2007). We use 'sensing' similarly to Teece: we emphasize the need for 'scanning, creation, learning, and interpretive activity' (2007: 1322) in markets that are in constant flux. Teece's seizing function is applicable to eINVs, but because of our more narrow focus, we concentrate here more narrowly on the scaling and spreading aspects of seizing an opportunity because they are uniquely crucial to digital firms. We expect reconfiguration – the ability 'to maintain evolutionary fitness and, if necessary, to try and escape from unfavorable path dependencies' (2007: 1335) – to be applicable to eINVs, as they are to any organizations, on the one hand. On the other hand, however, we see two potential differences in this context. The first is that digital artifacts are inherently unstable and easy to modify (Kallinikos et al. 2013), and so reconfiguring the routines of eINVs is likely to be substantially different than reconfiguring the routines of INVs. Second, the need for reconfiguration may be different for eINVs that benefit from herding behaviour, and early dominance of their market, than for those that do not. Although prior research indicates that platform ecosystems are subject to constant change (Lee and Mendelson 2008) and business models of internet-based businesses evolve continuously (Rindova and Kotha 2001), dominant eINVs such as Facebook, Twitter, eBay and Amazon have grown and internationalized with remarkably little change to their core nature. This suggests that there may be beneficial path dependencies for eINVs. For these reasons, we believe that the reconfigural aspects of eINVs represent a fruitful direction for future investigation.

We conclude our chapter by stressing once more that it is timely and important to think about, and to study, eINVs systematically. As we pointed out in our introduction, eINVs are a growing force in the global economy, which offers a pragmatic rationale for studying them carefully. A more theory-relevant reason for studying eINVs is that in doing so, our understanding of the nature and dynamics of international new ventures as a whole could be revised and expanded. For instance, as some of the examples here indicate, eINVs may be able to leverage sensing, scaling and spreading capabilities to win a major share of a global market in certain 'winner-takes-all' competitions; that is, they represent cases of international new ventures that rapidly become large and enjoy some advantages of a near-monopoly. This contrasts with earlier work on international new ventures suggesting that they are nearly always small, and that monopolistic advantages theories are therefore inapplicable to them (e.g. McDougall et al. 1994: 472). While observations such as these do not invalidate prior research on INVs, they sensitize us to the possibility that there may be boundary constraints on the applicability of earlier findings, and that our theories of new venture internationalization may need to be adapted to account fully for phenomena such as eINVs. This chapter constitutes a step in that direction.

Acknowledgements

The authors are grateful for the research assistance of Nicole Dolan and Cameron Salmers. Financial support from the Social Sciences and Humanities Research Council of Canada, the Adam Smith Research Foundation at the University of Glasgow, and the Work-Study Program at the University of Toronto is acknowledged with thanks.

Note

1 In this OECD report, the "internet firm" category is broader than our definition of eINVs, and includes firms that earn revenue from (a) internet-based activities; (b) internet intermediation; (c) providing services facilitating internet use; (d) providing internet-based software; (e) providing e-commerce platforms offline (OECD 2012: 43–44).

References

Adomavicius, G., Bockstedt, J.C., Gupta, A., and Kauffman, R. J. (2007) 'Technology Roles and Paths of Influence in an Ecosystem Model of Technology Evolution', *Information Technology and Management*, 8(2): 185–202.

Airbnb (2013a) 'Airbnb announcements new product advancements and $7.2m in Series A Funding to Accelerate Global Growth', http://assets.airbnb.com/press/press-releases/Airbnb_PressRelease_11112010.pdf (Accessed on 6 April 2013).

Airbnb (2013b) 'Airbnb's Global Growth', www.airbnb.com/global-growth (Accessed on 24 March 2013).

Aldrich, H.H. and Fiol, M. (1994) 'Fools Rush in? The Institutional Context of Industry Creation', *Academy of Management Review*, 19(4): 645–670.

Altshuler, L. and Tarnovskaya, V. (2010) 'Branding Capability of Technology Born Globals', *Journal of Brand Management*, 18(3): 212–227.

Alvarez, S.A. and Barney, J.B. (2007) 'Discovery and Creation: Alternative Theories of Entrepreneurial Action', *Strategic Entrepreneurship Journal*, 1(1/2): 11–26.

Amit, R. and Zott, C. (2001) 'Value Creation in e-Business', *Strategic Management Journal*, 22(6–7): 493–520.

Ashworth, C., Schmidt, R., Pioch, E. and Hallsworth, A. (2006) '"Web-weaving": An Approach to Sustainable e-Retail and Online Advantage in Lingerie Fashion Marketing', *International Journal of Retail & Distribution Management*, 34(6): 497–511.

Aspelund, A.T., Madsen, K. and Moen, O. (2007) 'A Review of the Foundation, International Marketing Strategies, and Performance of International New Ventures', *European Journal of Marketing*, 41(11/12): 1423–1444.

Autio, E., Sapienza H.J. and Almeida, J.G. (2000) 'Effects of Age at Entry, Knowledge Intensity, and Imitability on International Growth', *Academy of Management Journal*, 43(5): 909–924.

Banalieva, E.R. and Dhanaraj, C. (2013) 'Home-Region Orientation in International Expansion Strategies', *Journal of International Business Studies*, 44: 89–116.

Baron, R.A. and Ensley, M.D. (2006) 'Opportunity Recognition as the Detection of Meaningful Patterns: Evidence From Comparisons of Novice and Experienced Entrepreneurs', *Management Science*, 52(9): 1331–1344.

Barrutia, J.M. and Echebarria, C. (2007). 'A New Internet Driven Internationalisation Framework', *The Service Industries Journal*, 27(7): 923–946.

Bell, J. and Loane, S. (2010) 'New-Wave Global Firms: Web 2.0 and SME Internationalisation', *Journal of Marketing Management*, 26(3/4): 213–239.

Bilton, N. (2013) *Hatching Twitter: A True Story of Money, Power, Friendship and Betrayal*, New York: Portfolio/Penguin.

Bingham, C.B. (2009) 'Oscillating Improvisation: How Entrepreneurial Firms Create Success in Foreign Market Entries Over Time', *Strategic Entrepreneurship Journal*, 3(4): 321–345.

Blackett, T. and Boad, B. (1999) *Co-Branding: The Science of Alliance*, London: Macmillan Business.

Bock, A.J., Opsahl, T., George, G. and Gann, D.M. (2012) 'The Effects of Culture and Structure on Strategic Flexibility during Business Model Innovation', *Journal of Management Studies*, 49(2): 279–305.

Brown, T.J.P., Dacin, A., Pratt, M.G. and Whetten, D.A. (2006) 'Identity, Intended Image, Construed Image, and Reputation: An Interdisciplinary Framework and Suggested Terminology', *Journal of the Academy of Marketing Science*, 34(2): 99–106.

Buckley, P. and Casson, M. (1976) *The Future of the Multinational Enterprise*, New York: Holmes & Meier.

Buckley, P. and Casson, M. (2009) 'The Internalisation Theory of the Multinational Enterprise: A Review of the Progress of a Research Agenda after 30 Years', *Journal of International Business Studies*, 40(9): 1563–1580.

Cavusgil, T., Zou, S. and Naidu. G. (1993) 'Product and Promotion Adaptation in Export Ventures', *Journal of International Business Studies*, 24(3): 479–506.

Chandra, Y. and Coviello, N. (2010) 'Broadening the Concept of International Entrepreneurship: Consumers as International Entrepreneurs', *Journal of World Business*, 43: 228–236.

Chandra, Y., Styles, C. and Wilkinson, I.F. (2012) 'An Opportunity-based View of Rapid Internationalization', *Journal of International Marketing*, 20(1): 74–102.

Cornelissen, J.P. and Clarke, J.S. (2010) 'Imagining and Rationalizing Opportunities: Inductive Reasoning and the Creation and Justification of New Ventures', *Academy of Management Review*, 35(4): 539–557.

Coviello, N.E. (2006) 'The Network Dynamics of International New Ventures', *Journal of International Business Studies*, 37: 713–731.

Coviello, N.E. and Jones, M.V. (2004) 'Methodological Issues in International Entrepreneurship Research', *Journal of Business Venturing*, 19(4): 485–508.

Coviello, N.E. and Munro, H. (1997) 'Network Relationships and the Internationalisation Process of Small Software Firms', *International Business Review*, 6(4): 361–386.

Crick, D. and Spence, M. (2005) 'The Internationalisation of "High Performing" UK High-Tech SMEs: A Study of Planned and Unplanned Strategies', *International Business Review*, 14(2): 167–185.

Deutsch, Y., and Ross, T. (2003) 'You are Known by the Directors you Keep: Reputable Directors as a Signaling Mechanism for Young Firms', *Management Science*, 49(8): 1003–1017.

Dholakia, U.M. and Durham, E. (2010) 'One Café Chain's Facebook Experiment', *Harvard Business Review*, 88(3): 26.

Dimitratos, P. and Jones, M.V. (2005) 'Future Directions for International Entrepreneurship Research', *International Business Review*, 14: 119–128.

Duan, W. Gu, B. and Whinston, A.B. (2009) 'Informational Cascades and Software Adoption on the Internet: an Empirical Investigation', *MIS Quarterly*, 33(1): 23–48.

Dunning, J. H. (2009) 'Location and the Multinational Enterprise: John Dunning's Thoughts on Receiving the Journal of International Business Studies 2008 Decade Award', *Journal of International Business Studies*, 40(1): 20–34.

eBay Inc. (2005) eBay completes acquisition of Skype, http://investor.ebay.com/releasedetail.cfm?releaseid=176402 (Accessed on 24 March 2013).

Eisenmann, T. R., Parker, G., and Van Alstyne, M. W. (2011) 'Platform Envelopment', *Strategic Management Journal*, 32(12): 1270–1285.

Ellis, P.D. (2011) 'Social Ties and International Entrepreneurship: Opportunities and Constraints Affecting Firm Internationalization', *Journal of International Business Studies*, 42: 99–127.

Fernhaber, S.A. and McDougall-Covin, P.P. (2009) 'Venture Capitalists As Catalysts to New Venture Internationalization: The Impact of Their Knowledge and Reputation Resources', *Entrepreneurship Theory and Practice*, 33(1): 277–295.

Fernhaber, S.A. McDougall-Covin, P.P. and Shepherd, D.A. (2009) 'International Entrepreneurship: Leveraging Internal and External Knowledge Sources', *Strategic Entrepreneurship Journal*, 3(4): 297–320.

Financial Times (2012) 'A great British hope goes global', October 31, London: England.

Fischer, E. and Reuber, A.R. (2007) 'The Good, the Bad and the Unfamiliar: The Challenges of Reputation Formation Facing New Firms', *Entrepreneurship: Theory and Practice*, 31(1): 53–75.

Fischer, E. and Reuber, A.R. (2008) 'Survival of the Fittest: Which SMEs Internationalize Most Extensively and Effectively?' Publication 08–338, International Trade and Investment Centre, Conference Board of Canada, www.conferenceboard.ca/documents.aspx?DID=2821 (Accessed on 24 March 2013).

Fischer, E. and Reuber, R. (2012) 'Entrepreneurial Narratives Online: Influencing Stakeholder Engagement Through Twitter'. Paper presented at the Academy of Management Conference, Boston, MA.

Fischer, E. and Reuber, A.R. (2014) 'Online Entrepreneurial Communication: Mitigating Uncertainty and Increasing Differentiation Via Twitter', *Journal of Business Venturing*, 29(4): 565–583.

Fournier, S. and Avery, J. (2011) 'The Uninvited Brand', *Business Horizons*, 54: 193–207.

Friesl, M. and Larty, J. (2013) 'Replication of Routines in Organizations: Existing Literature and New Perspectives', *International Journal of Management Reviews*, 15: 106–122.

Gabrielsson, M. (2005) 'Branding Strategies of Born Globals', *Journal of International Entrepreneurship*, 3(3): 199–222.
Gabrielsson, M. and Gabrielsson, P. (2003) 'Global Marketing Strategies of Born Globals and Globalising Internationals in the ICT Field', *Journal of Euromarketing*, 12(3/4): 123–145.
Gabrielsson, M. and Kirpalani, V. (2004) 'Born Globals: How to Reach New Business Space Rapidly', *International Business Review*, 13(5): 555–571.
Gawer, A. and Cusumano, M.A. (2008) 'How Companies Become Platform Leaders', *MIT Sloan Management Review*, 49: 28–35.
George, G. and Bock, A.J. (2011) 'The Business Model in Practice and its Implications for Entrepreneurship Research', *Entrepreneurship Theory and Practice*, 35(1): 83–111.
George, G., Wiklund, J., and Zahra, S. (2005) 'Ownership and the internationalization of small firms', *Journal of Management*, 31(2): 210–233.
Grégoire, D.A., Barr, P.S. and Shepherd, D.A. (2010) 'Cognitive Process of Opportunity Recognition: The Role of Structural Alignment', *Organization Science*, 21(2): 413–431.
Guler, I. and Guillén, M.F. (2010) 'Institutions and the Internationalization of US Venture Capital Firms', *Journal of International Business Studies*, 41: 185–205.
Gurhan-Canli, Z. and Maheswaran, D. (2000) 'Determinants of Country-of-origin Evaluations', *Journal of Consumer Research*, 27(1): 96–108.
Hitt, M.A., Hoskisson, R.E. and Kim, H. (1997) 'International Diversification: Effects on Innovation and Firm Performance in Product-diversified Firms', *Academy of Management Journal*, 40(4): 767–798.
Humphery-Jenner, M. and Suchard, J.A. (2013) 'Foreign Venture Capitalists and the Internationalization of Entrepreneurial Companies; Evidence from China', *Journal of International Business Studies*, 44(6): 607–621.
Humphreys, A. (2013) 'The Creation of Value in Attention Economies', Working paper, Northwestern University.
Index Ventures (2004) 'SKYPE Closes "B" Round Funding from Top Venture Capitalists', www.indexventures.com/news/index/news_id/83 (Accessed on 6 April 2013).
Jiang, R.J., Beamish, P.W. and Makino, C. (2014) 'Time Compression Diseconomies in Foreign Expansion', *Journal of World Business*, 49(1): 114–121.
Johanson, J. and Vahlne, J.-E. (1977) 'The Internationalization Process of the Firm: A Model of Knowledge Development and Increasing Foreign Market Commitments', *Journal of International Business Studies*, 8: 23–32.
Johanson, J. and Vahlne, J.-E. (2009) 'The Uppsala Internationalization Process Model Revisited: From Liability of Foreignness to Liability of Outsidership', *Journal of International Business Studies*, 40: 1411–1431.
Jones, M.V. and Casulli, L. (2014) 'International Entrepreneurship: Exploring the Logic and Utility of Individual Experience Through Comparative Reasoning Approaches', *Entrepreneurship Theory and Practice*, 38(1): 45–69.
Jones, M.V., Coviello, N. and Tang, Y.K. (2011) 'International Entrepreneurship Research (1989–2009): A Domain Ontology and Thematic Analysis', *Journal of Business Venturing*, 26: 632–659.
Jonsson, A. and Foss, N.J. (2011) 'International Expansion Through Flexible Replication: Learning From the International Experience of IKEA', *Journal of International Business Studies*, 42: 1079–1102.
Kallinikos, J. (2009) 'On the Computational Rendition of Reality: Artefacts and Human Agency', *Organization*, 16(2): 183–202.
Kallinikos, J., Aaltonen, A. and Marton, A. (2013) 'The Ambivalent Ontology of Digital Artifacts', *MIS Quarterly*, 37(2): 357–370.
Kaufmann, L., Tritt, C., Bleckwenn, A., Dreiling, H., Jahn, F. and Jeschonowski, D. (2006) 'Jamba! Digital Internationalization', Case Study 806-046-1, WHU Otto Beisheim School of Management, www.ecch.com/educators/search/results?s=8D81CC88F2474492852743AF803C60B7 (Accessed on 20 April 2013).
Kobrin, S.J. (1991) 'An Empirical Analysis of the Determinants of Global Integration', *Strategic Management Journal*, 12: 17–31.
Kotha, S., Rindova, V.P. and Rothaermel, F.T. (2001) 'Assets and Actions: Firm-Specific Factors in the Internationalization of US Internet Firms', *Journal of International Business Studies*, 32(4): 769–791.
Kozinets, R.V., de Valck, K., Wojnicki, A.C. and Wilner, S.J.S. (2010) 'Networked Narratives: Understanding Word-of-Mouth Marketing in Online Communities', *Journal of Marketing*, 74 (March): 71–89.

Lee, D. and Mendelson, H. (2008) 'Divide and Conquer: Competing with Free Technology Under Network Effects', *Production and Operations Management*, 17(1): 12–28.
Levitt, T. (1983) 'The Globalization of Markets', *Harvard Business Review*, 61(3): 92–102.
Loane, S., McNaughton, R.B. and Bell, J. (2004) 'The Internationalizatoin of Internet-enabled Entrepreneurial Firms: Evidence from Europe and North America', *Canadian Journal of Administrative Sciences*, 21: 79–96.
Martens, M.L., Jennings, J.E., and Jennings, P.D. (2007) 'Do the Stories They Tell Get Them the Money They Need? The Role of Entrepreneurial Narratives in Resource Acquisition', *Academy of Management Journal*, 50(5): 1107–1132.
Martin, X., Swaminathan, A. and Mitchell, W. (1998) 'Organizational Evolution in the Interorganizational Environment: Incentives and Constraints on International Expansion Strategy', *Administrative Science Quarterly*, 43(3): 566–601.
Mathews, J.A. and Zander, I. (2007) 'The International Entrepreneurial Dynamics of Accelerated Internationalisation', *Journal of International Business Studies*, 38(3): 387–403.
McDougall, P.P., Oviatt, B.M. and Shrader, R.C. (2003) 'A Comparison of International and Domestic New Ventures', *Journal of International Entrepreneurship*, 1(1): 59–82.
McDougall, P.P., Shane, S. and Oviatt, B.M. (1994) 'Explaining the Formation of International New Ventures: The Limits of Theories From International Business Research', *Journal of Business Venturing*, 9(6): 469–487.
McMullen, J.S. and Shepherd, D.A. (2006) 'Entrepreneurial Action and the Role of Uncertainty in the Theory of the Entrepreneur', *Academy of Management Review*, 31(1): 132–152.
Melitz, M. (2003) 'The Impact of Trade on Intra-industry Reallocations and Aggregate Industry Productivity', *Econometrica*, 71(6): 1695–1725.
Nachum, L. and Zaheer, S. (2005) 'The Persistence of Distance? The Impact of Technology on MNE Motivations for Foreign Investment', *Strategic Management Journal*, 26(8): 747–767.
Nocke, V. and Yeaple, S. (2007) 'Cross-border Mergers and Acquisitions vs Greenfield Foreign Direct Investment: The Role of Firm Heterogeneity', *Journal of International Economics*, 72(2): 336–365.
OECD (2012) 'OECD Internet Economy Outlook 2012', OECD Publishing, Paris, http://dx.doi.org/10.1787/9789264086463-en. (Accessed on 24 March 2013).
Onetti, A., Zucchella, A., Jones, M.V. and McDougall-Covin, P.P. (2010) 'Internationalization, Innovation and Entrepreneurship: Business Models for New Technology-based Firms', *Journal of Management & Governance*, 16(3): 337–368.
Orlikowski, W.J. and Yates, J. (1994) 'Genre Repertoire: The Structuring of Communicative Practices in Organizations', *Administrative Science Quarterly*, 39: 541–574.
Oviatt, B.M. and McDougall, P.P. (1994) 'Toward A Theory Of International New Ventures', *Journal of International Business Studies*, 25(1): 45–64.
Oviatt, B.M. and McDougall, P.P. (2005) 'The Internationalization of Entrepreneurship', *Journal of International Business Studies*, 36(1): 2–8.
Ozgen, E. and Baron, R.A (2007) 'Social Sources of Information in Opportunty Recognition: Effects of Mentors, Industry Networks, and Professional Forums', *Journal of Business Venturing*, 22(2): 174–192.
Parker, G. and Van Alstyne, M.W. (2008) 'Managing Platform Ecosystems', *Proceedings of the 29th International Conference on Information Systems*, Paris, France, 14–17 December.
Petersen, B., Welch, L.S. and Liesch, P.W. (2002) 'The Internet and Foreign Market Expansion by Firms', *Management International Review*, 42(2): 207–221.
Pezderka, N. and Sinkovics, R.R. (2011) 'A Conceptualization of E-Risk Perceptions and Implications for Small Firms Active Online Internationalization', *International Business Review*, 20: 409–422.
Porter, M.E. (1986) 'Changing Patterns of International Competition', *California Management Review*, 28(2): 9–40.
Prashantham, S. (2005) 'Toward a Knowledge-Based Conceptualization of Internationalization', *Journal of International Entrepreneurship*, 3: 37–52.
Prashantham, S. and Dhanaraj, C. (2010) 'The Dynamic Influence of Social Capital on the International Growth of New Ventures', *Journal of Management Studies*, 47: 967–994.
Rangan, S. (2000) 'Search and Deliberation in International Exchange: Microfoundations to Some Macro Patterns', *Journal of International Business Studies*, 31(2): 205–222.
Rangan, S. and Sengul, M. (2009) 'Information Technology and Transnational Integration: Theory and Evidence on the Evolution of the Modern Multinational Enterprise', *Journal of International Business Studies*, 40(9): 1496–1514.

Read, S., Dew, N., Sarasvathy S., Song, M. and Wiltbank, R. (2009) 'Marketing Under Uncertainty: The Logic of an Effectual Approach', *Journal of Marketing*, 73(3): 1–18.
Reuber, A.R. and Fischer, E. (2005) 'The Company You Keep: How Young Firms in Different Competitive Contexts Signal Reputation Through their Customers', *Entrepreneurship Theory & Practice*, 29(1): 57–78.
Reuber, A.R. and Fischer, E. (2009) 'Signalling Reputation in International Online Markets', *Strategic Entrepreneurship Journal*, 3(4): 369–386.
Reuber, A.R. and Fischer, E. (2011a) 'International Entrepreneurship in Internet-enabled Markets', *Journal of Business Venturing*, 26(6): 660–679.
Reuber, A.R. and Fischer, E.F. (2011b) 'When Nobody Knows Your Name: Country-Of-Origin As a Reputational Signal For Online Businesses', *Corporate Reputation Review*, 14: 37–51.
Rialp, A., Rialp, J. and Knight, G.A. (2005) 'The Phenomenon of Early Internationalizing Firms: What do we Know after a Decade (1993–2003) of Scientific Inquiry?', *International Business Review*, 14(2): 147–166.
Ries, E. (2011) *The Lean Startup*, London: Crown Business.
Rindova, V.P. and Kotha, S. (2001) 'Continuous "Morphing": Competing Through Dynamic Capabilities, Form and Function', *Academy of Management Journal*, 44(6): 1263–1280.
Rothaermel, F.T., Kotha, S. and Steensma, H.K. (2006) 'International Market Entry by US Internet Firms: An Empirical Analysis of Country Risk, National Culture, and Market Size', *Journal of Management*, 32(1): 56–82.
Rugman, A.M. (1981) *Inside the Multinationals: The Economics of Internal Markets*, London: Croom Helm.
Rugman, A.M. and Verbeke, A. (2004) 'A Perspective on Regional and Global Strategies of Multinational Enterprises', *Journal of International Business Studies*, 35(1): 3–18.
Salomon R. and Wu, Z. (2012) 'Institutional Distance and Local Isomorphism Strategy', *Journal of International Business Studies*, 43: 343–367.
Samiee, S. and Roth, K. (1992), 'The Influence of Global Marketing Standardization on Performance', *Journal of Marketing*, 56(April): 1–17.
Sapienza, H.J., Autio, E., George, G. and Zahra, S.A. (2006) 'A Capabilities Perspective on the Effects of Early Internationalization on Firm Survival and Growth', *Academy of Management Review*, 31(4): 914–933.
Sarasvathy, S.D. (2001) 'Causation and Effectuation: Toward a Theoretical Shift From Economic Inevitability to Entrepreneurial Contingency', *Academy of Management Review*, 26(2): 243–263.
Schau, H., Muñiz, A. and Arnould, E. (2009) 'How Brand Community Practices Create Value', *Journal of Marketing*, 73(September): 30–51.
Shah, S.K. and Tripsas, M. (2007) 'The Accidental Entrepreneur: The Emergent and Collective Process of User Entrepreneurship', *Strategic Entrepreneurship Journal*, 1(1/2): 123–140.
Shane, S. and Cable, D. (2002) 'Network Ties, Reputation, and the Financing of New Ventures', *Management Science*, 48(3): 364–381.
Stuart, T.E., Hoang, H. and Hybels, R. (1999) 'Interorganizational Endorsements and the Performance of Entrepreneurial Ventures, *Administrative Science Quarterly*, 44(2): 315–349.
Szulanski, G. (1996) 'Exploring Internal Stickiness: Impediments to the Transfer of Best Practice Within the Firm', *Strategic Management Journal*, 17: 27–43.
Szulanski, G. (2000) 'The Process of Knowledge Transfer: A Diachronic Analysis of Stickiness', *Organizational Behavior and Human Decision Processes*, 82: 9–27.
Teece, D.J. (2007) 'Explicating Dynamic Capabilities: The Nature and Microfoundations of (Sustainable) Enterprise Performance', *Strategic Management Journal*, 28(13): 1319–1350.
Teece, D.J. (2010) 'Business Models, Business Strategy and Innovation', *Long Range Planning*, 43(2/3): 172–194.
Vermeulen, F. and Barkema, H. (2002) 'Pace, Rhythm, and Scope: Process Dependence in Building a Profitable Multinational Corporation', *Strategic Management Journal*, 23(7): 637–653.
Vermeulen, G.A.M. and Barkema, H.G. (2001) 'Learning Through Acquisitions', *Academy of Management Journal*, 44(3): 457–476.
Wang, X., Butler, B. and Ren, Y. (2013) 'The Impact of Membership Overlap on Growth: An Ecological Competition View of Online Groups', *Organization Science*, 24(2): 414–431.
West, J. (2003) 'How Open is Open Enough? Melding Proprietary and Open Source Platform Strategies', *Research Policy*, 32: 1259–1285.
Wind, Y. (1986) 'The Myth of Globalization', *Journal of Consumer Marketing*, 3(Spring): 23–26.
Winter, S.G. and Szulanski, G. (2001) 'Replication as Strategy', *Organization Science*, 12(6): 730–743.
Yamin, M. and Sinkovics, R.R. (2006) 'Online Internationalisation, Psychic Distance Reduction and the Virtuality Trap', *International Business Review*, 15: 339–360.

Zahra, S.A., Ireland, R.D. and Hitt, M.A. (2000) 'International Expansion by New Venture Firms: International Diversity, Mode of Market Entry, Technological Learning, and Performance', *Academy of Management Journal*, 43(5): 925–950.
Zeng, Y., Shenkar, O., Lee, S.-H. and Song, S. (2013) 'Cultural Differences, MNE Learning Abiliites, and the Effect of Experience on Subsidiary Mortality in a Dissimilar Culture: Evidence from Korean MNEs', *Journal of International Business Studies*, 44(1): 42–65.
Zott, C. and Amit, R. (2007) 'Business Model Design and the Performance of Entrepreneurial Firms', *Organization Science*, 18(2): 181–199.
Zott, C., Amit, R. and Massa, L. (2011) 'The Business Model: Recent Developments and Future Research', *Journal of Management*, 37(4): 1019–1042.
Zott, C. and Huy, Q.N. (2007) 'How Entrepreneurs Use Symbolic Management to Acquire Resources', *Administrative Science Quarterly*, 52: 70–105.

11
Venture capital and international entrepreneurship

Joseph A. LiPuma

Introduction

Venture capital is a key element to the development of entrepreneurial ventures, especially those that require significant initial investment, such as in technology industries. Technology products often have short lifecycles, requiring ventures based on such products to enter foreign markets at an early age to capture market share before substitute products appear. Companies that internationalize early in their lives are demographically similar to those that receive venture capital (VC)—young and in technology industries—underscoring the connection between VC and international entrepreneurship. Further, the success of the venture capital industry in the US has prompted other countries to develop domestic VC industries that vary significantly in their size, processes, and outcomes. No reviews of the myriad relationships between VC and international entrepreneurship exist, notwithstanding Terjesen et al.'s (2013) survey of literature on VC differences across countries.

This chapter synthesizes literature that explores the relationships between venture capital and international entrepreneurship. Specifically, I address literature in three areas: the relationships between venture capital and new venture internationalization, country differences and internationalization of the VC industry, and cross-border investing.[1] Each of these three dimensions provides different perspectives on the issues and opportunities facing entrepreneurs seeking to expand their ventures to foreign markets, investors seeking to profit from their support of new ventures, and governments seeking to enhance entrepreneurship.

Venture capital is "independent, professionally managed, dedicated pools of capital that focus on equity or equity-linked investments in privately held, high growth companies" (Gompers and Lerner 2001, p.146). Venture capital investing is commonly done in industries in which information asymmetries are high or where specialized assets are required (Amit et al. 1998). Venture capitalists (VCs), individuals who amass funds from investors (limited partners) and distribute the funds to their portfolio companies, have a critical role in resolving various agency issues between the investors and venture managers, as the contract specifying the funding terms reveals private information and helps to align incentives (Admati and Pfleiderer 1994).

Venture capital differs from other forms of equity investment, such as private equity (PE), which generally targets mature companies in industries with fewer information asymmetries, and angel financing, which is less formal in nature and driven more by individual action than by collective systematic processes. Venture capital and private equity investors have a differential impact on new venture performance (Bruton et al. 2010) and thus, for clarity and consistency, I focus exclusively on venture capital in this chapter.

Ventures may receive capital from independent VC firms[2] (IVCs), corporations via corporate venture capital (CVC) programs, universities, and government programs. The different ways in which these programs are funded, the investments managed, and the partners compensated result in varying allocations of control rights between the investor and the venture that, in turn, have considerations for how new ventures internationalize, investment differences across countries, and cross-border investing.

Gompers and Lerner (1999) note that venture capital dates back as far as Babylonian partnerships at the time of Hammurabi (Lutz 1932). In the past 35 years, VC investing has grown from a few dozen funds investing tens of millions of dollars to hundreds of funds worldwide investing over $200 billion at its peak during the internet bubble. In the US, VC-backed companies contribute a significant percentage of GDP, underscoring both the importance of VC as a driver of economic growth and the interest exhibited by other countries attempting to emulate the US and develop domestic VC industries.

In this chapter, I first present some literature on venture capital and entrepreneurship that relates to key elements in international entrepreneurship. I then synthesize key literature in cross-country differences in venture capital, followed by literature related to cross-border investment. I conclude the chapter by highlighting areas for fruitful research at the intersection of venture capital and entrepreneurship.

Venture capital and entrepreneurship

Early research in venture capital focused on studying why and how VCs operate (Bygrave 1987; Gompers 1995; Gompers and Lerner 2001; Lerner 1995) and with what effect and outcomes (e.g. Gulati and Higgins 2003; Sapienza 1992; Stuart et al. 1999). Early literature most relevant to entrepreneurship begins with Bygrave (1987) who observed that the need to share information led to syndication, whereby multiple investors participate in an investment. Gorman and Sahlman (1989), in answering the question "what do VCs do?" ranked VCs' assistance to new ventures as:

(1) help with getting additional financing;
(2) strategic planning;
(3) management recruiting;
(4) operational planning;
(5) introductions to potential customers and suppliers;
(6) resolving compensation issues.

This suggests that venture capitalists provide a bundle of value beyond financial capital. Due to the highly cyclical nature of the VC industry, VCs have more interest in adding such value when the supply of capital outstrips the demand (Sapienza 1992), as was the case during the internet boom in the late 1990s. Venture capitalists add greater value when communication between the entrepreneur and the VC investor is more frequent (as with highly innovative ventures), more open, and less contentious.

In an examination of the structure of VC investments, Gompers (1995) identified conditions, such as in early stage technology industries, in which information asymmetries allow entrepreneurs to have more discretion to invest in personally beneficial strategies at shareholders' expense. Venture capitalists can act to alleviate such information gaps normally present between entrepreneurs and their financiers (Gompers and Lerner 2001). The presence of these gaps makes imitability difficult, and VCs become boundary spanners, gaining idiosyncratic knowledge of the venture. Such detailed knowledge helps to keep return on investments for VC deals high by keeping poor deals from being done—the concept of "too much money chasing too few deals" (Gompers 1996). This highlights a nexus between the investor's opportunity and entrepreneur's opportunity, both necessary for investment, making the value of funding a new venture rare and inimitable.

New ventures, especially in young, technology-based industries, need capital to grow, as initial investment may greatly precede significant revenues. In such industries, information asymmetries are more pronounced (Amit et al. 1998) and agency problems more likely (Gompers 1995). While funding options of debt and equity exist for new ventures, banks and VC investors differ, and the choice of which source to use is based on the consequences of terminating the business and prior hold-up problems. Venture capitalists have better monitoring capabilities than banks and have higher cost of capital due to the illiquid nature of capital (Winton and Yerramilli 2008).

The nature of the contracts between the VC and the entrepreneur are designed to mitigate these agency problems by detailing control rights (Hellmann 1998) and their allocation. The division of control rights varies with firm features, and VCs have significant stakes and a considerable contingent element in the contracts (Kaplan and Strömberg 2003). Relevant firm features include internal risk, external risk, and project-related risk, which determine the allocation of cash flow rights, contingencies, control rights, and liquidation rights between VCs and entrepreneurs (Kaplan and Strömberg 2004).

Underpinning the solutions to agency-related issues between VCs and entrepreneurs is staged financing. Staged investments and VCs monitoring are designed to offset agency conflicts to keep incentives better aligned between startup investors and managers (Neher 1999). Early-stage ventures, in which information asymmetries and the potential for agency problems are greatest, have smaller financings, use cash more slowly, and have longer time between financings (Gompers 1995).

Game theory has also been used to examine the mechanism by which VCs and entrepreneurs cooperate. Using the "prisoner's dilemma" framework, Cable and Shane (1997) show that cooperation is the best mechanism for managing the relationship between the investor and the entrepreneur. Time pressure, payoff from cooperation, information, personal similarity, and transaction procedures are the main elements determining how the VC and entrepreneur should structure their relationship to maximize mutual cooperation and minimize defection. Both parties should increase the level and quality of information transfer to maximize mutual cooperation and minimize defection.

Performance

Entrepreneurs funded by VC come from a variety of sources, such as spin-offs (Fallick et al. 2006) and serial entrepreneurs (Gompers et al. 2010). Some types of opportunities are more suitable for VC financing than others, based on internal characteristics of management (Hall and Hofer 1993; MacMillan et al. 1985) or external market characteristics (Brander and De Bettignies 2009).

Venture capitalists spend significant amounts of time with portfolio companies (Sahlman 1990; Gorman and Sahlman 1989), and act to professionalize the ventures in which they invest, often by sharing their knowledge and other human capital (Hellman and Puri 2002). Venture capital helps to make ventures more innovative (Kortum and Lerner 2000), and sharing a common venture capitalist enhances strategic alliance formation among companies (Lindsey 2008).

The nature of the investing VC firm relates to the investment and its subsequent performance. Corporate venture capitalists invest less frequently in startup and mature private firms, choosing investment in later and larger financing rounds (Gompers 2002). Prominent VC partners facilitate access to resources that ventures need, and this access translates to enhanced new venture performance (Stuart et al. 1999).

The types of exits that new ventures experience (for example, initial public offering, acquisition, closure) vary by the nature of the VC arrangement. Companies backed by VC are more likely to go public, more likely to be acquired, and less likely to fail (Puri and Zarutskie 2012). Most exits occur through management buyouts or acquisitions rather than initial public offerings (IPOs), but the latter have returns higher than other forms of exit (Amit et al. 1998). Acquisitions are more likely when convertible securities are used (Cumming 2008). Ties to prominent VC firms are particularly beneficial to IPO success during cold markets (Gulati and Higgins 2003). While IPO success is important for new ventures, it is noteworthy that post-IPO performance of VC-backed companies is not significantly different from that of other public technology-based companies (Bottazzi and Da Rin 2002).

Spatial distribution

Venture capital investments are subject to spatial distribution factors. For example, the lack of an enforceable non-compete clause for employees in California resulted in employee mobility that led to technology spillovers which, in turn, fostered the development of technology clusters (Fallick et al. 2006). Silicon Valley benefited from California courts with a lax approach to trade secret enforcement and non-compete covenants (Gilson 1999).

VCs specializing in early stage ventures prefer a narrower geographic scope relative to other VCs, corporate VCs prefer broader geographic scope relative to international new ventures (INVs), and larger VC firms prefer broader geographic scope than do smaller VC firms (Gupta and Sapienza 1992). Broadly, venture capitalists exhibit a local bias (Cumming and Dai 2010), demonstrated by a preference for being near the companies in which they invest, resulting from the desire to establish and maintain relationships with new venture founders, communicate directly, and monitor the venture's activities (Sorenson and Stuart 2001). Inter-firm networks in the US VC market affect spatial patterns of exchange, resulting in geographic and industry-localized investing, which is a means to deal with information problems. Another means of addressing such problems is staging investments, which is more likely with greater geographic distance. Investors located farther away from an entrepreneurial venture finance the firm using more financing rounds, shorter durations between successive rounds, and smaller round size, on average (Tian 2011).

Venture capital and international entrepreneurship

The previous section provides insights into venture capital in the domain of entrepreneurship. Research examines factors such as (1) the resources needed for new venture development and expansion, (2) the issues of information asymmetries and agency, prompting both the need for venture capital and features such as staging and monitoring of investments, (3) knowledge as a key component for venture growth and as the basis for company geographic diversification, (4) the geography of venture capital, as the desire for communication, monitoring, and relationship building leads to proximity between investor and portfolio company, and (5) liabilities of newness faced by new ventures, who have limited legitimacy, especially in emerging industries, and liabilities of foreignness of companies entering foreign markets.

In this section, I examine how these aspects of venture capital are presented in the research domain of international entrepreneurship. International entrepreneurship is "the discovery, enactment, evaluation, and exploitation of opportunities—across national borders—to create future goods and services" (Oviatt and McDougall 2005: 540). International entrepreneurship has two main thrusts: comparative differences in entrepreneurship across countries and crossing-national-border entrepreneurial behaviors (e.g. new venture internationalization) (Jones et al. 2011). In terms of venture capital and international entrepreneurship, the former includes papers that examine differences in VC industries and practices across countries, which I address in a subsequent section.

The literature related to venture capital and international entrepreneurship is modest, at best, especially as to how venture capitalists and institutional investors influence new venture and SMEs' internationalization scale and scope (George et al. 2005). Studies of the relationship between the receipt of venture capital and new venture internationalization have been inconclusive (e.g. Burgel and Murray 1998) or inconsistent. Carpenter et al. (2003) suggest that VC backing is associated with greater risk-taking by the venture, and thus a greater willingness to enter international markets, as VC-backed new ventures are often in volatile or emerging industries requiring high initial costs. However, Carpenter et al. (2003) found that the impact of VC financing on internationalization was negative, whereas LiPuma (2006) found that not having VC was positively related to the intensity of new ventures' international activities.

Resources

Internationalization is expensive, requiring resources over and above those needed for solely domestic operations. Venture capital is one means by which new ventures access financial, knowledge, and network resources necessary for internationalization. Internationally experienced VCs can aid opportunity-seeking behaviors (Coviello and Munro 1995) of portfolio companies by identifying opportunities in foreign markets (Carpenter et al. 2003). As international networks of VCs grow due to internationalization of the VC industry and foreign syndication of deals, the number of internationally experienced VCs increases, thereby increasing their international knowledge relevant for opportunity identification.

Beyond being an impetus for internationalization, VC also allows new ventures to access resources necessary for increasing the intensity of their international activities (Preece et al. 1999). Different forms of VC may affect foreign market entry and growth in various ways. Corporate venture capital (CVC) may provide more introductions to foreign customers than independent venture capital (Maula et al. 2005), enhancing the internationalization of ventures receiving VC. Indeed, access to international contacts is a significant criterion of startup companies in selection of CVC investors (Chesbrough 2000). As CVC helps investor firms (Dushnitsky and Lenox 2005), and many CVC parent companies are multinational enterprises (MNEs), CVC investors may help themselves more by pulling their portfolio companies into foreign markets in which the MNEs operate. Receipt of foreign VC via cross-border investing can also affect the international activities of portfolio companies, as foreign investors can facilitate relationships with partner companies and customers in their home country.

Syndication is a function of the need to share information and knowledge (Bygrave 1987) critical to new venture internationalization. Opportunistic internationalizers (with low levels of foreign sales) have smaller investment syndicates doing each deal than solely domestic new ventures (LiPuma and Park, forthcoming), potentially limiting the resource stocks available for intensifying internationalization.

Information asymmetries and agency issues

Information asymmetries and agency issues between VCs and portfolio companies (PCs) in which they invest may be exacerbated when the new venture internationalizes. Such issues may result in increased staging or monitoring of the venture, which may be a substitute means of addressing agency issues (Tian 2011). LiPuma and Park (forthcoming) find that agency risk mitigation by VCs varies by the nature of the internationalization undertaken by the new ventures. Strategic internationalization, in which INVs employ specific strategies to intensify their foreign business to a significant degree, is associated with more rapid round staging, whereas opportunistic internationalizers with low levels of foreign sales experience slower staging and receive less funding per round, as compared to solely domestic ventures. Staging of investments by VCs is more likely with greater geographic distance (Tian 2011), although research has shown that US VCs investing in foreign ventures do not use greater staging as compared with their investments in US ventures (Guler and McGahan 2006).

Investment staging varies with the quality of the legal environment in which the portfolio company operates, with use of more staging when the portfolio company's country has better legal enforcement (Balcarcel et al. 2010). Higher quality legal environments mitigate VC–entrepreneur conflicts, as non-contractual governance mechanisms facilitate VCs' advice (Cumming and Johan 2007). With CVC, the limited partners (i.e. the parent company) and the managing partners (e.g. the CVCs) are in the same corporation, which may reduce agency problems via goal congruence (Maula and Murray 2002), suggesting that agency issues may be fewer for CVC-backed international new ventures.

Knowledge

Knowledge is central to a company's internationalization process (Autio et al. 2000; Casillas et al. 2009). While more mature internationalizers follow a process of internationalization based on existing knowledge from the domestic market that they extend via direct experiences through gradually increasing market commitment (Johanson and Vahlne 1977), young and rapidly internationalizing ventures enter and intensify foreign activities by largely capitalizing on the entrepreneur's existing, or congenital, knowledge base (Andersson 2000; Bruneel et al. 2010). This international knowledge is the cornerstone of new ventures' internationalization strategies. Knowledge from external sources such as VCs enriches the variety of new ventures' strategic repertoires (Larrañeta et al. 2012) and catalyzes new venture internationalization (Fernhaber and McDougall-Covin 2009).

International knowledge from VCs is especially important to those new ventures with limited prior international experience (Fernhaber et al. 2009). This is consistent with the observation that INVs often use congenital knowledge for internationalization, and if it is not internal to the venture, obtaining it from close outsiders facilitates its integration and use.

Geography and venture capital

The majority of VCs invest primarily in their home markets (Wright et al. 2005). Beyond issues of agency and information asymmetries attendant with cross-border investing, geographic considerations affect syndication size and composition which, in turn, can affect the internationalization of portfolio companies. Syndicates are generally smaller for ventures located outside the US than for those in the US (Guler and McGahan 2007). Geographic proximity is an important determinant of venture board membership, especially when the need for oversight is larger (Lerner 1995) as would be the case with internationalization. The distance between the local and foreign VCs in a syndicate is negatively correlated with a successful exit but the presence of a local syndicate partner is positively correlated with a successful exit (Chemmanur et al. 2010).

Some performance issues may relate to the quality of the legal regime in a country, resulting in corporate relocations. Venture capitalist behavior is driven by the internationalization of the VC industry and the role of property rights, legal systems, and economic conditions in facilitating successful VC exits. In order to mitigate associated risks in countries with weak institutions, VCs may force, prior to an exit, a portfolio company to relocate to a country with stronger legal protections and a more liquid exit market (Cumming et al. 2009).

New ventures in emerging countries face particular constraints that may relate to venture capital interaction with internationalization. Institutions affect new ventures and mature companies differently in their attempts to internationalize; in emerging economies, for example, limits on access to capital affect export performance for young ventures more so than for established companies (LiPuma et al. 2013). Limited capital access in developing economies may force new ventures to seek capital externally. Foreign venture capitalists from developed economies, based on a more strategic focus in assisting their emerging economy PCs in marketing and relationship building, may motivate new ventures from emerging economies to internationalize to developed economies (Yamakawa et al. 2008).

Liabilities of newness and foreignness

New ventures, with fewer embedded routines that can impede the internalization of knowledge, possess a learning advantage of newness (Autio et al. 2000) that facilitates internalization of VCs' international knowledge, However, new ventures face liabilities of newness (Singh et al. 1986) that are exacerbated by liabilities of foreignness (Zaheer 1995) when entering foreign markets. Associating with investors of high prominence or reputation can help new ventures overcome liabilities of newness (Stuart et al. 1999). Venture capitalists also provide reputation benefits that can help overcome liabilities of foreignness (Fernhaber and McDougall-Covin 2009). This is especially true for foreign VCs that add legitimacy in foreign markets (Makela and Maula 2005). In particular, legitimacy and reputation benefits from CVC investors in international settings may exceed those of independent VCs, since CVCs are often in more internationally known multinationals.

Industry characteristics and performance

Industry characteristics also relate to venture capital's effect on new venture internationalization. The age of an industry and its structure interact with the receipt ofVC to influence the likelihood of new venture internationalization (Fernhaber et al. 2007), as access to VCs who believe that internationalization presents an opportunity for a large return on investment may result in changes of managers in the company consistent with investors' desires. Asset specificity in some industries may affect new venture internationalization, consistent with VCs' objective to derive value at exit.

In addition, there are performance implications related to venture capital and internationalization. Investors may be sensitive to venture internationalization, as the initial public offering (IPO) performance of new VC-backed internationalized ventures often lags behind that of their solely domestic counterparts (LiPuma 2012). Indeed, VCs are reasoned risk-takers and, viewing early internationalization as too risky, may thus encourage their PCs to eschew foreign market entry and execute domestic strategies more in line with the firm's experience and understanding (Carpenter et al. 2003). This is consistent with the view that new ventures that internationalize may have lower survival but higher growth as compared to solely domestic new ventures (Sapienza et al. 2006).

Internationalization of the venture capital industry

Wright et al. (2005) reviewed international VC research across various disciplines and underscored the distinction between two facets of research relevant to international business: internationalization of the venture capital industry itself and cross-country differences in venture capital. Wright et al. (2005) note that a less developed research stream examined cross-border investments by VCs, including fund organization, motivations, and strategies (Guler and Guillen 2010a; Hall and Tu 2003), deal generation and screening (Makela and Maula 2008), valuation (Wright et al. 2002), and post-investment activities (Makela and Maula 2005). A more developed stream of research on cross-country comparisons considers development of VC industries, fund organization and fund raising (Bottazzi and Da Rin 2002; Megginson 2004), deal generation and screening (Knight 1994), valuation (Karsai et al. 1998), and post-investment activities (Bruton et al. 2005).

Cross-border investing

The venture capital industry is expanding internationally (Schilit 1992), and the decision to invest internationally is driven by the VC firm's human capital (Manigart et al. 2007). Specifically, the prior international experience of the VC firm's executives results in a higher probability of cross-border investing (Manigart et al. 2007). The preference for venture capitalists to be near the ventures in which they invest (Bygrave 1987; Gupta and Sapienza 1992; Stuart and Sorenson 2003) is evident in research on VC relationships and investments that cross national borders. Geographic distance, common language, and colonial ties predict higher trade flows between countries (Aizenman and Kendall 2012), and trust has a strong effect on cross-border investments (Bottazzi et al. 2011). Networks among VCs contribute to diffusing information about potential investments across geographic and sector boundaries, thus cross-border syndication at a distance is more likely to occur based on attributes of the portfolio company (Sorenson and Stuart 2008).

Guler and Guillen (2010b) find that VC firms invest in host countries characterized by institutions that create innovative opportunities, protect investors' rights, facilitate exit, and guarantee regulatory stability, and that as VC firms gain more international experience, they are more likely to overcome constraints related to these institutions. When formal institutions are weak, as is the case in emerging economies, networks and informal institutions supplement or replace the formal institutions (Ahlstrom and Bruton 2006). National factors associated with the portfolio company, such as military expenditure and financial market strength, a supportive business environment, and high-end human capital attract cross-border VC investment (Aizenman and Kendall 2012).

The willingness to invest overseas is directly related to the size of VC firms (measured by the funds available for investment), the number of offices they operate from, and the stage of development of their portfolio companies, and is inversely related to the length of time in which the venture capitalist had been in operation (Hall and Tu 2003).

Cross-border syndicates, in which local (to the portfolio company (PC)) venture capitalists co-invest with non-local investors, differentially affect portfolio companies. Involvement of foreign and local venture capitalists in investment syndicates is positively correlated with success

(Chemmanur et al. 2010). Further, the relationship between a venture's prospects and investors' commitment is amplified by geographic distance between them, and is mitigated by the investor's embeddedness in local syndication networks (Makela and Maula 2006).

Cross-country differences related to venture capital

A recent review for comparative international entrepreneurship (CIE)—cross-national comparisons of domestic entrepreneurship and of entrepreneurial internationalization—identified venture capital as a critical element in this stream (Terjesen et al. 2013). The VC industry varies by country, and Terjesen et al. (2013) note the differences in investment patterns by stage (Ooghe et al. 1991) and by the use of networks (Bruton and Ahlstrom 2003). Individual investors differ across countries in the number of opportunities they consider and their perception of performance (Harrison and Mason 1992), in their professionalism in investment activity (Landström 1993), in their means of navigating multiple institutional environments (Terjesen and Elam 2009), and in their reliance on market information (Zacharakis et al. 2007).

Institutional differences along normative, regulatory, and cognitive dimensions (Scott 1995) subject venture capitalists in various countries to different institutional forces that can affect venture capitalists' deal selection, interaction and governance, and value added (Bruton et al. 2005). In a study comparing the US and Sweden, Lerner and Tag (2013) examine how institutional differences such as historical government support for VC, financial market evolution (e.g. liberalization and deregulation of public pension funds), tax policy, labor regulations, and technology transfer policy (e.g. the Bayh-Dole Act in the US in 1980) differentially affected these two countries.

Stable, consistent, and predictable institutional environments are critical for economic functions (North 1986). Legal base and law enforcement determines the effectiveness of investment protection, and differences between country constitutions based on common law (British origins) versus various traditions of civil law (Roman origins) differentially affect the protection afforded investors (e.g. venture capitalists) and entrepreneurs (La Porta et al. 1998), and the success of investments. These differences can interact with the level of economic development of a country to affect investment deals and outcomes (Lerner and Schoar 2005).

Many institutional factors such as government interference with the private sector, output of public goods, size of public sector, political freedom, legal origin, and religion affect the quality of government in a systematic fashion across countries (La Porta et al. 1999). Government quality can positively affect entrepreneurship via policies such as innovation investment funds (essentially government-supplied venture capital), which facilitates investment in new ventures, underscoring the role that government venture capital (GVC) can play alongside IVC (Cumming 2007).

The role of banks also affects entrepreneurial systems and VC investing. Black and Gilson (1998) show that in contrast with bank-centric systems (e.g. Japan and Germany) in which buybacks are more common, market-centered systems (e.g. US) experience more IPOs, providing an incentive to entrepreneurs and VCs alike, thus fostering a vibrant VC market. Regarding such exits, Cumming et al. (2006) find that the quality of a country's legal system, as a mechanism to mitigate agency problems, is more directly connected to facilitating VC-backed IPO exits than the size of the country's stock market. This may relate to the ability to secure funding after failure, which may differ across countries.

In their annual assessment of the attractiveness of VC and PE markets globally, Groh et al. (2013) provide detailed country data related to the importance of economic activity (Gompers and Lerner 1998), depth of the capital market (Black and Gilson 1998), importance of taxation (Poterba 1989), investor protection and corporate governance (La Porta et al. 1998), the human and social environment (Black and Gilson 1998; Megginson 2004), and of entrepreneurial culture and deal opportunities (Kortum and Lerner 2000). This VCPE country attractiveness ranking of 118 countries most recently indicated that the US, Canada, UK, Japan, and Singapore are the most attractive countries for VC and PE investing.

Venture capital plays a role in economic development but the growth and health of a VC industry is dependent on multiple factors (Jeng and Wells 2000). IPOs are the strongest driver of VC investing, and government policy can have a strong impact, both by setting the regulatory stage, and by galvanizing investment during downturns.

Directions for future research

The preceding synthesis clearly shows that much research has been performed to further understand relationships between venture capital and international entrepreneurship; a number of interesting and important areas for study become apparent. Most striking is the limited development by international business scholars interested in international entrepreneurship, although venture capital is a value-laden resource bundle available for internationalization of new ventures. A recent paper by Manigart and Wright (2013) calls for research on the nature and processes of venture capital activity, syndication, returns to venture capital, and exit to augment evolving research in this area.

Venture capital and entrepreneurship

The importance of venture capital has been recently questioned (e.g. Lerner, 2009) and the number of venture capitalists in the US declined from 627 in 2007 to 522 in 2012 (NVCA). Does this suggest that other means of support are addressing capital needs of new ventures? Will new models of VC emerge? More research should focus on the relationship between the venture capitalist and the portfolio company to understand the dynamics of value provided to each partner in the transaction. As this is a value-laden exchange, what happens when the equity participation is disintermediated, as is the case with crowdfunding? Little work is done in this area, with only one paper (Mollick 2014) in a top academic journal. Will networks of investors provide differential value to that provided by traditional venture capitalists, be they independent or corporate?

Venture capital and international entrepreneurship

Much research examines the internationalization of the venture capital industry, and cross-country comparisons of venture capital practices and performance. While clearly important to the funding of ventures, this focus does not get to two of the central issues in international entrepreneurship: the role of opportunities (central to entrepreneurship) and the role of knowledge (central to international business). New venture internationalization, based on identifying foreign opportunities and pursuing them based on relevant knowledge, requires a focus on the relationship between the VC investor and the new venture receiving the associated financial, human, and social capital.

Additionally, little is known about how geographic diversification into countries outside of a venture's home market (Hitt et al. 2006) relates to IPO performance (Certo et al. 2009). As the existence of exit opportunities drives the development of venture capitalists, another fruitful area for study relates to the sources of the capital, including both the nature of the limited partners and of the manner in which it gets to the new venture (i.e., as IVC, CVC, government investment, or foreign venture capital (FVC)). The formation of new VC firms, their funding, and the experience of their executives relate to the firms' success (Walske and Zacharakis 2009), which may subsequently affect the financial, human, and social capital available to new ventures for their internationalization projects. The nature of the entity distributing the capital may affect its effect on new ventures and relate to the development of VC firms and industries in more countries. For example, as CVC providers are often multinational enterprises (MNEs), they may provide legitimacy in foreign markets or may facilitate portfolio companies following the MNE to foreign markets. Foreign venture capital similarly provides legitimacy or reputation benefits in the home country of the FVC provider, enhancing sales by the (foreign) PC and increasing its international intensity. As new ventures have limited resources for managing multiple relationships and limited attentional capabilities, understanding the complement or substitute effect of different sources of VC relevant for internationalization may enhance the efficiency of their funds and time.

Venture capital is but one means that new ventures use to support their international expansion activities. Other means, such as obtaining resources from alliance partners, permit ventures to access necessary internationalization resources without ceding equity or control. Examining the nature of the relationship of these two forms of resource acquisition may provide insights into the tradeoffs new ventures face in acquiring resources for internationalization (Hoehn-Weiss and LiPuma 2008).

Finally, as knowledge is key to internationalization, more work exploring the aspects of knowledge is warranted. The source of knowledge may affect perceptions about its usability (Shi et al. 2009), applicability (Peili and Zhonghong 2007), or judgment as to its relevance (Nguyen and Barrett 2006). Thus whether international knowledge comes from venture capitalist or entrepreneur may moderate its effect on internationalization. Additionally, the type of knowledge necessary for internationalization, such as know-how, know-why, know-who, know-what (OECD, 2000) may interact with the source to aid or hinder new venture internationalization.

Internationalization of venture capital and cross-border investing

Relationships between investor and new venture may vary significantly across countries based on cultural and regulatory differences. While Lerner and Tag (2013) examine institutional differences between two countries (the US and Sweden), a broader, multi-country study may unravel the relationships associated with VC in an institutional context. Beyond the institutional context, cultural differences such as individuality and long-term orientation may play into the nature of the VC–entrepreneur relationship and associated contract and control rights. Since associating with prominent partners facilitates access to resources that ventures need to enhance performance (Stuart et al. 1999), how might the role of prominence and its influence differ between individualist and collectivist, trust-based cultures? How might differences in long-term orientations relate to the timing of exits, and what effect might this have on the composition of cross-border VC syndicates?

Much of the international research on venture capital, including cross-country studies, such as that of Groh et al. (2013), combine venture capital and private equity into a common construct. This makes it difficult to compare, for example, studies of the US VC industry with those of European VC. Since the objectives and management for VC and PE differ, studies that distinguish venture capital from private equity would provide better insights for VC and provide a means for more complete and consistent cross-country studies of VC and its effect on internationalization of new ventures.

Notes

1 The entrepreneurship literature has much more to say about venture capital than does the international business (IB) literature, as evidenced by the paucity of papers on venture capital published in the top IB journals. This chapter reflects this trend and acknowledges the opportunities this presents for international business research.

2 I use the convention of "firm" for the investor or venture capitalist, and "venture" for the portfolio company in which the venture capitalist invests.

References

Admati, A.R. and Pfleiderer, P. (1994). "Robust Financial Contracting and the Role of Venture Capitalists." *The Journal of Finance* 49(2): 371–402.

Ahlstrom, D. and Bruton, G.D. (2006). "Venture Capital in Emerging Economies: Networks and Institutional Change." *Entrepreneurship: Theory & Practice* 30(2): 299–320.

Aizenman, J. and Kendall, J. (2012). "The Internationalization of Venture Capital." *Journal of Economic Studies* 39(5): 488–511.

Amit, R., Brander, J., and Zott, C. (1998). "Why do Venture Capital Firms Exist? Theory and Canadian Evidence." *Journal of Business Venturing* 13(6): 441–466.

Andersson, S. (2000). "The Internationalization of the Firm from an Entrepreneurial Perspective." *International Studies of Management and Organization* 30(1): 63–92.

Autio, E., Sapienza, H.J., and Almeida, J.G. (2000). "Effects of Age at Entry, Knowledge Intensity, and Imitability on International Growth." *Academy of Management Journal* 43(5): 909–924.

Balcarcel, A., Hertzel, M.G., and Lindsey, L.A. (2010). "Contracting Frictions and Cross-border Capital Flows: Evidence from Venture Capital," http://ssrn.com/abstract=1571928, accessed September 25, 2014.

Black, B.S. and Gilson, R.J. (1998). "Venture Capital and the Structure of Capital Markets: Banks Versus Stock Markets." *Journal of Financial Economics* 47: 243–277.

Bottazzi, L. and Da Rin, M. (2002). "Venture Capital in Europe and the Financing of Innovative Companies." *Economic Policy* 34: 229–269.

Bottazzi, L., Da Rin, M., and Hellmann, T.F. (2011). "The Importance of Trust for Investment: Evidence from Venture Capital." Cambridge, MA, National Bureau of Economic Research, Working Paper 16923.

Brander, J. and De Bettignies, J. (2009). "Venture Capital Investment: The Role of Predator–Prey Dynamics with Learning by Doing." *Economics of Innovation and New Technology* 18: 1–19.

Bruneel, J., Yli-Renko, H., and Clarysse, B. (2010). "Learning from Experience and Learning from Others: How Congenital and Interorganizational Learning Substitute for Experiential Learning in Young Firm Internationalization." *Strategic Entrepreneurship Journal* 4(2): 164–182.

Bruton, G. D., and Ahlstrom, D. (2003). "An Institutional View of China's Venture Capital Industry: Explaining the Differences Between China and the West." *Journal of Business Venturing* 18: 233–259.

Bruton, G.D., Filatotchev, I., Chahine, S. and Wright, M. (2010). "Governance, Ownership Structure, and Performance of IPO Firms: The Impact of Different Types of Private Equity Investors and Institutional Environments." *Strategic Management Journal* 31: 491–509.

Bruton, G.D., Fried, V.H., and Manigart, S. (2005). "Institutional Influences on the Worldwide Expansion of Venture Capital." *Entrepreneurship Theory & Practice* 29(6): 737–760.

Burgel, O. and Murray, G.C. (1998). *The International Activities of British Start-Up Companies in High-Technology Industries: Differences Between Internationalisers and Non-internationalisers.* Babson Kauffman Entrepreneurship Research Conference, Babson College.

Bygrave, W.D. (1987). "Syndicated Investments by Venture Capital Firms: A Networking Perspective." *Journal of Business Venturing* 2: 139–154.

Cable, D. and Shane, S. (1997). "A Prisoner's Dilemma Approach to Entrepreneur–Venture Capital Relationships." *Academy of Management Review* 22(1): 142–176.

Carpenter, M.A., Pollock, T.G., and Leary, M.M. (2003). "Testing a Model of Reasoned Risk-taking: Governance, the Experience of Principals and Agents, and Global Strategy in High-technology IPO Firms." *Strategic Management Journal* 24(9): 803–820.

Casillas J.C., Moreno A.M., Acedo F.J., Gallego M.A. and Ramos E. (2009). "An Integrative Model of the Role of Knowledge in the Internationalization Process." *Journal of World Business* 44(3): 311–322.

Certo, S.T., Holcomb, T.R., and Holmes, M.R. (2009). "IPO Research in Management and Entrepreneurship: Moving the Agenda Forward." *Journal of Management* 35(6): 1340–1378.
Chemmanur, T.J., Hull, T.J., and Krishnan, K. (2010). "Do Local and International Venture Capitalists Play Well Together? A Study of International Venture Capital Investments." Working Paper. Available at http://ssrn.com/abstract=1670319, accessed September 25, 2014.
Chesbrough, H.W. (2000). "Designing Corporate Ventures in the Shadow of Private Venture Capital." *California Management Review* 42(3): 31–49.
Coviello, N.E. and Munro, H.J. (2005). "Growing the Entrepreneurial Firm: Networking for International Market Development." *European Journal of Marketing* 29(7): 49–61.
Cumming, D.J. (2007). "Government Policy Towards Entrepreneurial Finance: Innovation Investment Funds." *Journal of Business Venturing* 22(2): 193–235.
Cumming, D.J. (2008). "Contracts and Exits in Venture Capital Finance." *Review of Financial Studies* 21: 1947–1982.
Cumming, D.J. and Dai, N. (2010). "Local Bias in Venture Capital Investments." *Journal of Empirical Finance*, 17: 362–380.
Cumming, D.J., Fleming, G., and Schwienbacher, A. (2006). "Legality and Venture Capital Exits." *Journal of Corporate Finance* 12: 214–245.
Cumming, D.J. and Johan, S.A. (2007). "Advice and Monitoring in Venture Finance." *Financial Markets and Portfolio Management* 21(1): 3–43.
Cumming, D.J., Sapienza, H.J., Siegel, D.S., and Wright, M. (2009). "International Entrepreneurship: Managerial and Policy Implications." *Strategic Entrepreneurship Journal* 3(4): 283–296.
Dushnitsky, G. and Lenox, M.J. (2005). "When Do Incumbents Learn from Entrepreneurial Ventures? Corporate Venture Capital and Investing Firm Innovation Rates." *Research Policy* 34(5): 615–640.
Fallick, B., Fleischman, C., and Rebitzer, J. (2006). "Job-hopping in Silicon Valley: Some Evidence Concerning the Microfoundations of a High-technology Cluster." *Review of Economics and Statistics* 88: 472–481.
Fernhaber, S.A., McDougall, P.P., and Oviatt, B. (2007). "Exploring the Role of Industry Structure in New Venture Internationalization." *Entrepreneurship Theory & Practice* 31(4): 517.
Fernhaber, S.A. and McDougall-Covin, P.P. (2009). "Venture Capitalists as Catalysts to New Venture Internationalization: The Impact of Their Knowledge and Reputation Resources." *Entrepreneurship Theory & Practice* 33(1): 277–295.
Fernhaber, S.A., McDougall-Covin, P.P., and Shepherd, D.A. (2009). "International Entrepreneurship: Leveraging Internal and External Knowledge Sources." *Strategic Entrepreneurship Journal* 3(4): 297–320.
George, G., Wiklund, J. and Zahra, S.A. (2005). "Ownership and the Internationalization of Small Firms." *Journal of Management* 31(2): 210–233.
Gilson, R. (1999). "The Legal Infrastructure of High Technology Industrial Districts: Silicon Valley, Route 128, and Covenants Not to Compete." *York University Law Review* 74: 575–629.
Gompers, P.A. (1995). "Optimal Investment, Monitoring, and the Staging of Venture Capital." *Journal of Finance* 50: 1461–1490.
Gompers, P.A. (1996). "Grandstanding in the Venture Capital Industry." *Journal of Financial Economics* 42: 133–156.
Gompers, P.A. (2002). "Corporations and the Financing of Innovation: The Corporate Venturing Experience." *Economic Review – Federal Reserve Bank of Atlanta* 87(4): 1–17.
Gompers, P.A. and Lerner, J. (1998). "What Drives Venture Fundraising?", in *Brooking Papers on Economic Activity, Microeconomics*. Washington DC: Brookings Institution Press. 149–192.
Gompers, P.A. and Lerner, J. (1999). *The Venture Capital Cycle*. Cambridge: MIT Press.
Gompers, P.A. and Lerner, J. (2001). "The Venture Capital Revolution." *Journal of Economic Perspectives* 15(2): 145–169.
Gompers, P., Lerner, J., Scharfstein, D., and Kovner, A. (2010). "Performance Persistence in Entrepreneurship." *Journal of Financial Economics* 96: 18–32.
Gorman, M. and Sahlman, W.A. (1989). "What Do Venture Capitalists Do?" *Journal of Business Venturing* 4(4): 231–248.
Groh, A., Liechtenstein, H., and Lieser, K. (2013). *The Venture Capital and Private Equity Country Attractiveness Index, 2013 Annual*, http://blog.iese.edu/vcpeindex/, accessed January 21, 2014.
Gulati, R. and Higgins, M.C. (2003). "Which Ties Matter When? The Contingent Effects of Interorganizational Partnerships on IPO Success." *Strategic Management Journal* 24: 127–144.
Guler, I. and Guillen, M.F. (2010a). "Home Country Networks and Foreign Expansion: Evidence from the Venture Capital Industry." *Academy of Management Journal* 53(2): 390–410.

Guler, I. and Guillen, M.F. (2010b). "Institutions and the Internationalization of US Venture Capital Firms." *Journal of International Business Studies* 41(2): 185–205.

Guler, I. and McGahan, A.M. (2006). "Do Investors Manage US Ventures Less Intensively Than Ventures in Other Regions of the World?" Working paper, available at ssrn.com/abstract=913042.

Guler, I. and McGahan, A.M. (2007). *Syndication in International Venture Investing*, Boston University.

Gupta, A.K. and Sapienza, H.J. (1992). "Determinants of Venture Capital Firms' Preferences Regarding the Industry Diversity and Geographic Scope of their Investments." *Journal of Business Venturing* 7(3): 347–362.

Hall, J. and Hofer, C. (1993). "Venture Capitalists' Decision Criteria in New Venture Evaluation." *Journal of Business Venturing* 8: 25–42.

Hall, G. and Tu, C. (2003). "Venture Capitalists and the Decision to Invest Overseas." *Venture Capital* 5(12): 181–190.

Harrison, R.T. and Mason, C.M. (1992). "International Perspectives on the Supply of Informal Venture Capital." *Journal of Business Venturing* 7: 459–475.

Hellmann, T. (1998). "The Allocation of Control Rights in Venture Capital Contracts." *RAND Journal of Economics* 29: 57–76.

Hellmann, T. and Puri, M. (2002). "Venture Capital and the Professionalization of Start-up Firms: Empirical Evidence." *The Journal of Finance* 57(1): 169–197.

Hitt, M.A., Tihanyi, L., Miller, T., and Connelly, B. (2006). "International Diversification: Antecedents, Outcomes, and Moderators." *Journal of Management* 32(6): 831–867.

Hoehn-Weiss, M.N. and LiPuma, J.A. (2008). "Better in Pairs? Interactions between Alliances and Corporate Venture Capital on New Venture Internationalization." In Zacharakis, A. et al. (Eds), *Frontiers of Entrepreneurship Research 2008*. Wellesley, MA: Babson College.

Jeng, L. and Wells, P. (2000). "The Determinants of Venture Capital Funding: Evidence Across Countries." *Journal of Corporate Finance* 6(1): 241–289.

Johanson, J. and Vahlne, J. (1977). "The Internationalization Process of the Firm: A Model of Knowledge Development and Increasing Foreign Commitments." *Journal of International Business Studies* 8(1): 23–32.

Jones, M.V., Coviello, N., and Tang, Y.K. (2011). "International Entrepreneurship Research (1989–2009): A Domain Ontology and Thematic Analysis." *Journal of Business Venturing* 26: 632–659.

Kaplan, S.N. and Strömberg, P. (2003). "Financial Contracting Theory Meets the Real World: An Empirical Analysis of Venture Capital Contracts." *Review of Economic Studies* 70: 281–315.

Kaplan, S.N. and Strömberg, P. (2004). "Characteristics, Contracts, and Actions: Evidence from Venture Capitalist Analyses." *Journal of Finance* 59(5): 2177–2210.

Karsai, J., Wright, M., Dudzinski, Z. and Morovic, J. (1998). "Screening and Valuing Venture Capital Investments: Evidence from Hungary, Poland and Sloavkia." *Entrepreneurship and Regional Development* 10: 203–224.

Knight, R. (1994). "Criteria Used By Venture Capitalists: A Cross Cultural Analysis." *International Small Business Journal* 13(1): 26–37.

Kortum, S. and Lerner, J. (2000). "Assessing the Contribution of Venture Capital to Innovation." *Rand Journal of Economics* 31: 674–692.

La Porta, R., Lopez-de-Silanes, F., Shleifer, A., and Vishny, R. (1998). "Law and Finance." *Journal of Political Economy* 106(6): 1113–1155.

La Porta, R., Lopez-de-Silanes, F., Shleifer, A., and Vishny, R. (1999). "The Quality of Government." *Journal of Law, Economics and Organization* 15(1): 222–279.

Landström, H. (1993). "Informal Risk Capital in Sweden and Some International Comparisons." *Journal of Business Venturing* 8: 525–540.

Larrañeta B., Zahra, S.A. and González, J.L.G. (2012). "Enriching Strategic Variety in New Ventures Through External Knowledge." *Journal of Business Venturing* 27(4): 401–413.

Lerner, J. (1995). "Venture Capitalists and the Oversight of Private Firms." *The Journal of Finance* 50(1): 301–318.

Lerner, J. (2009). *Boulevard of Broken Dreams: Why Public Efforts to Boost Entrepreneurship and Venture Capital Have Failed – and What to Do About It*. Princeton, NJ: Princeton University Press.

Lerner, J. and Schoar, A. (2005). "Does Legal Enforcement Affect Financial Transactions? The Contractual Channel in Private Equity." *Quarterly Journal of Economics* 120(1): 223–246.

Lerner, J. and Tag, J. (2013). "Institutions and Venture Capital." *Industrial and Corporate Change* 22(1): 153–182, doi: 10.1093/icc/dts050.

Lindsey, L. (2008). "Blurring Firm Boundaries: The Role of Venture Capital in Strategic Alliance." *Journal of Finance* 63: 1137–1168.
LiPuma, J.A. (2006). "Independent Venture Capital, Corporate Venture Capital, and the Internationalisation Intensity of Technology-based Portfolio Firms." *International Entrepreneurship and Management Journal* 2(2): 245–260.
LiPuma, J.A. (2012). "Internationalization and the IPO Performance of New Ventures." *Journal of Business Research* 65(7): 914–921.
LiPuma, J.A. and Park, S. (forthcoming). "Venture Capitalists' Risk Mitigation of Portfolio Company Internationalization." *Entrepreneurship Theory and Practice*, in press; doi: 10.1111/etap.12033.
LiPuma, J.A., Newbert, S.L., and Doh, J.P. (2013). "The Effect of Institutional Quality on Firm Export Performance in Emerging Economies: A Contingency Model of Firm Age and Size." *Small Business Economics* 40: 817–841.
Lutz, H.F. (1932). "Babylonian Partnerships." *Journal of Economic and Business History* 4: 552–570.
MacMillan, I., Siegel, R., and Narasimha, P. (1985). "Criteria Used by Venture Capitalists to Evaluate New Venture Proposals." *Journal of Business Venturing* 1: 119–128.
Makela, M.M. and Maula, M.V.J. (2005). "Cross-border Venture Capital and New Venture Internationalization: An Isomorphism Perspective." *Venture Capital* 7(3): 227–257.
Makela, M.M. and Maula, M.V.J. (2006). "Interorganizational Commitment in Syndicated Cross-border Venture Capital Investments." *Entrepreneurship Theory & Practice* 30(2): 273–298.
Makela, M.M. and Maula, M.V.J. (2008). "Attracting Cross-border Venture Capital: The Role of a Local Investor." *Entrepreneurship & Regional Development* 20: 237–257.
Manigart, S., Collewaert, V., Wright, M., Pruthi, S., Lockett, A., Bruining, H., Hommel, U., and Landstrom, H. (2007). "Human Capital and the Internationalization of Venture Capital Firms." *International Entrepreneurship and Management Journal* 3: 109–125.
Manigart, S. and Wright, M. (2013). "Venture Capital Investors and Portfolio Firms." *Foundations and Trends in Entrepreneurship* 9(4–5): 365–570.
Maula, M., Autio, E., and Murray, G. (2005). "Corporate Venture Capitalists and Independent Venture Capitalists: What Do They Know, Who Do They Know, and Should Entrepreneurs Care?" *Venture Capital* 7(1): 3–21.
Maula, M. and Murray, G. (2002). "Corporate Venture Capital and the Creation of US Public Companies: The Impact of Sources of Venture Capital on the Performance of Portfolio Companies." In Hitt, M.A., Amit, R., Lucier, C.E., and Nixon, R. D. (Eds), *Creating Value: Winners in the New Business Environment*. Oxford, UK: Blackwell Publishing.
Megginson, W. (2004). "Towards a Global Model of Venture Capital?" *Journal of Applied Corporate Finance* 17(1): 89–107.
Mollick, E.R. (2014). "The Dynamics of Crowdfunding: An Exploratory Study." *Journal of Business Venturing* 29(1): 1–16.
Neher, D.V. (1999). "Staged Financing: An Agency Perspective." *Review of Economic Studies* 66: 255–274.
Nguyen T. and Barrett N. (2006). "Internet-based Knowledge Internationalization and Firm Internationalization in Transition Markets." *Advances in International Marketing* 17: 369–394.
North, D.C. (1986). "The New Institutional Economics." *Journal of Institutional and Theoretical Economics* 142: 230–237.
OECD (2000). *Knowledge Management in the Learning Economy: Education and Skills*. Paris: OECD.
Ooghe, H., Manigart, S., and Fassin, Y. (1991). "Growth Patterns of European Venture Capital Industry." *Journal of Business Venturing* 6: 381–404.
Oviatt, B.M. and McDougall, P.P. (2005). "Defining International Entrepreneurship and Modeling the Speed of Internationalization." *Entrepreneurship Theory & Practice*: 537–553.
Peili, Y. and Zhonghong, F. (2007). "Knowledge Stickiness in the Process of Integrated Innovation: Performance and Countermeasures." R & D Management Year, 4: 75–80.
Poterba, J. (1989). "Venture Capital and Capital Gains Taxation." In Summers, L. (Ed.), *Tax Policy and the Economy*. Cambridge: Cambridge University Press, pp. 47–67.
Preece, S.B., Miles, G., and Baetz, M.C. (1999). "Explaining the International Intensity and Global Diversity of Early-stage Technology-based Firms." *Journal of Business Venturing* 14: 259–281.
Puri, M. and Zarutskie, R. (2012). "On the Lifecycle Dynamics of Venture-capital- and Non-venture capital-financed Firms." *Journal of Finance* 67(6): 2247–2293.

Sahlman, W. (1990). "The Structure and Governance of Venture-capital Organizations." *Journal of Financial Economics* 27: 473–521.
Sapienza, H. (1992). "When do Venture Capitalists Add Value?" *Journal of Business Venturing* 7(1): 9–27.
Sapienza, H. J., Autio, E., George, G., and Zahra, S.A. (2006). "A Capabilities Perspective on the Effects of Early Internationalization on Firm Survival and Growth." *Academy of Management Review* 31(4): 914–933.
Schilit, W.K. (1992). "The Globalization of Venture Capital." *Business Horizons* 35(1): 17–23.
Scott, W.R. (1995). *Institutions and Organizations*. Thousand Oaks, CA: Sage Publications.
Shi, Y.N., Sia, C.L., Banerjee, P., Luo, C., Tan, B.C.Y., and Chen, H. (2009). "Choice of Knowledge Source in Situations of Equivocality: Impact of Cultural Traits." Pacific Asia Conference on Information Systems Proceedings. Hong Kong: City University.
Singh, J.V., Tucker, D.J., and House, R.J. (1986). "Organizational Legitimacy and the Liability of Newness." *Administrative Sciences Quarterly* 31: 171–193.
Sorenson, O. and Stuart, T.E. (2001). "Syndication Networks and the Spatial Distribution of Venture Capital Investments." *American Journal of Sociology* 106(6): 1546–1588.
Sorenson, O. and Stuart, T.E. (2008). "Bringing the Context Back In: Settings and the Search for Syndicate Partners in Venture Capital Investment Networks." *Administrative Science Quarterly* 53: 266–294.
Stuart, T.E., Hoang, H., and Hybels, R.C. (1999). "Interorganizational Endorsements and the Performance of Entrepreneurial Ventures." *Administrative Science Quarterly* 44: 315–349.
Stuart, T.E. and Sorenson, O. (2003). "The Geography of Opportunity: Spatial Heterogeneity in Founding Rates and the Performance of Biotechnology Firms." *Research Policy* 32: 229–253.
Terjesen, S. and Elam, A.B. (2009). "A Development and Test of Practice Theory to Explore Transnational Entrepreneurs' Venture Internationalization." *Entrepreneurship Theory & Practice* 33: 1093–1120.
Terjesen, S., Hessels, J., and Li, D. (2013). "Comparative International Entrepreneurship: A Review and Research Agenda", *Journal of Management* doi: 10.1177/0149206313486259.
Tian, S. (2011). "The Causes and Consequences of Venture Capital Stage Financing." *Journal of Financial Economics* 101: 132–159.
Walske, J. and Zacharakis, A. (2009). "Genetically Engineered: Why Some Venture Capital Firms Are More Successful Than Others." *Entrepreneurship Theory & Practice* 33 (1): 297–318.
Winton, A. and Yerramilli, V. (2008). "Entrepreneurial Finance: Banks Versus Venture Capital." *Journal of Financial Economics* 88: 51–79.
Wright, M., Pruthi, S., and Lockett, A. (2002). "Internationalization of Western Venture Capitalists into Emerging Markets: Risk Assessment and Information in India." *Small Business Economics* 19(1): 13–29.
Wright, M., Pruthi, S., and Lockett, A. (2005). "International Venture Capital Research: From Cross-country Comparisons to Crossing Borders." *International Journal of Management Reviews* 7(3): 135–165.
Yamakawa, Y., Peng, M.W., and Deeds, D.L. (2008). "What Drives New Ventures to Internationalize from Emerging to Developed Economies?" *Entrepreneurship Theory & Practice* 32(1): 59–82.
Zacharakis, A.L., McMullen, J.S., and Shepherd, D.A. (2007). "Venture Capitalists' Decision Policies Across Three Countries: An Instructional Theory Perspective." *Journal of International Business Studies* 38: 692–708.
Zaheer, S. (1995). "Overcoming the Liability of Foreignness." *Academy of Management Journal* 38: 341–363.

12

International entrepreneurship in a world of broad triad regions

An international business perspective

Alan M. Rugman, In Hyeock (Ian) Lee and Siri Terjesen

Introduction: tensions in the IB and IE literatures

Although the world economy is characterized by firms of all sizes selling to customers overseas, it is noticeable that, despite multiple liabilities of newness, smallness, and foreignness, an increasing number of new and small ventures pursue international markets to sell their goods and services. Reflecting this recent trend, there is a large academic literature in international entrepreneurship (IE) that describes new and small firms as "born global" (Rennie 1993). The born global firm has also been termed an international new venture (INV): "a business organization that, from inception, seeks to derive significant competitive advantage from the use of resources and the sale of outputs in multiple countries" (Oviatt and McDougall 1994: p.49).

Although the definition of IE has been refined in order to apply to diverse contexts such as new ventures, small- and medium-sized enterprises (SMEs), and corporate entrepreneurship,[1] born global firms are described as typically taking three to six years from inception to initial foreign market entry (McDougall and Oviatt 2000). As "new" firms, the traditional Uppsala process theory of internationalization which suggests that firms must first develop in their home country market, and then go abroad to nearby countries at slow and incremental stages in order to learn about unfamiliar foreign markets, may not apply (Johanson and Vahlne 1977, 1990). There is no time for such learning to take place in INVs. This point has been largely ignored in the literature reviews which document a marked increase in studies of born global firms over the last 15 years (Coviello and Jones 2004; Rialp et al. 2005; Keupp and Gassmann 2009; Terjesen et al. 2013). Extant research typically examines only the scope, drivers, processes, characteristics, and impacts of cross-border activities by internationalized new and small firms, and does not consider the possibility of incremental learning related to INVs' young age. As a result, despite the increased interest in early internationalizing firms from policymakers, entrepreneurs, and scholars, there are still major gaps in our understanding (Keupp and Gassmann 2009).

This chapter is motivated by two developments in the international business (IB) field that have not yet been fully incorporated into the emerging research on born global firms. First, approximately half of extant IE research does not use a theoretical framework (Keupp and Gassmann 2009). Although, despite its young age as an academic domain, IE research is now offering several diverse but coherent thematic areas that are potentially rich for theoretical development (Jones et al. 2011; Terjesen et al. 2013), scholars have consistently called for better theories to explain IE (Autio 2005; Zahra 2005), particularly the integration of IB and entrepreneurship theories (Keupp and Gassmann 2009; Coviello and Jones 2004; Mathews and Zander 2007). Here, we demonstrate that INVs experience a liability of foreignness which is better analyzed within broad geographic regions of the triad (North America, Europe, Asia-Pacific), rather than globally. The most basic trade-off in the IB field is that the benefits of internationalization must exceed its costs. For international expansion to occur, firm specific advantages (FSAs) in the form of tacit knowledge, which needs to be internalized, must outweigh the perceived and actual liabilities of foreignness. Yet the born global literature tends to ignore the liability of foreignness by assuming that a firm can internationalize quickly to any country in the world from its inception. However, recent research indicates that even the world's largest multinational enterprises (MNEs) expand within their home region of the triad, rather than globally (Rugman and Verbeke 2004). This implies that there is a liability of inter-regional foreignness and that INVs are probably less equipped than large firms in dealing with this problem.

Second, scholars have appealed for better measures of the internationalization of new and small firms with more rigorous techniques, complementary studies, and multiple data sources (Coviello and Jones 2004). Specifically, another problem with research on born global firms is the overuse of an ambiguous scope metric for measuring their international activities. Recent literature reviews identify many inconsistencies in research (Coviello and Jones 2004; Keupp and Gassmann 2009), perhaps due to the fact that researchers have utilized scope measures (e.g., number of foreign countries, continents, and/or regions where new ventures entered) instead of scale metrics (e.g., amount of foreign sales, degree of internationalization or multinationality, and other scale ratios that new ventures achieved in foreign markets) (see Table 12.1 for a review of prior studies). As illustrated in Table 12.1, most INV studies simply count the number of countries in which a firm has exports (or foreign sales). This scope metric produces misleading results as it assumes that all countries are of equal size and of equal importance. This problem is exaggerated when the regional nature of IB is considered, since exports, foreign sales, and even outbound foreign direct investment (FDI) to geographically distant regions are more difficult than to intra-regional countries. Furthermore, scholars have called for research on the relationship between INVs' geographic context and firm performance (Rialp et al. 2005) and "different entry points and pathways into the global marketplaces, and their sustainability and performance implications" (Mathews and Zander 2007: 397). Indeed, a few recent empirical studies suggested that the relationship between INVs' internationalization and firm performance may be much more complicated than previously thought, such as M-shaped curves, especially when the regional dimension is considered (Almodóvar and Rugman 2013; Lee 2010, 2013).

In integrating these issues, this chapter makes three significant contributions to the literature. First, we extend earlier work on the regional nature of MNEs (Rugman and Verbeke 2004; Rugman 2005) reporting that of the world's 500 largest firms, 72 percent of their sales come from their home region. New and small firms are often started within clusters and networks led by large MNEs (Acs et al. 1997) which are regionally based. Second, we explore INV activity across different industries and regions of the triads. Third, we analyze new data on foreign over total (F/T) sales and outbound FDI amounts from both country and regional perspectives. Taken together, we significantly extend IE literature which examines INVs' international activities based on scope metrics.

This chapter proceeds as follows. First, we elaborate on the theories of liability of foreignness (LOF), transaction cost economics (TCE), and firm specific advantages (FSAs), and their impacts on the international activities of new and small firms. In the next two sections, we elaborate on these points in a detailed examination of the IE literature. Second, we put forward a notion that most new and small firms are actually "born regional" firms with a home region focus in terms of both *downstream* foreign export sales and *upstream* outbound FDI. We also examine the extent to which these INVs operate regionally or globally with data on Korean firms. Lastly, we conclude this chapter with a discussion of some limitations and future research directions.

Review of the previous literature: international activities of new and small firms

The born global subfield of IE has its origins in the now classic article by Oviatt and McDougall (1994) on the nature and growth of INVs (Autio 2005), awarded the *Journal of International Business Studies* Decade Award for being the most influential paper published in the journal that year. As of 2014, Google Scholar lists over 2,500 citations of Oviatt and McDougall (1994). To examine the insights of this path-breaking paper, we analyze thirty papers that were selected based on the following three criteria: (1) utilized empirical and quantitative research approaches; (2) cited Oviatt and McDougall (1994) as their theoretical foundation for conducting the empirical analyses; and (3) appeared in the most influential journals in management, entrepreneurship, IB, and international marketing.[2] See Table 12.1.

From Table 12.1, we observe that empirical IE research has been conducted on various topics with diverse samples from different countries, and in heterogeneous industry sectors. Most articles employ exports (or foreign sales), with only a handful exploring FDI, imports, and alliance relationships. We identify four critical issues from the studies listed in Table 12.1. First, in terms of the size and age of sampled companies, past empirical studies employ different thresholds: most use the common criteria in IE research for identifying new ventures as fewer than 500 employees (e.g. Zahra et al. 2000; Lu and Beamish 2001; Coviello 2006); however, based on our sample of selected empirical papers, we identified only six studies that unambiguously test "new" firms of under six years of age while nineteen explicitly test firms over six years of age which are no longer INVs. Three studies do not even report firm age used in their sampling process. As indicated in the last column of Table 12.1, differences between IE in new firms versus SMEs are inconclusive. In addition, with the exceptions of Zhou et al. (2010) and Khavul et al. (2010), most studies report only the age of firms as sample selection criteria, and do not clearly reveal the ventures' age at the time of internationalization.

Second, most empirical INV studies employ a broad country scope metric that weights large markets (e.g. USA) equally with small ones (e.g. Costa Rica). Internationalization is measured as the number of countries that new ventures entered at inception by the following: Coviello and Munro (1997); Burgel and Murray (2000); Shrader et al. (2000); Zahra et al. (2000); Lu and Beamish (2001); Kuemmerle (2002); Moen and Servais (2002); Coviello (2006); Mudambi and Zahra (2007); and Gabrielsson et al. (2008). Other studies use the number of continents or areas in which firms realize foreign sales, e.g. Reuber and Fischer (1997); Sapienza et al. (2005); Fernhaber et al. (2008); and Fernhaber et al. (2009). Several studies use a dummy to measure the internationalization achieved by INVs (Fan and Phan 2007; Coeurderoy and Murray 2008; Filatotchev et al. 2009; Carr et al. 2010; Fernhaber and Li 2010). Such scope metrics are limited because they explore only a count (of countries or other areas) and fail to measure the real "scale" of internationalization that new ventures achieved from their foreign business activities. Only four recent papers employ a scale measure of venture internationalization: Leiblein and Reuer (2004) use absolute foreign sales realized outside North America while Lopez et al. (2009) and Fernhaber et al. (2009) employ F/T and other scale ratios related to regional sales and costs; and Bruneel et al. (2010) adopt a measure that may capture both aspects

Table 12.1 Summary of previous studies citing Oviatt and McDougall 1994

Study	*Topic*	*Sample size (# of firms)*	*Industry sector*	*International activity*	*Internationalization metric(s)**	*Firm age*	*Firm size*	*Firm type*
Coviello and Munro (IBR, 1997)	Networks and internationalization	4 (Case studies)	Software	Exports	# of countries	Founded between 1978 and 1983	25–140 employees	SMEs
Reuber and Fischer (JIBS, 1997)	Top management team (TMT) and internationalization	49	Software	Exports	Composite measure: FS/TS and geographic scope	3–24 years	1–200 employees	SMEs
Autio et al. (AMJ, 2000)	International performance	59	Electronics	International sales	International sales growth	14.85 years (Mean)	106,600 Finnish markka (Mean)	SMEs
Burgel and Murray (JIM, 2000)	Entry mode decisions	362	High tech	Exports	Share of foreign revenue # of countries	1–10 years	More than 3 employees	SMEs
Knight (JIM, 2000)	Performance	268	Diverse industries	International sales	Composite survey measures: Globalization response and internationalization preparation	Not reported	1–500 employees	Unclear
Shrader et al. (AMJ, 2000)	International risk management	87	High tech and low tech	Exports, Licensing, Sales office, Joint venture and Production Subsidiary	# of countries FS/TS	1–6 years	$66 million (Mean, sales)	New ventures
Zahra et al. (AMJ, 2000)	Performance	321	High tech	Exports, Licensing, Acquisition and Start-ups	# of countries FS/TS	1–6 years	71.9 employees (Mean)	New ventures
Lu and Beamish (SMJ, 2001)	Performance	164	Diverse industries	Exports, FDI and Alliances	Export intensity # of countries	Not reported	1–500 employees	Unclear
Reuber and Fischer (ETP, 2002)	Firm growth	187	Software products and food processing	Foreign sales	Foreign sales growth	10.08 years (Mean)	1–200 employees	SMEs

(continued)

Table 12.1 Summary of previous studies citing Oviatt and McDougall 1994 (Continued)

Study	*Topic*	*Sample size (# of firms)*	*Industry sector*	*International activity*	*Internationalization metric(s)**	*Firm age*	*Firm size*	*Firm type*
Kuemmerle (JBV, 2002)	Internationalization	6 (Case studies)	Media, communication and service	Offices, Operations and Trips	# of countries	1–20 years	70–2,830 employees	SMEs
Moen and Servais (JIM, 2002)	Born global	677	Diverse industries	Exports	Export intensity # of countries	30–45 years (Mean)	33–84 employees (Mean)	SMEs
Fischer and Reuber (SBE, 2003)	SME internationalization	188	Diverse industries	Exports	FS/TS	9.5 years (Mean)	19 employees (Mean)	SMEs
Leiblein and Reuer (JBV, 2004)	Foreign sales development	101	Semiconductor	Exports	Foreign sales outside North America	1–50 years	$1.3–$13,500 million (Sales) $308 million (Mean, exports)	SMEs
Sapienza et al. (JBV, 2005)	International and domestic learning effort	90	Diverse industries	Exports	Composite measure: FS/TS and geographic scope of foreign sales	15.82 years (Mean)	1–1,000 employees	SMEs
Coviello (JIBS, 2006)	Network dynamics	3 (Case studies)	Software	Exports	# of countries	1–6 years	4–5 employees	New ventures
Fan and Phan (JIBS, 2007)	Internationalization	135	Airline	Allocation of seat capacity	Dummy (1 if international at birth; 0 otherwise)	Founded between 1996 and 2004	2,162 (Mean, seats per week)	SMEs
Mudambi and Zahra (JIBS, 2007)	Survival	51	Diverse industries	FDI	# of countries Export intensity	Less than 16 months	$52.479 (Mean, exports)	New ventures
Zhou et al. (JIBS, 2007)	Born global, social networks and performance	129	Diverse industries	Exports and imports	Composite measure	More than 5 years	50–500 employees 9.6 million yuan (Mean, sales)	SMEs

Coeurderoy and Murray (JIBS, 2008)	Location and timing of foreign market entries by new firms	375	High tech	Foreign sales	Dummy (1 if entered country j; 0 otherwise)	7.08 years (Mean, UK firms) 6.49 years (Mean, German firms)	3.5 employees (Mean)	SMEs
Fernhaber et al. (JIBS, 2008)	Clustering and internationalization	156	Information technology	Exports	FS/TS # of continents	3.59 years (Mean)	$32.02 million (Mean, sales)	Unclear
Gabrielsson et al. (IBR, 2008)	Born global	8 (Case studies)	Diverse industries	Exports	# of countries FS/TS (for 4 of the 8 cases)	5–54 years	40–450 employees	SMEs
Fernhaber et al. (SEJ, 2009)	International knowledge and internationalization	206	High tech	Foreign sales Foreign assets	FS/TS FA/TA # of continents Composite measure	1–6 years	$185.47 million (Mean, assets) $53.72 million (Mean, sales)	New ventures
Filatotchev et al. (JIBS, 2009)	Export orientation and performance	711	High tech	Exports	Dummy (1=exporting; 0 otherwise) Range of export sales (6 categories)	4.61 years (Mean)	50.21 employees (Mean)	Unclear
Knight and Kim (JIBS, 2009)	International business competence	354	Diverse industries	Foreign sales	International market share International sales growth International export intensity	Not reported	190 employees (Mean) $32 million (Mean, sales)	Unclear
Lopez, et al. (JIBS, 2009)	Born regional	40	Software	Exports	Export intensity FS/TS in the firm's first year % of current sales that are local, regional or global Foreign clients/Total customers	9.08 years (Mean)	2.43 employees (Mean)	SMEs

(continued)

Table 12.1 Summary of previous studies citing Oviatt and McDougall 1994 (Continued)

Study	*Topic*	*Sample size (# of firms)*	*Industry sector*	*International activity*	*Internationalization metric(s)**	*Firm age*	*Firm size*	*Firm type*
Carr *et al.* (SEJ, 2010)	Firm age and performance	787	Diverse industries	International revenues	Dummy (1=International revenues; 0 otherwise)	10.41 years (Mean)	4.39 (Mean, lnAssets)	SMEs
Fernhaber and Li (ETP, 2010)	Entry and Performance	150	Diverse industries	Entry in foreign markets	Dummy (1=International entry; 0 otherwise)	1–6 years	$255.38 million (Mean, assets)	New ventures
Khavul et al. (JBV, 2010)	Performance	166	Diverse industries	International sales	FS/TS; Blau's index by region	1–10 years	103.80 employees (Mean)	SMEs
Zhou et al. (JIBS, 2010)	Performance	436	Diverse industries	Exports	FS/TS	1–16 years	30–500 employees	SMEs
Bruneel et al. (SEJ, 2010)	Learning and internationalization	114	High tech	Foreign sales	Foreign sales weighted by the psychic and geographical distance of foreign markets	1–12 years	3.21 employees (Mean)	SMEs

Note: *FS/TS denotes the total foreign sales (including both exports and foreign subsidiary sales) divided by total sales whereas export intensity is calculated as exports divided by total sales. We note that they were used interchangeably in some studies.

of scale and scope metrics using foreign sales weighted by the psychic and geographical distance of foreign markets.

Third, although Oviatt and McDougall's (1994) seminal study did not mention Hymer's (1976) liability of foreignness, Table 12.1 makes it clear that the liability of foreignness applies even more to new and small firms, and that those firms may suffer additional liabilities in the internationalization process. Lu and Beamish (2001) find evidence that small firms face a liability of foreignness when they go abroad. Mudambi and Zahra (2007) also argue that firms are subject to the double liabilities of smallness and newness which inflate the liability of foreignness when entering foreign markets. These multiple disadvantages impose limitations on the global expansion of new ventures' foreign operations, especially when substantial dissimilarities exist between their home and host markets in terms of geographic, social, cultural, political, legal, and economic dimensions (Burgel and Murray 2000; Lu and Beamish 2001). Therefore, market potential perceived by INVs may be uneven across different regions (Gabrielsson et al. 2008).

Fourth, small and young firms face multiple liabilities during internationalization, and must possess something unique inside their firm boundaries (i.e. FSAs) to operate effectively in foreign markets. Leiblein and Reuer (2004) highlight the fundamental difference between non-equity and equity alliances, pointing out that since non-equity alliances do not provide full access to partners' complementary resources, new ventures should make "relationship-specific investments" when internationalizing. In a similar vein, several studies summarized in Table 12.1 stress the importance of FSAs to small and young firms' internationalization. Kuemmerle (2002) distinguishes between home base augmenting and home base exploiting activities undertaken by new ventures, arguing that the latter activities are resource intensive and require a substantial stock of product and process knowledge internalized inside the new ventures. Moen and Servais (2002) also find evidence that the basic resources and competencies of new ventures should be accumulated during the inception stage for their international competitiveness. Fernhaber et al. (2009) highlight the importance of international knowledge as a key intangible resource spurring new venture internationalization.

Therefore, the main contribution of Oviatt and McDougall (1994) is now clear from our critical review on the literature in Table 12.1: time is a major dimension in understanding new venture internationalization. By internationalizing into foreign markets from their inception, INVs cannot have the luxury of time to learn about unfamiliar foreign countries at incremental stages. As a result, the traditional Uppsala process theory of internationalization (Johanson and Vahlne 1977, 1990) does not apply to INVs, as INVs are conceptually "new" firms and there is not enough time for learning to take place in INVs. In short, the compressed and early timing of internationalization is the key element that distinguishes the subfield of IE from IB, as argued by several studies (e.g. Coviello and Munro 1997; Burgel and Murray 2000; Kuemmerle 2002; Moen and Servais 2002; Sapienza et al. 2005; Fan and Phan 2007). Scale-based metrics are more useful than scope-based metrics for empirical work on firm age and extent of internationalization after either three or six years. The present study uses a regional distribution of export sales and outbound FDI amounts across the triad to examine how and where new and small ventures internationalize through exporting and outbound FDI activities. We examine new firms that are under six years of age with fewer than 500 employees in multiple industry sectors of Korea. Korea has been recognized as one of the most entrepreneurial societies in the world (Kelley et al. 2011), demonstrating high rates of growth and industrialization in the past years; however, despite its entrepreneurial characteristics, the country is under-represented in the IE literature. We also explore the geographic distribution of exports and outbound FDI amounts across broad geographic regions of the triad (i.e. North America, Europe, Asia-Pacific) with diverse industrial sub-samples.

Regional internationalization of new ventures: some evidence from Korea

Firms can benefit from exporting their goods and services. Although theoretically firms could trade with countries around the world, Kenichi Ohmae (1985) argued that large firms face a "global impasse" in terms of difficulty replicating strong home region performance in other regions. More recent research indicates that the world is in a state of "semi-globalization" rather than full globalization due to costs emanating from cultural, administrative, geographic and economic distances (Ghemawat 2003). Regionalization is a form of semi-globalization.

Internalization theory describes how imperfections in the market increase the cost of transactions across markets, leading to the internalization of functions within the MNE (Rugman 1981). Despite possessing high levels of proactiveness and innovation, new and small firms face a liability of foreignness in overseas markets and must possess some distinct FSAs to overcome this liability. FSAs are unique capabilities that are proprietary to the organization and are based on technology, marketing or distribution skills. FSAs emerge from the internalization of an asset (e.g. knowledge, marketing capability) of which an organization has control. FSAs are reflected in the firm's success in coordinating activities, for example in production, sales, or distribution, and help to mitigate transaction costs.

While transaction cost economics (TCE) is mostly applied to help explain the internationalization of large firms, it is also an important framework for entrepreneurial firms (Zacharakis 1997). New ventures face TCE costs at both ex-ante (search, information, drafting, bargaining, decision, safeguarding) and ex-post (monitoring, enforcement, adaptation, haggling, bonding and mal-adaptation) stages (Zacharakis 1997). In the context of internationalization, transaction costs are driven by the need to manage complex coordination across diverse cultural environments and can be internal (related to developing higher coordination and control processes) or external (related to regulatory environment). TCE vary by national institutional environments: the more different the institutions, the higher the costs (Goerzen and Beamish 2003).

Generally transaction costs are lower within a triad region due to geographic proximity, ease of communication, more similar institutions and a longer history of cooperation and development. Compared to inter-region, intra-region transportation and communication is often easier, cheaper and more efficient. Regional trade agreements and associations such as NAFTA, EU, and ASEAN facilitate trade and FDI. For example, Rugman and Verbeke (2008) describe the EU region as characterized by efficient transportation networks, integrated institutions and increasingly irrelevant cultural distance.

Access to and processing of knowledge from other countries is critical for new venture creation (Kuemmerle 2002). Knowledge spillovers are geographically constrained (Acs et al. 1994). FSAs may emerge from knowledge-based advantages and are often location-bound and more easily exploited in the home region than globally. FSAs are more transferable when the institutional contexts are more similar. A large body of entrepreneurship research indicates that a firm is most likely to fail in its early years and the probability of survival increases with age. Thus managers of new firms may be interested in pursuing "safer" intra-region markets. Furthermore, the pursuit of international markets demands time, energy and other resources which are in short supply in a new venture. FSAs are more transferable when there is managerial slack in the firm (Bouquet et al. 2009). Nations also possess country specific advantages (CSAs) that can aid the performance of firms. In short the geographic location of firm activities within a triad region can affect firm outcomes such as the internationalization process and success.

Dunning (1998) categorizes four motives of FDI: market-seeking, resource-seeking, efficiency-seeking, and strategic asset-seeking. Considering that INVs are subject to multiple liabilities of newness, smallness, and foreignness, and that the IE literature has identified exporting as the most common step in their international expansion, most of the outbound FDI implemented by small and young firms should be to help them realize FSAs in downstream sales activities to achieve the market-seeking objective (Tatoglu and Glaister 1998a, 1998b), and this is best implemented in their home region.

In summary strategists in internationally oriented ventures seek rational choices based on trade-offs of FSAs such as knowledge and other resources against the costs of doing business abroad. This suggests that firms face a lower liability of foreignness within their home region than outside the region.

Regionalized foreign export sales

Extant qualitative and quantitative research provides competing evidence on the regionalization of new venture exports. For example, Prashantham and Dhanaraj (2010) and Terjesen et al. (2008) report a few case studies of Indian INVs in IT/software industries which internationalized into European and/or US markets from their inception. However, Coviello and Munro (1997) describe a New Zealand software firm with initial export markets in Japan and Australia. Lopez et al. (2009) also report that of 15 young Costa Rican software firms, 12 (80 percent) first export to another country within Latin America. The remaining three export to the USA (2) and Canada (1). As argued by Mathews and Zander (2007: 396–397), "As for the geographical location of activities, limited managerial resources and the complications associated with knowledge exchange and innovation across geographical distances may make entrepreneurs increasingly inclined to concentrate resources and activities closer to one distinct home base." Considering these arguments, we expect that new ventures are more likely to export to countries within their home region of the triad than to countries outside their home region.

In Table 12.2, we describe a regional distribution of export sales realized by 2,239 Korean INVs using Small and Medium Business Administration (SMBA) survey data in 2002.[3] We compare the geographic export sales segment data (i.e. scale metric) with the number of firms with within-triad international business (i.e. scope metric) to highlight the superiority of the scale metric in measuring the regional nature of INVs. We also explore multiple industries.

As shown in Table 12.2, approximately 92 percent of the total exports of $21.1 billion were made in Asia-Pacific, the home region of Korean INVs. Only 5.6 percent of total exports were made to North America, followed by 1.3 percent of exports to Europe. An important finding is that the scope metric (e.g. number of firms that export to each region of the triad) downplays the home region-oriented nature of the INVs' foreign operations. Approximately 54 percent of Korean INVs export to Asia-Pacific countries, but these Asia-Pacific sales constitute 91.9 percent of all exports. For comparison, 25.5 percent realize foreign export sales from North America, however this constitutes just 5.6 percent of all exports. The same table shows a similar picture to the INVs' internationalization tendency in manufacturing industries.

Some scholars purport that born globals are more likely to be found in high technology manufacturing sectors, partly due to the readily transferable nature of their FSAs (e.g. Burgel and Murray 2000). Table 12.2 reports a sub-sample of high technology manufacturing INVs' export sales over the triad. The data indicates that high technology manufacturing ventures' foreign export sales are more dispersed across the triad than their counterparts in non-high technology manufacturing, service, and IT industries. Contrary to prior scholarship, however, high technology manufacturing firms are still far from being "born global" as 74.2 percent of total exports are realized in Asia-Pacific and just 15.2 percent and 5.9 percent in North America and Europe respectively. Table 12.2 also shows that the scope metric may produce misleading results.

Table 12.2 Korean INVs' foreign export sales by triad

Industry	*Asia-Pacific*	*North America*	*Europe*	*Others*[a]	*Total*
All					
# of firms	1,210	571	176	286	2,243[b]
%	53.9	25.5	7.8	12.8	100
Export sales[c]	19.4	1.2	0.3	0.3	21.1
%	91.9	5.6	1.3	1.2	100
Manufacturing					
# of firms	757	373	126	173	1,429
%	53.0	26.1	8.8	12.1	100
Export sales	17.6	1.1	0.3	0.2	19.2
%	91.6	5.8	1.4	1.2	100
High technology manufacturing					
# of firms	471	271	97	113	952
%	49.5	28.5	10.2	11.9	100
Export sales	3.1	0.6	0.2	0.2	4.2
%	74.2	15.2	5.9	4.6	100
Service					
# of firms	423	183	44	110	760
%	55.7	24.1	5.8	14.5	100
Export Sales	1.8	0.05	0.01	0.02	1.9
%	95.4	2.8	0.7	1.1	100
IT service					
# of firms	368	149	33	92	642
%	57.3	23.2	5.1	14.3	100
Export sales	1.3	0.05	0.01	0.003	1.4
%	95.4	3.5	0.9	0.2	100

a Others include the regions of South America, Africa, and Middle East.
b 2,239 firms have international reaches in foreign countries with four ventures in two countries, resulting in 2,243 observations (= 2,239 + 4). This indicates that Korean new ventures choose a single country strategy for their internationalization through export at least for the first six years. Since the geographic segments of exports are not available, the four ventures are excluded when the amounts of exports are calculated.
c Export sales are in US$ billion.

Less than half (49.5 percent) report exports to Asia-Pacific, compared to 28.5 percent to North America, 10.2 percent to Europe, and 11.9 percent to other regions.

Table 12.2 also reports the data on foreign export sales over the triad in service industries. Not surprisingly, INVs exhibit a stronger home region orientation in service industries than in manufacturing industries. This is partly due to INVs' higher liability of foreignness in downstream activities than in upstream activities of their value chain when operating in unfamiliar and risky foreign markets (Rugman 2005). As such, INVs, like MNEs, may prefer the liability of intra-regional foreignness to that of inter-regional foreignness to reduce potential transaction costs (Rugman and Verbeke 2007). We find quantitatively and qualitatively similar results from the exports made by INVs in IT service industries.

Regionalized outbound FDI

Firms also use outbound FDI for their internationalization. Among large firms, FDI is carried out to increase or to exploit the firm's knowledge base, what Kuemmerle (2002) terms home base augmenting (HBA) and home base exploiting (HBE) investments, respectively. Managers of small- and medium-sized enterprises (SMEs) frequently choose the FDI entry mode to gain access to location specific advantages (CSAs) such as cheap labor, growing local markets, and/or intangible knowledge and information (Urata and Kawai 2000; Lu and Beamish 2001).

Transaction costs shaping FDI decisions are related to operating in the more unfamiliar and risky foreign markets, as discussed earlier. This liability of foreigness is expected to be significantly lower within the home region compared to across regions. Consistent with the earlier discussion, firms also possess FSAs that can lead to FDI, however these may be again better used within their home region. Anecdotal evidence from published IE case studies and research suggests that ventures' FDI is regional. For example, Kuemmerle (2002) profiles a Canada-based bakery and café entrepreneur who pursues franchising opportunities in the United States. Urata and Kawai (2000) document the evolution of Japanese SME FDI since the 1980s – first to Asian newly industrializing economies, and later to ASEAN, China and other countries in the Asia-Pacific. Following the above reasoning, we expect a similar regional pattern for FDI: small firms are more likely to make foreign direct investment in countries within their home region of the triad than in countries outside their home region.

In Table 12.3, we describe a regional distribution of outbound FDI activities implemented by Korean SMEs across the triad during 1990–2004 using the Export-Import Bank of Korea (EIBK) database. The EIBK SME sample does not provide firm-level information and therefore includes both INVs and SMEs. Since INVs are a subset of SMEs in terms of both size and age, this data constitutes a good approximation of Korean INVs' direct investments in foreign markets. We analyze the geographic segmentation of outbound FDI data by industries to determine whether there is a sectoral variation in the home region orientation of outbound foreign investment activities.

Across all industries, almost 60 percent of the total outbound FDI (i.e. $7.4 billion of $12.6 billion) were made within Asia-Pacific. The same table also shows that these regional FDI trends are driven by firms operating in manufacturing industries. In Asia-Pacific, outbound FDI by

Table 12.3 Korean SMEs' outbound FDI by triad (1990–2004)

Industry	*Asia-Pacific*	*North America*	*Europe*	*Others*[a]	*Total*
All industries					
Outbound FDI[b]	7.4	2.2	0.7	2.2	12.6
%	59.3	17.6	5.6	17.6	100
Manufacturing industry					
Outbound FDI	5.8	0.8	0.3	0.4	7.2
%	80.5	10.4	4.0	5.1	100
Retailing industry					
Outbound FDI	0.49	0.48	0.3	0.1	1.4
%	35.4	35.1	21.2	8.3	100
Publishing, broadcasting and information service industries					
Outbound FDI	0.21	0.16	0.003	0.08	0.45
%	46.6	35.4	0.8	17.3	100
Professional, science and technology service industries					
Outbound FDI	0.03	0.02	0.0007	0.004[c]	0.053
%	53.0	37.7	1.4	8.0	100

a Others include the regions of South America, Africa, and Middle East.
b Outbound FDI are in US$ billion.
c One outlier was removed from this calculation, i.e., an one-time investment of $1.4 billion in South America.

manufacturing SMEs constitutes a large share – over 80 percent for 1990–2004 ($5.8 billion of $7.2 billion). Although the regional trends for outbound FDI have been relatively weak in service industries compared to manufacturing industries, we see that Asia-Pacific is still the most popular region for the outbound FDI undertaken by Korean service SMEs. For example, 35.4 percent, 46.6 percent, and 53.0 percent of Korean SMEs' foreign investments were made in their home region of the triad in retailing industry, publishing, broadcasting and information service industries, and professional, science and technology service industries, respectively. Due to the liability of newness that most new ventures usually face from their inception, Korean INVs are expected to show a similar regional pattern of foreign investment activities made in upstream assets over the same time period.

Conclusions: future research directions

This chapter attempts to address confusions in the INV literature regarding the extent of regionalization versus globalization and the measurement of new venture internationalization. Specifically, we contribute to the current IE literature by integrating an IB perspective in a world of broad triad regions in the following ways. First, we extended earlier work on the regional nature of MNEs (Rugman and Verbeke 2004; Rugman 2005) to the domain of INVs. We showed that INVs are not "born global" but rather are "born regional," expanding internationally within their home region of the triad. The present chapter provided multiple sets of evidence that Korean INVs expand (in terms of both *downstream* foreign export sales and *upstream* outbound FDI) within the Asia-Pacific region. Second, we significantly extended the IE literature which examines INVs' international activities based on scope metrics. Our study indicated that the scale metrics (based on the distribution of foreign export sales across the triad) offer a better explanation of new venture internationalization than do the scope metrics (based on the count of countries) which seriously exaggerate the extent of so-called born global firms. Third, we explored INV activities across different industries and regions of the triad using outbound FDI in addition to foreign export sales from both country and regional perspectives.

We acknowledge three limitations of the present chapter. First, the SMBA data is based on the response of a single respondent (CEO) and at one point in time (2002). Second, while the EIBK database provides fifteen years of data, we aggregate this and do not examine longitudinal trends in the internationalization of firms. Third, the main findings in this chapter can be applied to other small-sized open economies which have overcome the limitation of insufficient domestic market size through aggressive exporting activities. Nevertheless, the chapter only utilizes data from a single country (Korea) and may not be generalizable to other countries and regions.

This chapter suggests a number of promising directions for future research. First, extant research on the internationalization of firm activities, including the present study, focuses primarily on exports; however internationalization could also be facilitated by other output modes such as FDI and indirect exports through export intermediary agents and distributors (Peng and York 2001; Terjesen et al. 2008). Future research could explore the patterns of regionalization among these direct and indirect entry modes. For example, firms operating outside of their home region may be more likely to use export intermediaries or distributors, while firms operating inside their home region may be more likely to export directly. Furthermore, firms may select export intermediaries and distributors located in a "key" or lead country in the region, such as the United States to access North America, or one of Europe's larger countries to access the Western and Eastern European market.

A second research direction is the examination of the regionalization of firm inputs such as indirect imports (i.e. import intermediary agents and distributors), licensing, and strategic alliances (Welch and Luostarinen 1988; Fletcher 2001). It is possible that small and medium-sized firms seeking to internationalize outside of their home regions may be more likely to use import intermediaries and distributors, licensors, or alliance partners, and may seek large, established firms with high levels of legitimacy and embeddedness.

Third, there is a need to integrate the scale-based degree of internationalization measurement (FS/TS) with the scope measurement (number of countries/regions) so that one can look into the percentage of foreign sales within a certain country and/or region of the triad. A new measure integrating both aspects of scale and scope metrics, such as the ratio of regional to total sales (RS/TS) suggested by Rugman and Verbeke (2007), may provide better insights and implications than just a single metric.

Fourth, researchers could explore the process of venture regionalization from one to many countries within the home region. There may be certain patterns of internationalization, beginning with one critical country and subsequently expanding via a particular blueprint of countries, perhaps related by language, geography or culture. This line of enquiry could utilize Johanson and Vahlne's (1977, 1990) stage theory.

Fifth, future research could explore the impact of regionalization on multiple levels of outcomes such as competitors' international strategies and local economic development. A firm's regional strategies may spur competitors to adopt similar strategies. Furthermore, regional strategies may lead to greater levels of local economic development due to the deep embeddedness of these firms in the economy.

Finally, additional empirical work could apply the principles outlined in this paper to INVs from other countries and regions. To an extent, the focus on the internationalization process of US INVs (e.g. as noted in Coviello and Jones 2004) may be misleading. As the US is the world's largest internal market and the region's other markets (Canada and Mexico) are significantly smaller, US firms may be less likely to be born regional than their counterparts in North America as well as in Europe, Asia-Pacific, and other regions. Thus studies of born regional firms should include firms from smaller economies.

Notes

1 McDougall and Oviatt (1997: 293) defined IE as "new and innovative activities that have the goal of value creation and growth in business organizations across national borders," and they changed it to "a combination of innovative, proactive, and risk-seeking behavior that crosses national borders and is intended to create value in organizations" (McDougall and Oviatt, 2000: 903). Oviatt and McDougall (2005: 540) further refined its definition as "the discovery, enactment, evaluation, and exploitation of opportunities – across national borders – to create future goods and services."

2 The following journals were selected on the criteria of high impact (Podsakoff et al. 2005) and a history of international entrepreneurship research (Coviello and Jones 2004; Keupp and Gassmann 2009): *Academy of Management Journal, Entrepreneurship Theory and Practice, International Business Review, Journal of Business Venturing, Journal of International Business Studies, Journal of International Marketing, Small Business Economics, Strategic Entrepreneurship Journal,* and *Strategic Management Journal.*

3 The Small and Medium Business Administration (SMBA) is a branch office of the Korean government in charge of supporting Korean small and medium-sized enterprises (SMEs) including new ventures. The SMBA conducted a nation-wide survey on those SMEs registered in 2002. This survey contained multiple firm-level items including the international activities of SMEs in foreign countries.

References

Acs, Z.J., Audretsch, D.B. and Feldman, M.P. (1994) R&D spillovers and recipient firm size. *Review of Economics and Statistics*, 100 (1), 336–367.

Acs, Z.J., Morck, R., Shaver, J.M. and Yeung, B. (1997) The internationalization of small and medium-sized enterprises: a policy perspective. *Small Business Economics*, 9 (1), 7–20.

Almodóvar, P. and Rugman, A.M. (2013) The M curve and the performance of Spanish international new ventures. *British Journal of Management*, DOI: 10.1111/1467-8551.12022.

Autio, E. (2005) Creative tension: the significance of Ben Oviatt's and Patricia McDougall's article 'Toward a theory of international new ventures.' *Journal of International Business Studies*, 36 (1), 9–19.

Autio, E., Sapienza, H.J. and Almeida, J.G. (2000) Effects of age at entry, knowledge intensity, and imitability on international growth. *Academy of Management Journal*, 43 (5), 909–924.

Bouquet, C., Morrison, A. and Birkinshaw, J. (2009) International attention and multinational enterprise performance. *Journal of International Business Studies*, 40 (1), 108–131.

Bruneel, J., Yli-Renko, H. and Clarysse, B. (2010) Learning from experience and learning from others: how congenital and interorganizational learning substitute for experiential learning in young firm internationalization. *Strategic Entrepreneurship Journal*, 4 (2), 164–182.

Burgel, O. and Murray, G.C. (2000) The international market entry choices of start-up companies in high-technology industries. *Journal of International Marketing*, 8 (2), 33–62.

Carr, J.C., Haggard, K.S., Hmieleski, K.M. and Zahra, S.A. (2010) A study of the moderating effects of firm age at internationalization on firm survival and short-term growth. *Strategic Entrepreneurship Journal*, 4 (2), 183–192.

Coeurderoy, R. and Murray, G. (2008) Regulatory environments and the location decision: evidence from the early foreign market entries of new-technology-based firms. *Journal of International Business Studies*, 39 (4), 670–687.

Coviello, N. (2006) The network dynamics of international new ventures. *Journal of International Business Studies*, 37 (5), 713–731.

Coviello, N.E. and Jones, M.V. (2004) Methodological issues in international entrepreneurship research. *Journal of Business Venturing*, 19 (4), 485–508.

Coviello, N.E. and Munro, H. (1997) Network relationships and the internationalization process of small software firms. *International Business Review*, 6 (4), 361–386.

Dunning, J.H. (1998) Location and the multinational enterprise: a neglected factor? *Journal of International Business Studies*, 29 (1), 45–66.

Fan, T. and Phan, P. (2007) International new ventures: revisiting the influences behind the 'born-global' firm. *Journal of International Business Studies*, 38 (7), 1113–1131.

Fernhaber, S.A., Gilbert, B.A. and McDougall, P.P. (2008) International entrepreneurship and geographic location: an empirical examination of new venture internationalization. *Journal of International Business Studies*, 39 (2), 267–290.

Fernhaber, S.A. and Li, D. (2010) The impact of interorganizational imitation on new venture international entry and performance. *Entrepreneurship Theory and Practice*, 34 (1), 1–30.

Fernhaber, S.A., McDougall-Covin, P.P. and Shepherd, D.A. (2009) International entrepreneurship: leveraging internal and external knowledge sources. *Strategic Entrepreneurship Journal*, 3 (4), 297–320.

Filatotchev, I., Liu, X., Buck, T. and Wright, M. (2009) The export orientation and export performance of high-technology SMEs in emerging markets: the effects of knowledge transfer by returnee entrepreneurs. *Journal of International Business Studies*, 40 (6), 1005–1021.

Fischer, E. and Reuber, A.R. (2003) Targeting export support to SMEs: owners' international experience as a segmentation basis. *Small Business Economics*, 20 (1), 69–82.

Fletcher, R. (2001) A holistic approach to internationalisation. *International Business Review*, 10 (1), 25–49.

Gabrielsson, M., Kirpalani, V.H.M., Dimitratos, P., Solberg, C.A. and Zucchella, A. (2008) Born globals: propositions to help advance the theory. *International Business Review*, 17 (4), 385–401.

Ghemawat, P. (2003) Semiglobalization and international business strategy. *Journal of International Business Studies*, 34 (2), 138–152.

Goerzen, A. and Beamish, P.W. (2003) Geographic scope and multinational enterprise performance. *Strategic Management Journal*, 24 (13), 1289–1306.

Hymer, S. (1976) *The international operations of national firms: a study of foreign direct investment*. Cambridge, MA: MIT Press. (Publication of his 1960 dissertation).

Johanson, J. and Vahlne, J.-E. (1977) The internationalization process of the firm: a model of knowledge development and increasing foreign market commitments. *Journal of International Business Studies*, 8 (1), 23–32.

Johanson, J. and Vahlne, J.-E. (1990) The mechanism of internationalization. *International Marketing Review*, 7 (4), 11–24.

Jones, M.V., Coviello, N.E. and Tang, Y.K. (2011) International entrepreneurship research (1989–2009): a domain ontology and thematic analysis. *Journal of Business Venturing*, 26, 632–659.
Kelley, D., Bosma, N. and Amorós, J. (2011) *Global entrepreneurship monitor report, executive report*. Babson Park, MA.
Keupp, M.M. and Gassmann, O. (2009) The past and future of international entrepreneurship: a review and suggestions for developing the field. *Journal of Management*, 35 (3), 600–633.
Khavul, S., Pérez-Nordtvedt, L. and Wood, E. (2010) Organizational entrainment and international new ventures from emerging markets. *Journal of Business Venturing*, 25 (1), 104–119.
Knight, G. (2000) Entrepreneurship and marketing strategy: the SME under globalization. *Journal of International Marketing*, 8 (2), 12–32.
Knight, G.A. and Kim, D. (2009) International business competence and the contemporary firm. *Journal of International Business Studies*, 40 (2), 255–273.
Kuemmerle, W. (2002) Home base and knowledge management in international ventures. *Journal of Business Venturing*, 17 (2), 99–122.
Lee, I.H. (2010) The M curve: the performance of born-regional firms from Korea. *Multinational Business Review*, 18 (4), 1–22.
Lee, I.H. (2013) The M curve and the multinationality–performance relationship of Korean INVs. *Multinational Business Review*, 21 (3), 214–231.
Leiblein, M.J. and Reuer, J.J. (2004) Building a foreign sales base: the roles of capabilities and alliances for entrepreneurial firms. *Journal of Business Venturing*, 19 (2), 285–307.
Lopez, L.E., Kundu, S.K. and Ciravegna, L. (2009) Born global or born regional? Evidence from an exploratory study in the Costa Rican software industry. *Journal of International Business Studies*, 40 (7), 1228–1238.
Lu, J.W. and Beamish, P.W. (2001) The internationalization and performance of SMEs. *Strategic Management Journal*, 22 (6/7), 565–586.
Mathews, J.A. and Zander, I. (2007) The international entrepreneurial dynamics of accelerated internationalisation. *Journal of International Business Studies*, 38, 387–403.
McDougall, P.P. and Oviatt, B.M. (1997) International entrepreneurship literature in the 1990s and directions for future research. In D.L. Sexton and R.W. Smilor (Eds) *Entrepreneurship 2000*, pp. 291–320. Chicago: Upstart Publishing.
McDougall, P.P. and Oviatt, B.M. (2000) International entrepreneurship: the intersection of two research paths. *Academy of Management Journal*, 43 (5), 902–906.
Moen, Ø. and Servais, P. (2002) Born global or gradual global? Examining the export behavior of small and medium-sized enterprises. *Journal of International Marketing*, 10 (3), 49–72.
Mudambi, R. and Zahra, S. (2007) The survival of international new ventures. *Journal of International Business Studies*, 38 (2), 333–352.
Ohmae, K. (1985) *Triad power: the coming shape of global competition*. The Free Press: New York.
Oviatt, B.M. and McDougall, P.P. (1994) Toward a theory of international new ventures. *Journal of International Business Studies*, 25 (1), 45–64.
Oviatt, B.M. and McDougall, P.P. (2005) Defining international entrepreneurship and modeling the speed of internationalization. *Entrepreneurship Theory and Practice*, 29 (5), 537–557.
Peng, M.W. and York, A.S. (2001) Behind intermediary performance in export trade: transactions, agents and resources. *Journal of International Business Studies*, 32 (2), 327–346.
Podsakoff, P.M., MacKenzie, S.M., Bachrach, D.G. amd Podsakoff, N.P. (2005) The influence of management journals in the 1980s and 1990s. *Strategic Management Journal*, 26, 473–488.
Prashantham, S. and Dhanaraj, C. (2010) The dynamic influence of social capital on the international growth of new ventures. *Journal of Management Studies*, 47, 967–994.
Rennie, M.W. (1993). Global competitiveness: born global. *The McKinsey Quarterly*, 4, 45–52.
Reuber, A.R. and Fischer, E. (1997) The influence of the management team's international experience on the internationalization behaviors of SMEs. *Journal of International Business Studies*, 28 (4), 807–825.
Reuber, A.R. and Fischer, E. (2002) Foreign sales and small firm growth: the moderating role of the management team. *Entrepreneurship Theory and Practice*, 27 (1), 29–45.
Rialp, A., Rialp, J. and Knight, G.A. (2005) The phenomenon of early internationalizing firms: what do we know after a decade (1993–2003) of scientific inquiry? *International Business Review*, 14 (2), 147–166.
Rugman, A.M. (1981) *Inside the multinational*. New York: Columbia University Press (reissued by Palgrave Macmillan in 2006).
Rugman, A.M. (2005) *The regional multinationals*. Cambridge: Cambridge University Press.

Rugman, A.M. and Verbeke, A. (2004) A perspective on regional and global strategies of multinational enterprises. *Journal of International Business Studies*, 35 (1), 3–18.

Rugman, A.M. and Verbeke, A. (2007) Liabilities of regional foreignness and the use of firm-level versus country-level data: a response to Dunning et al. *Journal of International Business Studies*, 38 (1), 200–205.

Rugman, A.M. and Verbeke, A. (2008) The theory and practice of regional strategy: a response to Osegowitsch and Sammartino. *Journal of International Business Studies*, 39, 326–332.

Sapienza, H.J., De Clercq, D. and Sandberg, W.R. (2005) Antecedents of international and domestic learning effort. *Journal of Business Venturing*, 20 (4), 437–457.

Shrader, R.C., Oviatt, B.M. and McDougall, P.P. (2000) How new ventures exploit trade-offs among international risk factors: lessons for the accelerated internationalization of the 21st century. *Academy of Management Journal*, 43 (6), 1227–1247.

Tatoglu, E. and Glaister, K.W. (1998a) An analysis of motives for western FDI in Turkey. *International Business Review*, 7 (2), 203–230.

Tatoglu, E. and Glaister, K.W. (1998b) Determinants of foreign direct investment in Turkey. *Thunderbird International Business Review*, 40 (3), 279–314.

Terjesen, S., Hessels, J. and Li, D. (2013) Comparative international entrepreneurship research: a review and research agenda. *Journal of Management*. Published online before print May 1, 2013, doi: 10.1177/0149206313486259.

Terjesen, S., O'Gorman, C. and Acs, Z.J. (2008) Intermediated mode of internationalization: new software ventures in Ireland and India. *Entrepreneurship & Regional Development*, 20 (1), 89–109.

Urata, S. and Kawai, H. (2000) The determinants of the location of foreign direct investment by Japanese small and medium-sized enterprises. *Small Business Economics*, 15 (2), 79–103.

Welch, L.S. and Loustarinen, R. (1988) Internationalization: evolution of a concept. *Journal of General Management*, 14 (2), 34–55.

Zacharakis, A. (1997) Entrepreneurial entry into foreign markets: a transaction cost perspective. *Entrepreneurship Theory & Practice*, 21 (3), 23–39.

Zahra, S.A. (2005) A theory of international new ventures: a decade of research. *Journal of International Business Studies*, 36 (1), 20–28.

Zahra, S.A., Ireland, R.D. and Hitt, M.A. (2000) International expansion by new venture firms: international diversity, mode of market entry, technological learning, and performance. *Academy of Management Journal*, 43 (5), 925–950.

Zhou, L., Barnes, B.R. and Lu, Y. (2010) Entrepreneurial proclivity, capability upgrading and performance advantage of newness among international new ventures. *Journal of International Business Studies*, 41 (5), 882–905.

Zhou, L., Wu, W. and Luo, X. (2007) Internationalization and the performance of born-global SMEs: the mediating role of social networks. *Journal of International Business Studies*, 38 (4), 673–676.

Part IV

Implications of entrepreneurial internationalization and future research

13

International entrepreneurship

Performance and survival implications

Per Servais and Erik S. Rasmussen

Background

Early and rapid internationalization has been the focus of increasing research interest over the last decade. However, despite the recent increase in 'born-global' studies there has been little research on how the scale and scope of being a born-global firm affects performance, survival and growth.

When measuring the performance of SMEs and especially international SMEs two measures are in focus: survival of the firm and growth (see, for example, Fernhaber, 2013, Jones et al., 2011, Prashantham and Young, 2011, Sapienza et al., 2006, Sleuwaegen and Onkelinx, 2014). Both can be measured in a number of ways – as we will discuss later on – but typically survival is seen in accordance with the initial public offering (IPO, the stock market launch) of the firm which can be a problem in countries where small firms are not going public. The second measure, growth, can be seen as, for example, growth in the number of employees or as sales growth, but also as growth in international sales. Both empirical results and theoretical models to a large extent depend on which definition is chosen and a clarification is highly needed. A third performance variable, profitability, is discussed in the chapter too.

The relation between internationalization and performance (understood as survival and growth and to some extent profitability) has been the subject for a large number of discussions and papers in international business and international entrepreneurship for several decades but empirically the subject has not been researched thoroughly with a few exceptions; for an overview see Jones et al., 2011, Prashantham and Young, 2011, Sapienza et al., 2006, Zahra, 2005. Most researchers agree that the relations are complex and cannot be seen as a simple linear relation as 'the more international the firm is at the founding the more it will grow'. Instead relations have been seen in the context of the MNE as shaped in a number of ways, for a discussion see Fernhaber, 2013. The relations have been seen as U-shaped, inverted U-shaped or S-shaped. It is not our intention to dig further into these models and results as they are related primarily to the large firm that several years after the founding begins its international operations. Instead the focus is on the international entrepreneurial firm – the type of firm that goes international right from the beginning. Whether internationalization has any effect on the performance of the small newly founded firm has been discussed, too. Internationalization has been seen as having no effect as in Fernhaber and Li (2010) and McDougall and Oviatt (1996), a negative as in Lu and Beamish (2001) or a positive relation as in Bloodgood et al. (1996) or Khavul et al. (2010).

Being an international firm in the current dynamic, complex and competitive market environment is often perceived as a critical ingredient of the firm strategy for achieving growth and above-the-average financial performance. Consequently, there is more and more empirical evidence on small firms which start to export almost immediately after being established (Knight and Cavusgil, 1996, Oviatt and McDougall, 1994). Although internationalization and its effect on firm performance has been a subject of intensive research throughout the last three decades (Fernhaber et al., 2009, Fernhaber et al., 2007, Sullivan, 1994) there is a scarcity on empirical research on when the rapid, accelerated internationalization is actually profitable. Lu and Beamish (2001) note that the scarcity of the studies concentrating especially on the effects of internationalization on small and medium-sized firms' performance is primarily due to the fact that detailed information is hard to obtain. Another problem is the actual measurement of performance, i.e. how the performance of the firm should be measured as a function of rapid internationalization. Focusing on this gap, these questions form the main target of the chapter.

One of the most used definitions of international entrepreneurship is the following: 'international entrepreneurship is a combination of innovative, proactive, and risk seeking behaviour that crosses national borders and is intended to create value in organizations' (McDougall and Oviatt, 2000). In addition Zahra and George (2002) define international entrepreneurship as a process in which firms would discover and exploit opportunities in the international marketplace. In these definitions authors do not identify the arena of research in terms of size or age, but they seek to capture the entrepreneurial behaviour of any firm abroad.

The ability to internationalize successfully in foreign markets is a function of the internal capabilities of the firm (Autio et al., 2000, McDougall et al., 1994, Zahra et al., 2000). The importance of internal capabilities is rooted in evolutionary economics. This means that the ability to sustain innovation and create new knowledge leads to the development of capabilities, consisting of competences and routines. The knowledge accumulation, the organizational capabilities, financial resources, the equipment and other physical resources are the main arsenal that the older firms have built up in order to perform in foreign markets, but young firms lack them. They rely upon intangible knowledge-based capabilities in approaching foreign markets entry. Capabilities-based resources are particularly important to SMEs, because they are poor in tangible resources and they deal with different environments in different countries around the world (Knight and Cavusgil, 2004). Wolff and Pett (2000) argue that export strategy is the primary foreign-market entry mode used by small businesses in their internationalization efforts (Leonidou and Katsikeas, 1996) with a greater degree of flexibility, offering an effective means for firms to achieve an international position without overextending their capabilities or resources (Young et al., 1989). Exporting thus represents also the predominant international activity of small firms (Fernhaber and McDougall-Covin, 2009, Kundu and Katz, 2003, Tesar and Moini, 1998, Westhead et al., 2001). Some studies have demonstrated that a firm's size and export intensity – as measured by the ratio of exports to sales – are not correlated (Bonaccorsi, 1992, Calof, 1994, Wolff and Pett, 2000, Zucchella et al., 2007) underlining that the smallest firms are not necessarily prevented from being strong exporters. The importance of entrepreneurs has been dealt with in many studies, and the findings reveal a positive relationship between entrepreneurs' international attitude, orientation, experience and network and positive international development (Andersson and Wictor, 2003, Fernhaber and Li, 2013, Kuemmerle, 2002, Preece et al., 1999, Westhead et al., 2001).

It is generally affirmed that entrepreneurship can have a positive influence on the performance of the firm (Covin and Slevin, 1991). If entrepreneurship is the key factor to innovate, to exploit new economic opportunities and to introduce new ideas in the market, this means that entrepreneurship is a driver to create value operating both on the domestic and on the foreign markets. This evidence is supported by a number of studies linking entrepreneurship with export performance (Balabanis and Katsikea, 2003, Dimitratos et al., 2004, Ibeh, 2003, Knight, 2001, Oviatt and McDougall, 1995, Zahra et al., 1997); these studies point out that a global vision at the firm's inception is probably the most important characteristic associated with born global entrepreneurs. They argue that the creation of international ventures is due to the founder's ability to see market opportunities in a cross-national context. Prior international activities can equip entrepreneurs with language skills and skills in accessing national networks of contacts to access resources. McDougall et al. (1994) and Madsen and Servais (1997) both concluded that the background and experience of the entrepreneurs had a major influence on the emergence of born globals. Market knowledge, personal networking of the entrepreneur, personal contact and experience, other prior jobs, relations and education are examples of international skills gained before the establishment of the firm.

As this chapter intends to show there are a large number of articles that deal with the subject of performance of the international firm but relatively few that specifically deal with international entrepreneurship. From a theoretical point of view one of the best articles on this subject is Sapienza et al. (2006), which from a capabilities perspective develops a model of the effects of early internationalization on the survival and growth of firms. The moderating variables in the model are stated as organizational age, managerial experience and resources.

The model has been empirically tested in a number of articles of which one of the most important is Fernhaber (2013). This research clearly shows two different types of relations between internationalization and survival/growth. The survival of the firms is highest at moderate levels of internationalization (an inverted U-shape) while sales growth is highest at either low or high levels of internationalization (U-shape).

Another article that attempts to test the model from Sapienza et al. (2006) is Schueffel et al. (2011), which with data from UK firms shows that there is no linear relation between internationalization and the firm's survival or growth. Instead the authors propose a U-shaped or S-shaped relation instead. Furthermore they find a negative relation between managerial experience and survival in contrast with the classical assumptions. Another article using the Sapienza framework is Carr et al. (2010), which with US data also demonstrates that the model cannot be confirmed. The results are unclear but one point is important: young firms have to find a balance between survival and growth, especially firms that are internationalizing rapidly.

Problems for the firms in balancing between survival and growth can be seen too in Sleuwaegen and Onkelinx (2014). The highly international firms – the global start-ups – have the highest commitment and growth on the international markets but the lowest survival rate, too. But it is important to stress – as the authors do – that the failure rate of the most internationalized firms is not higher than for other young firms.

IE and survival

The basic question can be stated as whether the internationalization of a new venture will increase or decrease its chance of survival (Fernhaber, 2013). Survival is a real threat for new firms and the argument is that a new firm lacks the legitimacy of an older firm and has limited resources (Stinchcombe, 1965 and Westhead et al., 2001). Especially for the international new firm, entering a number of markets will create a shock for the firm (Sapienza et al., 2006) require new routines and in the end make substantial investments necessary (Zaheer, 1995 and Zott, 2003). But as exporting is typically chosen as the road to internationalization for the young firm and exporting is not that resource demanding, the survivability of the firm will not

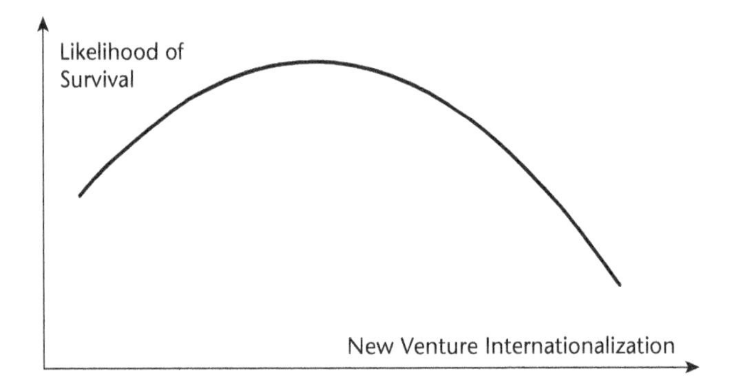

Figure 13.1 Likelihood of survival following internationalization

be influenced at the first and low levels of internationalization (Fernhaber, 2013 and Fernhaber and Li, 2013).

In Fernhaber (2013) survivability is argued to peak at moderate levels of internationalization where the associated resources and risk are balanced between local and foreign markets but will be lower later in the process of internationalization of the firm with more resources committed and a higher risk. The hypothesis in Fernhaber (2013) is thus that the internationalization of the firm will have a positive influence on the survival of the new firm up to an optimal point where more internationalization will lead to a decline in the survival.

Very few studies exist except Fernhaber (2013) that have focussed on how small, international and entrepreneurial firms survive. Mudambi and Zahra (2007: 333) conclude that we do not know much about the survival rates of INVs. Cesinger et al. (2012) builds upon secondary data from 1992–96 and a mail survey in Britain supplemented with interviews in 1997. The data show that INVs have a lower survival probability than other types of firms. But the differences in survival probabilities disappear when the firms' competitive strategies are considered. When compared with FDI undertaken by established firms, INVs have about the same survival probability. The conclusions from Mudambi and Zahra (2007) can be seen as a complement to McDougall and Oviatt (1996) who state that there is no difference between INVs and domestic firms regarding performance.

Two articles from respectively 2011 and 2012 come to two opposing conclusions. Lee et al. (2012) finds a positive relationship from a survey of Korean SMEs and that internationalization is associated with better survival prospects. Furthermore it is shown that R&D alliances are directly linked with survival, which supports the liabilities of newness and smallness views that external relationships can help counter survival threats. In contrast to these findings Giovannetti et al. (2011) show from data from Italy that internationalized firms have a higher failure risk, but large internationalized firms are more likely to survive. Internationalizing (either by exporting or FDI) has a negative effect on the survival of the firms. More specifically the data shows that to export increases the risk of failure by 32 per cent and to invest abroad by 38 per cent. But firms that export high-tech goods are less vulnerable and their probability of survival increases by roughly 33 per cent. The best survival strategy for Italian exporters is thus to be in a high-tech industry and the second best as it is shown in Giovannetti et al. (2011) is to become larger.

A lot of research in the field of INVs has focussed on high-tech firms and it is thus interesting to see that in the results from Italy in Giovannetti et al. (2011) the differences between international and domestic firms regarding their survival almost disappear when the focus is solely on high-tech industries.

An older article which does not directly focus on INVs but instead on exporting versus non-exporting firms is Westhead et al. (2001). Data for the article comes from a sample of SMEs in Great Britain in 1990/91 and again in 1997. One of the aims of the article was to explain variations in the propensity to export reported by surviving independent firms in 1997. The hypothesis was that firms that were exporters in 1990/91 were more likely to have survived seven years later, but contrary to the expectation of the authors, the propensity to export in 1990/91 did not significantly encourage subsequent sales and employment growth or survival over the following seven years. What the researchers found, though from a limited number of firms, was that firms with older founders, with more resources, denser information and contact networks, and considerable management know-how were significantly more likely to be exporters, and that firms with founders that had considerable industry-specific knowledge were more likely to be exporters. This research is interesting because it focuses on small firms – exporters or non-exporters – and because survival is measured as whether the firm is still active and in existence and not whether it is still gone public.

In Sapienza et al. (2006) a theoretical discussion of the relation between early internationalization and the survival and growth of firms is outlined. This is done from a dynamic capabilities perspective and the arguments are that the commitment to internationalization for a new venture will be resource intensive and demanding for the management and thus reduce the survival opportunities of the firm in the short run (but at the same time the use of resources will improve venture growth).

As we are interested in young firms the age at the initiation is not in focus. Instead we will take a look at the two other intermediary variables: managerial experience and resources. Both are expected to decrease firm survival and increase firm growth. Initiation of international entry is also expected to decrease firm survival and increase the growth of the firm. As all variables are clearly defined the article ought to lead to a number of empirical tests. But this has been done in two cases only: Schueffel et al., 2011 and Fernhaber, 2013. We will take a closer look at the results from both papers.

Schueffel et al. (2011) is a direct attempt at testing the conceptual model from Sapienza et al. (2006). The data comes from a database of all UK registered companies, the focus was on start-ups and the time horizon was set to six years. Contrary to the model suggested by Sapienza et al. (2006) none of the propositions were confirmed. There was no linear relation between internationalization and a small firm's survival or growth seen over a six-year time span but the authors suggest that the relations could be U-shaped or S-shaped instead. Furthermore for the control variables they find no relation between size of the firm and survival but a negative relation between managerial experience and survival contrasting the classical assumption that experience is good.

The results from Fernhaber (2013) have been outlined. With data from US-based firms that have been through an IPO she clearly demonstrates that internationalization of the firm has a positive influence on firm survival up to a certain point (approximately 50 per cent foreign sales) and then a negative influence. The dataset is quite small though and it can be difficult to generalize the results to other countries or to firms that have not been through an IPO.

Summing up the discussions above the question regarding survival of INVs can be stated as whether internationalization from the beginning of a new firm will increase or decrease its survival – or if there is any relation at all.

IE and growth

Studying growth as a performance variable has of course been of high importance for all kinds of business research whether it has focussed on business generally, entrepreneurship,

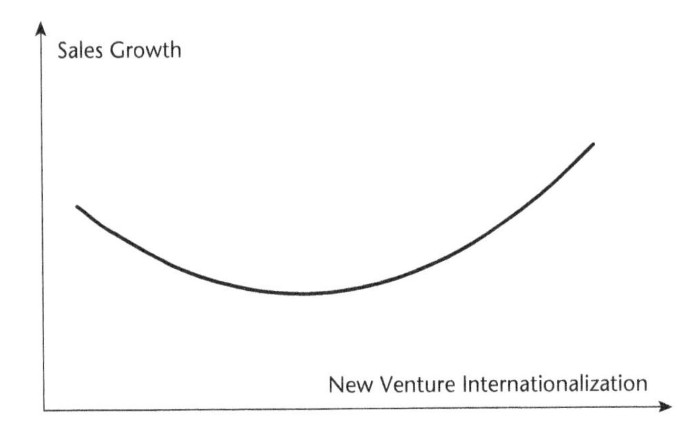

Figure 13.2 Sales growth following internationalization (adapted from Fernhaber 2013)

internationalization or SMEs (Brush and Vanderwerf, 1992, McDougall and Oviatt, 1996, Zahra et al., 2000). Especially for small firms internationalizing from the founding, growth can be a problematic issue where the management needs to develop new routines and adapt to an uncertain environment (Hagen et al., 2012 and Lu and Beamish, 2006). This learning process is in several cases seen as challenging, leading to a negative development in sales growth (Mort et al., 2012, Prange and Verdier, 2011, Sapienza et al., 2006, Weerawardena et al., 2007). But at the same time it is often suggested that internationalization at high levels will lead to an increase in the sales growth of the firm (Sapienza et al., 2006). This leads Fernhaber (2013) to hypothesize that sales growth during the internationalization process will be decreasing to a certain point from which higher levels of internationalization will lead to sales growth increase.

As presented above, data for Fernhaber (2013) comes from a small number of US-based firms that have been through an IPO, but from these data she clearly demonstrates the hypothesized model with an inflection point around 50 per cent. This demonstrates that firms that are 'stuck in the middle' between the home market and the international markets have the lowest growth in sales. The strategy recommended in the article is thus to develop the home market first, which is only realistic with a large home market like the US, or to focus on the international markets right from the beginning. As previously discussed both strategies can be problematic when the focus is on survival and not sales growth.

There have been a large number of articles focussing on internationalization and growth over more than 20 years. The articles have quite different definitions of both internationalization and especially growth and we will take a closer look at some of these articles, their definitions and the results.

One of the articles that clearly presents a theoretical framework is Sapienza et al. (2006). The expectations of the authors were that the early internationalization would lead to higher growth and that managerial experience and access to resources would have a positive influence.

As with survival a test of these assumptions was done in Schueffel et al. (2011). Both managerial experience and resources had, contrary to expectations, a negative influence on firm growth and none of the propositions outlined in Sapienza et al. (2006) could be confirmed. Internationalization could thus not be shown to have any influence on the probability of growth – or as previously discussed – on the probability of survival. The authors conclude that INVs do not become international for performance reasons contrary to, for example, the view of McDougall and Oviatt, 1996, Oviatt and McDougall, 1994, Oviatt and McDougall, 1995.

In Keen and Etemad (2012) the focus was on high growth and rapid internationalization starting with SMEs from Canada that have shown exceptionally high growth rates. The conclusion is that rapid growing enterprises and rapid internationalizing enterprises are two distinctive types of firms and that rapid growth and rapid internationalization are not interlinked. Furthermore they conclude that firms with rapid growth are found across all industries, sizes and regions in Canada.

Two articles from 2002 and 2010 with respectively a quantitative and a qualitative perspective have international growth as their focus and dependent variable. Prashantham and Dhanaraj (2010) explores how new ventures seek international growth through the use of social capital using a number of longitudinal case studies in the software industry. The conclusion is that network learning plays a critical role in new ventures' ability to realize the potential contribution of social capital to international growth. The other paper by Yli-Renko et al. (2002) is a quantitative study of the international growth of technology-based new firms. The theoretical model of the paper aims at explaining the role of intra- and inter-organizational relationships in achieving international growth. The conclusion shows that by developing the social capital within the firm and in external relationships, the firm can achieve international growth. It is interesting that these two papers, even if one is quantitative and the other qualitative, and takes place in different research settings, come to almost the same conclusion regarding the role of networks and learning (the ability to achieve new knowledge) in facilitating international growth – while ensuring survival.

IE and profitability

While survival and growth are the two performance outcomes of international ventures mostly considered in the research, profitability is the most common measurement of performance when looking at the international business literature in general.

Two of the IE and IB papers that deal with profitability as a performance outcome are Fernhaber and Li (2010) and Lu and Beamish (2001). The article by Lu and Beamish (2001) discusses and explores the effects of internationalization seen as an entrepreneurial strategy employed by small and medium-sized enterprises on firm performance. Using a sample of Japanese SMEs the authors find that the positive impact of internationalization on performance extends primarily from the extent of a firm's FDI activity. When firms first begin FDI activity, profitability declines, but greater levels of FDI are associated with higher performance. Exporting moderates the relationship FDI has with performance, as pursuing a strategy of high exporting concurrent with high FDI is less profitable than one that involves lower levels of exports when FDI levels are high. The authors find that making alliances with partners with local knowledge can be an effective strategy to overcome the deficiencies small firms face in resources and capabilities when they expand into international markets.

One of the conclusions in the article is that in the initial stages of internationalization, performance declines as the firm has problems with the liability of foreignness. But, performance improves as new knowledge and the firm's capabilities are developed. Furthermore competitiveness is enhanced and market opportunities are captured by the firm's activities in international markets. In the end, performance declines due to the complexity coming from managing a number of subsidiaries in dissimilar markets.

The other article by Fernhaber and Li (2010) examines the impact of interorganizational imitation on new venture international entry and subsequent performance. The authors find that new venture internationalization is to a large extent an imitative response to the internationalization of other firms. This interorganizational imitation moderates the relationship between internationalization and profitability, but not the relationship between internationalization and sales growth. The conclusion of the article is that interorganizational imitation of internationalization leads to higher profitability by conforming to industry internationalization norms.

A number of articles from the IB literature and general strategy and organization discuss profitability as part of the performance of a firm. One of these is Richard et al. (2009) that through a review of a number of studies shows that performance is multidimensional, related predominately to stakeholders, heterogeneous product market circumstances, and time. Their review of the operationalization of performance highlights the lack of a universally accepted measurement.

Another article that discusses the differences between growth and profitability is Pett and Wolff (2009), which focuses on the process by which small firms aim at growth or profitability. Internationalization and innovation have a positive relationship to product improvements and process improvements, while environmental uncertainty, internationalization and product improvement have positive relationships with growth as a performance dimension.

A classic article in this field is McDougall et al. (1992), which examined the relative role of strategy, industry structure, and origin on the profitability growth of new ventures. The aim of the study was to simultaneously examine origin, strategy, and industry structure as well as the interaction between strategy and industry structure. The study found that variability in new venture performance was better 'accounted for' when all three factors were included in a statistical model. Overall, the results suggested that new venture strategy and industry structure and their interaction are essential for understanding new venture performance while origin is secondary (more important in explaining market share growth than higher profitability). These findings can be seen as a supplement to, for example, Brush and Vanderwerf (1992).

As discussed in Lee (2010) the relationship between internationalization and performance is not necessarily linear but can be seen as shaped in many different ways – U-shaped, inverted U-shaped or even M-shaped as Lee (2010) suggests.

Performance (growth) and survival

In a number of newer articles the relation between the internationalization of the firm and the performance and survival of the firm is empirically studied. We have previously looked at some of these in the chapter but will now take a closer look at the newer articles that can supplement the discussion.

In Carr et al. (2010) the focus is on how the age of the firm can moderate the survival and growth of the firm after internationalization. In tune with the classical 'liability of newness' argument they propose that firm age will have a negative effect on short-term growth after the internationalization and a positive effect on survival in line with the argument in Sapienza et al. (2006). Using longitudinal data from a large number of US firms of which approximately half of them had internationalized they tested these hypotheses but the conclusion is not clear. Younger firms had higher rates of short-term growth than older firms but failing to internationalize is likely to enhance the odds of long-term survival. This dilemma – balancing the internationalization of the firm between survival and growth – can be solved, as the authors suggest, by creating a balanced set of capabilities and managerial competence which has been suggested by, for example, Sapienza et al. (2006) too. Timing of internationalization is thus extremely important and has to be in focus to secure survival and growth of young, international firms.

Sleuwaegen and Onkelinx (2014) analyse empirically the post-entry development of three types of newly internationalized firms following the definition by, for example, Oviatt and McDougall (1994): international new ventures or global start-ups that from the foundation export on a global scale, the geographically focused start-ups that export to a smaller number of countries in the same region and thirdly the traditional exporters, firms that start exporting after some time and after having established themselves on the home market. Based on longitudinal data from Belgian firms the authors can clearly show a major difference between the INVs on the one side and the two other types on the other. The global start-ups have a very strong commitment to internationalization with a large initial investment, a fast growth in foreign markets and continuation of export over time. But this commitment has a problematic side too, which can be seen from the survival rate of the firms. The traditional exporters have the highest survival rate (or lowest failure rate) of all three groups, but it is important to notice (as the authors do) that all three groups have a failure rate that is not higher than other young firms, meaning that rapid internationalization does not add further risk to the survival of a young firm.

The conclusions from Sleuwaegen and Onkelinx (2014) can thus be divided into four parts: First their research clearly shows that most international firms, the global start-ups, export to more markets than the other two types of firms, they have the highest initial exports and they continue to increase their commitment over time. Second, early internationalization is typically associated with faster overall export growth of the firm. And again it is the global start-up firm that exhibits the highest growth rates. And third, the high initial commitment of the global start-ups is also associated with a high likelihood of continuation of the exports. As the fourth conclusion, the authors find that the failure rates for the internationalized firms are not different from the domestic new ventures. The global start-ups, the geographically focused start-ups and the domestic new ventures all have high failure rates compared to the traditional exporters, which is consistent with a 'liability of newness' effect as previously discussed. Their research shows, too, that the difference in failure rate between global start-ups and geographically focused start-ups is insignificant.

In Efrat and Shoham (2012) the difference between short- and long-term performance drivers of born global firms is discussed in relation to Israeli firms. In the initial stages of internationalization external factors are dominant and the performance of the born global firms is improved in growing markets with high technological turbulence and reduced in markets with a high country risk. In the long run the environmental factors' importance is diminished and the firm's internal capabilities become more important. The main assets for the firms in the long run are marketing, management and technological competence, all of which can improve the survival rates of the firms. In short, the born global firms have to react to the market factors in the initial stages of their development but can be more proactive in the further development of the firm.

Discussion and future research directions

If any conclusion regarding the relation between the international entrepreneurial firm and the performance of the firm seen as survival and growth (and profitability) is possible, then the conclusion is that the relation is much more complex than previously thought. The results from Fernhaber (2013) confirm clearly from empirical data that new venture internationalization shows an inverted U-shaped relationship with survival, while the opposite U-shaped relationship is found with sales growth. But the context of the paper and the data for the paper has some problems. The data comes from US-based firms meaning that the home market is huge and typically will exist for all types of firms regardless of product, service or industry. Whether the relation exists for firms from small economies with a very limited home market is not clear. Furthermore all firms have gone public and have been through an IPO. This is often seen in the US but not to any extent among, for example, firms based in Europe. If the focus is on survival seen as not related to IPO but just to the existence of the firm would the results then change? Again this is an open question which is not able to be answered before we have data from a large number of countries and firms.

For a small entrepreneurial firm from, for example, New Zealand or one of the Nordic countries, the discussion whether to establish itself on the home market before expanding to the international markets is redundant as the home market often doesn't exist or consists of very few customers. The firms will be highly international – not necessarily global but often regional – right from day one and the management's focus will be on a number of international markets.

In Kuivalainen et al. (2012) the focus is on what happens after the foundation and internationalization of knowledge-intensive SMEs from Finland. The strategies are divided in three types of pattern: the traditional internationalization model, the born global model and the born again global model. The article demonstrates that even if the born global strategy involves a high risk the survival result is positive as most of the firms survive during the first five years. This is related to the 'learning advantage of newness' which has previously been discussed in this chapter. The born global firms are fast in utilizing any 'window of opportunity' and to build relations and networks to key customers. They typically follow a niche strategy and are able to grow fast in this niche globally. In contrast to these firms the traditional international firms have done worse – both in survival and growth – and many of them have de-internationalized their sales. Internationalization in small steps is thus – in this research – not an adequate strategy if you want rapid growth.

International entrepreneurial firms such as the ones we are dealing with in this chapter (and in the book) typically act in a very complex context where technological competences, market orientation and entrepreneurial orientation are interweaved on a global scale. As, for example, Zahra (2008) points out the performance of the firm is highly dependent on the management's capability to link the entrepreneurial spirit of the firm with market orientation on a global scale and of course a high technological competence. The problem for many of the small, highly international firms is a lack of a systematic process for the internationalization of the firm, but as, for example, Yip et al. (2000) demonstrate the performance of the firms improves the more systematic the approach.

As a summary of this chapter we would like to present four themes that in our opinion can be seen as the most important:

The context

The question here is under what conditions does the internationalization of a firm increase or decrease the vulnerability of the firm leading to better or worse performance? The region in which a firm internationalizes can increase or decrease its odds of survival, for example, to markets with a low or high psychic distance (Almodóvar and Rugman, 2013, Oh and Rugman, 2012, Prashantham and Floyd, 2012, Prashantham and Young, 2011, Rugman and Verbeke, 2004, Rugman et al., 2011). As described above the conclusions on relations between internationalization and performance are highly context dependent. There is a huge difference between a firm operating in the US or in a smaller European country regarding, for example, the size of the market or the opportunities in the market. A home market first strategy can be useful for a firm in the US, even if it is in a small niche market, while the same strategy would be a disaster for a firm from, for example, Sweden, Belgium or New Zealand. Cross-country studies with a number of different settings – small versus large countries or rich countries versus emerging economies – would be useful in determining how important the context is. Another difference is between research that focuses on newly established firms and research that studies firms that have been through an IPO. It is both a question about the research setting – e.g. the time period from the foundation to the study – and again the context.

Newness

The studies are mostly about newly established firms and newness is in many of the papers seen as both an advantage and a liability. To be a newly established firm can be an advantage as all decisions are new and not bounded in old routines. Instead the management can have a clear and fresh look at the decision and there are no sunk cost commitments to influence the rational decision making. But newness can be a problem, too, making it difficult to enter new markets, get access to new customers and establish relations and networks. Almost all the sales in the first period of the firm's life are dominated by 'cold canvas' where every customer is new.

Choice of entry mode

How the choice of entry mode can affect the performance of newly established and fast internationalizing firms has not been studied to any extent. A few exceptions are Dimitratos et al. (2004), Zahra and Garvis (2000) and Zahra et al. (2000).

Export or other international activities

Another limitation of most of the research on performance in relation to the internationalization of smaller firms is that the type of international activity researched is almost always export. Activities like sourcing, research and development or foreign direct investment are seldom part of either the theoretical or the empirical research setting. One exception is an older article about Japanese SMEs and their foreign direct investments (Lu and Beamish, 2001). In this article the authors find that the positive impact of the internationalization of the firms on performance comes from the extent of the firms' FDI activities. In the beginning of the FDI activity performance declines but higher levels of FDI lead to higher performance.

It is thus important for future research in this field to consider how important the context is for the conclusions and to establish research across different settings – small and large countries, different stages of the firm's development and whether the firm has been through an IPO. It is also necessary that the discussion of the advantage or liability of the newness of the firm becomes more empirically founded and furthermore that the focus is on other ways of internationalizing than export.

This discussion can be seen as part of a larger discussion of the cost of internationalization of new ventures and especially how to reduce these costs through learning. As Zhou et al. (2010) – see Yi and Wang, 2012 too – points out, young international new ventures can have a learning advantage of newness and thus avoid the liability of newness and foreignness. This can be done by upgrading the knowledge and network capability of the INV. The firms can thus use the entrepreneurial dynamics of a new, international firm through a learning process to achieve growth.

In relation to this perspective it can be important, too, to distinguish between two phases in the internationalization of an INV (Sasi and Arenius, 2008). In the first phase the firm is focussed on getting access to the international markets through exiting ties and networks and in a second phase the focus is on global growth adding new relations. Research from Finland (Sasi and Arenius, 2008) demonstrates that the first phase is completed successfully by firms that primarily rely on dyadic relations. But these relations typically become a problem in the second phase where the firms need to develop a multilateral network to achieve growth. It can thus be important to see the growth and development of the INV not as a linear process but as a transition from one phase to another.

References

Almodóvar, P. and Rugman, A. M. 2013. The M curve and the performance of Spanish international new ventures. *British Journal of Management*, 25, S6–S23.

Andersson, S. and Wictor, I. 2003. Innovative internationalisation in new firms: born globals – the Swedish case. *Journal of International Entrepreneurship*, 1, 249–275.
Autio, E., Sapienza, H. and Almeida, J. G. 2000. Effects of age at entry, knowledge intensity, and imitability on international growth. *Academy of Management Journal*, 43, 909–924.
Balabanis, G. I. and Katsikea, E. 2003. Being an entrepreneurial exporter: does it pay? *International Business Review*, 12, 233–252.
Bloodgood, J. M., Sapienza, H. J. and Almeida, J. G. 1996. The internationalisation of new high-potential US ventures: antecedents and outcomes. *Entrepreneurship Theory and Practice*, 20, 61–76.
Bonaccorsi, A. 1992. On the relationship between firm size and export intensity. *Journal of International Business Studies*, 23, 605–635.
Brush, C. G. and Vanderwerf, P. A. 1992. A comparison of methods and sources for obtaining estimates of new venture performance. *Journal of Business Venturing*, 7, 157–170.
Calof, J. L. 1994. The relationship between firm size and export behavior revisited. *Journal of International Business Studies*, 25, 367–387.
Carr, J. C., Haggard, K. S., Hmieleski, K. M. and Zahra, S. A. 2010. A study of the moderating effects of firm age at internationalization on firm survival and short-term growth. *Strategic Entrepreneurship Journal*, 4, 183–192.
Cesinger, B., Danko, A. and Bouncken, R. 2012. Born globals: (almost) 20 years of research and still not 'grown up'? *International Journal of Entrepreneurship and Small Business*, 15, 171–190.
Covin, J. G. and Slevin, D. P. 1991. A conceptual model of entrepreneurship as firm behavior. *Entrepreneurship Theory and Practice*, 16, 7–25.
Dimitratos, P., Lioukas, S. and Carter, S. 2004. The relationship between entrepreneurship and international performance: the importance of domestic environment. *International Business Review*, 13, 19–41.
Efrat, K. and Shoham, A. 2012. Born global firms: the differences between their short- and long-term performance drivers. *Journal of World Business*, 47, 675–685.
Fernhaber, S. 2013. Untangling the relationship between new venture internationalization and performance. *Journal of International Entrepreneurship*, Online first, 1–23.
Fernhaber, S. A. and Li, D. 2010. The impact of interorganizational imitation on new venture international entry and performance. *Entrepreneurship Theory and Practice*, 34, 1–30.
Fernhaber, S. A. and Li, D. 2013. International exposure through network relationships: implications for new venture internationalization. *Journal of Business Venturing*, 28, 316–334.
Fernhaber, S. A., McDougall, P. P. and Oviatt, B. M. 2007. Exploring the role of industry structure in new venture internationalization. *Entrepreneurship Theory and Practice*, 31, 517–542.
Fernhaber, S. A. and McDougall-Covin, P. P. 2009. Venture capitalists as catalysts to new venture internationalization: the impact of their knowledge and reputation resources. *Entrepreneurship Theory and Practice*, 33, 277–295.
Fernhaber, S. A., McDougall-Covin, P. P. and Shepherd, D. A. 2009. International entrepreneurship: leveraging internal and external knowledge sources. *Strategic Entrepreneurship Journal*, 3, 297–320.
Giovannetti, G., Ricchiuti, G. and Velucchi, M. 2011. Size, innovation and internationalization: a survival analysis of Italian firms. *Applied Economics*, 43, 1511–1520.
Hagen, B., Zucchella, A., Cerchiello, P. and De Giovanni, N. 2012. International strategy and performance-clustering strategic types of SMEs. *International Business Review*, 21, 369–382.
Ibeh, K. I. N. 2003. Toward a contingency framework of export entrepreneurship: conceptualisations and empirical evidence. *Small Business Economics*, 20, 49–68.
Jones, M. V., Coviello, N. and Tang, Y. K. 2011. International entrepreneurship research (1989–2009): a domain ontology and thematic analysis. *Journal of Business Venturing*, 26, 632–659.
Keen, C. and Etemad, H. 2012. Rapid growth and rapid internationalization: the case of smaller enterprises from Canada. *Management Decision*, 50, 569–590.
Khavul, S., Pérez-Nordtvedt, L. and Wood, E. 2010. Organizational entrainment and international new ventures from emerging markets. *Journal of Business Venturing*, 25, 104–119.
Knight, G. A. 2001. Entrepreneurship and strategy in the international SME. *Journal of International Management*, 7, 155–171.
Knight, G. A. and Cavusgil, S. T. 1996. The born global firm: A challenge to traditional internationalization theory. *Advances in International Marketing*, 8, 11–26.
Knight, G. A. and Cavusgil, S. T. 2004. Innovation, organizational capabilities, and the born-global firm. *Journal of International Business Studies*, 35, 124–141.

Kuemmerle, W. 2002. Home base and knowledge management in international ventures. *Journal of Business Venturing*, 17, 99–122.
Kuivalainen, O., Saarenketo, S. and Puumalainen, K. 2012. Start-up patterns of internationalization: a framework and its application in the context of knowledge-intensive SMEs. *European Management Journal*, 30, 372–385.
Kundu, S. K. and Katz, J. 2003. Born-international SMEs: BI-level impacts of resources and intentions. *Small Business Economics*, 20, 25–47.
Lee, H., Kelley, D., Lee, J. and Lee, S. 2012. SME survival: the impact of internationalization, technology resources, and alliances. *Journal of Small Business Management*, 50, 1–19.
Lee, I. H. 2010. The M curve: the performance of born-regional firms from Korea. *Multinational Business Review*, 18, 1–22.
Leonidou, L. C. and Katsikeas, C. S. 1996. The export development process: an integrative review of empirical models. *Journal of International Business Studies*, 27, 517–551.
Lu, J. W. and Beamish, P. W. 2001. The internationalization and performance of SMEs. *Strategic Management Journal*, 22, 565–586.
Lu, J. and Beamish, P. 2006. SME internationalization and performance: growth vs. profitability. *Journal of International Entrepreneurship*, 4, 27–48.
Madsen, T. K. and Servais, P. 1997. The internationalization of born globals: an evolutionary process? *International Business Review*, 6, 561–583.
McDougall, P. P. and Oviatt, B. M. 1996. New venture internationalization, strategic change, and performance: a follow-up study. *Journal of Business Venturing*, 11, 23–40.
McDougall, P. P. and Oviatt, B. M. 2000. International entrepreneurship: The intersection of two research paths. *Academy of Management Journal*, 43, 902–906.
McDougall, P. P., Robinson, R. B., Jr and Denisi, A. S. 1992. Modeling new venture performance: an analysis of new venture strategy, industry structure, and venture origin. *Journal of Business Venturing*, 7, 267–289.
McDougall, P. P., Shane, S. and Oviatt, B. M. 1994. Explaining the formation of international new ventures: the limits of theories from international business research. *Journal of Business Venturing*, 9, 469–487.
Mort, G. S., Weerawardena, J. and Liesch, P. W. 2012. Advancing entrepreneurial marketing evidence from born global firms. *European Journal of Marketing*, 46, 542–561.
Mudambi, R. and Zahra, S. A. 2007. The survival of international new ventures. *Journal of International Business Studies*, 38, 333–352.
Oh, C. H. and Rugman, A. M. 2012. Regional integration and the international strategies of large European firms. *International Business Review*, 21, 493–507.
Oviatt, B. M. and McDougall, P. P. 1994. Toward a theory of international new ventures. *Journal of International Business Studies*, 25, 45–64.
Oviatt, B. M. and McDougall, P. P. 1995. Global start-ups: entrepreneurs on a worldwide stage. *The Academy of Management Executive*, 9, 30–43.
Pett, T. L. and Wolff, J. A. 2009. SME opportunity for growth or profit: what is the role of product and process improvement? *International Journal of Entrepreneurial Venturing*, 1, 5–21.
Prange, C. and Verdier, S. 2011. Dynamic capabilities, internationalization processes and performance. *Journal of World Business*, 46, 126–133.
Prashantham, S. and Dhanaraj, C. 2010. The dynamic influence of social capital on the international growth of new ventures. *Journal of Management Studies*, 47, 967–994.
Prashantham, S. and Floyd, S. W. 2012. Routine microprocesses and capability learning in international new ventures. *Journal of International Business Studies*, 43, 544–562.
Prashantham, S. and Young, S. 2011. Post-entry speed of international new ventures. *Entrepreneurship Theory and Practice*, 35, 275–292.
Preece, S. B., Miles, G. and Baetz, M. C. 1999. Explaining the international intensity and global diversity of early-stage technology-based firms. *Journal of Business Venturing*, 14, 259–281.
Richard, P. J., Devinney, T. M., Yip, G. S. and Johnson, G. 2009. Measuring organizational performance: towards methodological best practice. *Journal of Management*, 35, 718–804.
Rugman, A. M. and Verbeke, A. 2004. A perspective on regional and global strategies of multinational enterprises. *Journal of International Business Studies*, 35, 3–18.
Rugman, A. M., Verbeke, A. and Nguyen, Q. T. K. 2011. Fifty years of international business theory and beyond. *Management International Review*, 51, 755–786.

Sapienza, H. J., Autio, E., George, G. and Zahra, S. A. 2006. A capabilities perspective on the effects of early internationalization on firm survival and growth. *Academy of Management Review*, 31, 914–933.
Sasi, V. and Arenius, P. 2008. International new ventures and social networks: advantage or liability? *European Management Journal*, 26, 400–411.
Schueffel, P., Amann, W. and Herbolzheimer, E. 2011. Internationalization of new ventures: tests of growth and survival. *The Multinational Business Review*, 19, 376–403.
Sleuwaegen, L. and Onkelinx, J. 2014. International commitment, post-entry growth and survival of international new ventures. *Journal of Business Venturing*, 29, 106–120.
Stinchcombe, A. L. 1965. Social structure and organizations. In March, J. G. (ed.) *Handbook of Organizations*. Chicago: Routledge.
Sullivan, D. 1994. Measuring the degree of internationalization of a firm. *Journal of International Business Studies*, 25, 325–342.
Tesar, G. and Moini, A. H. 1998. Planning for product development among smaller manufacturing enterprises: a longitudinal study. *Journal of Global Marketing* [GLO], 11, 95–106.
Weerawardena, J., Mort, G. S., Liesch, P. W. and Knight, G. A. 2007. Conceptualizing accelerated internationalization in the born global firm: a dynamic capabilities perspective. *Journal of World Business*, 42, 294–306.
Westhead, P., Wright, M. and Ucbasaran, D. 2001. The internationalization of new and small firms: a resource-based view. *Journal of Business Venturing*, 16, 333–358.
Wolff, J. A. and Pett, T. L. 2000. Internationalization of small firms: an examination of export competitive patterns, firm size, and export performance. *Journal of Small Business Management*, 38, 34–47.
Yi, J. and Wang, C. 2012. The decision to export: firm heterogeneity, sunk costs, and spatial concentration. *International Business Review*, 21, 766–781.
Yip, G. S., Biscarri, J. G. and Monti, J. A. 2000. The role of the internationalization process in the performance of newly internationalizing firms. *Journal of International Marketing*, 8, 10–35.
Yli-Renko, H., Autio, E. and Tontti, V. 2002. Social capital, knowledge, and the international growth of technology-based new firms. *International Business Review*, 11, 279–304.
Young, S., Hamill, J., Wheeler, C. and Davies, R. 1989. *International market entry and development*, Englewood Cliffs, NJ: Prentice Hall.
Zaheer, S. 1995. Overcoming the liability of foreignness. *The Academy of Management Journal*, 38, 341–363.
Zahra, S. A. 2008. Being entrepreneurial and market driven: implications for company performance. *Journal of Strategy and Management*, 1, 125–142.
Zahra, S. A. and Garvis, D. M. 2000. International corporate entrepreneurship and firm performance: the moderating effect of international environmental hostility. *Journal of Business Venturing*, 15, 469–492.
Zahra, S. A. and George, G. 2002. International entrepreneurship: The current status of the field and future research agenda. *Strategic Entrepreneurship: Creating an Integrated Mindset*, 255–288.
Zahra, S. A., Ireland, R. D. and Hitt, M. A. 2000. International expansion by new venture firms: international diversity, mode of market entry, technological learning, and performance. *Academy of Management Journal*, 43, 925–950.
Zahra, S. A., Neubaum, D. O. and Huse, M. 1997. The effect of the environment on export performance among telecommunications new ventures. *Entrepreneurship Theory and Practice*, 22, 25–46.
Zhou, L. X., Barnes, B. R. and Lu, Y. A. 2010. Entrepreneurial proclivity, capability upgrading and performance advantage of newness among international new ventures. *Journal of International Business Studies*, 41, 882–905.
Zott, C. 2003. Dynamic capabilities and the emergence of intraindustry differential firm performance: insights from a simulation study. *Strategic Management Journal*, 24, 97–125.
Zucchella, A., Palamara, G. and Denicolai, S. 2007. The drivers of the early internationalization of the firm. *Journal of World Business*, 42, 268–280.

14

Policy implications of international entrepreneurship

Rod B. McNaughton and Juan Pellegrino

Introduction

Smaller and younger firms face resource constraints, and lack experience and credibility. Internationalization further challenges them with an exponentially more complex and vastly expanded range of potential markets. Despite these challenges, some SMEs are able to take advantage of international opportunities, entering multiple international markets soon after founding. Policy interest in such firms was sparked two decades ago when Rennie (1993), conducting research for the Australian Manufacturer's Association, discovered a group of "born global"[1] firms that began exporting within two years of their founding, when the average firm in his sample served the domestic market for 27 years before initiating export activity. The following year, Oviatt and McDougall (1994) published their seminal article on "international new ventures," spawning a now substantial stream of research focused on firms that pursue opportunities in international markets soon after their founding.

Surprisingly, however, few studies explicitly address the policy issues raised by born globals. Recent reviews of the literature on international entrepreneurship by Jones et al. (2011) and Keupp and Gassmann (2009) demonstrate that the field has grown exponentially. Yet Jones et al.'s (2011: 5) thematic map of the international entrepreneurship domain does not include a strand of policy research (indeed, the word "policy" does not occur in the text of their review). Keupp and Gassmann's (2009: 605) organizing framework includes "government policy" as an industry-level antecedent of international entrepreneurship, but there is no detailed discussion of which papers address government policy, or the nature of those policies. Most researchers explore the policy implications of their empirical findings in a few sentences, and few have tried to bring together these fragmented observations in a systematic way to provide guidance to policy-makers, or stimulate more policy-relevant research.

This inattention to policy issues is surprising because born globals have exciting policy implications. Small firms pose a challenge for developed economies: they account for a disproportionate number of new jobs, but a relatively smaller share of both value-added and export earnings. Across the OECD, SMEs make up over 95 percent of enterprises and account for up to 80 percent of jobs, yet only account for between 50 and 60 percent of value-added (OECD, 2005: 17–21), and 15–50 percent of exports (OECD, 1998, 2000), with the ranges accounting for differences between countries and industries. The share of employment in small firms vastly exceeds their economic contribution, implying lower labour productivity than in larger firms; yet paradoxically new firms are important to productivity *growth* as they challenge and displace incumbent firms (OECD, 1998). Policies that foster born globals, with their promise of growth and early export earnings, appear to offer a resolution to this long-standing dilemma. Despite McDougall and Oviatt's (1996: 23) observation almost two decades ago that "Although many scholars, business experts, and government agencies enthusiastically advise all firms, including new and small ventures, to internationalize, such advice does not appear to be based on empirical evidence," the policy implications of such advice are still not well studied.

This chapter is an attempt to summarize the policy issues raised by born global firms. It begins the task of organizing the fragmented observations about policy implications raised by recent empirical studies of early and rapid internationalization into a cogent set of themes. The body of the chapter is arranged into three parts. The first briefly reviews the literature on early and rapid internationalization to summarize specific program recommendations that emerge from empirical studies, the second identifies forms of support that may benefit born globals, and the third discusses broad issues that characterize discussions of international entrepreneurship policy. The chapter concludes with suggestions for research focused on the policy interests and program needs of early and rapidly internationalizing firms.

Policy in born global research

The absence of a distinct stream of policy-related research in the contemporary born global literature is perplexing as a substantial literature built up during the 1980s and early 1990s on export promotion, and the unique needs of SMEs was clearly a theme in this literature. Rather than evolving into the literature on born globals, however, this literature remained largely separate, and the number of contributions peaked and then began to decline in the late 1990s. This is particularly interesting as some of the contributors to this literature (e.g. Bell, 1994) went on to make significant contributions to the study of different internationalization paths (e.g. Bell, 1995, 1997).

Seringhaus and Rosson's (1990) book is the archetype of these export promotion studies, providing a comprehensive summary of international programs, both direct (e.g. research support, export preparation, and export market entry programs) and indirect (e.g. policy support on issues such as productivity, R&D, innovation, work force planning, fiscal measures, or regional development). Much of the literature in this vein was comparative, describing the nature and scope of export assistance between countries (e.g. Seringhaus, 1987; Elvey, 1990; Camino, 1991; Diamantopoulos et al., 1993; Bell, 1994). Outside of the focus on export promotion, a number of papers during this period considered issues of SME internationalization more broadly (e.g. Boter and Holmquist, 1996; Acs et al., 1997; Bell, 1997).

Two recent studies continue the tradition of this literature by evaluating the influence of export promotion programs on SME export activity (Freixnet, 2012; Durmuşoğlu et al., 2012). Freixnet's (2012) literature review illustrates how the number of studies of export promotion organizations has declined (Table 1, p. 1068; see also Appendix A). Using data collected from SMEs in Spain, Freixnet concluded that export promotion programs are most helpful for firms initiating exporting, but paradoxically firms at later stages know more about the programs and make greater use of them. The primary recommendation is that programs need to communicate more with potential users, and target their offerings by stage of internationalization. Freixnet also suggests reducing bureaucracy, increasing flexibility, and strengthening coordination between programs, along with directing resources toward programs with the highest impact: sponsored international trade shows, trade missions, and information programs. In the context of SMEs in Turkey, Durmuşoğlu et al. (2012) also found a positive role for export promotion programs, reporting that use of programs is associated with their performance, and achievement of various management objectives including relationship development, development of new management skills, and organizational learning. Neither paper develops a link to the literature on born globals, illustrating that these two streams of literature remain largely separate.

One explanation for the paucity of policy-related research in the born global literature is that a unifying and powerful theory of the formation and behaviour of these firms has yet to emerge. In contrast, the Uppsala model provided a coherent model of incremental internationalization that significantly influenced the design of export promotion programs throughout the 1980s and 1990s. This model, originally developed by Johanson and Wiedersheim-Paul (1975) and Johanson and Vahlne (1977) posited that a lack of foreign market knowledge is the critical hurdle for the internationalization of a firm, and that relevant knowledge is primarily acquired through experiential learning. In the Uppsala model, firms enter psychically close markets before those more distant, and gradually commit more resources as they gain knowledge about a market. Following this thinking, many government programs to promote and support exporting assumed that firms must achieve a threshold size and gain sufficient knowledge in the domestic market before cautiously entering nearby markets. For policy-makers it justified programs that were orderly (based on a series of stages), scalable (by providing standardized knowledge about markets and internationalization challenges at each stage) and relatively inexpensive (as the primary constraint to internationalization was assumed to be knowledge and experience since firms bootstrap their expansion from one market to the next).

Born globals challenge all of these assumptions. They are heterogeneous, exhibit different internationalization patterns, are not solely dependent on experiential learning, have rich and deep knowledge about their global niche, move quickly, often behave opportunistically, and typically rely on external investors to fund their growth. Bell and McNaughton (2000) were among the first to explore the policy implication of such complex internationalization patterns, and to suggest that born global firms are not well-served by traditional export development programs. They noted the influence of the Uppsala model on the design of such programs, and the resulting emphasis on the pre-export phase and stimulating interest in exporting, along with providing standardized information about national markets. They argued that born globals were already highly motivated to internationalize and recognize the benefits of doing so, and that a focus on global niches meant that standardized country-level data was of little value. In addition, the speed with which born globals enter markets is challenging for the timing of government programs, and exacerbates the need for financial rather than information assistance, as expansion cannot be bootstrapped.

Wright et al. (2007), writing several years later, also analyzed the implications of international entrepreneurship for export promotion and policy, identifying seven themes: timing, intensity and sustainability, mode, influence of domestic context, levering external resources, unit of analysis, and the effect on performance. Reviewing the literature within these themes, Wright et al. concluded that market imperfections exist and governments are justified in providing programs to aid SME internationalization, but that existing programs are not aligned with the needs of small and rapidly internationalizing firms. They made a series of recommendations to policy-makers with respect to scope, dynamism, mode of entry, use of domestic and international resources and the need to pay more attention to the role of the individual entrepreneur. Similarly, Fischer and Reuber (2008) reviewed the literature to identify factors associated with extensive and effective internationalization by SMEs, and concluded that government agencies should focus on selectively supporting firms with the greatest potential to internationalize successfully, recognize that some internationalization opportunities are opportunistic, and lever support within industrial networks and clusters.

What support do born globals need?

Despite the absence of a holistic explanation of born global behaviour, the empirical literature on born globals contains some common themes about the policy interests and program needs of these firms. These can be characterized at the level of the environment, firm, and management team (Fischer and Reuber, 2008). At the environmental level, literature from an institutional perspective points to the need to make laws, regulations, and policies relating to international trade accessible for smaller firms and to reduce compliance costs (e.g. Szyliowicz and Galvin, 2010). Intellectual property rights and incentives for R&D are posited to have important policy implications for born globals. In their review, Fischer and Reuber (2008) cited evidence that SMEs are more likely to internationalize if they are innovative and have significant new knowledge. Oesterle (1997) and others have argued that born globals internationalize as a way to appropriate the benefits of their investment in R&D through early mover advantage. This argument contrasts with earlier analyses, which claimed the costs of enforcing passive intellectual property rights are a barrier to small firm internationalization (e.g. Acs et al., 1997).

The most frequent theme at the environment level relates to the role of networks, both domestic and international, in facilitating internationalization. The literature on the role of networks in early and rapid internationalization began soon after the recognition of born globals (e.g. Coviello and Munro, 1997), and calls for government facilitation of collaboration which continues to the present day (e.g. Kyvik et al., 2013). The evidence is that reasonably concentrated clusters enhance opportunities for SME internationalization through a variety of both active and passive externalities (Brown et al., 2010), but that too much competition can negate some of these benefits (Fernhaber et al., 2008).

The notion of supporting born globals through cluster facilitation is second only to the Uppsala model in its impact on government policy and programs. Indeed, the importance of this perspective is such that Johanson and Vahlne (2009) revisited the original Uppsala model to incorporate the importance of relationships in networks, proposing that "outsidership" to networks, perhaps more so than even psychic distance, is a source of uncertainty for the internationalizing firm. However, the popularity of this approach likely owes more to Porter's (1990) research, than it does to the literature on internationalization. Denmark, one of the original ten countries studied by Porter, was the first in the early 1990s to turn the notion of industrial clustering into a program to facilitate economic development and export activity. Adaptations of the Danish model quickly spread to other developed countries, resulting in a plethora of programs to facilitate bottom-up collaboration between industry groups, and clusters of co-located firms (Goldfinch and Perry, 1996, 1997). Such programs explicitly recognized the limitations of smaller firms, and the potential of levering resources in the local environment, including subsidiaries of MNEs, through collaboration.

The idea that networks of firms could combine their efforts to address international market opportunities was a significant departure from export promotion and development programs focused on government services provided through local offices and overseas embassies and consulates (Brown and McNaughton, 2003). However, most cluster-based programs have since terminated, or are now much smaller and administered at a regional level. In part, this was planned as cluster programs are typically designed to initiate but not sustain clusters. In addition, the outcome of clustering is often serendipitous, making it difficult to provide evidence of success. Despite this, no alternative approach has since captured the attention of policy-makers on such a broad scale.

At the firm level, much discussion surrounds the issue of whether governments can or should "pick winners." The empirical literature on born globals suggests that firms likely to internationalize early and successfully are innovative, with small domestic markets, large and growing foreign markets, produce goods, and are led by internationally experienced managers (Fischer and Reuber, 2008). All small and young firms are not equally positioned or prepared to do well in international markets, and the success and even survival of some firms might be challenged by internationalizing or doing so too soon. This suggests that programs, especially those involving subsidies to help alleviate the resource constraints of small internationalizing firms, should be highly targeted (Baum et al., 2011). However, governments find this difficult to do from both a practical perspective (actually identifying high potential born global firms) and a political one (being seen to show favouritism to some industries or even entrepreneurs over others). This is especially so as the ability to obtain funding is the primary constraint on the growth of rapidly internationalizing firms (McNaughton and Bell, 2004; Gabrielsson et al., 2004), and governments are loathe to invest directly in firms.

Finally, there are also significant policy recommendations at the level of the management team or entrepreneur. Numerous studies confirm the importance of the founders in both motivating internationalization, and providing the initial knowledge and contacts to enter international markets. A substantial stream of literature seeks to understand how born globals learn, given that they clearly do not learn incrementally through experience as postulated by the Uppsala model. The policy recommendations that come from this literature suggest programs that can be tailored for each entrepreneur/management team to identify gaps in learning and develop knowledge management systems to support internationalization (e.g. Fletcher and Prashantham, 2011; Fletcher and Harris, 2012; Kyvik et al., 2013). More broadly, some authors recommend indirect policies aimed at cultivating international entrepreneurial mind-sets from a young age (e.g. Kaur and Sandhu, 2013). A focus on the entrepreneur/management team, tailored programing, early intervention, and multiple forms of learning is different to the approach used by Uppsala model inspired programs that targeted firms with a threshold of experience, and provided standardized knowledge about markets and internationalization challenges at different stages.

There is evidence that governments are responding to these insights about the needs of born globals. Most developed countries have a portfolio of export promotion and support programs that attempt to address different resource deficiencies. Increasingly these also target the unique needs of particular sectors, especially emerging fields at the interface between new technologies and new markets. The variety of programs in different countries offers considerable collective experience for going forward. Reports by the OECD (2008, 2009) present the results of surveys of both SMEs and export promotion agencies across OECD countries. The findings reveal some differences between the views of SMEs and policy-makers. SMEs stress financial and market access barriers and only later become concerned about internal capabilities, and the business environment (e.g. government regulations and economic conditions). Policy-makers, on the other hand, stress barriers created by lack of knowledge and limited resources both financial and human. Not surprisingly, policy-makers rated external barriers, especially those created by governments, lowly.

Challenges for policy-makers

This section identifies a number of broad policy implications of international entrepreneurship. At the pinnacle of these is debate over the extent to which governments should have a role in promoting or supporting the internationalization of firms. One view is that governments should take a hands-off approach, limiting their role to ensuring a competitive and level playing field. However, from a practical perspective, governments at various levels in almost all developed economies take an active role, and intervene with a range of programs that address various perceived market failures. A related issue is that both inward and outward internationalization may be encouraged; the former represented by the attraction of foreign investment, and the latter by export development programs. In general, explicit interventions that promote outward internationalization are most relevant to born globals. However, foreign investment can have valuable spin-off effects for endogenous firms, which may become indirect exporters by supplying local subsidiaries of multi-national firms (Prashantham and McNaughton, 2006), or be pulled into international markets through relationships with a subsidiary and its international network (Bell and McNaughton, 2000). Additional benefits may be realized through opportunities for import substitution and inward technology transfer.

A second issue is that born globals conflate promoting and supporting entrepreneurial firms with internationalizing firms. The born global literature largely focuses on entrepreneurial small firms, usually new ventures, though as Keupp and Gassmann (2009: 602) argue, this focus may be limiting as opportunities for both entrepreneurship and internationalization exist across the range of firm size and age. Traditionally, export promotion programs focused on helping established medium to larger sized firms enter international markets; and while there may still be a need to do so as many large firms do not export, there is also a need to assist the internationalization of new and small firms. In parallel, there are programs focused on assisting start-ups, and these must now deal with new ventures that are also internationalizing.

Born globals make the policy arena more complex by expanding the interstice between internationalization and domestic economic development. Born globals illustrate that internationalizing firms are much more heterogeneous than previously thought, and that using criteria like age and size to segment and target programs may not be appropriate. Born globals are distinct from both larger firms, and from their peer group of newer and younger firms, suggesting they may benefit from specialized programs that respond to the simultaneous challenges of high growth and internationalization. Heterogeneity makes it difficult for governments to respond with scalable and cost-effective programs. It also has implications for which government departments fund programs, as a different ministry or department often administers assistance for start-ups versus internationalization. In addition, as local governments are frequently involved in assisting start-ups, lower levels of government are increasingly drawn into the international realm, once the sole purview of national governments.

New ventures that internationalize rapidly are frequently also high growth firms, which themselves pose interesting policy challenges (Mason and Brown, 2013). High growth firms are outliers in the population of small firms. They seek to create a large firm from a small base, whereas many small firms try to create sustained income for their owners with stable or limited growth. The policy interests and program requirements of high growth and traditional small firms are not necessarily aligned. For example, small firms might be concerned with the minimum wage and interest rates, whereas high growth firms, needing talent and capital, might be concerned about immigration for skilled workers, R&D tax credits and an active market for private equity.

A final issue is the challenge of gathering empirical evidence to inform policy and program development. Much of the literature on born globals is cross-sectional and based on small-scale surveys or qualitative research. This body of evidence is weak with respect to two important questions. First, governments want to know if they should foster and support born globals. Do born globals indeed perform above average and produce the hoped for effect on productivity?

Second, they need to know the number of born globals within their border and their rate of creation.

Answers to these questions require authoritative evidence based on a census or at least a large random sample of firms. Ideally, to understand how firm size, age and internationalization are interwoven over time in a population of firms, the national business registry (which identifies all firms in an economy along with their demographic characteristics) needs to be merged with the export registry (which provides details of the products and services exported by firms). This has proven difficult in a majority of countries for reasons that include the data being managed by different ministries or departments, databases designed for administrative rather than research purposes, lack of resources, and various laws limiting the use of data disclosed by firms (Niroui, 2011).

It is also important that data be longitudinal to assess patterns of internationalization, and the effect of internationalization on firm performance. The view that internationalizing firms have superior performance is widely accepted (Wright et al., 2007). However, there is no clear evidence of a positive relationship, and the emerging consensus is that the relationship is likely an inverted-U, where firms benefit from internationalization up to a point, and then experience disadvantages because of costs and uncertainty (Bausch and Krist, 2007; Fischer and Reuber, 2008). A related issue is the lack of consensus on how to define and measure both the phenomenon of early/rapid internationalization and internationalization performance. In both cases, a proliferation of measures makes it difficult to compare between studies and countries (Madsen, 2013; Katsikeas et al., 2000). Without authoritative information on the number of born globals and their performance, it is difficult for governments to justify and design programs that foster and support these firms.

Conclusions

As smaller and younger organizations, born globals have advantages of innovativeness and agility, but also face limitations because of constrained resources and/or lack of experience. Sometimes SMEs cannot obtain the additional resources they require in the market, or from appropriate partners, because of information asymmetry and perceived risks that increase the costs of the resources. This is most evident in the market for financial capital, as firms require additional financing for international activities, but have difficulty arranging it through traditional sources. However, firms also experience similar gaps in the markets for social and intellectual capital and most developed countries have multiple programs that address these gaps. These market failures may be addressed through various policies and programs that promote and support SME exporting.

The rationale for government involvement in this area is that export activity contributes to the public good through increased employment, innovation, and export earnings. Still, governments face limitations in their ability to help. SMEs, for example, lack credibility and reputation, but for political reasons governments find it difficult to "pick winners" that they can promote and vouch for in international markets. Equally, it is politically difficult to address directly the financial limitations experienced by born globals. Entrepreneurs can be suspicious of government programs, finding them insufficiently flexible (Knight et al., 2003), and employees of export development programs often lack industry-specific knowledge. Thus, they are helpful with legal and administrative issues, but not sector-specific in-market knowledge. In response to these and other concerns, programs are becoming more flexible, involving industry groups in their design, hiring ex-entrepreneurs, and sometimes outsourcing their delivery to the private sector.

Though these programs seem promising, the evaluation of their return on public investment remains difficult. The effect of facilitating networks, for example, may take a long time to appear, and serendipity plays a significant role. In addition, most countries do not have good data for matching firm characteristics to export activity. Thus, it is difficult to justify many export development programs using quantitative criteria. One implication is that government commitment tends to remain small and support for specific programs frequently wanes. Thus, the singular research opportunity is to access and analyze longitudinal records from national business and export registries, and compare patterns of internationalization and export performance. On the theoretic side, understanding of born global behaviour cries out for a unifying framework, which if simple and clear, would likely have significant influence on the way policy-makers think about born globals and the design of programs that target their needs. It is not simply that born globals internationalize differently; after 20 years of research it remains difficult to explain their complex behaviour, and thus to provide clear guidance for the design of policy and programs (Cesinger et al., 2012).

The absence of policy as a theme in the recent reviews of the international entrepreneurship literature undertaken by Jones et al. (2011) and Keupp and Gassmann (2009) illustrates the gap in the literature on born globals with respect to policy and promotion or support programs. Studies of export promotion are amongst the ancestors of contemporary research about born globals. However, a cogent stream of research on the policy implications and program needs of born globals has yet to arise. A portfolio of such research would be valuable, from both the perspectives of entrepreneurs and policy-makers, addressing issues at the level of the environment, firm and individual. This research should be sensitive to the heterogeneity of firms described in this chapter, and distinguish the interests of born globals from both other SMEs and different internationalization paths. Even within the broad category of "born global," the literature recognizes several patterns of early and rapid internationalization, each of which may have nuanced differences in their policy interests and support needs. Thus, there is considerable scope for policy-related research on born globals, and potential to affect both scholarly understanding of these organizations, and how they are supported by governments around the world.

Note

1 A number of names, definitions, and measures are used to describe the phenomenon of early and rapidly internationalizing firms. Some studies use the terms "born global" and "international new ventures" interchangeably, while others make nuanced distinctions between them. For these authors, the issue is often the spatial scale of the internationalization; whereas "global" suggests selling everywhere in the world (or at least in more than one major world region), "international" could be limited to one or a few countries within a major region (Crick, 2009). We do not distinguish studies of born globals from those of INVs in this chapter, and generally refer to both as "born globals." However, there is merit in future research attempting to unpack potential differences in the policy implications and support needs of these and other closely related internationalization paths.

References

Acs, Z.J., Morck, R. Shaver, M. and Yeung, B. (1997) The internationalization of small and medium sized enterprises: a policy perspective, *Small Business Economics*, 9, 7–20.

Baum, M., Schwens, C., and Kabst, R. (2011) A typology of international new ventures: empirical evidence from high-technology industries, *Journal of Small Business Management*, 49(3), 305–330.

Bausch, A. and Krist, M. (2007) The effect of context-related moderators on the international-performance relationship: evidence from meta-analysis, *Management International Review*, 47(3), 319–347.

Bell, J. (1994) The role of government in small-firm internationalization: a comparative study of export promotion in Finland, Ireland, and Norway with specific reference to the computer software industry. Ph.D. Thesis, University of Strathclyde.

Bell, J. (1995) The internationalization of small computer software firms: a further challenge to "stag"' theories, *European Journal of Marketing*, 29(8), 60–75.
Bell, J. (1997) A comparative study of export problems of small computer software exporters in Finland, Ireland, and Norway, *International Business Review*, 6(2), 1–20.
Bell, J., and McNaughton, R. (2000) "Born-global" firms: a challenge to public policy in support of internationalization, *Marketing in Global Economy Conference Proceedings*, American Marketing Association, Buenos Aires, 175–185.
Boter, H. and Holmquist, C. (1996) Industry characteristics and internationalization processes in small firms, *Journal of Business Venturing*, 11(6), 471–487.
Brown, P. and McNaughton, R.B. (2003) Cluster development programmes: panacea or placebo for promoting SME growth and internationalization? in *Globalization and Entrepreneurship: Policy and Strategy Perspectives*, H. Etemad, and R. Wright, eds. Cheltenham: Edward Elgar, 106–124.
Brown, P., McNaughton, R.B., and Bell, J. (2010) Marketing externalities in industrial districts: evidence from the Christchurch NZ electronics cluster, *Journal of International Entrepreneurship*, 8(2), 168–181.
Camino, D. (1991) Export promotion in Spain and other EEC countries: systems and performance, in *Export Development and Promotion: The Role of Public Organizations*, F.H.R. Seringhaus and P.J. Rosson, eds. Boston: Kluwer Academic Publishers, 119–144.
Cesinger, B., Danko, A., and Bouncken, R. (2012) Born globals: (almost) 20 years of research and still not "grown up"? *International Journal of Entrepreneurship and Small Business*, 15(2), 171–190.
Coviello, N. and Munro, H. (1997) Network relationships and the internationalisation process of small software firms, *International Business Review*, 6(4), 361–386.
Crick, D. (2009) The internationalization of born global and international new venture SMEs, *International Marketing Review*, 26(4/5), 453–476.
Diamantopoulos, A., Schlegelmilch, B.B., and Katy Tse, K.Y. (1993) Understanding the role of export marketing assistance: empirical evidence and research needs, *European Journal of Marketing*, 27, 5–18.
Durmuşoğlu, S.S., Apfelthaler, G., Nayir, D.Z., Alvarez, R., and Mughan, T. (2012) The effect of government-designed export promotion service use on small and medium-sized enterprise goal achievement: a multidimensional view of export performance, *Industrial Marketing Management*, 41, 680–691.
Elvey, L.A. (1990) Export promotion and assistance: a comparative analysis, in *International Perspectives on Trade Promotion*, S.T. Cavusgil and M.R. Czinkota, eds. Westport, CT: Quorum Books, 133–148.
Fernhaber, S.A., Gilbert, B.A., and McDougall, P. (2008) International entrepreneurship and geographic location: an empirical examination of new venture internationalization, *Journal of International Business Studies*, 39(2), 267–290.
Fischer, E. and Reuber, B. (2008) *Survival of the Fittest: Which SMEs Internationalize Most Extensively and Effectively?* The Conference Board of Canada, December.
Fletcher, M. and Harris, S. (2012) Knowledge acquisition for the internationalization of the smaller firm: content and sources, *International Business Review*, 21(4): 631–47.
Fletcher, M. and Prashantham, S. (2011) Knowledge assimilation processes of rapidly internationalising firms, *Journal of Small Business and Enterprise Development*, 18(3): 475–501.
Freixnet, J. (2012) Export promotion programs: their impact on companies' internationalization performance and competitiveness, *International Business Review*, 21, 1065–1086.
Gabrielsson, M., Sasi, V., and Darling, J. (2004) Finance strategies of rapidly-growing Finnish SMEs: born internationals and born globals, *European Business Review*, 16(6), 590–604.
Goldfinch, S. and Perry, M. (1996) Developing small business networks in New Zealand, *Policy, Organisation & Society*, 12(winter), 64–88.
Goldfinch, S. and Perry, M. (1997) Promoting business networks, *New Zealand Geographer*, 53(1), 41–46.
Johanson, J. and Vahlne, J.-E. (1977) The internationalization process of the firm: a model of knowledge development and increasing foreign market commitments, *Journal of International Business Studies*, 8(1), 23–32.
Johanson, J. and Vahlne, J.-E. (2009) The Uppsala internationalization process model revisited: from liability of foreignness to liability of outsidership, *Journal of International Business Studies*, 40(9), 1411–1431.
Johanson, J. and Wiedersheim-Paul, F. (1975) The internationalization of the firm: four Swedish cases, *Journal of Management Studies*, 12(3), 305–22.
Jones, M.V., Coviello, N., and Tang, Y. (2011) International entrepreneurship research (1989–2009): a domain ontology and thematic analysis, *Journal of Business Venturing*, 26(6), 632–659.

Katsikeas, C.S., Leonidou, L.C., and Morgan, R.E. (2000) Firm-level export performance assessment: review, evaluation and development, *Journal of the Academy of Marketing Science*, 28(4), 493–511.
Kaur, S. and Sandhu, M.S. (2013) Internationalisation of born global firms: evidence from Malaysia, *Journal of the Asia Pacific Economy*, DOI: 10.1080/13547860.2013.818426.
Keupp, M.M. and Gassmann, O. (2009) The past and the future of international entrepreneurship: a review and suggestions for developing the field, *Journal of Management*, 35(3), 600–633.
Knight, J., Bell, J., and McNaughton, R.B. (2003) Satisfaction with paying for government export assistance, in *Advances in International Business*, I. Greaves, and C. Wheeler, eds. Basingstoke, UK: Palgrave Publishers, 223–240.
Kyvik, O., Saris, W., Bonet, E., and Felício, J.A. (2013) The internationalization of small firms: the relationship between the global mindset and firms' internationalization behavior, *Journal of International Entrepreneurship*, 11, 172–195.
Madsen, T.K. (2013) Early and rapidly internationalizing ventures: similarities and differences between classifications based on the original international new venture and born global literatures, *Journal of International Entrepreneurship*, 11(1), 65–79.
Mason, C. and Brown, R. (2013) Creating good public policy to support high-growth firms, *Small Business Economics*, 40, 211–225.
McDougall, P.P. and Oviatt, B.M. (1996) New venture internationalization, strategic change, and performance: a follow-up study, *Journal of Business Venturing*, 11(1), 23–40.
McNaughton, R. and Bell, J. (2004) Capital structure and the pace of SME internationalisation, in *International Entrepreneurship in Small and Medium Size Enterprises: Orientation, Environment and Strategy*, E. Hamid, ed. Cheltenham, UK: Edward Elgar Publishers, 57–71.
Niroui, F. (2011) Access to government microdata for SME internationalization research, Masters thesis, Department of Management Sciences, University of Waterloo, Canada.
OECD (1998) Small businesses, job creation and growth: facts, obstacles and best practices, downloaded from www.oecd.org/industry/smes/2090740.pdf, November 1, 2013.
OECD (2000) Policy brief: small and medium sized enterprises: local strength, global reach, June, downloaded from www.oecd.org/regional/leed/1918307.pdf, November 1, 2013.
OECD (2005) OECD small and medium enterprise outlook, downloaded from www.camaras.org/publicado/europa/pdf/8505011E.pdf, December 10, 2013.
OECD (2008) Removing barriers to SME access to international markets, downloaded from www.oecd-ilibrary.org/industry-and-services/removing-barriers-to-sme-access-to-international-markets_9789264045866-en, November 1, 2013.
OECD (2009) Top barriers and drivers to SME internationalisation, downloaded from www.oecd.org/cfe/smes/43357832.pdf, November 1, 2013.
Oesterle, M. (1997) Time-span until internationalization: foreign market entry as a built-in mechanism of innovations, *Management International Review*, 37(2), 125–149.
Oviatt, B.M. and McDougall, P.P. (1994) Toward a theory of international new ventures, *Journal of International Business Studies*, 25(1), 45–64.
Porter, M.E. (1990) *The Competitive Advantage of Nations*. New York: Free Press.
Prashantham, S. and McNaughton, R.B. (2006) Facilitation of links between multinational subsidiaries and SMEs: the Scottish Technology and Collaboration (STAC) Initiative, *International Business Review*, 15(5), 447–462.
Rennie, M.W. (1993) Global competitiveness: born global, *McKinsey Quarterly*, 4, 45–52.
Seringhaus, F.H.R. (1987) Export promotion: the role and impact of government services, *Irish Marketing Review*, 2, 106–116.
Seringhaus, F.H.R. and Rosson, P.J. (1990) *Government Export Promotion: A Global Perspective*. London: Routledge.
Szyliowicz, D. and Galvin, T. (2010) Applying broader strokes: extending institutional perspectives and agendas for international entrepreneurship research, *International Business Review*, 19(4), 317–332.
Wright, M., Westhead, P., and Ucbasarand, D. (2007) Internationalization of small and medium-sized enterprises (SMEs) and international entrepreneurship: a critique and policy implications, *Regional Studies*, 41, 1013–1029.

15

Future agenda for research design in international entrepreneurship

Niina Nummela

Introduction

International entrepreneurship is a relatively young field (Jones et al. 2011) and understandably therefore in the process of development. In earlier discussions, a number of scholars have addressed challenges that need to be resolved for the field to become rigorous, well-established and well-respected. The most frequently discussed area is probably the methodological approaches employed in international entrepreneurship research. Research design, applied methods in data collection and analysis, and means to improve the validity and reliability of the research process and output are all decisive in assessing whether a study is of high quality or not. This is naturally not only a challenge for international entrepreneurship but for all fields of research, and particularly important to young, emerging fields.

Concern for methodological rigour in international entrepreneurship research is not new. On the contrary, it has been highlighted in all the literature reviews conducted within the field (e.g. Terjesen et al. 2013; Jones et al. 2011; Coombs et al. 2009; Keupp and Gassmann 2009; Rialp et al. 2005), and one review has even chosen it as its focus (Coviello and Jones 2004). And yet it seems that we have not advanced a great deal, as most reviews seem to draw the same conclusions in terms of methods in future international entrepreneurship studies. The open questions remain (1) how should international entrepreneurship be studied in the future and (2) what are the principle challenges yet to be overcome?

This chapter builds on existing knowledge but also delivers novel insights. First, it provides an insider perspective on research methods in international entrepreneurship research by presenting the kinds of study international entrepreneurship researchers would welcome. As such, it deviates from earlier reviews in which the author(s) summarise their perception on the extant research. Second, it takes the preferred methodological approaches and digs deeper into the challenges of these strategies than does any previous review. Understanding the problems, pitfalls and suggested solutions hopefully facilitates the adoption of these strategies and will increase their popularity.

Initially, a systematic literature review was conducted on prior studies on international entrepreneurship. Instead of collecting a new set of articles on the topic for this purpose, it was decided that the analysis would rely on previous work by Jones et al. (2011). That review was chosen for three reasons: (1) it is recent, (2) it is comprehensive, as it covers 20 years of work and a huge number of publications ranging from the well-established journals to those that are emerging, and (3) the data collection process has been described in a highly systematic and transparent manner, thus enabling replication and verification of the process.

It should also be mentioned that the chosen review is very clear on defining the field, which seems to be a common problem in earlier reviews (Keupp and Gassmann 2009). To define the field, the review combines two definitions: the first formal definition of the field (McDougall and Oviatt 2000) and also a later revised definition (Oviatt and McDougall 2005). Thus, it focuses on studies that:

- combine "innovative, proactive and risk-seeking behavior that crosses national borders and is intended to create value in organisations" (McDougall and Oviatt 2000, 903);
- focus on "the discovery, enactment, evaluation and exploitation of opportunities – across national borders – to create future goods and services" (Oviatt and McDougall 2005, 540).

This approach has two notable benefits. First, it enables the inclusion of an important sub-branch of international entrepreneurship, comparative international entrepreneurship, which focuses on cross-national comparisons of domestic entrepreneurship (cf. Terjesen et al. 2013). Second, the definition does not contain any limitation on company size, which has been considered a problem by some scholars (Keupp and Gassmann 2009). By taking these aspects into account, the adopted approach captures earlier research that studies entrepreneurial aspects of internationalisation which cannot be explained separately by either international business or entrepreneurship theories, as both are needed (Mathews and Zander 2007).

What are we calling for?

A look back: a literature review

The 323 international entrepreneurship studies identified by Jones et al. (2011) were the starting point of our analysis. In line with earlier reviews, a focus on journal articles was considered appropriate because of their impact on the field and also the validity check they provide through their peer-review process (cf. Podsakoff et al. 2005). These studies were systematically reviewed (cf. Petticrew and Roberts 2006) to determine the kind of methodological suggestions international entrepreneurship researchers were proposing for future research.

To assess these studies as systematically as possible, each study was read and the content analysed (cf. Krippendorff 1980) to find methodological suggestions for future research. Although, in principle, these suggestions can be found at any part of the study, typically, they were placed at the end of the article, for example, as part of the conclusions, discussion on limitations of the focal study or as a separate section on suggestions for future research. The suggestions were coded inductively; however, saturation level was quickly reached and the number of new codes added remained modest after analysing the first 25 articles. Altogether, 48 codes were employed in the analysis (Table 15.1) and the coding was conducted with QSR Nvivo.

For the sake of clarity, Table 15.1 includes only the most popular codes of the analysis. Codes which received four or fewer references have been combined into the category 'other'. This group comprises a number of diverse codes, such as calls for cross-cultural measures, secondary data, exploratory research, more complex research designs and research on managerial or individual levels. Furthermore, in some cases, two codes were combined due to their notable similarity or assumed overlap. For example, the category 'call for longitudinal studies' also includes references

Table 15.1 Codes employed in the IE literature analysis

Code: Call for ...	*Number of references*
cross-context comparison	99
cross-country comparison	99
longitudinal studies	94
larger samples	42
quantitative research	38
qualitative research	32
case studies	28
methodological rigour	16
additional measures	13
targeted samples	7
firms in different stages of internationalisation	7
definitional rigour	6
multidisciplinary research	6
network-based research	6
interviews	5
single-industry studies	5
other	36
no methodological suggestions for future research	101

in which calls were made for dynamic studies (i.e. eight references) and research on multiple time periods (i.e. one reference).

In addition, the type of study was coded as it was assumed that this might impact the kind of methodological suggestions made. Studies were classified into six categories: quantitative study, qualitative study, mixed method study, literature review, conceptual paper and other. Furthermore, as a validity check, after careful reading and content analysis, each article was also searched mechanically as a Word document for selected keywords such as 'method', 'design', 'future', 'further' and 'suggest*'. This led to the identification of additional suggestions in a few cases, particularly in exceptional parts of the manuscript. However, this validity check confirmed the original coding in the majority of cases.

The outcome of the analysis was very clear. Although approximately one third of studies had no methodological suggestions for future research, of those making a suggestion, the 'top three' were clearly visible: researchers called for cross-cultural studies, cross-context comparison and longitudinal studies (Table 15.1). All other codes received significantly fewer references.

The outcome was not altogether a surprise. Similar calls for future research have often been raised and are also under discussion in other fields. However, the question remains, why have these long-standing calls not elicited responses? These calls are raised typically in the context of limitations of a focal study; however, if scholars recognise the need for these studies, why are they so rare? What makes them so difficult? Next, the challenges for each suggested research design in future international entrepreneurship research are addressed.

Longitudinal research design

International entrepreneurship, as with many other research fields, has been criticised by several scholars as being dominated by static, cross-sectional studies (Coombs et al. 2009; Keupp and Gassmann 2009; Rialp et al. 2005; Coviello and Jones 2004) and the calls for longitudinal research designs have been persistent. However, what is actually meant by longitudinal research and what does it require from researchers who want to conduct such a study?

Longitudinal research commonly refers to a research design that concentrates on the observation, description and analysis of an organisational process (Kimberly 1976) or processes (Hassett and Paavilainen-Mäntymäki 2013). It typically utilises process data, a data set including observations at multiple points in time (Welch and Paavilainen-Mäntymäki 2014), to produce process theory. Given that the process of entrepreneurial internationalisation is at the heart of international entrepreneurship research (cf. Jones and Coviello 2005), it is quite natural to assume that this research design would be most appropriate for the field.

Conducting longitudinal research does not only require collecting process data but also introducing a temporal dimension to the whole research design, ranging from research questions to methods and conclusions (Langley et al. 2013). Traditionally, researchers have applied the Western understanding on time in international entrepreneurship research, according to which, development in time is a linear process and advances in the process can be measured chronologically (Hurmerinta-Peltomäki 2003). This has resulted in an objective study on internationalisation, based on clock time (Middleton et al. 2011). However, the extension of international entrepreneurship studies to emerging markets has put pressure on taking a more cyclical and subjective understanding on time into account. Another issue supporting cyclical understanding of time is that researchers have acknowledged the fact that internationalisation is not always an onward moving, continuous process of growth and development, but also that there are discontinuities (see, for example, Vissak and Francioni 2013) and the process can actually comprise alternating periods of de- and re-internationalisation (Welch and Welch 2009).

Studying international entrepreneurship requires, in addition to time and process, that we also take another temporal dimension into account: the speed or pace of internationalisation. In the international entrepreneurship literature, this aspect has been discussed either as the time lag between company establishment and first international operations (Christensen 1991; Hurmerinta-Peltomäki 2001) or the speed of a firm's subsequent growth (Autio et al. 2000). In other words, one can distinguish between early and rapid internationalisation (Prashantham and Young 2011; Zucchella et al. 2007), which do not necessarily co-exist. At the heart of investigating both early and rapid internationalisation lies the concept of speed, which attempts to capture the change in selected dimensions over a time period (Chetty et al. 2014; Casillas and Acedo 2013).

In principle, it can be argued that any attempt to explain behaviour or phenomena relating to international entrepreneurship would benefit from a research design that is temporally sensitive and longitudinal in nature. This is not only a theoretically sound argument but also important from the perspective of managerial relevance. After all, instead of know-what knowledge, it enables the opportunity to provide know-how knowledge that managers find particularly valuable (Langley et al. 2013).

Nevertheless, after all this praise for longitudinal research design, it is also fair to point out a few caveats that researchers are bound to encounter with this approach. First, researchers should be aware of the huge variation in longitudinal research designs ranging from repeated cross-sectional studies to those that are real-time and retrospective (cf. Hassett and Paavilainen-Mäntymäki 2013). Although the number of alternatives offers a freedom of choice for an interested researcher, it also simultaneously means that there is no 'correct' way to conduct a study. In practice, it will not be easy to replicate the study or find practical advice on how to proceed. Fortunately, interest in both longitudinal and process research has increased over recent years and the situation in terms of support and guidance has gradually improved.

Second, incorporating time into the research design of an empirical study is not an easy task. Longitudinal research design involves not only data collection at multiple points in time, but the temporal aspect also needs to be extended to the analysis and theorisation. In analysing longitudinal data, temporal bracketing[1] has become quite popular when comparing successive time periods, and it does work well in within-case analysis. However, in a study attempting to compare processes across cases, problems arise because temporal brackets of two cases are not necessarily directly comparable. For example, it would be quite unwise to compare the rapid internationalisation process of two companies in a situation when one internationalised recently and the other ten years ago. A solution to this kind of challenge might be to employ reference time[2] instead of chronological time as the measure for time when comparing the cases.

Third, although not all, many studies with longitudinal research design are qualitative case studies. These studies often struggle with the difficult task of balancing the rich data collected and the problem of making a single-case study sufficiently interesting for publication (for challenges, see for example, Siggelkow 2007). Unfortunately, this can lead authors to focus completely on convincing their readers of the representativeness of their respective cases and to forget that the decisive element in a process study is the number of temporal observations, not the number of cases (Langley et al. 2013). In other words, if the story is interesting and the research process is described in a rigorous and transparent manner, the study should be relevant to an academic audience.

Fourth, researchers should ensure that their research design enables the identification, observation and investigation of the discontinuities and cyclic development of international entrepreneurial companies. The discovery of anomalies in behaviour or breaks in evolution is, in fact, often the source for novel insights and both would offer valuable contributions to our current understanding. However, this would require process thinking; that is, focusing on movement, activity, events and change both in the data collection and analysis (Langley 2007), and bringing these elements back to the analysis and findings of the study.

Nevertheless, time is not only an element of longitudinal research design but is also an element of context (Michailova 2010; Welter 2011). The systematic literature review also identified a number of calls for studies that include cross-context comparison, which will be addressed next.

Cross-context comparison

Researchers often call for contextualisation; that is, the focal phenomenon should be studied within a context and preferably even across different contexts. Earlier international entrepreneurship research has been argued to lack cross-contextual studies (Rialp et al. 2005; Coviello and Jones 2004). This argument was supported in the analysis of previous international entrepreneurship research that indicated a strong call for cross-context studies in future research. Almost one third of the reviewed studies recommend a cross-contextual approach in future studies (see Table 15.1). However, the suggestions for contextualisation were diverse, including, for example, comparisons across:

- industries (consumer vs. B-2-B; manufacturing vs. services)
- products (high-tech vs. low-tech)
- regions
- company size (small vs. large)
- company age (new vs. mature ventures)
- internationalisation phase (domestic vs. international new ventures; early vs. mature internationalising companies)
- survivorship (success vs. failure)
- ownership (private vs. public vs. state-owned enterprises)
- gender (male vs. female entrepreneurs).

The list above demonstrates well that, as a field of research, international entrepreneurship investigates phenomena embedded in multiple contexts; a feature shared with two closely related fields of research: entrepreneurship and international business (cf. Welter 2011; Michailova 2010). Interestingly, the context also seems to have clear layers; in addition to the often employed classification of inner and outer context (cf. Pettigrew 1987), we can see that the strong interest in entrepreneurial behaviour also highlights the individual-level context.

Unfortunately, the list also demonstrates well the narrow understanding on contextualisation among international entrepreneurship researchers, for whom it seems that context is something that can be measured and compared, with the resulting outcome enabling us to assess better whether our findings are generalisable or not. However, contextualisation could be much more. The context of a study can be understood as the dynamic collection of factors, processes and events that influence the phenomenon under investigation (Michailova 2010). Thus, contextualisation might range from the early phases of the research process to the interpretation of findings and conclusions, and provide not only a thick description of the research setting but also an analysis of contextual effects (Rousseau and Fried 2001). For example, in entrepreneurship research, the need for understanding entrepreneurial behaviour in its historical, institutional, spatial and social context has already been recognised (Welter 2011). Therefore, it is quite alarming that international entrepreneurship research has been described as context-specific while, at the same time, aiming for universal explanations (Coviello and Jones 2004; Rialp et al. 2005; Keupp and Gassmann 2009).

What might contextualisation be in practice? At least, when conducting their research, international entrepreneurship researchers should make their research process transparent concerning the contextual dimensions of 'who', 'where' and 'when' (cf. Whetten 1989). Currently, research seems to be quite actor-centric (concerned with who) and more or less context-free (ignoring where and when). Yet, as all behaviour is embedded in the institutional, social and historical environment, the audience should be made aware of the impacts of this embeddedness. However, the degree of awareness and the role of context can vary. For example, Tsui (2004) differentiates between context-sensitive and context-embedded research. Whereas context-sensitive research is aware of the context-specific elements of the research design, context-embedded research employs the context as the study's primary explanatory variable (Tsui 2004). The latter approach comes close to contextualised explanation (Welch et al. 2011), which aims at in-depth knowledge on the context, thus expanding the transferability of the findings.

In principle, all research should be context-sensitive, ranging from formulation of the research question to selection of an appropriate theory, data collection and analysis and presentation of findings and conclusions (Whetten 2009). The need for contextualisation is not limited only to qualitative research; quantitative researchers should also take its challenges seriously (Michailova 2010). From the perspective of international entrepreneurship research, it is important to shift from a passive understanding on context as a research setting to its more active utilisation. In line with the thoughts of Langley et al. (2013), it is time to move from a noun to a verb – from context to contextualisation in international entrepreneurship research.

As mentioned above, contextualisation can be embedded in research design from the outset. There are also concrete ways to make a study context-rich over the process; an example of which is to make visible the embeddedness of the phenomenon. For example, network researchers increasingly visualise their research objects with network pictures (Ramos and Ford 2011; Ford and Redwood 2005). Similar efforts to visualise the contexts in which international entrepreneurship phenomena are embedded would be welcome. Nevertheless, the focus should be on active interpretation of the context. In other words, we should move our interest from the 'boxes' of our models to the 'arrows' between them (cf. Langley et al. 2013).

One of the most important contexts of international entrepreneurship research, its *international* dimension, has not yet been discussed in this section on context. Compared to any other type of context, the need for studying the phenomenon across borders was clearly recognised among international entrepreneurship researchers (see Table 15.1). The reason for this might be very simple as the importance of context is often better understood when the context is unfamiliar (Welter 2011). The next section discusses in detail the calls for comparative international entrepreneurship studies.

Cross-country comparison

Most organisational and managerial theories originate from developed economies, particularly from North America and Western Europe (Whetten 2009; Tsui 2004). Although interest in other geographic areas has been increasing, the collected data predominantly originate from the same areas. This is particularly worrying as this problem is seldom acknowledged (Michailova 2010) and, thus, important questions on novel contexts can be ignored (Tsui 2007).

In this respect, compared to many other fields of research, international entrepreneurship has a clear advantage as, over the years, its knowledge base has been built around the world. Although this stream of research has been particularly popular in small, open, Western economies (Rialp et al. 2005), empirical studies recently have been conducted also in emerging economies (e.g. Prashantham 2011; Zhou et al. 2010; Zou and Ghauri 2010; Lopez et al. 2009; Karra et al. 2008). Nevertheless, international entrepreneurship research also suffers from the fact that theories and constructs have been developed in the West and, occasionally, they do not match well to the context of other countries. As an example, in a recent study on Chinese international new ventures, Vissak et al. (2012) found that market knowledge, a key concept in the internationalisation process literature, did not play any significant role in the early phases of the companies' internationalisation.

The great majority of international entrepreneurship research seems to focus on a single context; comparative studies are a minority (Jones et al. 2011). Yet our systematic literature review revealed that a great number of authors were suggesting that there should be more cross-country studies in the future (see Table 15.1). However, these calls were surprisingly brief and straightforward, often only suggesting that there should be additional studies in similar or different countries to make the findings of the authors' respective studies more generalisable. In many cases, which countries these might be was not even clearly stated; instead the authors refer rather ambiguously to 'countries at similar levels of economic development' or 'other small and open economies'. In studies in which countries were mentioned, even listed, the authors did not provide much argument on why they would be the most suitable. Furthermore, the suggestions for future comparative research were not accompanied by a discussion of what this would require in practice. This is surprising as the importance of comparative international entrepreneurship research was recognised early (Coviello and Jones 2004), not only as a means to improve the generalisability of findings but more to identify fundamental differences in entrepreneurial activity across countries (Terjesen et al. 2013).

What is required to encourage this kind of research? First, the field would need to undergo an attitudinal change. International entrepreneurship research seems to suffer from the same problem as international business and management research: the international context has been understood in a rather narrow way (Michailova 2010; Tsui 2004). Most researchers appear to have accepted an etic approach to knowledge (Coviello and Jones 2004); that is, concepts and behaviour are assumed to have some universal characteristics which hold true independent of the culture and environment in which they have been embedded. This kind of thinking is heavily criticised in other fields of research. For example, the approach is more emic[3] in cultural anthropology; that is, culture, people and their behaviour are all in constant interaction and shaped by each other and, therefore, generalisation is impossible. The emic approach is much more aligned with thoughts on increasing contextualisation in international entrepreneurship research.

Second, the change would need to be accompanied by rigorous development of key concepts and measures. According to the emic approach, comparison of cultural entities is either very challenging or often even impossible (Hui and Triandis 1985) and all concepts employed in theorisation are culturally bound (Triandis 1983). As Coviello and Jones (2004) point out, many of the instruments employed in international entrepreneurship research are culture-bound; however, researchers seldom discuss the related problems. Thus, to advance the field methodologically, there is a strong need for culturally sensitive measures that can then be employed in context-sensitive studies.

Third, there is a more practical hurdle to overcome: namely, conducting cross-country research would greatly benefit from researcher triangulation (Denzin 1978), so that different team members represent different cultural backgrounds. These members would be able to cross social, linguistic and semantic boundaries and, thus, better read and understand the context (Michailova 2010). However, building and maintaining a well-functioning cross-cultural team has its own challenges over the whole research process. A team with great diversity (e.g. nationality, age, gender, culture, and education) needs a clear code of conduct, sufficient time and constant interaction to turn its heterogeneity into an asset and team members into cultural interpreters (Salmi 2010). Even then, there is no guarantee that the research output will be context-sensitive if the challenges of conducting cross-cultural research are not made transparent (Michailova 2010).

Discussion

Based on the literature review, researchers seem to agree that there is a considerable need for context-sensitive research, including also the temporal and cultural dimensions of the context. The number of such studies remains limited although, increasingly, researchers taking this approach are combining multiple methods as part of their research design. These mixed-methods studies are typical when conducting research in emerging or transition economies as they enable better contextualisation (Hurmerinta-Peltomäki and Nummela 2006) and also a combination of emic and etic approaches (Polsa 2013). In addition, they seem appropriate for investigation on processes and applying process theorisation (Langley et al. 2013). In sum, there are a number of issues favouring this research design in international entrepreneurship research.

The potential of mixed-method research design has been raised in earlier reviews on the field. For example, Rialp et al. (2005) and Terjesen et al. (2013) point out the relatively small number of these studies and recommend that mixed methods should be applied in future studies. Interestingly, some of the most impactful studies in international entrepreneurship research are mixed-methods studies (e.g. Autio et al. 2000; Bell 1995; Coviello and Munro 1995; Jones 1999; Knight and Cavusgil 2004), suggesting that it is possible to obtain knowledge which is both new and valuable for the field with such an approach.

The status of the research field itself would also support this kind of approach. When analysing methodological fit in management research, Edmonson and McManus (2007) point out that a combination of quantitative and qualitative methods would be particularly beneficial in fields that are in an intermediate state; that is, when theories are characterised by provisional explanations for phenomena and models that propose relationships between a focal phenomenon and established questions. As a field, international entrepreneurship research seems to fit this description well. According to Edmonson and McManus (2007), hybrid research designs that draw on the best sides of both approaches can shed light in a rigorous manner on the underlying mechanisms.

However, the mixed-methods research strategy involves many challenges (Jick 1979; Hurmerinta-Peltomäki and Nummela 2006). In addition, international entrepreneurship as a research field and researchers active within the field carry with them a strong legacy of research design; that is, existing routines and norms concerning how rigorous research should be conducted. A review of the international entrepreneurship research confirms that it is strongly dominated by quantitative research, data collected either with a postal survey or from various databases, such as the Global Entrepreneurship Monitor. Both the challenges and the legacy encourage researchers to remain within the mainstream and continue following the same research strategies that have proven successful in terms of publishing. The legacy is also noticeable in suggestions for future research; novel methodological insights are seldom put forward. It is to be hoped that researchers at least follow their own recommendations otherwise the field will not progress.

Notes

1 Temporal bracketing refers to a data-driven research strategy in which data are decomposed in successive periods based on continuities and discontinuities in data and/or events instead of a theoretical framework (e.g. Langley 1999).
2 Whereas chronological time is fundamental and the same for all firms, employing reference time means that the selected event is positioned in terms of a firm's history or other historical background (Jones and Coviello 2005). For example, instead of describing the growth of a born global firm in chronological years, the year count could start from the foundation of the company.
3 Management researchers have adopted the terms 'emic' and 'etic' from anthropology to distinguish between studies with insider's (emic) and outsider's (etic) perspectives on reality (Morey and Luthans 1984). For more on the history and development of the concepts, see Harris (1976).

References

Autio, E., Sapienza, H.J. and J.G. Almeida, 'Effects of age at entry, knowledge intensity, and imitability on international growth', *Academy of Management Journal*, 43, 2000, 909–924.
Bell, J., 'The internationalization of small computer software firms: a further challenge to "stage" theories', *European Journal of Marketing*, 29, 1995, 60–75.
Casillas, J.C. and F.J. Acedo, 'Speed in the internationalization process of the firm', *International Journal of Management Reviews*, 15, 2013, 15–29.
Chetty, S., Johanson, M. and O. Martin Martin, 'Speed of internationalization: conceptualization, measurement and validation', *Journal of World Business*, 49(4), 2014, 633–650.
Christensen, P.R., 'The small and medium-sized exporters' squeeze: empirical evidence and model reflections', *Entrepreneurship and Regional Development*, 3, 1991, 49–65.
Coombs, J.E., Sadrieh, F. and M. Annavarjula, 'Two decades of international entrepreneurship research: what have we learned – where do we go from here?' *International Journal of Entrepreneurship*, 13, 2009, 23–64.
Coviello, N. and M.V. Jones, 'Methodological issues in international entrepreneurship research', *Journal of Business Venturing*, 19, 2004, 485–508.
Coviello, N.E. and H.J. Munro, 'Growing the entrepreneurial firm: networking for international market development', *European Journal of Marketing*, 29, 1995, 49–61.
Denzin, N.K., *The research act: a theoretical introduction to sociological methods*, 1978. New York: McGraw-Hill.
Edmonson, A.C. and S.E. McManus, 'Methodological fit in management field research', *Academy of Management Review*, 32, 2007, 1155–1179.
Ford, D. and M. Redwood, 'Making sense of network dynamics through network pictures: a longitudinal case study', *Industrial Marketing Management*, 34, 2005, 648–657.
Harris, M., 'History and significance of the emic/etic distinction', *Annual Review of Anthropology*, 5, 1976, 329–350.

Hassett, M. and E. Paavilainen-Mäntymäki, 'Longitudinal research in organizations: an introduction', In: *Handbook of longitudinal research methods in organisation and business studies*. Cheltenham, UK: Edward Elgar Publishing, 2013, pp. 1–22.
Hui, C.H. and H.C. Triandis, 'Measurement in cross-cultural psychology: a review and comparison of strategies', *Journal of Cross Cultural Psychology*, 16, 1985, 131–152.
Hurmerinta-Peltomäki, L., 'Time and internationalisation. The shortened adoption lag in small business internationalisation', Publications of the Turku School of Economics and Business Administration, Series A-7, 2001, Turku, Finland.
Hurmerinta-Peltomäki, L., 'Time and internationalisation: theoretical challenges set by rapid internationalisation', *Journal of International Entrepreneurship*, 1, 2003, 217–236.
Hurmerinta-Peltomäki, L. and N. Nummela, 'Mixed methods in international business research: a value-added perspective', *Management International Review*, 46, 2006, 1–21.
Jick, T.D., 'Mixing qualitative and quantitative methods: triangulation in action', *Administrative Science Quarterly*, 24, 1979, 602–611.
Jones, M.V., 'The internationalization of small high-technology firms', *Journal of International Marketing*, 7, 1999, 15–41.
Jones, M.V. and N.E. Coviello, 'Internationalization: conceptualising an entrepreneurial process of behavior in time', *Journal of International Business Studies*, 36, 2005, 284–303.
Jones, M.V., Coviello, N. and Y.K. Tang, 'International Entrepreneurship research (1989–2009): A domain ontology and thematic analysis', *Journal of Business Venturing*, 26, 2011, 632–659.
Karra, N., Phillips, N. and P. Tracey, 'Building the born global firm: developing entrepreneurial capabilities for international new venture success', *Long Range Planning*, 41, 2008, 440–458.
Keupp, M.M. and O. Gassmann, 'The past and the future of international entrepreneurship: a review and suggestions for developing the field', *Journal of Management*, 35, 2009, 600–633.
Kimberly, J., 'Issues in the design of longitudinal organizational research', *Sociological Methods and Research*, 4, 1976, 321–347.
Knight, G.A. and S.T. Cavusgil, 'Innovation, organizational capabilities, and the born-global firm', *Journal of International Business Studies*, 35, 2004, 124–141.
Krippendorff, K., *Content analysis: an introduction to its methodology*. Beverly Hills, CA: Sage Publications, 1980.
Langley, A., 'Strategies for theorizing from process data', *Academy of Management Review*, 24, 1999, 691–710.
Langley, A., 'Process thinking in strategic organization', *Strategic Organization*, 5, 2007, 271–282.
Langley, A., Smallman, C., Tsoukas, H., A.H. and Van de Ven, 'Process studies of change in organization and management: unveiling temporality, activity, and flow', *Academy of Management Journal*, 56, 2013, 1–13.
Lopez, L.E., Kundu, S.K. and L. Ciravegna, 'Born global or born regional? Evidence from an exploratory study in the Costa Rican software industry', *Journal of International Business Studies*, 40, 2009, 1228–1238.
Mathews, J.A. and I. Zander, 'The international entrepreneurial dynamics of accelerated internationalisation', *Journal of International Business Studies*, 38, 2007, 387–403.
McDougall, P.P. and B.M. Oviatt, 'International entrepreneurship: the intersection of two research paths', *Academy of Management Journal*, 43, 2000, 902–906.
Michailova, S., 'Contextualizing in international business research: why do we need more of it and how can we be better at it?', *Scandinavian Journal of Management*, 27, 2010, 129–139.
Middleton, S., Liesch, P.W. and J. Steen, 'Organizing time: internationalization narratives of executive managers', *International Business Review*, 20, 2011, 136–150.
Morey, N.C. and F. Luthans, 'An emic perspective and ethnoscience methods for organizational research', *Academy of Management Review*, 9, 1984, 27–36.
Oviatt, B.M. and P.P. McDougall, 'Defining international entrepreneurship and modeling the speed of internationalization', *Entrepreneurship Theory & Practice*, 29, 2005, 537–553.
Petticrew, M. and H. Roberts, *Systematic reviews in the social sciences: a practical guide*. Malden, MA: Blackwell Publishing Ltd, 2006.
Pettigrew, A.M., 'Context and action in the transformation of the firm', *Journal of Management Studies*, 24, 1987, 649–670.
Podsakoff, P., MacKenzie, S., Bachrach, D. and N. Podsakoff, 'The influence of management journals in the 1980s and 1990s', *Strategic Management Journal*, 26, 2005, 473–488.
Polsa, P., 'The crossover-dialog approach: the importance of multiple methods for international business', *Journal of Business Research*, 66, 2013, 288–297.
Prashantham, S., 'Social capital and Indian micromultinationals', *British Journal of Management*, 22, 2011, 4–10.

Prashantham, S. and S. Young, 'Post-entry speed of international new ventures', *Entrepreneurship Theory and Practice*, 35, 2011, 275–292.

Ramos, C. and I.D. Ford, 'Network pictures as a research device: developing a tool to capture actors' perceptions in organizational networks', *Industrial Marketing Management*, 40, 2011, 447–464.

Rialp, A., Rialp, J. and G.A. Knight, 'The phenomenon of early internationalizing firms: what do we know after a decade (1993–2003) of scientific inquiry?' *International Business Review*, 14, 2005, 147–166.

Rousseau, D.M. and Y. Fried, 'Location, location, location: contextualizing organizational research', *Journal of Organizational Behavior*, 22, 2001, 1–13.

Salmi, A., 'International research teams as analysts of industrial business networks', *Industrial Marketing Management*, 39, 2010, 40–48.

Siggelkow, N., 'Persuasion with case studies', *Academy of Management Journal*, 50, 2007, 20–24.

Terjesen, S., Hessels, J. and D. Li, 'Comparative international entrepreneurship: a review and research agenda', *Journal of Management*, 2013. Published online before print May 1, 2013, doi: 10.1177/0149206313486259.

Triandis, H., 'Dimensions of cultural variation as parameters of organisational theories', *International Studies of Management & Organization*, 12, 1983, 139–169.

Tsui, A.S., 'Contributing to global management knowledge: a case for high quality indigenous research', *Asia Pacific Journal of Management*, 21, 2004, 491–513.

Tsui, A.S., 'From homogenization to pluralism: international management research in the academy and beyond', *Academy of Management Journal*, 50, 2007, 1353–1364.

Vissak, T. and B. Francioni, 'Serial nonlinear internationalization in practice: a case study', *International Business Review*, 22, 2013, 951–962.

Vissak, T., Zhang, X. and K. Ukrainski, 'Successful born globals without experiential market knowledge: survey evidence from China', In: *Handbook of Research on Born Globals*. Cheltenham, UK: Edward Elgar Publishing, 2012, pp. 353–380.

Welch, C. and E. Paavilainen-Mäntymäki, 'Putting process (back) in: research on the internationalization process of the firm', *International Journal of Management Reviews*, 16, 2014, 2–23.

Welch, C., Piekkari, R., Plakoyiannaki, E. and E. Paavilainen-Mäntymäki, 'Theorising from case studies: towards a pluralist future for international business research', *Journal of International Business Studies*, 42, 2011, 740–762.

Welch, C.L. and L.S. Welch, 'Re-internationalisation: exploration and conceptualisation', *International Business Review*, 18, 2009, 567–577.

Welter, F., 'Contextualizing entrepreneurship: conceptual challenges and ways forward', *Entrepreneurship Theory & Practice*, 35, 2011, 165–184.

Whetten, D.A., 'What constitutes a theoretical contribution?', *Academy of Management Review*, 14, 1989, 490–495.

Whetten, D.A., 'An examination of the interface between context and theory applied to the study of Chinese organizations', *Management and Organization Review*, 5, 2009, 29–55.

Zhou, L., Barnes, B.R. and Y. Lu, 'Entrepreneurial proclivity, capability upgrading and performance advantage of newness among international new ventures', *Journal of International Business Studies*, 41, 2010, 882–905.

Zou, H. and P.N. Ghauri, 'Internationalizing by learning: the case of Chinese high-tech new ventures', *International Marketing Review*, 27, 2010, 223–244.

Zucchella, A., Palamara, G. and S. Denicolai, 'The drivers of the early internationalization of the firm', *Journal of World Business*, 42, 2007, 268–280.

Index

Note: page references in *italic* refer to tables; those in **bold** refer to figures; those followed by 'n' refer to notes.